THE ARDEN SHAKESPEARE

GENERAL EDITOR: RICHARD PROUDFOOT

LOVE'S LABOUR'S LOST

THE ARDEN SHAKESPEARE

All's Well That Ends Well: edited by G. K. Hunter
Antony and Cleopatra: edited by M. R. Ridley
As You Like It: edited by Agnes Latham
The Comedy of Errors: edited by R. A. Foakes
Coriolanus: edited by Philip Brockbank
Cymbeline: edited by J. M. Nosworthy
Hamlet: edited by Harold Jenkins
Julius Caesar: edited by T. S. Dorsch
King Henry IV, Parts 1 & 2: edited by A. R. Humphreys
King Henry V: edited by J. H. Walter
King Henry VI, Parts 1, 2 & 3: edited by Andrew S. Cairncross
King Henry VIII: edited by R. A. Foakes
King John: edited by E. A. J. Honigmann
King Lear: edited by Kenneth Muir

King Richard II: edited by Peter Ure
King Richard III: edited by Antony Hammond
Love's Labour's Lost: edited by Richard David
Macbeth: edited by Kenneth Muir
Measure for Measure: edited by J. W. Lever
The Merchant of Venice: edited by John Russell Brown
The Merry Wives of Windsor: edited by H. J. Oliver
A Midsummer Night's Dream: edited by Harold F. Brooks
Much Ado About Nothing: edited by A. R. Humphreys
Othello: edited by M. R. Ridley
Pericles: edited by F. D. Hoeniger
The Poems: edited by F. T. Prince
Romeo and Juliet: edited by Brian Gibbons
The Taming of the Shrew: edited by Brian Morris
The Tempest: edited by Frank Kermode
Timon of Athens: edited by H. J. Oliver
Titus Andronicus: edited by J. C. Maxwell
Troilus and Cressida: edited by Kenneth Palmer
Twelfth Night: edited by J. M. Lothian and T. W. Craik
The Two Gentlemen of Verona: edited by Clifford Leech
The Winter's Tale: edited by J. H. P. Pafford

THE ARDEN EDITION OF THE
WORKS OF WILLIAM SHAKESPEARE

LOVE'S LABOUR'S LOST

Edited by
RICHARD DAVID

METHUEN
LONDON and NEW YORK

The general editors of the Arden Shakespeare have been
W. J. Craig (1899–1906), R. H. Case (1909–44),
Una Ellis-Fermor (1946–58), Harold F. Brooks (1952–82),
Harold Jenkins (1958–82) and Brian Morris (1975–82)

Present general editor: Richard Proudfoot

This edition of *Love's Labour's Lost*, by Richard David,
first published in 1951 by
Methuen & Co. Ltd
11 New Fetter Lane, London EC4P 4EE

Fifth edition 1956
Reprinted four times

First published as a University Paperback in 1968
Reprinted three times
Reprinted 1983

Published in the USA by
Methuen & Co.
in association with Methuen, Inc.
733 Third Avenue, New York, NY 10017

ISBN 0 416 47310 5 (hardback edition)
ISBN 0 416 10440 1 (paperback edition)

Printed and bound in Great Britain by
Richard Clay (The Chaucer Press), Ltd
Bungay, Suffolk

TO

MY MASTERS

G. H. W. R.
H. G. B.
J. D. W.

CONTENTS

	PAGE
GENERAL EDITOR'S PREFACE	ix
PREFACE TO FIFTH EDITION	xii
LIST OF ABBREVIATIONS	xii
INTRODUCTION	xiii
I. THE PLAY	xiii
2. THE TEXT	xvi
2.1. The Quarto of 1598	xvi
2.2. The Printing of the Quarto	xvii
2.3. The Folio of 1623	xvii
2.4. The Copy for the Quarto	xviii
2.5. Evidence of revision:	xviii
2.51. Doublets	xix
2.52. The 'Katharine–Rosaline tangle' in II. i	xx
2.53. The recasting of the 'Worthies'	xxi
2.54. A lost Armado scene	xxii
2.55. Variant speech-headings	xxii
2.56. Variations in typography	xxii
2.57. Conflicting allusions	xxiii
3. THE DATE OF COMPOSITION	xxiii
3.1. External evidence	xxiii
3.2. Internal evidence:	xxiv
3.21. Style	xxiv
3.22. Allusions	xxv
3.221. Navarre 3.222. Anti-alien riots	
3.223. Plague 3.224. Morocco	
3.225. Cowdray 3.226. Pierce Penilesse	
3.227. Ralegh 3.228. Gray's Inn	

3.3. Conclusions   xxvii

4. THE SOURCES   xxviii
   4.1. A hypothetical source   xxviii
   4.2. The historical basis   xxix
   4.3. Dramatic models: xxx
       4.31. John Lyly   xxx
       4.32. The *Commedia dell' Arte*   xxxi
       4.33. The Queen's Progresses   xxxii

5. THE TOPICAL CONTEXT   xxxii
   5.1. Evidences of hidden meaning   xxxii
   5.2. Suggested explanations: xxxiii
       5.21. Individual identifications   xxxiii
       5.22. Harvey and Nashe   xxxiv
       5.23. Ralegh and the 'Schoole of Night'   xxxvii
       5.24. John Eliot and the Earl of Northumberland xxxix
       5.25. Conclusions   xli

6. THE OCCASION   xliii

ACKNOWLEDGEMENTS   xliii

LOVE'S LABOUR'S LOST   I

GENERAL EDITOR'S PREFACE

THE first volumes of the original series of the Arden edition of Shakespeare's works appeared in 1899, fifty years before the first volume in the present series. It has not, until now, been possible to alter what was originally set up except by the addition of such footnotes and brief appendices as were supplied at successive revisions by the editors themselves or the general editors. Some of the latest volumes in the original series were not gravely affected by this, as they already had the solid body of twentieth-century scholarship behind them when they were first produced. But the earliest of that series, even if edited by the most distinguished scholars of their day, have inevitably become to varying degrees outmoded by investigations that have followed their publication. It was to remedy this that the publishers proposed a new revision, of which the first volumes were to appear in 1949.

Two facts governed the nature of this revision, as indeed, of the original edition. The first was the need to offer to the senior pupils of schools and to university students as much as could be presented in brief and intelligible form of the immense body of scholarship which the first half of the twentieth century has contributed to the field of Shakespeare studies. The second was the need to present a reliable text within the limits imposed by modernization, with its inevitable effects upon spelling, punctuation,[1] and, less directly, upon collation.

Working within these conditions, the revising editors have adopted in general the following methods of treating text, collations, and annotations.

The modernized text which formed the basis of the original series was that of the Cambridge edition of 1891–3. For the present edition we have reached the following agreement:

1. To follow the substantive text (if that was easily determined, as

1. Some change is unavoidable in substituting modern, grammatical punctuation for the pointing of Elizabethan dramatic texts. This is more generally understood now than in the early years of this century, but comments on the problems of individual passages or plays will be found in the separate volumes.

in the case of 'Folio only' plays), except for obvious and agreed errors, spelling variants, mispunctuation, and mislineation. (It will be at once recognized that the connotations of the words 'obvious' and 'agreed' admit a wide solution and allow of some dispute.)

2. To follow, in cases where there was divergence between a F and a good Q text (or between a F, good Q, and bad Q), the generally accepted blend of the two which had been used by the Cambridge editors, except where fresh light had since been thrown on the relative validity of the source texts.[1] It has rested with the individual editors to determine when changes were necessary. There has been a tendency to interpret this in the direction of a return to F or Q readings in place of traditional emendations.[2]

The collations were affected by the use of a modernized text, as in all such editions of the work of Elizabethan dramatists, but, with due allowance for this, they have been arranged in the customary way. Sometimes this has meant little alteration of those of the original Arden volume, but sometimes, where a subsequent textual discovery has modified the evidence, complete recasting has been necessary.

The annotations have been designed to cover, as before, description of specific textual problems including classical emendations, the elucidation of obscure passages with comments on syntax and vocabulary, explanation of references to customs and events that are no longer familiar to modern readers, quotation of illustrative parallels from other sixteenth- and seventeenth-century writers, and brief comments, if the editors so wished, on a few aspects of the thought or dramatic technique. These subjects necessarily receive different emphases in different volumes. The extent to which individual editors have found themselves able to adopt or obliged to modify the work of their predecessors in this section has varied so widely that it is left to each editor to indicate in his own introduction the nature of his indebtedness.

In the appendices each revising editor has included as full representation as possible of source material and in the introductions (in necessarily varying proportions) description of the text of each

1. As, for example, in the case of certain good Quartos, whose reputation has improved during the past fifty years.

2. A minor example may be given from *Macbeth*, the first volume in the new series. At II. iv. 4, all former editors followed Rowe in the slight alteration involved in emending *Ha,* to *Ah!* The present editor restores the reading of the Folios.

play and its problems, discussion of the evidence for its date, some critical comment on the play as a work of art and in relation to its sources, and any further comment which, in the view of that editor, is proper to a full understanding of the lines along which the student may most profitably continue his work.

UNA ELLIS-FERMOR

London, 1949

PREFACE TO FIFTH EDITION

THE occasion of reprinting allows me to correct some errors (many of my own, a few of the printers') and to add notes on two or three discoveries and interpretations made since the previous edition appeared. There has been no change in the general plan or substance of the book.

18 August 1955   R. D.

LIST OF ABBREVIATIONS

E.E.T.S.	Early English Text Society.
E.H.	*England's Helicon*, 1600, ed. Bullen 1887.
M.L.N.	*Modern Language Notes.*
M.L.R.	*Modern Language Review.*
N. & Q.	*Notes and Queries.*
N.E.D.	*A New English Dictionary*, 13 vols., 1933.
R.E.S.	*Review of English Studies.*
Shakes. Lib.	*Shakespeare's Library*, ed. W. C. Hazlitt, 1875.
Tilley	M. P. Tilley, *A Dictionary of the Proverbs in England in the Sixteenth and Seventeenth Centuries*, 1950.
T.L.S.	*The Times Literary Supplement.*

The abbreviations of the titles of Shakespeare's plays and poems follow C. T. Onions, *Shakespeare Glossary*, p. x.

INTRODUCTION

'If we were to part with any of the author's comedies it should be this,' wrote Hazlitt of *Love's Labour's Lost*, and his opinion was shared by most critics between Shakespeare's day and our own. Their reason was partly the belief that this was one of the earliest of Shakespeare's plays, if not the very earliest, a beginner's clumsy effort, full of stilted rhyming couplets and over-elaborate puns, the characters unlifelike, and the action constantly held up for skirmishes of what the uneducated countryman from Stratford mistakenly took for wit. Pope found the comic scenes so generally barren that he cut whole pages of them out of his text, printing them at the page-foot for those curious archaeologists who might wish to see what blunders Shakespeare made before he learnt his business. Actors took it for granted that the play could not be 'good theatre'; the general reader gave thanks that here at least was one work of Shakespeare which it was not considered necessary to read.

Recently there has been a change of feeling. Scholars have come to the conclusion that, in spite of some misleading signs, *Love's Labour's Lost* is not one of Shakespeare's earliest plays, but belongs rather with *Richard II*, *Romeo and Juliet*, and *A Midsummer Night's Dream*, a group written in the same heat as Shakespeare's essays in pure poetry, *Venus and Adonis*, *Lucrece*, and perhaps the sonnets, and with the same sheer lyrical power carrying off occasional unpractised crudities in the action. At the same time a number of revivals on the stage, both professional and amateur, have shown that as entertainment and as drama *Love's Labour's Lost* is still very much alive; the fault is rather too much exuberance—individual characters are lost in the sparkle of quirks and comicalities and personal touches, and the jokes are crammed into the dialogue four deep. Yet this excess of high spirits and invention has its own charm. Shakespeare, it is clear, hugely enjoyed writing the play, and his gusto, his drive, his delighted discovery of the buoyancy of his own genius, carries his audience away with him. It is fascinating, too, to recognize here, so tightly packed on each other that they have no space to develop, the seeds of so many characters and situations to which Shakespeare in later plays was to give full elbow room. Rosaline is clearly a portrait of his own Dark Lady, but from her, and her fellows in the Princess's retinue, stems a whole race of heroines, Portia and Nerissa, Beatrice, Rosalind. Berowne, likewise, is 'father to a line' of gallants. The clowns' mistaking of words reappears in Dogberry and Verges, their play of the Nine Worthies in Bottom's Pyramus and Thisbe. Holofernes is a great-uncle of Dr Caius, and even the mighty Falstaff has a trick of accent and gesture that proclaims him a direct descendant of Armado. Dr Johnson, no kinder than other critics to the play as a whole, is compelled to admit that there is no work that has 'more evident marks of the hand of *Shakespeare*'.

If this were all, if the play were interesting only in the light of the better use to which Shakespeare was later to put some of its material, it might well be left to scholars and to dramatic societies with antiquarian tastes. But *Love's Labour's Lost* stands firmly in its own right. No play of Shakespeare is more distinct, has more a character and 'aura' of its own, and in few is the spell of personality so strong. The attraction springs from a unique combination of formality and actuality, fantastication and common sense. This quality, or balance of qualities, has been admirably characterized by Granville Barker in one of the best of all his *Prefaces to Shakespeare* (First Series, 1927, pp. 1–50). He points to 'style' as the quality above all that a production of this play must achieve if it is to be successful, and 'style' as the essence of the play itself. The situations, for all their flippancy and extravagance, are designed with admirable economy and dovetail with perfect precision. What could be neater than the main plot, with the young men's pious resolutions inviting their discomfiture, the ladies and their suit held off at arm's length, and then the tables turned? What more telling single effects than Jaquenetta's sudden appearance with the letter that pricks the bubble of Berowne's self-righteousness, Costard's interruption, which finally takes the wind out of Armado, or Marcade's, which in a moment swings the play from farce to earnest? Old stage-tricks and gags are used, but with the bravado of genius that can change a damp squib into a rocket—as when the stock eavesdropping scene is multiplied by three and becomes not, as sublunary arithmetic would make it, just trebly boring but a star of mirth. The dialogue, too, has always the controlled energy of fine musical phrasing, whether it be the elegant banter of Navarre and his peers, the quicksilver repartee of the 'mocking wenches', or the fine flights of Armado's and Holofernes' disordered fancies; and the characters, for all that many of them are fantastic, have a method in their madness, a consistency in their exaggeration, which is again the mark of 'style'.

This play then has, like opera, its conventions, which we must accept at the outset if we are not to be merely bewildered and antagonized by their apparent unreality; but having accepted them we start at once on a higher plane, from which we can proceed to explore the remoter ranges of imagination and feeling and are spared the laborious climb up from the jungle of everyday trivialities. The comparison between *Love's Labour's Lost* and a work of music is inescapable. To quote again from Granville Barker, the play is 'never very far from the actual formalities of song and dance. The long last act is half mask and half play; and in song and dance the play ends.' And in another passage he says that 'the actor, in fine, must think of the dialogue in terms of music; of the time and rhythm of it as at one with the sense—in telling him what to do and how to do it, in telling him, indeed, what to be.'

It is this musical quality, evident in both construction and language, that gives the play its buoyancy, its coherence, and its feeling of release, but this must not be taken to suggest that its effect is of a purely formal and artificial beauty. If it is likened to an opera, it must be to one of Mozart's Italian comedies in which perfection of form is combined with shrewdness of characterization and humanity of feeling: to *Figaro*, or to that *Così fan Tutte* for so long misjudged by those who missed the understanding that fills out the modish satire of the plot and the tenderness that informs the elegant melodic line. Armado, like his countryman, Don Quixote, inspires affection as well as mirth. Even Holofernes, conceited, misguided, intolerant, cannot fail to win our sympathy with his final 'This is not generous, not gentle, not humble'; and Nathaniel, bowler or no bowler (see 2.53), has it from the start, though practically he is no more than an ineffectual toady. It is usual to dismiss the secondary heroes and heroines as indistinguishable shadows and reflections one of another, but this is to disregard the delicate touches with which Shakespeare has established a definite personality and even physical character for each: the over-tall and slightly quizzical Longaville, Dumain, impetuous but not quite sure of himself, the red and gold charm of Katharine, and the brusquer Maria. As for Berowne and his Rosaline, there is nothing to touch their genuineness, their completeness as human beings, and their 'high seriousness' till we come to *As You Like It*.

As You Like It, again, is the only Shakespearean comedy earlier than the late romances that in total impression can match this for imaginativeness and variety of mood, or so strongly suggest that beneath the shimmering surface the waters are deep. Anyone who has seen *Love's Labour's Lost* acted will admit the powerful effect of Marcade's entrance in Act v, Scene ii, not only as a superb *coup de théâtre* but as setting up an ever-present pressure of reality through-out the rest of the play until it fades out in bird-calls. And yet this sudden enrichment of the texture has been anticipated again and again in earlier scenes, as in the tale of Katharine's sister or in Berowne's set speeches. In a flash we are back to earth, and it is all the more solid and immediate for our absence and for the suddenness of our return.

There is perhaps another reason, less reputable, for the revival of interest in *Love's Labour's Lost*. In this age of detective stories, who does not enjoy a good 'mystery'? And not only is this, of the men behind the masks of Armado and Holofernes, one of the best, but it is linked more or less directly with the series of unsolved puzzles that makes the literary history of the early 1590's sound like a collection of Father Brown's cases: the elusive Martin Mar-prelate, the lost years of William Shakespeare, the secret society of Sir Walter Ralegh, the stabbing of Christopher Marlowe, the riddle of Willobie and his Avisa, to say nothing of the ubiquitous Francis Bacon and other such unhistorical mystifications. This is the attraction that has brought cranks swarming about *Love's Labour's Lost* and strange indeed is some of the honey they have distilled from it. Behind this, however, lies a more genuine interest. Of all Shakespeare's plays this is the most personal; a solution of the puzzle he has set here (and I had better say at once that I can-not provide it) would not only satisfy the most rabid detective ardour but illuminate Shakespeare's own early life and the condi-tions that shaped his career and his first plays—an essential back-ground of which at present absolutely nothing is known.

2. THE TEXT

2.1. THE QUARTO OF 1598

The earliest surviving text of the play is the edition in Quarto dated 1598. The title-page reads: *A* / PLEASANT / Conceited Comedie / CALLED, / Loues Labors lost. / As it vvas presented before her Highnes / this last Christmas. / Newly corrected and augmented / *By W. Shakespere.* / [ornament] / Imprinted at London by *W. W.* / for *Cutbert Burby.* / 1598.

The phrase 'newly corrected and augmented' reappears on the title-page of the 'good' Quarto of *Romeo and Juliet*, also published by Burby (1599) and, like *Love's Labour's Lost*, never entered on the

Stationers' Register. The 'good' Quarto of *Romeo and Juliet* was evidently issued to supplant the 'bad' Quarto printed by Danter in 1597, and no doubt it was the existence of this earlier edition that made registration, for licensing purposes, unnecessary. Since Burby's *Love's Labour's Lost* appears so similar to his *Romeo and Juliet* it is likely that it was issued with the same purpose, to replace a 'bad' Quarto of which no copy has survived.

2.2. THE PRINTING OF THE QUARTO

The printer of the 1598 Quarto was William White. Dover Wilson's researches, the results of which are given in his Note on the Copy in the New Cambridge edition of the play, have established a remarkably clear picture of what went on in the shop of this printer, and have presented succeeding editors with all the evidence they need to judge how closely White's text is likely to have followed Shakespeare's original.

White had in 1598 only just set up as a printer, and *Love's Labour's Lost* must have been one of the very first books he printed. His compositor was obviously very inexperienced. Misprints abound, mostly 'literals'—one letter used for another, either because the compositor's hand was not sufficiently practised to go to the right compartment of his 'case' for the letter required (as a bungling typist will hit the wrong key) or because the case was 'foul', the type used for an earlier printing and subsequently broken up having been sorted back into the wrong compartments. Many letters again are 'turned', i.e. they were placed the wrong way up in the composing-stick, very much a beginner's blunder. The punctuation is chaotic; not even the most advanced theories of Elizabethan 'rhetorical punctuation' can make it consistent even with itself. Most significant of all, the compositor had not learnt to 'lock up' his type properly, so that when it was shaken, either in being carried to the press, on being dabbed with the inking balls, or under the stress of the actual impression, the letters tended to fall apart from each other or were even jerked out altogether. There are frequent blanks in the Quarto where letters have disappeared; and it is clear that the type became looser and looser as printing proceeded, since in the Bodleian copy and in those held by the British Museum and Trinity College, Cambridge, these blanks become progressively more extensive. (For a note on the status of the 'Devonshire' copy see IV. iii. 179.)

2.3. THE FOLIO OF 1623

It is this peculiarity that provides the proof that the First Folio text of the play was set up not, as Hart supposed, from an independent (and more authoritative) manuscript but from a copy of the 1598 Quarto; for the word 'venew' (v. i. 55) appears in the Quarto as two words, 'vene we', the type having fallen apart in the middle, and this error is exactly reproduced in the Folio. Now it is inconceivable that the same accident should have happened in the same place of the same work in two independent printings; and, besides, Jaggard's compositors were experienced men who did not allow their type to remain loose. Clearly they were merely following what was in the Quarto (which they must therefore have been using as 'copy'), without realizing that it was a misprint.

True, the Folio occasionally improves on the Quarto, correcting 'literals', replacing turned letters, making good the obvious gaps; but none of these improvements is beyond the scope of an experienced printer, and several are quite clearly honest, but weak, patchwork which could never have come from the author (see v. ii. 808). Of the two major alterations, the Folio's 'That were to climb o'er the house to unlock the gate' (I. i. 109) is ill-fitting and flat beside the Quarto's 'Climb o'er the house to unlock the little gate'; and the extra line, 'You that way; we this way,' at the end of the play has presumably been added to make possible an orderly *Exeunt*. It has charm—it may be Shakespeare's; but, like the other improvements, it is well within the capacity of an intelligent prompter or stage-manager.

2.4. THE COPY FOR THE QUARTO

Dover Wilson believed that the 1598 Quarto was set up from a manuscript of Shakespeare's, whose oddities of spelling and handwriting are reflected in the printed text (see notes on I. i. 165, II. i. 34, IV. ii. 35, IV. ii. 52, and IV. iii. 13). Miss Greta Hjort has argued (*Modern Language Review*, XXI, 1926) that the 'good' Quarto of *Romeo and Juliet* was set up from a corrected copy of the 'bad' Quarto, and that the same procedure is likely to have been followed with *Love's Labour's Lost*. But the peculiarities and corruptions that can only be due to a manuscript original are surely too many to be explained either (*a*) as originating entirely from the mere MS. *corrections* made in the margin of the 'bad' Quarto to bring that corrupt version up to standard, or (*b*) as a reflection of the eccentricities of the MS. copy for the 'bad' Quarto which, to survive two printings, must have been more pronounced even than Shakespeare's, and in the same kind.

2.5. EVIDENCE OF REVISION

A decision on this point is vital. If Dover Wilson is right, the two distinct kinds of material evident in the play, and at times conflicting with each other, can only be Shakespeare's original version and a later revision of it. The words on the title-page are then to be taken at their face value: some years ('newly') after first writing the play, Shakespeare revised and augmented it. If on the other hand Miss Hjort is right, the phrase is merely the normal indication that the text that bears it is a 'good' Quarto, i.e. a text authorized by its proprietor and with those passages restored that were garbled or cut in the corrupt version. The two strands in the play would then be Shakespeare's re-established text and surviving traces of the 'bad' Quarto.

I find it impossible to accept Sir Walter Greg's contention (*The Editorial Problem in Shakespeare*, 1942, p. 127) that the two elements represent first and second thoughts in Shakespeare's original draft, and that the Quarto preserves both because it was set up, deletions and all, from his 'foul papers'. As will be seen, the differences not only in style but in intention are too great to be included in a single act of composition.

2.51. *Doublets*. The most striking instances of the double nature of the play are those first noticed by Capell in iv. iii. 285–361 and a similar passage at v. ii. 809, where alternative versions of an identical speech are retained side by side. It is a matter of opinion whether the shorter version of Berowne's speech in iv. iii is best explained as an early draft of Shakespeare's on the basis of which he later elaborated the longer version, or merely as a pirate's corruption of this. Dover Wilson makes much of the meaningless fragment, 'with ourselves', which appears in early texts tacked on at the end of the shorter version (line 312). To explain it he produces the plausible theory that Shakespeare marked the earlier version for deletion not by scoring it through but by enclosing it in a bracket, the lower arm of which cut into the last line. The compositor could not miss the mutilated line, and duly omitted all but the two words that had escaped Shakespeare's reckless stroke; he did miss the main span of the bracket running up the margin and failed to realize that all the lines embraced by it should have been omitted too. This agrees well with Shakespeare's known carelessness, the compositor's known lack of experience, and the undoubted existence of more than one passage that should have been deleted but was not. To Miss Hjort, however, the fragment 'with ourselves' is one of the loose ends and misunderstandings with which all 'bad' Quartos abound.

It is noteworthy that a passage constantly quoted as parallel to this of Berowne's, namely, the speech with which Theseus opens Act v of *A Midsummer Night's Dream*, appears to have undergone a precisely similar expansion. Theseus' speech in its original version clearly dealt only with lover and madman. The poet is an afterthought, and the lines that describe him are purple patches, of a later and richer material, added to the original, which makes connected sense even if these are detached (see New Shakespeare edition, pp. 80–3). The joins in Berowne's speech are less obvious, but we can guess that it was constructed on the same principle.

The fuller treatment of Berowne's exchange with Rosaline in v. ii shows a change of intention as to how the scene is to develop and can surely only be due to author's revision. Supporters of Miss Hjort's view would still point to passages in the *Contention* and in the 'bad' Quarto of *Hamlet* as equally radical perversions of the Shakespearean scenes.

2.52. *The 'Katharine–Rosaline tangle' in II. i.* Failure to cancel a rejected draft must also be responsible for this famous puzzle. At II. i. 113 begins a conversation between Berowne and a lady who is designated Katharine in the Quarto, Rosaline in the Folio. Editors, with the exception of Capell, have followed the Folio, and it certainly looks as if Berowne should be skirmishing with his own lady at this point. Yet it is odd that he should have another encounter with her at line 179, while the other pairs of lovers are never given a turn to speak; and the situation is further complicated by both Quarto and Folio reading Rosaline at line 194 where we should expect Dumain to be told of his own lady, Katharine, and Katharine at line 209, where Berowne's inquiry should surely be for his Rosaline.

This muddle has been variously put down to printers' errors (that easy cutting of every Gordian Knot), and to an early version of the play in which there were only three pairs of lovers, Berowne's opposite being the fair Katharine who, by an oversight of the reviser, still usurps Rosaline's place in this scene and elsewhere sometimes lends her her attributes (e.g. the 'white hand' of III. i. 162 and 'whitely' complexion of III. i. 191—see notes). This theory is developed at length by H. D. Gray in *The Original Version of 'Love's Labour's Lost'* (Stanford University, 1918), and on rather different lines, with a dark Katharine, by Dr Janet Spens (*Review of English Studies*, VII. 1931).

It was Capell who suggested that this scene was originally one of cross-purposes, the ladies wearing masks (which still persist at line 123) and each lover being put off with the wrong opposite. On this assumption Berowne first tackles Katharine thinking she is Rosaline, discovers his mistake, and leaves her; next approaches Rosaline, who succeeds in hiding her identity, so that, convinced again that he has hit on the wrong person, Berowne leaves her too; finally he asks Boyet who the third lady is and, on being told 'Katharine', sees he has been made game of, and goes off in a huff. In the same way Dumain and Longaville, inquiring after their ladies, are given misleading answers.

That this was originally the intention of the scene is clear from the survival of the allusion to masking, but Capell's explanation still does not account for the Rosaline in line 194 (line 61 has already established that it *must* be Katharine who is associated with Alençon) and he too is forced to attribute this to a printer's error. Nor can it be that in the scene as it stands now the lovers are intended to be left mystified, since in IV. iii they have no difficulty in addressing their sonnets to the right ladies.

The most satisfactory solution is that put forward by H. B. Charlton in *The Library*, 8 (1917), p. 355, and elaborated by Dover Wilson (New Shakespeare edition, pp. 120 ff.). It is that in revising the play Shakespeare decided to transfer his comedy of mistaken identities, originally placed here in II. i, to Act v, Scene ii, where it becomes the fooling of the 'Muscovites'. To transform the present scene into one of straightforward exposition certain adjustments were necessary: Berowne's exploratory conversations with Katharine at line 113 and with Rosaline at line 179 had to be cut out, and at the end of the scene each lover must be made to inquire after and be informed of his own lady. Shakespeare, however, scrawled his cancellation so roughly, as in IV. iii and v. ii, that the compositor missed the indication that the passages were to be deleted, and set them both up in his text; and the vital change of Katharine to Rosaline was made in the wrong line (194 instead of 209).

2.53. *The recasting of the 'Worthies'*. Traces of a change of plan can also be found in the pageant of the Nine Worthies and in the winding up of the action. In first casting his players (v. i. 118) Holofernes gives the parts of Joshua and Judas to actors who do not in the event play them, and apparently leaves his own role undecided; and it has been suggested by H. D. Gray (*op. cit.*) that Alexander was originally played by Dull, a more likely person than Nathaniel to be commended by Costard for his skill at bowls and his neighbourliness, and to possess that strong smell always associated by Shakespeare with 'the base vulgar'. Furthermore the Princess's reference (v. ii. 731) to her 'great suit so easily obtain'd' seems inexplicable in the play as we have it. Did Marcade originally bring the Princess not the news of her father's death but the missing document required to establish her claim? And did the play end

> *Berowne.* Our wooing doth not end like an old play;
> Jack hath not Jill: these ladies' courtesy
> Might well have made our sport a comedy.
> *King.* Come, sir, it wants a twelvemonth and a day,
> And then 'twill end.
> *Berowne.*   That's too long for a play?

2.54. *A lost Armado scene.* Again, at the end of iv. i Costard's words (lines 145–8) suggest that he and the audience have recently been watching some comic business performed by Armado and his page; but these two characters do not appear at all in the scene as it stands now.

2.55. *Variant speech-headings.* The speech-headings also suggest two different drafts. Their variations have been studied at length by Dover Wilson (New Shakespeare edition, pp. 109–13). Certain characters, including Navarre but particularly the group of comics —Armado, Moth, Costard, Dull, Holofernes, Nathaniel—appear sometimes under their personal names, sometimes with the generic titles of King, Braggart, Boy, Clown, Constable, Pedant, and Curate. For the most part the names, generic or personal, remain constant for any one scene: Navarre is Navarre (or Ferdinand) for the first two acts, King for the rest of the play; Armado and Moth his Page are so called in i. ii and the second half of iii. i but appear as Braggart and Boy for the first sixty-six lines of that scene and for the whole of Act v. There are, however, scenes in which both types of heading are used indiscriminately. Dover Wilson's analysis of these shows that speeches essential to the structure and continuity of the scene are invariably headed by personal names; the speeches, and parts of speeches, headed by type-names might all be additions to the original material. This sounds more like a man touching up and expanding his own first draft than the correction of another's garbled version. It also suggests that some time had elapsed between the writing and the re-writing, so that the author had come to remember his *dramatis personæ* by their general characters and not by the particular names he had given them.

2.56. *Variations in typography.* Peculiarities of typography and lining may imply that the printer's copy was not uniform. We have seen (2.2) that the compositor was a beginner but, perhaps for that very reason, he seems (except in the matter of punctuation) to have followed his copy slavishly. Hence Armado's letter in i. i, set in italic with an ornament at the head, may represent an original elaborately written out in Italian hand. The letter in iv. i is in roman like the rest of the text; here Shakespeare cannot have bothered to distinguish the inset letter from the dialogue, but wrote all out in his normal English script. The change of practice, supported by a difference in the spelling of Armado's signature, suggests a lapse of time between the writing of the two scenes.

In several places, notably v. ii. 1–4 and 15–17, the Quarto prints verse-speeches as prose. These are all points at which revision is suspected on other grounds, and Dover Wilson suggests that the new material was written crabbedly in the margin, so that the compositor was unable to distinguish any line-division.

2.57. *Conflicting allusions.* Finally, it is difficult to reconcile with a single date of composition the various allusions to contemporary events that have been detected in the play. The Navarre setting must belong to some date earlier than 1594, by which time the real King of Navarre had ceased to be an ally of Elizabeth and the doings of a Navarrese court would no longer arouse friendly interest in England; the hunting scene appears very close to the account of Elizabeth's entertainment at Cowdray, published in 1591; and if, as has been suggested, the play is partly ridicule of Ralegh and his 'school' of mathematicians and atheists, it cannot be much later than Ralegh's disgrace in 1592, and the official inquiry into the school held in 1594. On the other hand the scene of the masque of Muscovites in v. ii if, as seems probable, it bears a reference to the Gray's Inn Revels of Christmastide 1594, cannot have been written earlier than the summer of 1595. We may therefore expect to find indications of two distinct dates for the writing of *Love's Labour's Lost.*

3. THE DATE OF COMPOSITION

3.1. EXTERNAL EVIDENCE

The *terminus ante* is given by the first Quarto, dated 1598 and carrying a reference to a performance at Christmas. Since the year in the old style ran from March to March, this performance may have been either at Christmas 1598 or Christmas 1597, and the play in its present form completed autumn 1598 or 1597. The earlier dates are more probable. References to the play by name occur in Francis Meres's *Palladis Tamia* (published 1598, probably in October) and in Robert Tofte's *Alba* (also dated 1598). The wording of the latter is

> Loues Labour Lost, I once did see a Play
> Ycleped so, so called to my paine.

The 'once' suggests some time long before the time of writing, but it is just possible that it means 'on one occasion only'.

It has been suggested that Robert Southwell's poem, *St Peter's Complaint*, with its play, in stanzas 56 and 57, on eyes and stars, borrows from *Love's Labour's Lost*. It was published in 1595, but Southwell had been kept a close prisoner since 1592 and can hardly have read, much less seen the play after that date. It is, of course, arguable that Shakespeare borrowed from Southwell, or that the similarity is pure coincidence.

The joke about 'remuneration' and 'guerdon' (III. i. 164) appears in the anonymous *A Health to the gentlemanly profession of serving-men* (1598), where it is said to have been told to the author 'not long since by a friend'. It may have been taken from *Love's Labour's Lost*; but may equally well have been traditional.

3.2. INTERNAL EVIDENCE

3.21. *Style*. According to the metrical tests invented by Fleay, whose ranging of the plays in chronological order by this means has been largely confirmed by other evidence, *Love's Labour's Lost* is the earliest of the series. The proportion of rhymed lines, end-stopped lines, and doggerel metres is very high. The play has, however, a highly artificial theme to which these metrical devices are particularly appropriate; for the special subject-matter Shakespeare may well have revived a technique which he had otherwise discarded.

The same considerations apply to the play's structure. T. W. Baldwin, in *Shakspere's Five-Act Structure*, 1947, argues that this is the most primitive, the least classical in form of all Shakespeare's plays, and therefore the earliest. Its peculiarities of construction may just as well be due to a special purpose for which it was designed. They are certainly not such overwhelming proofs of early date as to justify Baldwin's, to my mind, petulant refusal to study the other evidence impartially.

Love's Labour's Lost is intensely lyrical and teems with echoes of the non-dramatic poems of Shakespeare, particularly *Lucrece*, and of the sonnets. The most striking resemblances, involving both thought and expression, are those between the 'Dark Lady' sonnets (especially 127 and 132) and Berowne's praise of 'blackness' in IV. iii; and between Sonnet 21 and several passages in the play similarly decrying flattery (II. i. 13–16, IV. iii. 236). Other examples are given in the notes, and a long list has been collected by C. F. McClumpha in *Modern Language Notes*, xv, no. 6 (1900). The date of composition of individual sonnets is of course not known, but *Venus and Adonis* was printed in 1593 and *Lucrece* in 1594. Until Hotson brings forward weightier evidence than appears in *Shakespeare's Sonnets Dated* (1949) for the ante-dating of Shakespeare's non-dramatic (and with it much of his dramatic) work, it is to

1593–4 that the stylistic affinities of *Love's Labour's Lost* would seem to attach it.

3.22. *Allusions*

3.221. *Navarre*. It was Joseph Hunter who first suggested that the characters of the play are historical, though he failed to realize that they were Shakespeare's contemporaries. There was a real King of Navarre, very much in the Elizabethan news, who possessed many of the characteristics of the King in the play, though his name was Henri and not Ferdinand. The Duc de Biron and the Duc de Longueville were his faithful supporters; and though the Duc de Mayenne was not a supporter, but his bitterest enemy, this name too was constantly linked with the King's (see particularly 4.2 below), and may also have been confused with that of d'Aumont, a trusted general of the King's who was especially well known to Englishmen. Gossip about life at the court of Navarre might have been available to an English author at any time after 1586, or even earlier, but the period in which it would be appreciated with sympathy by an English audience is more limited. The question has been carefully explored by H. B. Charlton (*Modern Language Review*, XIII, 1918). He recalls that it was in October 1589 that English troops, under Lord Willoughby, were first sent openly to help the Protestant Henri to enforce, in the face of the Catholic League, his claim to the throne of France; that Henri's popularity in England was at its height in August 1591 (when Essex played a flamboyant but not very effective part in the campaign for the capture of Rouen), but was forfeited in July 1593 when, coming to terms with the League, Henri renounced his Protestantism and was received into the Catholic church; and that the English troops supporting him were finally withdrawn in November 1593. A playwright would therefore be most tempted to write a play about Navarre in 1591–3, when Englishmen were fighting with his troops as allies in a popular cause.

3.222. *Anti-alien riots*. The same dates fit the other apparent references to historical events. Moth's joke at III. i. 6 about a 'French brawl' has been taken as referring to the London riots against foreign refugees, many of them Huguenots, whose competition for the city's accommodation, food, and employment was much resented. These riots recurred at intervals in the 'eighties and 'nineties. There was an abortive anti-alien plot in September 1586, and more open demonstrations in May 1593. The serious outbreak of June 1595, followed by a savage execution of the ringleaders, seems to have been directed more against profiteering tradesmen than against aliens.

3.223. *Plague*. The plague, to which much reference is made in
v. ii. 419 ff., was also particularly violent in the years 1591–4, but it
was many years earlier that the phrase 'Lord have mercy upon us'
(quoted at v. ii. 419) was first widely used as the sign, painted on
house doors, that those within were infected. See note on the passage.

3.224. *Morocco*. The 'dancing horse' of I. ii. 50 is usually taken
to be Banks's famous 'Morocco'. The earliest certain reference to
him is dated 1591, but there was a performing horse, Morocco or
another, at the Cross Keys theatre as early as 1588 (see note on the
passage) and Banks's animal was still doing tricks in 1600. In view
of this long span of activity, no precise date can be deduced for
Moth's allusion.

3.225. *Cowdray*. Hart believed that the unnecessarily elaborate
treatment of the hunting-scene (IV. i, ii) owed something to the
publication in 1591 of an account of the *Queen's Entertainment at
Cowdray*. The details of the erection of 'stands', the shooting with
cross-bows, the use of hounds, etc., are certainly similar to those in
the play, but the methods may well have been those generally accepted for ceremonial hunting parties of this kind. As Sir Edmund
Chambers acidly remarks (*William Shakespeare*, I. 335), 'There is
no reason whatever to suppose that Elizabeth shot a deer with a
cross-bow for the first or the last time at Cowdray in 1591.'

3.226. *Pierce Penilesse*. Hart was also responsible for calling attention to the echoes in *Love's Labour's Lost* of the pamphlet war between Gabriel Harvey and Thomas Nashe, of which more below
(5.22). The battle proper began with the appearance of Robert
Greene's *A Quip for an Upstart Courtier*, Nashe's *Pierce Penilesse his
Supplication to the Divell*, and Harvey's answer to both in *Foure Letters
. . . especially touching Robert Greene*, all in the autumn of 1592. The
probable references are to *Pierce Penilesse* and to Harvey's second
major pamphlet, *Pierce's Supererogation*, almost certainly published
in October 1593; but some ears have detected faint echoes of
Nashe's rejoinder, *Have With You to Saffron Walden*, which was not
ready until spring 1596.

3.227. *Ralegh*. Allusions have also been suspected (see 5.23) to
Sir Walter Ralegh's fall from favour on account of his liaison with
the Queen's maid of honour, Elizabeth Throgmorton (afterwards
Lady Ralegh); to his circle of mathematicians and philosophers
whose 'atheism', notorious for several years before, could only be
openly investigated after the disgrace had removed Ralegh's protection; and to the poem, *The Shadow of Night*, written by George
Chapman apparently in honour of this circle. Now Ralegh was
sent to the Tower in July 1592, the investigation into his atheistical
associates was set on foot in March 1594, and Chapman's poem,

published in 1594, had been entered on the Stationers' Register in December 1593 and probably seen in manuscript by Marlowe before his death in June.

3.228. *Gray's Inn.* Many have wondered why the lords should choose in Act v, Scene ii, to appear in *Russian* disguises. Russia, like Navarre, had been in the news during the 'eighties and 'nineties. The voyages of Richard Chancellor and the Burroughs had opened up trade with Russia and a trading company, the Company of Muscovy Merchants, was formed in 1584. There had been an exchange of ambassadors between England and Russia and in 1583 a special envoy was sent by Czar Ivan the Terrible to ask for the hand of Lady Mary Hastings in marriage. The lady was nicknamed at court the 'Empress of Muscovia' and was much teased about the wooing, which was conducted with elaborate and, on the part of the English, mock ceremony. Sir Sidney Lee was convinced that this incident lay behind the scene in the play. In 1591 appeared Giles Fletcher's detailed account of Russia and Russian customs, *Of the Russe Common Wealth*; and it was perhaps the reading of this work that inspired a remarkable 'revel' at Gray's Inn during the Christmas season of 1594–5. Attention was first drawn to this by E. K. Chambers in his *William Shakespeare*, and it has been independently studied in detail by R. Taylor (*The Date of Love's Labour's Lost*, 1932). There are two main points of contact with the masque in *Love's Labour's Lost* over and above the fact that a mock embassy of Muscovites appears in both. The 'Russians' of the present play are accompanied, rather strangely, by blackamoors, who *may* be a reflection of the 'Negro Tartars' of the Gray's Inn revel; and Rosaline's jibe at v. ii. 393, 'sea-sick, I think, coming from Muscovy', may be an echo of the excuse made by the Prince of Purpoole (the director of the Christmas merry-making elected each year by the benchers) who, on his return from a 'visit' to Russia, declared that he must forgo certain ceremonies on account of his exhaustion 'by length of my Journey, and my sickness at Sea'. Shakespeare may have had particular reason to bear this Gray's Inn revel in mind. During the same Christmas festivities the benchers put on, as the climax to an evening's rag, a 'play of Errors'. On that day, 28 December 1594, Shakespeare's company performed his *Comedy of Errors* before the Queen at Greenwich; and it is generally assumed that it was a repeat performance of this play that was given at Gray's Inn that night, with the same actors, among whom may well have been Shakespeare himself.

3.3. CONCLUSIONS

The occurrence in *Love's Labour's Lost* of many ideas and images from Shakespeare's poems, here wrought into the very fabric of the play, suggest that it was written at the same time as they were, viz. 1593–4. The historical events which are also found woven into the pattern belong, with the exception of the Gray's Inn revel, to the same years; the interest in Navarre would be cold before 1594, but on the other hand Shakespeare could hardly have seen *Pierce's Supererogation* or *The Shadow of Night* before the autumn of 1593. To that season, then, the date of composition of the main body of the play is best assigned.

The reference to the Gray's Inn revel, if it is accepted, must be a later touch added to the original play, and the doublets in the text, the apparent reshaping of certain scenes, and the variations in speech-headings also point to a revision. The date of this must fall between February 1594/5 (the date of the revel) and Christmas 1597 (the presumed date of the performance before the Queen). Since this introduction was first written, Mr J. W. Lever's discovery in Gerard's *Herball* (see note on v. ii. 887–8) has come to support a revision of the play in 1597.

4. THE SOURCES

4.1. A HYPOTHETICAL SOURCE

No written source is known from which the plot might have been borrowed; there is, however, some reason to think that such a source did exist but is now lost. For every other play Shakespeare is known to have used some documentary original. Moreover the description on the title-page of the 1598 Quarto—'newly corrected and augmented'—suggests the existence of an earlier printed edition, and it would appear that such a 'bad' Quarto might sometimes be compiled on the basis of an earlier 'non-copyright' version of the play. This discarded piece would be brought into some sort of conformity with the modern work that had superseded it by the addition of scenes and dialogue supplied either by actors willing to give away their parts in the new play or by the writer's own memory of performances he had attended. The foundation can be clearly traced in other 'bad' Quartos. If then there was a 'bad' Quarto of *Love's Labour's Lost*, it may be that this too was constructed on a similar basis, viz. an earlier play with the same plot.

It is possible also that such things as the confusion between the Princess's ladies, and the doggerel of Costard (IV. i. 141–9) and Nathaniel (IV. ii. 23–32)—surprising even in such a confirmed experimenter as Shakespeare—go back not to an early Shakespearean draft but to this pre-Shakespearean play.

4.2. THE HISTORICAL BASIS

Shakespeare's play follows historical fact remarkably closely. The real King of Navarre received two embassies from France, either of which might have served as a model for that in *Love's Labour's Lost*. In one the ambassador was indeed a Princess of France, Marguerite de Valois (daughter of Catharine de Médicis and herself married to Henri), who came with her mother in 1578; in the other it was the Queen of France, Catharine herself (and in several places the Quarto reads 'Queen' for 'Princess') who met Henri at Saint Bris in 1586. In both discussions probably, and certainly in the earlier one, an important topic was Marguerite's dowry, which included Aquitaine (compare II. i. 128 ff.). On both occasions the royal envoy, reinforcing diplomacy by coquetry, was supported by that famous bevy of ladies-in-waiting who for their grace and flightiness were known as 'l'escadron volant'. Abel Lefranc, who first drew attention to the earlier embassy (*Sous le Masque de William Shakespeare*, 1918), points out that negotiations were conducted at Nerac in an atmosphere of pageantry, gallantry, and continual entertainment which is strikingly similar to that of *Love's Labour's Lost*. Sully wrote of the occasion: 'On se livra au plaisir, aux festins et aux fêtes galantes, ne nous amusant tous qu'à rire, danser et courir la bague.' In the years immediately preceding this visit, Marguerite had made journeys exactly corresponding to those referred to by the Princess and her ladies in Act II, Scene i, of the play: to Alençon (Marguerite's brother François was Duc d'Alençon) in 1578 and to Liége (Brabant) in 1577. It was at Liége that Hélène de Tournon, daughter of one of Marguerite's ladies-in-waiting, died of love for a young nobleman, the Marquis de Varembon. The Marquis was not in Liége at the time of her death, and learnt of it only when, returning, he met the funeral procession. It is highly probable that this incident suggested not only the decline of Katharine's sister (v. ii. 14) but the story of Ophelia in *Hamlet*.

The King's 'Achademe' is also a reflection of history. In 1583 the English ambassador to the court of France reported to Walsingham that Navarre 'has furnished his Court with principal gentlemen of the Religion, and reformed his house'; and in the autumn of 1582 Marguerite herself had written to Henri: 'Si vous etiez honete homme vouz quitteriez l'agriculture et l'humeur de Timon pour venir vivre parmi les hommes.' Navarre had in fact followed a widespread fashion and become royal patron of an academy. Miss F. A. Yates, in her *French Academies* (1947), has described how the example of Plato first fired renaissance scholars in Italy to found these, in essence, philosophical debating societies;

how the vogue spread to France and was there fostered by the
Medicis, who no doubt remembered how their ancestors had been
patrons of the movement in its cradle, Florence; and how Navarre
was inspired (probably through the Huguenot poet d'Aubigné, a
member of the Palace Academy) to emulate his brother-in-law
Henri III. It is perhaps significant that Henri III's academy had
extended its field of interest to philology and music, and the poets
and artists who composed it were largely responsible for the court
entertainments. In such elaborate masques as, for instance, those
devised for the wedding of Henri of Navarre and Marguerite,
Catholic and Huguenot nobles met on an equal footing. The only
milieu in which Navarre and de Mayenne might have been found
side by side was one, like that of the play, closely associated with
both masquing and academies. It is, however, extremely unlikely
that Shakespeare had any direct knowledge of Navarre's academy,
of which neither the Duc de Biron nor the Duc de Longueville were
members. His idea of it most probably came from Pierre de la
Primaudaye's *L'Académie françoise*, a generalized account of the
French movement which was translated in 1586 and became very
popular. The model academy described is composed by *four* young
idealists of Anjou.

A great many other correspondences are listed in Professor Lefranc's book: the King's impetuous riding (IV. i. 1–2) and his
covering of the whole sheet, 'margent and all', in his letter-writing
(V. ii. 8) were actual habits of Henri of Navarre; and the names
Boyet, Marcadé, and de la Mothe appear in contemporary regis-
ters of court officials. Others of these examples are not so convincing,
and we can smile at the contention that Armado's fixing of the
position where he caught Costard and Jaquenetta—'north north-
east and by east from the west corner of thy curious-knotted garden'
—is navigationally correct. In his anxiety to prove that *Love's
Labour's Lost* was written by someone with intimate and first-hand
knowledge of Navarre and its court, Lefranc overstates a case already established by the Hélène de Tournon story, which was not
published until it appeared in Marguerite de Valois's own memoirs
(1628). A suggestion has been made, and is noted in 5.25 below,
as to the channel through which even Shakespeare may have obtained it, together with the rest of the Navarre material which any
unbiased reader of Lefranc must recognize as a source of the play.

4.3. DRAMATIC MODELS

4.31. *John Lyly.* That *Love's Labour's Lost* is an imitation of Lyly's
plays is as much a commonplace of criticism as that it is a satire
on Lyly's affected language, his 'Euphuism'. It is constantly re-

peated that Armado and Moth are copied from Sir Thopas and his page Epiton in *Endymion*. But in fact there is no real similarity between Shakespeare's play and those of Lyly, which belong to an older and more courtly *genre* even than *Love's Labour's Lost*, Shakespeare's most courtly play; the ridiculous language of Armado and Holofernes is much nearer to Sidney's *Arcadia* than to Lyly's *Euphues*, and the resemblance between Armado and Sir Thopas exists not because one is an imitation of the other but because both can be traced back, though by different channels, to a common source.

4.32. *The Commedia dell' Arte*. Lyly's plays derive from the academic *Commedia Erudita* (itself based on classical originals), with its formalized plot and characters, and its simplified staging in which a separate 'house' (though all are set together on the same stage) symbolizes the location of each group of characters. Shakespeare's play lacks this stylization altogether, but it does owe something to the *Commedia dell' Arte*, which replaced the *Commedia Erudita* on the popular stages. The distinguishing mark of the *Commedia dell' Arte* was the entirely improvised dialogue in which the stock plots, of much the same character as those of the 'learned' plays, were elaborated. The professional actors who in Italy developed this form of drama specialized each one in the presentation of a particular figure from among the group of conventional types that formed the *dramatis personæ*. Thus Francesco Andreini, chief of the Gelosi company which visited France and possibly England in the last quarter of the sixteenth century, was famous for his Braggart. This character, derived from the Miles Gloriosus of Plautine comedy, had already been transformed in Italian comedy into a Spanish soldier of fortune, a familiar figure in an Italy much of it garrisoned by Spanish armies. The role was played by Andreini in a multitude of different plays, but always under the same name, Capitano Spavento del Vall' Inferno; and he built up the character by a series of highly elaborate set speeches, which took infinite study and pains to compose and which were so popular that Andreini published two collections of them.

Armado would have been impossible without the Captain and his kin; and in the same way Holofernes, with his scraps of languages, his false etymologies, and his blunders over technical terms, is an English version of the pedant, Doctor Graziano, as Costard of the rustic servant Zanni and the yes-man Nathaniel of the parasite. The line of descent is not always direct. Armado, in love with a bumpkin, and finding classical precedents for his predicament, is nearer Doctor than Captain; but though the family character-

istics may be mixed the Italian parentage of all the comic supporting characters in *Love's Labour's Lost* cannot be denied. For a detailed analysis of the debt see O. J. Campbell's *Love's Labour's Lost
Restudied* (University of Michigan Studies in Shakespeare, Milton
and Donne, 1925).

4.33. *The Queen's Progresses*. Professor Campbell has also described
another probable influence in the make-up of Shakespeare's play
—the elaborate entertainments, often prolonged over several days,
which were presented to the Queen at the rich houses which she
visited on 'progress'. These entertainments were made up of a
number of dissimilar but largely standardized elements. Among
them constantly figure masques of courtiers, disputations both
serious and burlesque, dancing and song, and a play presented in
all earnestness by local talent (often led by the schoolmaster) to be
duly mocked by the Queen and her retinue with all the brutality
accorded here to Holofernes' pageant. No doubt Shakespeare, as
Campbell suggests, in devising a suitable entertainment for the
reception of a Princess of France would naturally turn to what was
provided *de rigueur* for her English counterpart. Hence the episodical
nature of the play and the accumulation of set pieces that so prolong its final section. Bookish critics have called it a lack of proportion, but it is precisely this, with its recollection of Elizabeth's *al
fresco* diversions, that gives the play its delightful air of formal in-
formality.

5. THE TOPICAL CONTEXT

5.1. EVIDENCES OF HIDDEN MEANING

Neither the historical events on which the play is based nor the
dramatic models by which it is shaped can provide the full explanation of its purpose and point; and that these must lie deeper than
the superficial import of the words, often vapid and sometimes
completely senseless, is clear from the indefinable impression of a
coherent intention with which the reader of the play is left. The
more he enjoys the play the more (in the words of 'Q') 'he will be
teased by afterthoughts of meanings missed, and will long to go
back and solve them'. There are, for example, nine passages which
must embody some contemporary joke now lost to us. These are:

(*a*) Armado and Moth's play with the words 'tender Juvenal'
(I. ii. 8 ff.).

(*b*) Armado's resentment of Moth's allusion to an eel (I. ii. 29).

(*c*) The constant punning on 'penny' and 'purse' (III. i. 25, v. i.
66–7) and particularly the flourish on the phrase 'piercing a hogshead' (IV. ii. 84).

(*d*) The doggerel on the Fox, the Ape, and the Humble-bee (III. i. 82).

(*e*) The reference (if it is not a misprint) to a 'Schoole of Night' (IV. iii. 251).

(*f*) Armado's pronunciation of 'Sirrah' as 'Chirrah' (V. i. 31).

(*g*) The reference to a 'charge-house' on a 'mountain', where Holofernes teaches (V. i. 74–5).

(*h*) The unorthodox inclusion of Hercules and Pompey among the Nine Worthies (V. i. 120–1).

(*i*) The connection of Holofernes with Judas Iscariot (V. ii. 590 ff.).

Any key to the general mystery we may think we have found must be tested on these nine locks.

5.2. SUGGESTED EXPLANATIONS

Incidental suggestions go back almost within reach of Shakespeare's own day, but it is only recently that connected explanations of the play's meaning have been put forward.

5.21. *Individual identifications.* The first note (1747) comes from Warburton, who stated bluntly, without citing any authority, 'By *Holofernes* is designed a particular character, a pedant and schoolmaster of our author's time, one *John Florio*, a teacher of the *Italian* tongue in *London*, who has given us a small dictionary of that language under the title of *A world of words*.' This derivation for Holofernes was blown upon by Dr Johnson, but scholars have continued to canvass it. Even anagrams have been rushed to its support, but the arguments brought against it are hardly less feeble. It has been said, for instance, that Shakespeare would hardly have risked offending his patron Southampton by attacking Florio, a member of the Earl's household; but in fact he may have hoped to curry favour by doing just this, since Florio was almost certainly placed in that household by Burghley, presumably to keep a severe and Protestant eye on his young Catholic ward. It is certainly curious that, in the preface to the 1598 edition of his dictionary, Florio combines abuse of his chief detractor H(ugh) S(anford), with a savage sneer at '*Aristophanes* and his comedians' who '*make plaies, and scowre their mouthes on Socrates*'. This looks like a reference to an actual attack by a playwright on that famous teacher, John Florio. In connecting it specifically, as he does, with *Love's Labour's Lost*, Warburton may be following an old and authentic tradition. If so, crux (*g*)—the 'charge-house on the mountain'—might be explained as a pun on Florio's work on *Montaigne*; but there are perhaps better solutions of this puzzle.

Some of these incidental suggestions, as that Holofernes is a caricature of the schoolmaster who taught Shakespeare at Stratford, spring too plausibly from the facts. Others are too fanciful. Lefranc's contention, that Holofernes must be one Richard Lloyd, the pedantic tutor of the sixth Earl of Derby, rests on the fact that Lloyd actually composed a pageant of the Nine Worthies, in which each character introduces himself with the words 'I am', and the arms of Alexander are described as in *Love's Labour's Lost*. J. H. Roberts has shown (*Modern Philology*, XIX, 1921–2) that this formula of introduction is common to a host of sixteenth-century didactic poems including the *Mirrour for Magistrates*, and that Alexander's arms are those generally given for him in the heraldic textbooks of the period. Equally lacking in solid foundation is Fleay's identification of the comic characters of the play with the protagonists in the pamphlet-war between the Puritans, their unauthorized and unidentified champion 'Martin Marprelate', and the defenders of the established church. The Marprelate scandals, as Fleay justly points out, would be a likely subject for a topical play in the early 'nineties. There may indeed be something in the general suggestion, though nothing in Fleay's detailed correspondences.

5.22. *Harvey and Nashe*. Fleay had maintained that Moth represents Thomas Nashe, the young 'University wit' whose part in the tracts written against Martin, though never yet clearly defined, is generally recognized to have been extensive. In the first Arden edition of *Love's Labour's Lost* H. C. Hart confirmed that there were traces of Nashe in the play, but detailed investigation appeared to show that these led back not to the Marprelate controversy but to its sequel, Nashe's long drawn-out battle with the Cambridge don, Gabriel Harvey. This conclusion was awkward for Hart who, like Fleay, held the then orthodox view that the play must be dated about 1590; now that we believe it was written in 1593 Hart's findings are just what we should expect.

The Harvey–Nashe quarrel, then, is a solid foundation, the first to be offered to theory-builders. For this reason, and for its complexity, it deserves examination in some detail. In origin it goes back to 1580, when the Earl of Oxford quarrelled violently (on the tennis-court) with Sir Philip Sidney. Gabriel Harvey was a protégé of the Earl of Leicester and his nephew Sidney (both of Puritan sympathies) and now wrote a lampoon which might be construed as an attack on Oxford's Italianate airs, his political trickery, and his irreligion, though Harvey afterwards denied this interpretation. The poem was brought to Oxford's attention through the malice of his secretary, John Lyly, the dramatist and novelist, and Harvey had an unpleasant time of it until he had made his peace.

Nine years later Lyly was one of the hacks hired on behalf of the bishops of the established church to answer Marprelate in his own vein; and in his pamphlet, *Pappe with an Hatchet*—out of sheer devilment it seems—he dared his old victim to undertake the Puritan defence. Harvey prepared his reply but for some reason kept it by him and did not publish it. Instead he preferred (or so Lyly and his friends believed) to make his contribution to the controversy by collaborating with his brother Richard in the writing of *Plaine Percevall* and *The Lambe of God*, two pamphlets in which impartial rebuke of Martinists and anti-Martinists is coupled with specific condemnation of Nashe and of the playwright Robert Greene. (Both had probably had a hand in the anti-Martinist tracts though the connection is never made explicit.)

Greene and Nashe took two years to mature their answers, but in 1592 came Greene's *A Quip for an Upstart Courtier* in which he managed to insert a sneering passage about the whole Harvey family and their humble origin. Gabriel Harvey threatened physical and legal reprisals and Greene, now on his deathbed, was frightened into cancelling the libellous passage and almost certainly into printing a warning to his young friend Nashe against the danger of being 'too bitter against scholars'. Nashe, however, disregarded it and his *Pierce Penilesse his Supplication to the Divell* carried a withering retort to the criticisms that had appeared in *Plaine Percevall* and *The Lambe of God*. This induced Harvey to expand the pamphlet he had in hand against the dead Greene, and his *Foure Letters* eventually included a severe sermon to Nashe as well.

The battle was now joined. In April 1593 Nashe brought out his *Strange Newes of the intercepting Certaine Letters*, or *The Four Letters Confuted*, an uproarious and outrageous guying of Harvey and all his works. Friends of both sides then tried to bring about a reconciliation and Nashe was even persuaded to print an apology to Harvey in the preface to his *Christ's Teares* (September 1593); but that only gave Harvey an opportunity to get his own back. In *A New Letter* he pounced with ridicule on Nashe's apology, and followed this up with a lengthy, circuitous, and obscure attack on Nashe and his allies, *Pierce's Supererogation*, into which he worked the unpublished reply to Lyly's *Pappe*, written four years before.

In the spring of 1594 *Christ's Teares* was reprinted with, of course, a violent onslaught on Harvey in place of the apology; but Nashe's full rejoinder was delayed till 1596 and in any case *Pierce's Supererogation* is the last of this series of pamphlets to contain any striking parallel to a passage in *Love's Labour's Lost*.

Shakespeare's echoes of the controversy are manifold and are catalogued (many of them are harder to catch than a bat's squeak) in R. Taylor's *The Date of Love's Labour's Lost*. Two major ones, about which there can be no doubt, should be enough to prove that Harvey and Nashe are behind some of the fooling in the play. In III. i Armado addresses Moth as 'tender juvenal', and this is elaborated in a long interchange. Now 'gallant young juvenal' was to be the title given to Nashe by Francis Meres in his catalogue of writers, *Palladis Tamia* (1598); and it is all but certain that Nashe again is the 'Young Iuvenall, that byting Satyrist' whom Greene in his deathbed tract, *Greene's Groatsworth of Wit* (1592), warned against baiting scholars, i.e. Harvey. Moth, therefore, here is Nashe. Furthermore, it is Moth who is perpetually the centre of the puns about purses and pennies, many of them close echoes of those which Harvey and Nashe himself made about the title of Nashe's first anti-Harvey pamphlet, *Pierce Penilesse*. As evidence, the cumulative effect of these parallels seems to me overwhelming, even though we must now perhaps discount the reference to 'piercing a hogshead', which has for long seemed the most striking of all (see note on IV. ii. 80–4).

This disposes of two of the text cruces, (*a*) and (*c*); it may also explain (*d*), the Fox and Ape rhyme. Dover Wilson has already suggested (privately) that this jingle may have something to do with the Marprelate controversy, in the course of which such motto-rhymes were freely adopted by both sides. Compare this, from the title-page of the anti-Martinist *Martin's Months Minde*

Martin the ape, the dronke, and the madde
The three Martins are, whose workes we have had,
If Martin the fourth comes, after Martins so euill
Nor man, nor beast comes, but Martin the devill.

'Martin' was, incidentally, Elizabethan slang for a monkey or ape.

I believe that the connection between the Fox and the Ape and Marprelate is at one remove, through Nashe who, in his *Pierce Penilesse*, inserted a mysterious fable which can best be explained as another anti-Martinist tract in disguise. In it (after some satire on the Bear, Leicester, who favoured Puritans) he describes the conspiracy of the Bear's creatures, the Fox and the Chameleon, the second of whom had an especial aptitude for intrigue since he could vary his colour and shape and, indeed, for a large part of the story puts on the form of an Ape. These evil beasts try to persuade the Husbandman that he can have good honey without keeping bees—at a pinch wasps will do as well. The allegory is surely transparent, with the Husbandman standing for authority, honey for

true religion, the bees for the bishops, and the wasps for the 'pres-
byters' the Puritans would substitute for them. The Chameleon
can only be Martin in his various disguises; while the Fox I presume is some Puritan dignitary like Thomas Cartwright who, not
himself Martin, was thought by many to be directing the campaign.

Shakespeare's rhyme plays on this: the Puritan party, Marprelate, and the bishops were quarrelling; how could they be anything but 'at odds', since there were three of them? The appearance of a fourth party to the controversy 'stays the odds'. I return
to Dover Wilson for the suggestion that the Goose is Gabriel
Harvey, who with his brother Richard had in *Plaine Percevall* advo-
cated a middle way and sought to reconcile the quarrellers. For
is it not precisely Goose that Harvey is called in Nashe's *Have With
You to Saffron Walden*, in a passage which, like Shakespeare's, cari-
catures 'envoys', a form of composition to which Harvey was
partial?

> Gabriel Harvey, fames duckling,
> hey noddie, noddie, noddie:
> Is made a gosling and a suckling,
> hey noddie, hey noddie.

Here is merely a suggestion; let no scepticism about this conclusion affect the earlier proof that Moth in some ways reflects Thomas
Nashe. Who then is to be cast for Harvey? Both Armado and Holofernes (but particularly Armado) have some of his affectations of
language, both have the wizened mahogany face so praised by the
Queen (she took Harvey for an Italian) and so cruelly mocked by
Nashe in *Have With You*. It is Armado to whom Moth is more particularly attached in the play, Holofernes whom he more unmerci-
fully mocks—and indeed the very name Holofernes might be one
of the distortions to which Nashe subjects that of Harvey. Holofernes is attended by an obsequious clerical shadow, just as Gabriel
was by his parson brother Richard. Armado pawns his linen, as
Harvey was said to have done to pay his printer, and is as stingy
as Harvey to his dependants. The objections to each identification
are equally extensive, not the least being the strength of the rival
claim. To note only single difficulties in addition, Holofernes' precise pronunciation seems as remote from Harvey (who wrote
'dettor' and was all for modernity) as does Armado's romantic
passion for Jaquenetta. In *Love's Labour's Lost* Harvey is still to seek.

5.23. *Ralegh and the 'Schoole of Night'*. To Arthur Acheson is largely
due the discovery of a second clue that seems to lead some way into
the labyrinth. Professor Minto had suggested, in his *Characteristics*

of the English Poets (1885), that Chapman was the 'rival poet' of Shakespeare's sonnets, and Chapman's *Shadow of Night* (published 1594), the poem whose 'proud full sail' challenged Shakespeare's. Following this hint, Acheson was struck by a curious opposition between the theme of this *Shadow of Night* and that of *Love's Labour's Lost*. Chapman's poem is a eulogy of contemplation, study, knowledge (often symbolized as astronomy) as opposed to the life of pleasure and practical affairs. It appears that in composing it Chapman hoped to curry favour with a group of noblemen—'most ingenious Darby, deep-searching Northumberland, and skill-embracing heir of Hunsdon'—and with this end in view addressed an introductory letter to Matthew Roydon, a minor poet who had connections with the group. The central theme of *Love's Labour's Lost* is ridicule of the academic affectations of a group of noblemen, and the words

> Never durst poet touch a pen to write
> Until his ink were temper'd with Love's sighs

with which Berowne dissolves the academy and turns its members back to real life might well be a specific answer to Chapman's

> No pen can anything eternal write
> That is not steep'd in humour of the Night.

Now Roydon's particular patron was Sir Walter Ralegh. With Ralegh himself and others of his protégés, such as Marlowe and the mathematician Thomas Harriot (both 'soul-loved friends' of Chapman), Roydon made up a little 'academy' for philosophical and scientific discussion which in 1592 was branded by a pamphleteer as 'Sir Walter Rauley's Schoole of Atheisme' and in 1594, after Ralegh's disgrace, subjected to the attentions of a special commission appointed by the Privy Council to investigate its heresies. Harriot, with Walter Warner and Thomas Hughes, two other mathematicians of the group, later transferred his service to a close friend of Ralegh's, the very Earl of Northumberland mentioned by Chapman in his dedication of *The Shadow of Night*; another indication that the circle which Chapman sought to approach through Roydon, and which he hoped to flatter by praise of the studious and contemplative life, was Ralegh's circle.

The dedication to Roydon contains the following sentences:

How then may a man stay his marvailing to see passion-driven men, reading but to curtail a tedious hour, and altogether hidebound with affection to great men's fancies, take upon them as killing censures as if they were judgment's butchers, or as if the life of truth lay tottering in their verdicts.

Now what a supererogation in wit this is, to think Skill so
mightily pierced with their loves, that she should prostitutely
show them her secrets, when she will scarcely be looked upon by
others but with invocation, fasting, watching.

This may be a general censure of uninstructed critics, but it
looks rather more like resentment at a particular attack, made by
an uneducated hack in the payment of a rival group, upon Chapman's own poem before publication. This attack, says Acheson, is
no other than *Love's Labour's Lost*, the hack is Shakespeare, and the
rival group that of Southampton and his friend Essex, who was in
perpetual rivalry with Ralegh at court. The attack on *The Shadow
of Night* is essentially an attack on Ralegh; the over-serious academe is Ralegh's 'schoole', and it is his three famous mathematicians that are mocked in the comic characters who, as Dover
Wilson has pointed out, are so hopeless at sums.

It is even possible that Ralegh's circle is explicitly named in the
play. What could the mysterious 'schoole of night' (crux (*e*)) of IV.
iii. 251 more fitly be than the 'Schoole of Atheisme' in whose
honour had been written *The Shadow of Night*? And does the sneer
(II. i. 16) in 'Beauty . . . not utter'd by base sale of *chapmen's* tongues'
pun on the name of that poem's author? Acheson believed that
Chapman himself figured in *Love's Labour's Lost*, as Holofernes, but
it is hardly Chapman's style that is parodied in the poem on the
pricket, nor Chapman's pronunciation (he rhymed 'debtor' with
'better') in Holofernes' orthographical pedantries. With more
probability Dover Wilson puts forward Thomas Harriot himself
as Holofernes' original. He was a schoolmaster, he was for a long
time living at Sion House, Northumberland's residence at Isle-
worth (perhaps the 'mountain' of crux (*g*)), he scribbled doggerel
poems, full of mathematical puns, upon his scientific papers, and
he was attended by a clerical toady whose name was the Reverend
Nathaniel Torporley.

5.24. *John Eliot and the Earl of Northumberland.* A synthesis of the
Harvey–Nashe and the School of Night theories was attempted by
Miss F. A. Yates in *A Study of Love's Labour's Lost* (1934), still the
most complete summary of the researches and speculations that
have been devoted to this play. She introduces two new elements.
The first is a certain John Eliot, a teacher of French and compiler
for the printer Wolfe of a London news-letter on French affairs.
In dudgeon at the challenge to his livelihood offered by refugees
who set up as language teachers, he published in April 1593 his
Ortho-Epia Gallica, superficially another French phrase-book in dialogue form but also a satire on the foreigners and a parody of the

method of teaching favoured by such noted educationalists among them as Florio and, earlier, Vives.

There appears to be a reference to the preface of this book in Harvey's *Pierce's Supererogation* (printing at the same time and at the same printers) in connection with an acquaintance Harvey had recently met and of whom he quotes a long speech. This acquaintance, Miss Yates believes, was therefore Eliot himself; the speech, which praises Nashe, the champion of 'real life', at the expense of more academic writers, agrees with Eliot's line in *Ortho-Epia Gallica* and incidentally with Shakespeare's in *Love's Labour's Lost*. Furthermore it may be noticed that Chapman, in the passage from the dedication of his *Shadow of Night* quoted in 5.23 above, drags in the words 'supererogation' and 'pierced', and it is impossible not to believe that this must be a deliberate reference to Harvey's pamphlet, particularly as the argument of Harvey's anonymous friend there reproduced is precisely the view Chapman is concerned to refute. The two camps thus become more clearly defined; on the one side the practical writers, the 'reporters', Eliot, Nashe, Shakespeare; on the other the conscious artists, the academicians, Harvey, Chapman (with the School of Night behind him), and (if Harvey's acquaintance *is* Eliot) Florio and Vives.

Miss Yates's second link is more certain and more far-reaching. It lies in an essay, discovered by Miss Yates in the Record Office, and written by Ralegh's friend the Earl of Northumberland to prove to his lady the infinite superiority of the attractions of learning over those of any female whatsoever. The essay cannot be dated, but it sums up Northumberland's attitude (which we know from contemporary reports) to his own wife Dorothy Devereux, whom he married about the year 1594. Dorothy was of course the sister of the Earl of Essex and of the more famous Penelope Devereux, Lady Rich, whose identity with the 'Stella' of Sidney's sonnet-sequence is now confirmed. 'Stella' had already suffered, from another academician, the same insult now offered to her sister by Northumberland's essay; for in 1585 the Italian astronomer Giordano Bruno, who had connections with the French Palace Academy and was at that time in England on secret business for the French King, dedicated to Sidney his *De gli eroici furori*, a bitter condemnation of romantic love (and in particular sonnet-writing) as standing in the way of the pursuit of higher knowledge. The slight to the object of Sidney's own love and love-poems was hardly redeemed by Bruno's perfunctory conclusion, in which he added that English women were exceptions to his rule, being celestial creatures, stars (with perhaps a pun on the name 'Stella'). Bruno's strictures on women were revived, significantly enough, by Florio, his friend and housemate during his London visit, in his *Second Fruits* (1591), one of the very dialogues directly parodied by Eliot's *Ortho-Epia Gallica*.

Here, then, is the plot of *Love's Labour's Lost* as Miss Yates sees it: Essex is insulted by Ralegh, his sisters, famous beauties, by Ralegh's friends, the members and correspondents of Ralegh's pretentious study-circle; their defence is undertaken by Shakespeare, protégé of Essex's friend Southampton. 'Women *are* stars' is the theme of the play; 'men derive more light, warmth, and inspiration from them than from the cold and distant objects to which these astronomers devote themselves.'

5.25. *Conclusions.* Some of Miss Yates's evidences are shaky. In particular the convenient ubiquity of Eliot is suspect for there is hardly a corner of all this intrigue in which his traces have not been seen —he might, for instance, have so easily provided Shakespeare with the French gossip on which *Love's Labour's Lost* is founded. The very words 'Schoole of Night' may be an invention not of Shakespeare's but of his commentators (see note on IV. iii. 251). Yet even the loss of this piece of corroborative evidence would not annul either the fact that Ralegh's 'school' existed, or the apparent links between school and play brought out by Acheson. There can be little doubt that Shakespeare's butts are the superior persons who exalt art and learning above nature and common sense, and that among them he intended his audience to recognize some living people of the time—Harvey, Chapman, Florio, Thomas Harriot's 'schoole', and its patron, Sir Walter Ralegh. If these are the enemy, it is clear on whose behalf the play must have been written: Essex, and the young noblemen of his party, Bedford, Rutland, and Southampton.

The key to many of the interrelations of these two groups, if we could only grasp it, is, I am sure, that elusive and engaging person Thomas Nashe. Just as Moth has an equivocal position in the play, attached to Armado and yet twitting him and Holofernes as openly as do the King and his lords, so Nashe shifted between the two parties in real life. It is not known who was his patron before the summer of 1592; *Pierce Penilesse* was then dedicated to 'Amyntas', presumably the same as the Amyntas of Spenser's *Colin Clout's Come Home Again*, that is Ferdinando, Lord Strange, later the 'ingenious Darby' mentioned by Chapman in his dedication of *The Shadow of Night*, and so connected with the Ralegh group. The 'Lord S.', of Lancastrian blood, for whom Nashe's *The Choise of Valentines* was written, can only be the same person. In 1593 Nashe had passed under the protection of Sir George Carey who, as Hunsdon, is named by Chapman in the same breath as Ferdinando Stanley and

Northumberland, but was later to be the Lord Chamberlain who gave his name and his protection to Shakespeare's company of actors. While with Carey, Nashe was persuaded by the 'motive inspiration' of some person unnamed to write a tract significantly called *The Terrors of the Night*, which ridicules the pretensions of 'conjurers' (the name had been applied to Harriot), reproves the follies of atheists, and rails at the neglect of patrons who are more interested in being accounted *Gloriosos* at court than in rewarding real merit. In the next year Nashe finally crosses the dividing line between the two camps and dedicates his *Unfortunate Traveller* to Southampton, although it appears that the overture was not well received since the dedication was dropped from later editions of the book.

Does Nashe's conscientious renunciation of the properties of the Night suggest that he had been more closely connected with its School than has been suspected? It is odd how the memory of an unkind and vainglorious patron is associated in his mind with atheism—not only in the *Terrors*, but in *Pierce Penilesse* and *Christ's Teares* as well. Was Nashe's first patron Ralegh himself?

Confirmation of this guess would strengthen our appreciation of the general sense of the play, but it would not be likely to help much in revealing exact correspondences. It is doubtful if any discovery could do this, since it is highly probable that they do not exist. Navarre and his friends are not actual portraits of Ralegh, Derby, Northumberland, and Hunsdon any more than the Princess's ladies, for all the punning on 'rich' at v. ii. 158–9, number among them the real Stella. It is tempting to see something of Ralegh in Armado. The 'Chirrah' of v. i. 31 *may* be a jibe at the Wessex accent that Ralegh kept all his life, and Armado's predicament with Jaquenetta is exactly that which brought about Ralegh's disgrace in 1592—the taunt 'the eel is quick' that so upsets him in Act I may be only a variant of Costard's 'the party is gone', which repeats the process in Act v. It would be tidy if it were so, but the Elizabethans were not tidy. It is clear from Spenser's *Faerie Queene* that they were capable of assimilating a multiple allegory, in which a fictional character can stand simultaneously for two persons in real life, themselves exemplars of an abstract virtue. It may well be that Shakespeare ridiculed Ralegh's academic pretensions by presenting him as the pedant Harvey, himself disguised as Armado; and Holofernes may be all the 'masters' of Ralegh's school, Bruno, Florio, Harriot, Chapman, rolled into one. It does not matter. Though odd lines may puzzle us and some of our nine locks remain unopened, the point of the play is clear, and it is a point worth writing a play about.

6. THE OCCASION

All the evidence, then, goes to show that *Love's Labour's Lost* was a battle in a private war between court factions. This confirms the indications, from other sources, that it was written for private performance in court circles. The artificiality of its form and tone, though not immediately borrowed from Lyly, are clearly directed at Lyly's audience. The large number of parts for which boy-players would be required—the Princess and her ladies, Jaquenetta, Moth—points away from the regular actors' companies to some great household where a troupe of choristers was maintained; for the professional children's companies were out of action between 1590, when the combined company under Giles and Lyly was suppressed, and 1599–1600, when Evans and Giles were granted licences to reconstitute the Paul's and Chapel children respectively.

Austin K. Gray, in *Publications of the Modern Language Association*, xxxix (September 1924), has put the case for a first performance of the play in Southampton's house at Titchfield on the occasion of the Queen's visit 'on progress' in 1591; but, as has been seen, the writing of the play as we have it must be later than this date, and a more likely occasion would be an entertainment in a private house at Christmas 1593, when the regular theatres were all closed because of the plague.

Though the title-page of the second Quarto (1631) declares that it was publicly acted 'at the Blacke-Friers and the Globe', *Love's Labour's Lost* retained its peculiar connection with the court. The first Quarto title-page bears witness to a performance before Queen Elizabeth in 1597 or 1598. In 1604, when Southampton, who for three years had been imprisoned in the Tower for his part in Essex's rebellion, was released by James I and wished to entertain the royal party at his house, the play chosen for their delight was *Love's Labour's Lost*. We have already guessed at the personal associations that may have induced Southampton to put the play on; the reasons given by Burbage to the Chamberlain of the exchequer are more lasting and more essential—that 'for wytt and mirthe' it would 'please exceedingly'.

ACKNOWLEDGEMENTS

There is nothing new or startling in this Introduction, nor in the recension of the text and the notes that follow. I believe that an edition of this kind, intended in the first place for students, should not parade new theories, though it should contain a summary of any genuinely fruitful work in this kind that has been done by previous editors. For the same reason my text is conservative. As a devoted disciple of McKerrow, I have kept to the only primary text we have, the 1598 Quarto, wherever a conceivable explanation can be made out for its reading, while recording as fully as possible the emendations and elucidations that have been suggested by more adventurous editors as solutions of the undoubted difficulties.

In accordance with the general style of the Arden edition, spelling and punctuation are modernized throughout, and this means that sometimes a definite sense must be given to a passage that Shakespeare left ambiguous. Thus the spelling 'loose' was used by the Elizabethans for both 'loose' and 'lose', and the question mark did duty equally for the exclamation; an editor who uses modern spelling must make up his mind which of the two meanings Shakespeare intended by such symbols, for example at I. i. 72, I. ii. 4, IV. iii. 70, and V. ii. 224.

My debts are enormous and obvious. The greatest is to Dr Dover Wilson, and it is a double one—a general, shared with all other editors who may succeed to his masterly investigation into text and copy, and a personal, for his typical generosity not only in answering all my questions but in putting at my disposal unpublished notes prepared for his own edition.

The second debt I owe is to my predecessor in the editing of this play for the Arden series, H. C. Hart. His notes, particularly those on parallels of language and thought between *Love's Labour's Lost* and other Elizabethan writings, are still of the highest value, and I have not hesitated to take advantage of the Arden tradition and preserve much of his work verbatim. For anything so reprinted I take, of course, full responsibility, and in those instances where I do not entirely share Hart's view, I have made it quite clear where his opinion ends and mine begins.

Finally, I should like to say how grateful I am to the general editor for setting an inspiring standard of thoroughness; to Mr John Crow for a wealth of references and examples that have saved my notes from at least some indiscretions; to Miss Agnes Latham, to Miss F. A. Yates, and to Professor F. P. Wilson for helping me in my chase of various quarries—eels, libbards, and, I fear, wild geese; to Professor J. A. K. Thomson for coaching me in the Latin of Elizabethan schools; to George Rylands for patiently correcting at least some of my errors in the use of English, as well as one in entomology; and to my wife for cheerfully supporting both the natural grumblings of an editor and the theorizings that this play inevitably provokes.

July 1951   R. D.

LOVE'S LABOUR'S LOST

DRAMATIS PERSONÆ[1]

KING FERDINAND OF NAVARRE.

BEROWNE,
LONGAVILLE, } *Lords attending on the King.*
DUMAIN,

BOYET,
MARCADE, } *Lords attending the Princess of France.*

DON ADRIANO DE ARMADO, *a fantastical Spaniard.*

SIR NATHANIEL, *a Curate.*

HOLOFERNES, *a Schoolmaster.*

DULL, *a Constable.*

COSTARD, *a Clown.*

MOTH, *Page to Armado.*

A Forester.

THE PRINCESS OF FRANCE.

MARIA,
KATHARINE, } *Ladies attending on the Princess.*
ROSALINE,

JAQUENETTA, *a country Wench.*

Officers and others, Attendants on the King and Princess.

SCENE: *The King of Navarre's park.*

[1] The *dramatis personæ* were first listed by Rowe. Their names, as given in stage-directions and speech-headings, are widely varied in Q. In the directions to Act I, Scene i, the King is called Ferdinand, and again in II. i. 128–66; but the name is not found elsewhere in the directions or at all in the dialogue of the play. Similarly the Princess's speeches are sometimes headed 'Queen'—on her first appearance in II. i, throughout IV. i, and once in V. ii. For the variations in the speech-headings for Armado and the other comics see Intro. 2.55.

Some modern editors are at pains to correct the Q spellings of all the French names as being mere archaisms. It is, however, arguable that Shakespeare's intention was to *anglicize* them; certainly the original form of, e.g., Berowne, gives the clearer indication of how the name must be pronounced in the play (it rhymes with 'moon' at IV. iii. 228). For 'Marcade' see note on V. ii. 708.

LOVE'S LABOUR'S LOST

ACT I

SCENE I

Enter FERDINAND, *King of Navarre*, BEROWNE, LONGAVILLE, *and*
DUMAIN.

King. Let fame, that all hunt after in their lives,
　　Live register'd upon our brazen tombs,
　　And then grace us in the disgrace of death;
　　When, spite of cormorant devouring Time,
　　Th' endeavour of this present breath may buy　　　　5
　　That honour which shall bate his scythe's keen edge,
　　And make us heirs of all eternity.
　　Therefore, brave conquerors—for so you are,
　　That war against your own affections
　　And the huge army of the world's desires—　　　　10
　　Our late edict shall strongly stand in force:
　　Navarre shall be the wonder of the world;
　　Our court shall be a little academe,

ACT I
Scene 1

S.D. BEROWNE] *Qq,F1; Biron, Ff2,3,4.*　　1. *King.*] *Ferdinand Ff,Qq, throughout
the scene.*　　5. Th' endeavour] *Ff;* Thendeuour *Q1.*　　13. academe] *Q2,F2;*
Achademe *Q1,F1;* Academy *Ff3,4.*

3. *in the disgrace*] in the midst of, or in
spite of, the degradation (loss of physical beauty and material honour) that
death will bring us.

4. *cormorant*] ravenous. Elsewhere
Shakespeare has 'cormorant war' and
'cormorant belly'. Nashe frequently
uses the noun for a rapacious person.

5. *Th' endeavour of this present breath*]
Our efforts while we are alive will earn
us fame after death.

6. *bate*] dull, deaden or lessen.

13. *academe*] a poetic form of 'academy'. The name, originally that of
Plato's school at Athens, was adopted
by the Medicis for the circle of poets
and savants which gathered in Flor-

3

Still and contemplative in living art.
You three, Berowne, Dumain, and Longaville,   15
Have sworn for three years' term to live with me,
My fellow-scholars, and to keep those statutes
That are recorded in this schedule here:
Your oaths are pass'd; and now subscribe your names,
That his own hand may strike his honour down   20
That violates the smallest branch herein:—
If you are arm'd to do, as sworn to do,
Subscribe to your deep oaths, and keep it too.
Long. I am resolv'd; 'tis but a three years' fast:
The mind shall banquet, though the body pine: 25
Fat paunches have lean pates, and dainty bits
Make rich the ribs, but bankrupt quite the wits.
Dum. My loving lord, Dumain is mortified:
The grosser manner of these world's delights
He throws upon the gross world's baser slaves: 30
To love, to wealth, to pomp, I pine and die;
With all these living in philosophy.

18. schedule] sedule *Q1;* scedule *Q2,Ff.*   23. oaths] oath *Steevens* (*1793*).
it] *Qq,F1;* them *Ff3,4.*   27. bankrupt quite] bancrout quite *Q1;* banerout
quite *Q1* (*Devon copy*), *Furnivall;* bankerout *Ff.*   31. pomp] pome *Q1.*   32.
living] lyning *Q1* (*Devon copy*).

ence under their patronage; and it
became the standard term for the
societies set up in imitation of the
Medicis at other European courts for
the discussion of philosophy and art.
De la Primaudaye's fictional account
of the movement in France, englished
as the *French Academy* by Thomas
Bowes in 1586, became favourite reading in fashionable Elizabethan circles;
with Sidney's *Arcadia* it was prescribed
for the instruction of the 'Knights of
the Helmet' in the Gray's Inn rag of
1594 (*Gesta Grayorum,* Malone Society,
ed. W. W. Greg, pp. 29–30). See Intro.
4.2 and, for details, Miss F. A. Yates's
French Academies (1947).

14. *living art*] J. S. Reid thinks this is
a rough translation of 'ars vivendi', the
crowning (ethical) study in the Stoic
discipline. The threefold vow and the
'still and contemplative' method certainly sound like Stoicism, which the
Elizabethans knew from such Latin
writers as Cicero and Seneca. But the
translation is excessively rough, and
the phrase may mean no more than
'vital learning'.

26. *Fat paunches have lean pates*] The
sentiment may have come, with the
rest of the academy, from De la
Primaudaye who has (T. B.'s translation, ch. xx): 'For (as Plato saith) . . .
gluttonie fatteth the bodye, maketh
the minde dull and unapt, and which
is worse, undermineth reason.' After
Shakespeare the phrase became proverbial.

28. *mortified*] dead to worldly desires
and temptations. Cf. Marlowe, *Jew of
Malta,* i. ii. 342: 'She has mortified
herself. . . . And is admitted to the
Sisterhood.'

32. *all these*] his companions.

Ber. I can but say their protestation over;
　　　So much, dear liege, I have already sworn,
　　　That is, to live and study here three years.   35
　　　But there are other strict observances;
　　　As not to see a woman in that term,
　　　Which I hope well is not enrolled there:
　　　And one day in a week to touch no food,
　　　And but one meal on every day beside;   40
　　　The which I hope is not enrolled there:
　　　And then to sleep but three hours in the night,
　　　And not be seen to wink of all the day,
　　　When I was wont to think no harm all night,
　　　And make a dark night too of half the day,   45
　　　Which I hope well is not enrolled there.
　　　O, these are barren tasks, too hard to keep,
　　　Not to see ladies, study, fast, not sleep.
King. Your oath is pass'd to pass away from these.
Ber. Let me say no, my liege, an if you please.   50
　　　I only swore to study with your grace,
　　　And stay here in your court for three years space.
Long. You swore to that, Berowne, and to the rest.
Ber. By yea and nay, sir, then I swore in jest.
　　　What is the end of study, let me know?   55
King. Why, that to know which else we should not know.
Ber. Things hid and barr'd, you mean, from common sense?

57. barr'd] bard *Q1*; hard *Q1 (Devon copy)*.

37. *not to see a woman*] Greene, in *The Royal Exchange*, 1590 (Grosart, vii. 314) says that 'Plato admitted no Auditour in his *Academie*, but such as while they were his schollers woulde abstaine from women: for he was wont to say that the greatest enemie to memorie, was venerie.'

43. *of all the day*] in, or during all the day. Cf. *Ham.*, I. v. 60.

44. *think no harm all night*] sleep well, from the proverb 'He that sleeps well thinks no harm' (Tilley, H 169).

48. *Not to see ladies*] In *Gesta Grayorum*, 1594, 'the sixth Counsellor, persuading pass-time and sport', says: 'What, nothing but tasks? nothing but working days? No feasting, no music, no dancing, no triumphs, no comedies, no love, no ladies? Let other men's lives be as pilgrimages, but Princes' lives are as Progresses, dedicated only to variety and solace' (Nichols's *Progresses*, iii. 295). The previous counsellors had recommended War, Fame, State, Virtue, and Philosophy.

54. *By yea and nay*] The injunction in Matt., v. 37, 'let your communication be, Yea, yea; Nay, nay' came to be taken by the simple-minded as a formula for a particularly earnest oath. Both Shallow and Quickly so use it in *Wiv.* Berowne is making play with its apparent equivocation.

57. *common sense*] ordinary perception, average intelligence. A parallel

King. Ay, that is study's god-like recompense.
Ber. Come on, then; I will swear to study so,
    To know the thing I am forbid to know;   60
    As thus,—to study where I well may dine,
    When I to feast expressly am forbid;
    Or study where to meet some mistress fine,
    When mistresses from common sense are hid;
    Or, having sworn too hard a keeping oath,   65
    Study to break it and not break my troth.
    If study's gain be thus, and this be so,
    Study knows that which yet it doth not know.
    Swear me to this, and I will ne'er say no.
King. These be the stops that hinder study quite,   70
    And train our intellects to vain delight.
Ber. Why! all delights are vain, but that most vain,
    Which with pain purchas'd doth inherit pain:
    As, painfully to pore upon a book
    To seek the light of truth; while truth the while   75
    Doth falsely blind the eyesight of his look:
    Light seeking light doth light of light beguile:
    So, ere you find where light in darkness lies,
    Your light grows dark by losing of your eyes.
    Study me how to please the eye indeed,   80
    By fixing it upon a fairer eye,
    Who dazzling so, that eye shall be his heed,

---

59. Come on] Com' on *Q1.*   62. feast . . . forbid] *Theobald et seq.;* fast . . . forbid *Qq,Ff;* fast . . . forebid *Theobald conj.*   65. hard a keeping] hard-a-keeping *Hanmer.*   72. Why!] Why? *Qq,Ff;* Why, *Pope, Steevens, et seq.* but] *Q1, Camb., New;* and *Ff,Q2.*   77. of light] *Qq,F1; not in Ff2,3,4.*

passage in Golding's *Ovid* (1567) suggests that Navarre's academe was in part derived from Numa, the Roman king who retired to the country to study philosophy, and 'taught his silent sort . . . what shakes the earth: what law the starres doo keepe theyr courses under, and what soever other *things is hid from common sence*' (xv. 80).

59. *Come on*] The Q spelling suggests that Berowne is punning on '*common* sense'.

71. *train*] allure, entice.

73. *inherit*] possess. See IV. i. 20.

Berowne is condemning activities that, painful in themselves, achieve ('purchase') only more pain as their reward.

76. *falsely*] treacherously.

77. *Light seeking light*] while the eyes seek wisdom from books they lose their sight with too much reading.

80. *Study me*] study for me (the 'ethic dative').

82. *Who dazzling so*] the man who is thus dazzled. Cf. *Ven.,* 1064: 'her sight dazzling makes the wound seem three'.

heed] explained by *N.E.D.* as 'that which one heeds'; but more probably

And give him light that it was blinded by.
Study is like the heaven's glorious sun,
That will not be deep-search'd with saucy looks;   85
Small have continual plodders ever won,
Save base authority from others' books.
These earthly godfathers of heaven's lights,
That give a name to every fixed star,
Have no more profit of their shining nights   90
Than those that walk and wot not what they are.
Too much to know is to know nought but fame;
And every godfather can give a name.

King. How well he's read, to reason against reading!
Dum. Proceeded well, to stop all good proceeding!   95
Long. He weeds the corn, and still lets grow the weeding.
Ber. The spring is near, when green geese are a-breeding.
Dum. How follows that?
Ber.   Fit in his place and time.
Dum. In reason nothing.
Ber.   Something then in rhyme.
King. Berowne is like an envious sneaping frost   100
    That bites the first-born infants of the spring.
Ber. Well, say I am; why should proud summer boast
    Before the birds have any cause to sing?
    Why should I joy in any abortive birth?

104. any] *Qq,Ff;* an *Pope.*

'that which takes heed of one', a guard-ian. Cf. the *Lay Folks Catechism* (1357), 200: 'Our gastly fadirs that has hede of us'.

86. *plodders*] Cf. Nashe, *The Unfortunate Traveller,* 1594 (McKerrow, ii. 251): 'Grosse plodders they were all, that had some learning and reading, but no wit to make use of it.'

95. *Proceeded*] Johnson suggests here the academical sense of taking a degree in a university. Cf. Ascham, *Scholemaster* (Arber, p. 24): 'untill the Scholar be made able to go to the Universitie, to procede in Logik, Rhetoricke, and other kindes of learning'.

97. *green geese*] young geese of the previous autumn, fit for sale about

Whitsuntide. Green Goose Fair, or Goose Fair, held on Whit Monday when they were in season, is constantly referred to by Elizabethan and Jacobean writers as a festive occasion. Berowne is perhaps hinting that his earnest companions are young fools who do not know what is in store for them.

99. *reason . . . rhyme*] The phrase 'neither *rhyme* nor *reason*' was already current. It occurs in *Err.,* II. ii. 48.

100. *sneaping*] biting, nipping. A rare word outside Shakespeare, who always uses it of the effect of frost (cf. *Lucr.,* 333, and *Wint.,* I. ii. 13). *N.E.D.* gives this and the kindred 'snaping' as forms of 'snubbing'.

104. *any*] Dover Wilson suggests that

At Christmas I no more desire a rose   105
Than wish a snow in May's new-fangled shows;
But like of each thing that in season grows.
So you, to study now it is too late,
Climb o'er the house to unlock the little gate.
King. Well, sit you out: go home, Berowne: adieu!   110
Ber. No, my good lord; I have sworn to stay with you:
And though I have for barbarism spoke more
Than for that angel knowledge you can say,
Yet confident I'll keep what I have sworn,
And bide the penance of each three years' day.   115
Give me the paper; let me read the same;
And to the strict'st decrees I'll write my name.
King. How well this yielding rescues thee from shame!
Ber. [*reads*]. Item: that no woman shall come within a
mile of my court,—Hath this been proclaimed?   120
Long. Four days ago.
Ber. Let's see the penalty—on pain of losing her tongue.
Who devised this penalty?
Long. Marry, that did I.
Ber. Sweet lord, and why?   125
Long. To fright them hence with that dread penalty.
Ber. A dangerous law against gentility!
    Item: if any man be seen to talk with a woman
    within the term of three years, he shall endure such
    public shame as the rest of the court can possibly   130
    devise.
    This article, my liege, yourself must break;

---

106. shows] *Qq,Ff;* earth *Theobald;* mirth *S. Walker conj., Globe.*   109. Climb
. . . gate] *Q1;* That were to climb o'er the house to unlock the gate *Ff,Q2.*
110. sit] *Qq,Ff2,3,4;* fit *F1.*   114. sworn] *Qq,F1;* swore *Ff2,3,4, Cambridge,*
New.   127. *Ber.*] *Theobald; Qq,Ff* assign this (*as far as* devise) *to Longaville.*
130. can] *Q1;* shall *Ff,Q2.*   possibly] *Ff,Q2;* possible *Q1, New.*

the Q compositor caught *any* from the
preceding line. This is plausible; but
where the Q reading makes sense, it is
better retained.

107. *like of*] occurs several times in
Shakespeare. Hart quotes 'Rosalynd's
Madrigal' from Lodge's *Euphues Golden*
Legacie: 'Then sit thou safely on my
knee, And let thy bower my bo-

some be; Lurke in my eies, I like of
thee.'

109. *Climb . . . gate*] See Intro. 2.3.

112. *barbarism*] lack of culture, phili-
stinism. Cf. Dekker, *Gulls' Horn Book,*
1609: 'You shall never be good Gradu-
ates in these rare Sciences of Bar-
barisme and Idiotisme.'

127. *gentility*] good manners.

For well you know here comes in embassy
The French king's daughter with yourself to speak—
A maid of grace and complete majesty—   135
About surrender up of Aquitaine
To her decrepit, sick, and bed-rid father:
Therefore this article is made in vain,
Or vainly comes th' admired princess hither.
King. What say you, lords? why, this was quite forgot.   140
Ber. So study evermore is overshot:
While it doth study to have what it would,
It doth forget to do the thing it should;
And when it hath the thing it hunteth most,
'Tis won as towns with fire, so won, so lost.   145
King. We must of force dispense with this decree;
She must lie here on mere necessity.
Ber. Necessity will make us all forsworn
Three thousand times within these three years' space;
For every man with his affects is born,   150
Not by might master'd, but by special grace.
If I break faith, this word shall speak for me,
I am forsworn on mere necessity.
So to the laws at large I write my name;
And he that breaks them in the least degree   155
Stands in attainder of eternal shame:
Suggestions are to other as to me;
But I believe, although I seem so loath,
I am the last that will last keep his oath.
But is there no quick recreation granted?   160
King. Ay, that there is. Our court, you know, is haunted

154.] *Subscribes and gives back the Paper. Capell; Subscribes. mod. edd.*   157. other]
Q1; others *Ff,Q2.*

145. *won as towns with fire*] i.e. de-
stroyed in the taking.

146. *of force*] necessarily.

147. *lie*] dwell, stay.

150. *affects*] passions. Cf. *Oth.,* I. iii.
264: 'the young affects in me defunct'.

156. *Stands in attainder of*] stands condemned and disgraced. The offender
would be guilty of treason against the
vows sworn to the king and so liable to
the normal penalty for treason—the

forfeit of all honours and all rights to
property. Shakespeare here uses 'attainder' almost in its technical sense.
Elsewhere it stands for 'disgrace' or
'stain' generally.

157. *Suggestions*] temptations. The
usual sense in Shakespeare.

161. *haunted with*] frequented or
visited by. Cf. Sidney's *Arcadia,* bk I
(Feuillerat, i. 12): 'a man who for his
hospitalitie is so much haunted that no

With a refined traveller of Spain;
A man in all the world's new fashion planted,
That hath a mint of phrases in his brain;
One who the music of his own vain tongue   165
Doth ravish like enchanting harmony;
A man of complements, whom right and wrong
Have chose as umpire of their mutiny:
This child of fancy, that Armado hight,
For interim to our studies shall relate   170
In high-born words the worth of many a knight
From tawny Spain, lost in the world's debate.
How you delight, my lords, I know not, I;
But I protest I love to hear him lie,
And I will use him for my minstrelsy.   175
Ber. Armado is a most illustrious wight,
A man of fire-new words, fashion's own knight.
Long. Costard the swain, and he, shall be our sport,
And so to study three years is but short.

162. refined] *Qq,F1*; conceited *Ff2,3,4*.   165. One who] *F1*; On who *Q1*; One whom *Ff2,3,4*.   177. fire-new] fire, new *F1*.

newes sturre but comes to his eares'.

162. *refined*] delicate, cultivated. The metaphorical sense is unusual at this date; Shakespeare generally uses the word literally, as in 'refined gold'.

165. *One*] regularly spelt 'on' by Harvey, and perhaps by Shakespeare too.

167. *complements*] This word did duty both for 'fulfilment' (as now) and for 'courtesy', until the late seventeenth century when the French 'compliment' was introduced to carry the second meaning. The sense here probably inclines towards 'affected manners', and the modernized spelling 'compliments' might be justified, as in IV. ii. 137; but it may be merely 'accomplishments' as in Jonson's *Every Man Out of his Humour* (1600), I. ii: 'All the rare qualities, humours and complements of a Gentleman'.

169. *hight*] is named.

170. *interim*] interval of relaxation, interlude. Cf. Jonson, *Cynthia's Revels*, I. i (1600): 'in which disguise, during

the interim of these revels, I will get to follow some one of Diana's maids'.

171. *high-born*] high-borne may be correct. 'Born' is usually spelt *borne* at this time, so that the choice lies between high-birth and high-bearing.

172. *tawny Spain*] the colour of the people given to their country, sunburnt clime. Cf. Greene, *Never Too Late* (Grosart, viii. 200): 'Flora in tawnie hid up all her flowers . . . upon the barren earth.' Elsewhere Greene applies the epithet to autumn leaves, and to eyes.

world's debate] warfare. Lyly employs the word *debate* with the same meaning in *The Woman in the Moone*, II. i (*ante* 1595): 'What telst thou me of love. . . . Fyre of debate is kindled in my hart.'

177. *fire-new*] fresh from the mint. The expression appears again in *R3*, *Tw.N.*, and *Lr.* It appears to be a Shakespearean coinage.

179. *and so to study*] i.e. with these provisions for our recreation. Many

Enter DULL *with a letter, and* COSTARD.

Dull. Which is the duke's own person?　　　180

Ber. This, fellow. What would'st?

Dull. I myself reprehend his own person, for I am his
　　grace's farborough: but I would see his own person
　　in flesh and blood.

Ber. This is he.　　　185

Dull. Signior Arm—Arm—commends you. There's vil-
　　lany abroad: this letter will tell you more.

Cost. Sir, the contempts thereof are as touching me.

King. A letter from the magnificent Armado.

Ber. How low soever the matter, I hope in God for high　　190
　　words.

Long. A high hope for a low heaven: God grant us pa-
　　tience!

Ber. To hear? or forbear hearing?

Long. To hear meekly, sir, and to laugh moderately; or　　195
　　to forbear both.

Ber. Well, sir, be it as the style shall give us cause to
　　climb in the merriness.

Cost. The matter is to me, sir, as concerning Jaquenetta.
　　The manner of it is, I was taken with the manner.　　200

Ber. In what manner?

---

179. S.D. *Enter . . .* COSTARD] *Malone; Enter a Constable with Costard with a letter*
Qq,Ff.　　　180. duke's] *Qq,Ff;* King's *Theobald.*　　　183. farborough] *Q1;*
tharborough *Ff.*　　　192. heaven] having *Theobald.*　　　194. hearing] *Qq,Ff,*
Steevens (1793); laughing *Capell and some modern edd.*

---

editors make it an exhortation:
'And so to study! Three years is but
short.'

182. *reprehend*] represent. Dull's
'mistaking of words' anticipates Dogberry's in *Ado.*

183. *farborough*] thirdborough; a
petty constable. In Blount's *Glosso-*
graphia (1656) the term is used inter-
changeably with 'headborough'. But
Jonson in his *Tale of a Tub* (1633) dis-
criminates these officers, high constable, headborough, petty constable,
and thirdborough. He places these on
the stage, the lowest in rank being the
thirdborough, a tinker.

188. *contempts*] Slender is credited
with a similar confusion in *Wiv.,* I. i.
258.

189. *magnificent Armado*] This form
of the magnificent Armada of Spain
occurs twice in Greene's *Spanish Mas-*
querado (1589) and in the second part
of Marlowe's *Tamburlaine,* I. ii.

200. *taken with the manner*] more properly 'mainour', i.e. hand-work, an
old form of 'manœuvre'. Taken in the
act. Palsgrave's *Lesclaircissement* (1530)
has 'I take with the maner, as a thefe is
taken with the thefte, or a person in the
doyng of any other acte, *Je prens sur lé*
faict.' A legal expression.

Cost. In manner and form following, sir; all those three:
   I was seen with her in the manor-house, sitting with
   her upon the form, and taken following her into the
   park; which, put together, is in manner and form   205
   following. Now, sir, for the manner,—it is the manner of a man to speak to a woman; for the form,—
   in some form.

Ber. For the following, sir?

Cost. As it shall follow in my correction; and God defend   210
   the right!

King. Will you hear this letter with attention?

Ber. As we would hear an oracle.

Cost. Such is the simplicity of man to hearken after the
   flesh.   215

King. [*reads*]. Great deputy, the welkin's vicegerent,
   and sole dominator of Navarre, my soul's earth's
   God, and body's fostering patron.

Cost. Not a word of Costard yet.

King. So it is,—   220

Cost. It may be so; but if he say it is so, he is, in telling
   true, but so.

222. true, but so] true: but so *Qq,Ff;* true, but so so *Hanmer.*

205–6. *in manner and form following*]
another set expression of the time.
Craig refers to Nashe's *Unfortunate
Traveller* (McKerrow, ii. 248), 1594.
There is an earlier example in the
N.E.D. from T. Washington's trans. of
Nicholay's Voyage, 1585: 'Over their
shoulders in the fourme and maner as
the picture following doth shew'. And
see Lyly's *Mydas,* v. ii (? 1589): 'you
shall have the beard, in manner and
form following.'

210. *correction*] punishment.

210–11. *God defend the right*] See *R2,*
I. iii. 101; *2H6,* II. iii. 55; the formal
prayer made before a trial by combat.
Costard is quite ready with his defence.

216. *welkin*] sky. See IV. ii. 5.

vicegerent] seems to have been a term
affected by Philip of Spain. Greene in
The Spanish Masquerado, 1589 (Grosart,
v. 245, 281) refers twice to his 'Vice-

gerentes of his Indies'. In the transferred sense here it is used by Stubbes,
Anatomie of Abuses, ii. 104: 'The Devill
himselfe, whose Vice-gerent . . . he
showes himselfe to be' (1583).

217. *dominator*] lord, ruler. The word
occurs again in *Tit.,* II. iii. 31, in an
astrological sense. The only example
of the word prior to Shakespeare, in
the *N.E.D.,* is from *Mirour Saluacioun*
(*c.* 1450), applied to the Deity. Shakespeare is likely to have met it in
Puttenham's *Arte of English Poesie;*
chap. xvi is headed 'In what forme of
Poesie the great Princes and domi-
nators of the world were honored'.

221. *It may be so; but if he say it is so*]
This recalls the jingle in *Ado,* I. i. 219:
'Like the old tale, my lord; it is not so,
nor 'twas not so, but indeed God forbid
it should be so.'

222. *but so*] indifferent, not worth

King. Peace!

Cost. Be to me and every man that dares not fight.

King. No words!   225

Cost. Of other men's secrets, I beseech you.

King. So it is, besieged with sable-coloured melancholy,
    I did commend the black oppressing humour to the
    most wholesome physic of thy health-giving air;
    and, as I am a gentleman, betook myself to walk.   230
    The time when? About the sixth hour; when beasts
    most graze, birds best peck, and men sit down to
    that nourishment which is called supper: so much
    for the time when. Now for the ground which?
    which, I mean, I walked upon: it is ycleped thy   235
    park. Then for the place where? where, I mean, I
    did encounter that obscene and most preposterous
    event, that draweth from my snow-white pen the
    ebon-coloured ink, which here thou viewest, be-
    holdest, surveyest, or seest. But to the place where: 240
    it standeth north-north-east and by east from the

much. Equivalent to our 'but so so',
which occurs frequently in Shakespeare. The phrase 'no more but so'
was a favourite with Marlowe.

230. *as I am a gentleman*] frequent in
Shakespeare. It occurs twice in *Wiv.*

231–6. *The time when . . . the place
where*] An early example of this classical mode of speech is in Gabriel
Harvey's celebrated *Judgement of
Earthquakes* (Grosart, i. 63), 1580: 'We
are to judge of as advisedly and pro-
vidently, as possible we can, by the
consideration and comparison of circumstances, the tyme when: the place
where: the qualities and dispositions
of the persons, amongst whom such.'
Cf. Wilson's *Art of Rhetorique* (1553):
'Seven circumstances whiche are to be
considered in diverse matters . . . Who,
what, and where, by what helpe and
by whose: Why how and when, doe
many thinges disclose' (1562 ed., fol.
9). This was also the standard form for
a legal indictment. Hotson (*Shakespeare's Sonnets Dated*, 1949, p. 55)

quotes the model indictment for theft
given in William West's *Symboleo-
graphie* (1590): '*Quis*. The person with
his name, surname, addicion of the
Towne, Countie, Arte, and degree.
Quando. The day and yeare. *Ubi*. The
place, Towne, and Countrie. *Quid*.
The thing taken, the colour, the
marke, the price and value. *Cuius*. The
owner of the thing and whose it was.
Quomodo. The manner of the doing and
how. *Quare*. The entent, which is com-
prised in this word (*Felonicè*).' The
proximity of Costard's play on 'manner and form following' suggests that
Armado's rigmarole is also a skit on
legal phraseology.

237. *preposterous*] entirely out of
place, highly improper. Cf. *Oth.*, I. iii.
62: 'For nature so preposterously to
err . . . Sans witchcraft could not.'

239. *ebon-coloured*] Cf. Greene, *Tullies
Love* (Grosart, vii. 146), 1589: 'Hir
eyes like Ariadnes sparkling Starres
Shone frome the Ebon Arches of hir
browes.'

west corner of thy curious-knotted garden: there
did I see that low-spirited swain, that base minnow
of thy mirth,—

Cost. Me?   245

King. that unlettered small-knowing soul,—

Cost. Me?

King. that shallow vassal,—

Cost. Still me?

King. which, as I remember, hight Costard,—   250

Cost. O! me.

King. sorted and consorted, contrary to thy established
proclaimed edict and continent canon, which with

245, 247, 249. Me? . . . Me? . . . me?] *Ff,Q2*; Me? . . . me? . . . me *Q1,
New*; Me . . . Me . . . me. *Hanmer, Steevens, Craig.*   253. which] with,
Theobald.

242. *curious-knotted garden*] labyrinths
and intricate patterns amongst the
flower beds were the glory of early gar-
deners. Bacon, *Essay of Gardens*, writes:
'for the *Making of Knots*, or Figures,
with Diuers Coloured Earths . . . they
be but Toyes: You may see as good
sights, many times in Tarts' (1625).
And cf. Shirley, *Gentleman of Venice*, i.
ii: 'When I am digging, he is cutting
unicorns, And lions in some hedge, or
else devising New knots upon the
ground, drawing out crowns, And the
duke's arms, castles and cannons in
them: Here gallies, there a ship giving
a broadside: Here out of turf he carves
a senator With all his robes, making
a speech to Time That grows hard
by, and twenty curiosities,—I think
he means to embroider all the garden.'

243. *low-spirited*] base. Armado cor-
rects here the modern use.

minnow] a contemptible little person, a shrimp. Nashe, speaking of
Gabriel Harvey, says: 'Let him denie
that there was another Shewe made of
the little Minnow his Brother. . . .
Whereupon Dick came and broke the
Colledge glasse windowes' (*Have With
You to Saffron Walden* [McKerrow, iii.
80], 1596).

246. *unlettered*] illiterate, ignorant.
See *Sonn.* lxxxv. 6, and again in this
play, IV. ii. 18; and *H5*, I. i. 55, where
the company kept by Prince Hal is
described as 'unletter'd, rude and
shallow'. Nashe uses the term in *A
Wonderfull Prognostication* (McKerrow,
iii. 390), 1591: 'insomuch that sundrie
unlettered fooles should creepe into the
ministerie'.

248. *vassal*] a country bumpkin, or
clown. Collier's 'Corrector' would
read 'vessel' here, which Dyce adopted. Cf. Lodge's *Euphues Golden Legacie*
(*Shakes. Lib.*, 1875, p. 21), 1590: 'In
this humour was Saladyne making his
brother Rosader his foote boy . . . as if
he had been the sonne of any country
vassal.'

252. *sorted*] associated.

253. *continent canon*] restraining
canon; or canon enforcing restraint.
This is the usual explanation, or choice
of explanations, of Armado's words.
But he may mean merely, in his
pedantic way, the edict and the law
contained therein. Jonson uses the
word similarly in *Every Man out of his
Humour*, Induction: 'So in every
human body, The choler, melancholy
. . . flow continually In some one part
and are not continent.'

—O! with—but with this I passion to say where-
with,—   255

Cost. With a wench.

King. with a child of our grandmother Eve, a female;
or, for thy more sweet understanding, a woman.
Him, I, as my ever-esteemed duty pricks me on,
have sent to thee, to receive the meed of punish-   260
ment, by thy sweet grace's officer, Anthony Dull, a
man of good repute, carriage, bearing, and estima-
tion.

Dull. Me, an't shall please you; I am Anthony Dull.

King. For Jaquenetta—so is the weaker vessel called—   265
which I apprehended with the aforesaid swain, I
keep her as a vessel of thy law's fury; and shall, at
the least of thy sweet notice, bring her to trial. Thine
in all compliments of devoted and heart-burning
heat of duty,   270

DON ADRIANO DE ARMADO.

Ber. This is not so well as I looked for, but the best that
ever I heard.

King. Ay, the best for the worst. But, sirrah, what say
you to this?   275

Cost. Sir, I confess the wench.

---

258. sweet] *not in Ff2,3,4.*   267. keep] *Qq,Ff2,3,4;* keeper *F1.*   vessel] vassal
Theobald.   271. ADRIANO] *Qq; Adriana Ff.*

254. *passion*] grieve, as in *Ven.*, 1059.
Cf. Nashe, *The Unfortunate Traveller*,
1594: 'Having passioned thus a while,
she hastely ranne and lookt herselfe in
her glasse.'
   265. *weaker vessel*] See 1 Pet., iii. 7,
for the expression applied to a wife.
But the term was proverbial for any
woman earlier than the time of this
play. Greene has it twice in *Mamillia*
(Grosart, ii. 95, 255), 1583: 'They say
a woman is the weaker vessel, but sure
in my judgement it is in the strength of
her body, and not in the force of her
minde'; and 'women sure, whom they
count the weake vessels, had more
neede to be counselled than condemned.' Lyly has it also in *Euphues*

(Arber, p. 78): 'men are always laying
baites for women, which are the
weaker vessels'; and again, in *Sapho
and Phao*, I. iv (1584): 'I cannot but
oftentimes smile to myselfe to heare
men call us weaker vessels.'
   274. *the best for the worst*] Cf. Dekker's
Strange Horse-Race (Grosart, iii. 364):
'The Masquers . . . not needing any
Vizards (their owne visages beeing
good enough because bad enough)'.
But Lyly gives the best parallel:
'[*Perim danceth*] How like you this;
doth he well? *Diog.* The better, the
worse' (*Campaspe*, v. i). Greene quotes
this in *Tritameron* (Grosart, iii. 88),
1584: 'I thinke of lovers as Diogenes
did of dancers . . . the better the worse.'

King. Did you hear the proclamation?

Cost. I do confess much of the hearing it, but little of the marking of it.

King. It was proclaimed a year's imprisonment to be   280
  taken with a wench.

Cost. I was taken with none, sir: I was taken with a
  demsel.

King. Well, it was proclaimed damsel.

Cost. This was no damsel neither, sir: she was a virgin.   285

King. It is so varied too, for it was proclaimed virgin.

Cost. If it were, I deny her virginity: I was taken with a
  maid.

King. This maid will not serve your turn, sir.

Cost. This maid will serve my turn, sir.   290

King. Sir, I will pronounce your sentence: you shall fast
  a week with bran and water.

Cost. I had rather pray a month with mutton and porridge.

King. And Don Armado shall be your keeper.   295
  My Lord Berowne, see him deliver'd o'er:
  And go we, lords, to put in practice that

---

283. demsel] *Q1;* damosell *Ff,Q2.* 284, 285. damsel] *Q1;* damosel *Ff,Q2.*

---

283. *demsel*] Costard's malaprop-isms are better credited to Shake-speare's art than to the compositor's blunder. Cf. this play below, v. ii. 500, and note on Holofernes' quota-tions at IV. ii. 90. The word 'dam-sel' was in ordinary use earlier than this time; the F spelling need not be taken as implying a specialized mean-ing.

286. *varied*] diversified in language. Cf. *Sonn.*, cv. 10, and see this play below, IV. ii. 9.

290. *serve my turn*] satisfy me. Costard twists the King's sentence—'This play with the letter of the law will not pro-vide the excuse you need'—to a bawdy sense.

292. *bran and water*] Cf. *Meas.*, IV. iii. 160; and Nashe, *Summer's Last Will* (McKerrow, iii. 260), 1592: 'Thou

witholdest both the mault and flowre, And giv'st us branne, and water, (fit for dogs).'

293-4. *mutton and porridge*] mutton-broth. 'Porridge' and 'pottage' were used synonymously, the former prob-ably formed in imitation of the latter from *purée.* Cotgrave has '*La purée de pois:* Pease strained, Pease pottage'; and 'Potage: Pottage, porridge'. Nashe speaks of this good nourish-ment: 'Amongst all other stratagems . . . to pumpe over mutton and por-ridge into Fraunce? this coolde weather our souldirs . . . have need of it, . . . they have almost got the colicke and stone with eating of provant' (*Foure Letters Confuted* [McKerrow, i. 331], 1593). 'Mutton' was also a cant term for a whore, and Costard may be punning on this.

Which each to other hath so strongly sworn.

> [*Exeunt King, Longaville, and Dumain.*

Ber. I'll lay my head to any good man's hat,

These oaths and laws will prove an idle scorn.   300

Sirrah, come on.

Cost. I suffer for the truth, sir: for true it is I was taken

with Jaquenetta, and Jaquenetta is a true girl; and

therefore welcome the sour cup of prosperity! Afflic-

tion may one day smile again; and till then, sit thee   305

down, sorrow!   [*Exeunt.*

SCENE II

Enter ARMADO *and* MOTH.

Arm. Boy, what sign is it when a man of great spirit grows

melancholy?

Moth. A great sign, sir, that he will look sad.

Arm. Why! sadness is one and the self-same thing, dear

imp.   5

Moth. No, no; O Lord, sir, no.

301.] *Given to Dull in the Collier MS.*   304–5. Affliction] afflicio *Q1 (Devon copy).*

Scene II

Scene II] *Capell; Scene* III. *Pope.*   S.D. *Enter* ARMADO . . .] *Enter Armado a Braggart*
F2.   3. *Moth.*] *Rowe et seq. and throughout scene; Boy Q1,F1.*   4, 7, 11, *etc.*
Arm.] *Qq; Brag., Bra., or Br. Ff.*   4. Why!] Why? *Qq,Ff.*

---

299. *lay*] offer a bet. 'I take six to one
saies the Gripe, I lay it saies the vin-
cent, and so they make a bet' (Greene,
second part of *Conny-catching* [Grosart,
x. 84], 1592). On the title-page of the
same tract Greene has: 'if you reade
without laughing, Ile give you my cap
for a noble'; and in *A Looking Glass for
London and England* (1594) he has: 'I
hold my cap to a noble.' See v. ii. 556
(note), and Beaumont and Fletcher,
Knight of the Burning Pestle, III. ii: 'I hold
my cap to a farthing he does.'

303. *true*] honest.

305–6. *sit . . . sorrow*] The source of

this saying is not known. It occurs
again at IV. iii. 3–4.

Scene II

5. *imp*] primarily a sapling, a young
shoot; then a child, especially of noble
origin; and, commonly, any child,
though now chiefly limited to a 'child
of the devil'. Cf. *Euphues* (Arber, p.
108): 'This is therefore to admonish all
young Imps and novices in love, not to
blow the coales of fancy with desire.'

6. *O Lord, sir*] surely, certainly. Cf.
Jonson, *Every Man out of his Humour*, II.
i: 'His lady! what, is she fair, splendi-

Arm. How canst thou part sadness and melancholy, my
    tender juvenal?
Moth. By a familiar demonstration of the working, my
    tough Signor.   10
Arm. Why tough Signor? why tough Signor?
Moth. Why tender juvenal? why tender juvenal?
Arm. I spoke it, tender juvenal, as a congruent epitheton
    appertaining to thy young days, which we may
    nominate tender.   15
Moth. And I, tough Signor, as an appertinent title to
    your old time, which we may name tough.
Arm. Pretty, and apt.
Moth. How mean you, sir? I pretty, and my saying apt?
    or I apt, and my saying pretty?   20
Arm. Thou pretty, because little.
Moth. Little pretty, because little. Wherefore apt?
Arm. And therefore apt, because quick.

10, 11, 16. Signor] signeor *Q1*; signeur *Ff*.   13. epitheton] *Ff2,3,4*; apethatoa
Q1; apethaton *Q1* (*Devon copy*); apathaton *F1,Q2*.

dious, and amiable? *Gent.* O Lord,
sir!' The ejaculation here may merely
express impatience; cf. Jonson's *Cynthia's Revels*, Induction: 'What shall I
do with it? *Child.* O Lord, Sir! will you
betray your ignorance so much?' It
might serve almost any purpose; see
also v. ii. 485 ff.

8. *juvenal*] youth. It is possible that
this term, with a pun on the name of
the Roman satirist, was commonly
used as a nickname for Nashe: 'As
Acteon was worried of his owne
hound: so is Tom Nash of his *Isle of
Dogs. Dogges* were the death of Euri-
pides, but bee not disconsolate gallant
young Iuvenall, Linus the sonne
of Apollo died the same death'
(Meres, *Wits Treasurie*, 1598); and
Greene speaks of 'young Iuvenal
that byting Satyrist' in a well-known
passage in his *Groatsworth of Wit*
(Grosart, xii. 143), which probably
(in spite of Dyce) refers to Nashe.
Shakespeare has this word for a youth
again in this play (iii. i. 63) and in
1H4, i. ii. 22, and *MND.*, iii. i. 97,

with no reference to the proper name.
    9. *working*] operation.
    10. *Signor*] To emend the title, so
clearly indicated in both Q and F, to
'Senior', as many editors do, is to emphasize the obvious half of the pun at
the expense of the less apparent. The
joke, and the editorial blunder, are
repeated at iii. i. 177.
    13. *congruent*] suitable. Jonson uses
the word in *Discoveries* (p. 131): '*De
Stylo.* The congruent and harmonious
fitting of parts in a sentence.' We have
this word again from Holofernes, v. i.
84. See note for other examples.
    epitheton] an adjective indicating
some characteristic quality or attribute (*N.E.D.*). The earliest form of the
word 'epithet'. Cf. Greene, *Planetomachia* (Grosart, v. 101), 1585: 'which
naturall and proper qualitie in my
judgement caused the auncient Poets
to attribute this Epitheton unto *Venus:
Alma.*'
    16. *appertinent*] belonging. See *2H4*,
i. ii. 194: 'the other gifts appertinent to
man'.

Moth. Speak you this in my praise, master?

Arm. In thy condign praise.   25

Moth. I will praise an eel with the same praise.

Arm. What! that an eel is ingenious?

Moth. That an eel is quick.

Arm. I do say thou art quick in answers: thou heat'st my
  blood.   30

Moth. I am answered, sir.

Arm. I love not to be crossed.

Moth. He speaks the mere contrary: crosses love not him.

                                                            [*Aside*

Arm. I have promised to study three years with the duke.

Moth. You may do it in an hour, sir.   35

Arm. Impossible.

Moth. How many is one thrice told?

Arm. I am ill at reckoning; it fitteth the spirit of a tapster.

---

27. ingenious] *Q1,F4;* ingenuous *Q2,Ff1,2,3.*   33. mere contrary] *Qq,F1;*
clean contrary *Ff2,3,4.*   34. three] *Q1;* iii *Ff1,2,Q2;* 3 *Ff3,4.*   duke] King
Theobald.   38. fitteth] *Q1;* fits *Ff,Q2.*

---

25. *condign*] well-merited. Commonly used as here at this time. 'Condigne
thankes' occurs in Greene's *Planetomachia* (Grosart, v. 85), 1585.

28. *an eel is quick*] There must be a
topical hit here since Armado so much
resents it ('thou heat'st my blood').
John Crow suggests that the reference
is to the proverb 'to get a woman by the
waist or a quick eel by the tail', and
that Moth means to imply that
Armado is always running after
women. This seems to me a very long
way round, even for *LLL*. See Intro.,
5.25, and also William Bullein, *A Dialogue* against the Fever Pestilence, 1564
(E.E.T.S., p. 91): '*Vxor.* There is also
painted a lustie young man, stouping
downe to a vessell, in which swimmeth
bothe Eles and Snakes; he seemeth to
catche one of them: what meaneth
that? *Ciuis.* Ha, ha, ha! it is merrily
handled; forsothe, it is one that is ouer
come either with loue or coueteous-
nesse [of a wower how he sped] He
goeth a woyng, my dyng, dyng; and
if he spedeth, my dearlyng, what get-
teth he, my swetyng? Forsoth, either
a serpente that will styng hymn all his
life with cruell words, or els a swete
harte with pleasant speache, that when
hee thinketh her moste sure, hee hath
but a quicke Ele: you knowe where.
[Ha, ha, ha! well fished]'.

33. *crosses*] coins, from many kinds
bearing the representation of a cross.
A venerable and threadbare pun. Perhaps the commonest form is 'The devil
may dance in his pocket for he has
never a cross there.' It occurs in
Hoccleve (*c.* 1420). Nashe (Mc-
Kerrow, i. 305), 1593, says it 'hath
been a graybeard Proverbe two hundred yeares before Tarlton was borne.'

34. *duke*] See above, I. i. 180. The
king. The term was commonly used of
a sovereign prince, as in *Tp.*, I. ii. 54,
58, etc. Sidney, in *Arcadia* (bk v), calls
King Basilius 'the duke'.

38. *tapster*] a 'tapster's arithmetic' is
mentioned again in *Troil.*, I. ii. 123.
A 'tapster' was regarded as a very
ignorant person. Nashe, in his Introduction to Greene's *Menaphon* (1589),

Moth. You are a gentleman and a gamester, sir.

Arm. I confess both: they are both the varnish of a com-   40
plete man.

Moth. Then I am sure you know how much the gross sum
of deuce-ace amounts to.

Arm. It doth amount to one more than two.

Moth. Which the base vulgar do call three.   45

Arm. True.

Moth. Why, sir, is this such a piece of study? Now here is
three studied ere ye'll thrice wink; and how easy it is
to put years to the word three, and study three years
in two words, the dancing horse will tell you.   50

45. do] *Q1; not in Ff, Q2.*

speaks of 'tapsterly terms' as befitting the 'mind of the meanest'. See Intro., 5.23.

39. *gamester*] player, gambler. So in Cooke's *Greene's Tu Quoque*: 'Primero! why I thought thou hadst not been so much gamester as to play at it.'

45. *vulgar*] the common people. Cf. Henry Porter's *Two Angry Women of Abingdon* (Malone Soc., ed. Greg, ll. 401 ff.): *'Comes.* Faith sir like a poore man of service. *Philip.* Or servingman. *Comes.* Indeed so called by the vulgar. *Philip.* Why where the divell hadst thou that word?' There is also a hint of the meaning 'vernacular speech'. Cf. iv. i. 69.

50. *dancing horse*] The description fits Morocco, Banks's trick-performing horse, which is famous in Elizabethan literature and on down to the middle of the seventeenth century. Halliwell quotes from a MS. diary kept by a native of Shrewsbury: 'September, 1591. This yeare . . . Master Banckes, a Staffordshire gentile brought into the town of Salop a white horse which would doe wonderfull and strange things, as these—wold in a company or prese tell how many peeces of money by hys foote were in a mans purce . . . many people judgid that it were impossible to be don except he had a famyliar, or don by the arte of magicke.' A tract with an illustration

(reproduced by Chambers, *Book of Days*, i. 225) was published in 1596, under the title of '*Moroccus Exstaticus: or Bankes Bay Horse in a Traunce*' (in the diary the animal is said to be white). The cut shows the horse on his hind legs, and at his feet two dice, one of which has ace uppermost, the other the deuce to the front. Evidently what his master had taught him was to beat out with his hoof any suggested number; and this talent was used in what would now be called a thought-reading act. The entry in the Shrewsbury diary for September 1591 is the first certain reference to this accomplished animal and this has been taken by several editors as evidence that *LLL.* could not have been written earlier than that year; but William Clowes, in *A Prooued Practise for all Young Chirurgians* (1588) speaks of a quack being 'as cunning, as the Horsse at the Crosse Keyes', which may have been the same. There may also have been other dancing horses. Morocco was still going strong in 1600, when his master took him on to the roof of St Paul's and caused a sensation—as the author (? Dekker) of the *Owle's Almanack* has it (1606): 'The dancing horse stood on the top of Powles whilst a number of asses stood braying below.' According to Jonson (*Epigram 133*) Banks and his horse were eventually

Arm. A most fine figure!

Moth. To prove you a cipher.   [*Aside*

Arm. I will hereupon confess I am in love; and as it is
base for a soldier to love, so am I in love with a base
wench. If drawing my sword against the humour   55
of affection would deliver me from the reprobate
thought of it, I would take Desire prisoner, and ran-
som him to any French courtier for a new-devised
courtesy. I think scorn to sigh: methinks I should
outswear Cupid. Comfort me, boy. What great men   60
have been in love?

Moth. Hercules, master.

Arm. Most sweet Hercules! More authority, dear boy,
name more; and, sweet my child, let them be men
of good repute and carriage.   65

Moth. Samson, master: he was a man of good carriage,
great carriage, for he carried the town-gates on his
back like a porter; and he was in love.

burned together beyond sea for one
witch, but the date of this is not given.

51. *figure*] a turn of rhetoric or of
logic. See v. ii. 408.

52. *cipher*] a nothing, a nonentity.

58-9. *French courtier . . . courtesy*] a
bow or complimentary acknowledge-
ment after any of the new French
fashions. Cf. *R3*, I. iii. 39: 'French nods
and apish courtesy'; and Jonson's *Case
is Altered*, II. iii (1598): 'And she should
make French court'sies so most low
That every touch should turn her over
backward.' Montaigne (1580-8) refers to our 'kissing the hands . . . our
low-lowting courtesies' (bk II, chap.
xii in Florio's translation).

59. *think scorn*] scorn, disdain. A frequent expression in Shakespeare, Jonson (*Cynthia's Revels*, v. ii), and others
of the time. So Lyly in *Euphues and his
England* (Arber repr., p. 424), 1580:
'Hee that never tooke the oare in his
hand must not thinke scorn to bee
taught'; and Sir Philip Sidney's
Arcadia, bk I: 'thinking foule scorne
willingly to submit my selfe to be
ruled'.

60. *outswear Cupid*] 'surpass in swearing', according to some commentators
and *N.E.D.*; 'conquer by swearing',
Schmidt. I prefer the latter sense, i.e.
forswear. Cf. II. i. 103, where the expression 'sworn out housekeeping'
obviously means forsworn, renounced.

64. *sweet my child*] The inversion is
common; so 'good my knave', III. i.
147.

67. *carried the town-gates*] A passage
in Middleton's *Family of Love*, I. iii
(1607), recalls this about Samson:
'from what good exercise come you
three? *Gerardius.* From a play where
we saw most excellent Sampson excel
the whole world in gate-carrying . . .
Believe it we saw Sampson bear the
town-gates on his neck from the lower
to the upper stage, with that life and
admirable accord, that it shall never
be equalled, unless the whole new
livery of porters set their shoulders'.
Henslowe paid for the book of a play
called *Samson* (now lost) in July 1602.
See W. W. Greg, *Henslowe's Diary*, i.
169 and ii. 223. This may be referred
to by Middleton as Greg points out.

Arm. O well-knit Samson! strong-jointed Samson! I do
    excell thee in my rapier as much as thou didst me in   70
    carrying gates. I am in love too. Who was Samson's
    love, my dear Moth?
Moth. A woman, master.
Arm. Of what complexion?
Moth. Of all the four, or the three, or the two, or one of   75
    the four.
Arm. Tell me precisely of what complexion.
Moth. Of the sea-water green, sir.
Arm. Is that one of the four complexions?
Moth. As I have read, sir; and the best of them too.   80
Arm. Green indeed is the colour of lovers; but to have
    a love of that colour, methinks, Samson had small
    reason for it. He surely affected her for her wit.

70. *my rapier*] This was becoming the fashionable weapon, introduced, along with the dress and manners of the continent, by the 'Italianate' fops so often satirized by Elizabethan writers. Though the models for this fashion were largely French or Italian the rapier seems to have been regarded as peculiarly Spanish. Giles du Guez, *Introductione . . . for to speke Frenche, c.* 1530, has 'the Spanische sworde, la rapiere'. Cotgrave (1611) gives 'Espa Espagnole—A Rapier or Tuck'.

74–5. *complexion? Of all the four*] The commonest sense of 'complexion' in Shakespeare is the colour of the skin; but the word can also mean either a 'humour' (Phlegm, Blood, Choler, or Melancholy) or the peculiar mixture of them in an individual that determined his character. For Moth's quibbling cf. Dekker: '*Bellafront.* Is my glass there? and my boxes of complexion? *Roger.* Yes forsooth: your boxes of complexion are here I thinke: yes 'tis here: here's your two complexions, and if I had all the foure complexions, I should nere set a good face upon't, some men I see are borne under hard-favoured planets' (*Honest Whore* [Pearson, ii. 25]).

78. *sea-water green*] Holland has this

expression (our 'sea-green') in Pliny's *Naturall History*, trans. 1601 (bk XXXVII, chap. v, p. 613): 'Beryls . . . which carrie a sea-water green'. In Jonson's *Part of the King's Entertainment*, 1604, Tamesis has 'a mantle of sea-green or water-colour'. The name lives in the 'Aquamarine', a gem, which is mentioned in Stow's *Survey* (1598) as being 'of a sea-water green colour'. It is mentioned as an artist's colour in Rider's *Bibliotheca Scholastica*, 1589: 'A certain medly colour, made of hony, rain water, and sea water'.

81. *Green . . . colour of lovers*] This statement is supported by a reference to 'Green sleeves'; not only does the lady wear green but the lover puts his men in green for her sake. Green was commonly the colour of hope and of rejoicing. If Moth is Nashe, there may well be a pun here on Robert Greene, author of love-romances and, until his death in 1592, chief adversary of the Harveys. Nashe uses the quibble to sneer at writers 'who with Greene colours seeke to garnish such Gorgon-like shapes' (McKerrow, I. 16), i.e. 'gloss over Woman's natural deformity by describing her in the romantic terms invented by Greene'; and Gabriel Harvey has it often.

Moth. It was so, sir, for she had a green wit.

Arm. My love is most immaculate white and red.　　85

Moth. Most maculate thoughts, master, are masked
　　under such colours.

Arm. Define, define, well-educated infant.

Moth. My father's wit and my mother's tongue assist me!

Arm. Sweet invocation of a child; most pretty and pathe-　90
　　tical!

Moth.　　　　If she be made of white and red,
　　　　　　Her faults will ne'er be known,
　　　　　　For blushing cheeks by faults are bred,
　　　　　　　　And fears by pale white shown:　　95
　　　　　　Then if she fear, or be to blame,
　　　　　　　　By this you shall not know,
　　　　　　For still her cheeks possess the same
　　　　　　　　Which native she doth owe.

A dangerous rhyme, master, against the reason of　100
white and red.

---

86. maculate] *Q1, Pope et seq.;* immaculate *Ff,Q2.*　　94. blushing] *Ff2,3,4;*
blush-in *Qq,F1.*

84. *green wit*] Grant White saw an
allusion here to the green withes with
which Samson was bound. But 'Green
wit' was a common expression, bound
to be suggested by the context. Cf.
Greene's *Never Too Late* (Grosart, vii.
44), 1590: 'his grave wisdome exceedes
thy green wit'; and his *Mamillia*
(1583): 'your talk . . . sheweth surely
but a green wit, not so full of gravity,
as . . . age requires' (p. 46); and again
on pp. 49, 79, in the same tale.
In Lyly's *Euphues* 'green' is used of
a wit that remains fresh in spite of
age.

85. *white and red*] Cf. *A Twelfe Night
Merriment (Narcissus)*, 1602 (ed. M.
Lee, p. 12): 'Leave off to bragg thou
boy of Venus breadd, I am as faire as
thou for white and red.' See *Per.,* iv.
vi. 27: 'flesh and blood, sir, white and
red'.

88. *define*] explain your meaning.

90–1. *pathetical*] touching. An early

form of 'pathetic' introduced by
Gabriel Harvey, with the original
meaning of 'passionate'. He has it
several times in his *Letters to Spenser*:
'Dionisius . . . is reported in a certain
Patheticall Ecstasie to haue cryed out'
('Earthquake Letter') (Grosart, i. 57),
1580; and earlier, in 1573, *Letter-Book*
(Camden Soc.). Chapman has 'pretty
and pathetical' twice, in *An Humourous
Day's Mirth,* i. i. 36, of the posy engraved on an agate, and in *Widow's
Tears,* iii. i. 129. Shakespeare uses it,
each time colloquially or playfully,
again in *AYL.,* iv. i. 196, as well as
later in this play (iv. i. 149).

99. *owe*] own. Cf. ii. i. 6.

101. *white and red*] alluding to the
two 'complexions' or cosmetics, as in
the quotation from Dekker above (l.
74); the 'Ceruse and Vermillion' of
the same author in his *Gull's Horn
Book.* Ceruse was known as 'Spanish
white'.

Arm. Is there not a ballad, boy, of the King and the
  Beggar?

Moth. The world was very guilty of such a ballad some
  three ages since; but I think now 'tis not to be   105
  found; or, if it were, it would neither serve for the
  writing nor the tune.

Arm. I will have that subject newly writ o'er, that I may
  example my digression by some mighty precedent.
  Boy, I do love that country girl that I took in the   110
  park with the rational hind Costard: she deserves
  well.

Moth. To be whipped; and yet a better love than my
  master.   [*Aside*

Arm. Sing, boy: my spirit grows heavy in love.   115

Moth. And that's great marvel, loving a light wench. [*Aside*

Arm. I say, sing.

Moth. Forbear till this company be past.

            Enter DULL, COSTARD, *and* JAQUENETTA.

Dull. Sir, the duke's pleasure is that you keep Costard
  safe: and you must suffer him to take no delight   120
  nor no penance, but a' must fast three days a week.

109. precedent] *Johnson;* president (*or* prescedent) *Qq,Ff.*   113. love] *Ff2,3,4;*
loue *Qq;* ioue *F1.*   118. S.D. *Enter . . .*] *Steevens (1793); Enter Clown, Constable,
and Wench Qq,Ff.*   120. suffer him to] *Q1;* let him *Ff,Q2.*   121. a'] *Q1;*
hee *Ff.*

102–3. *King and the Beggar*] See note
at IV. i. 66, 67.

106–7. *serve . . . tune*] The song is out
of date, says Moth; neither words nor
music would pass muster now.

109. *digression*] deviation from the
proper course; transgression. See *Lucr.*,
202. Jonson has the word in a similar
sense in *Cynthia's Revels*, I. i, in a speech
full of affectations by Amorphus.
N.E.D. has an early example from
Hawes (1509).

111. *rational hind*] intelligent clown.
Theobald suggested a quibble on the
two senses of *hind*, rustic and stag.

116. *light*] wanton.

121. *penance*] Perhaps Dull was

thinking of 'pleasance', a Shakespearean word.

three days a week] In 1580–1 Elizabeth
re-enacted certain Acts (1549 and
1564) relating to fishing and fisher-
men. They prescribed that Wednesday
and Saturday in every week (except
Christmas week and Easter week)
should be observed as 'Fish Days'.
Those who failed to make fish the main
item of their diet on these days were
subject to the penalties laid down for a
similar offence on Friday, the official
fast-day of the Church, although the
new Fish Days were expressly dis-
sociated from religious observances,
being instituted for 'the maintenance

For this damsel, I must keep her at the park; she is
allowed for the day-woman. Fare you well.

Arm. I do betray myself with blushing. Maid.

Jaq. Man.   125

Arm. I will visit thee at the lodge.

Jaq. That's hereby.

Arm. I know where it is situate.

Jaq. Lord, how wise you are!

Arm. I will tell thee wonders.   130

Jaq. With that face?

Arm. I love thee.

Jaq. So I heard you say.

Arm. And so farewell.

Jaq. Fair weather after you!   135

127. hereby] *Qq; here by Ff.*   131. that] *Q1,Ff2,3,4;* what *F1,Q2.*

and increase of the navy', and the pre-
servation of young cattle. Costard's
penance is doubtless a reflection of
these regulations, though the Wednesday had been remitted in 1585.

123. *allowed for the day-woman*] admitted or passed as dairymaid. Under
day-woman (correctly *dey*) and *dey-wife,*
N.E.D. gives examples of this variant
of dairy-woman as early as 1398 and as
late as Scott (*Fair Maid of Perth,* 1828).
It is in a list of Gloucester dialect words
dated 1890.

127. *That's hereby*] No doubt Jaquenetta has some vulgar wit here, such as
'over the left shoulder' or 'the left-hand
way', but confirmation is lacking.
Schmidt (with no authority) says 'that
as it may be'. He adopted it from
Steevens. For this scene between
Jaquenetta and Armado there is a
close parallel in one between Silena
and Candius in Lyly's *Mother Bombie*
(about 1589), ii. 3. Silena has 'rackt
together all the odde blinde phrases
that help them that know not how to
discourse, but when they cannot
answer wisely, either with gybing
cover their rudenesse, or by some new
coined by word bewray their peevish-
nesse'.

131. *With that face?*] a piece of slang

equivalent to 'you don't mean it!'
'you're not the man', etc. Steevens,
Dyce, and Craig refer to Fielding's
Joseph Andrews, rather a long way down
the time. Steevens says it has no meaning and was still in use. Cf. Heywood,
Fair Maid of Exchange (Pearson, p. 11),
1607: 'Come, come, leave your jesting,
I shall put you downe. *Mall.* With that
face! away, you want wit'; and Killi-
grew's *Parson's Wedding* (Hazlitt's
Dodsley, xiv. 532), 1663: '*Parson.* Sir,
my business is praying, not epilogues.
Captain. With that face?' There is a
side note to the line 'Despatch him,
therefore, while we are alone', of
Woodes's *Conflict of Conscience* (Hazlitt's
Dodsley, vi. 53), 1581: 'Hipocrisy
[aside] On your face, sir', which is the
same expression slightly altered.

133. *So I heard you say*] another rural
witticism. It occurs in Jonson's *Bartholomew Fair,* Act iii: '*Waspe.* Yet these
will serve to pick the pictures out of
your pockets, you shall see. *Cokes.* So I
heard them say. Pray thee mind him
not, fellow.' The meaning may be
paraphrased by our 'you don't say so.'

134–5. *farewell. Fair weather after you*]
Jaquenetta, who has been very ill-
treated by the commentators, completes the rustic saw. Cf. *Arden of*

Dull. Come, Jaquenetta, away! [*Exeunt Dull and Jaquenetta.*

Arm. Villain, thou shalt fast for thy offences ere thou be
pardoned.

Cost. Well, sir, I hope when I do it I shall do it on a full
stomach.   140

Arm. Thou shalt be heavily punished.

Cost. I am more bound to you than your fellows, for they
are but lightly rewarded.

Arm. Take away this villain: shut him up.

Moth. Come, you transgressing slave: away!   145

Cost. Let me not be pent up, sir; I will fast, being loose.

Moth. No, sir, that were fast and loose: thou shalt to
prison.

Cost. Well, if ever I do see the merry days of desolation
that I have seen, some shall see—   150

Moth. What shall some see?

Cost. Nay, nothing, Master Moth, but what they look
upon. It is not for prisoners to be too silent in their
words, and therefore I will say nothing: I thank
God I have as little patience as another man, and   155
therefore I can be quiet.   [*Exeunt Moth and Costard.*

Arm. I do affect the very ground, which is base, where

136. *Dull*] *Q1 gives this to Clown.*   146. fast] be fast *Ff2,3,4.*   153. not] *not in*
Q2.   be too silent] *Q1*; be silent *Ff,Q2.*   154. words] wards *Johnson conj.*
156. *Exeunt . . . Costard*] *Exit Q1.*

Faversham, iv. 3 (1592): 'See you follow
us. . . . *Michael.* So. Fair weather after
you!'; and *Wily Beguiled* (Malone Soc.,
ed. Greg, ll. 607–9), 1606: 'Come,
follow us, good Wench. *Peg.* I, farewell, faire weather after you.' It occurs
also in Middleton. Silena in *Mother
Bombie*, ii. 3, has another form, 'farewell frost'.

139–40. *on a full stomach*] There is a
quibble between the literal meaning
and the sense 'proudly', 'courage-
ously', which can be seen in Palsgrave's
Lesclaircissement, p. 230 (1530), '*Full-
stomacht*', 'Full-stomacht' occurs in
Greene and Nashe; and cf. *Captain
Smith* (Arber, p. 864), 1629: 'Excellent,
swift, stomack full, Tartarian horse.'
With a good heart.

142. *fellows*] servants. See *1H4*, IV.
ii. 68: 'Tell me, Jack, whose fellows are
these that come after? *Falstaff.* Mine,
Hal, mine.'

147. *fast and loose*] a cheating trick.
Most of the early examples refer it to
the gipsies, as in *Ant.*, IV. x. 41. Cf.
Whetstone, *Promos and Cassandra* (pt i),
ii. vi (Hazlitt, *Shakes. Lib.*, vi. 226),
1578: 'At fast or loose, with my Gip-
tian, I meane to have a cast: Tenne to
one I read his fortune by the Marymas
fast' (spoken by a hangman); and
Lyly, *Euphues and his England*, 1580:
'Thus with the Ægyptian thou playest
fast or loose' (Arber, p. 326). And
Jonson assigns it to a gipsy in his
Masque of the Metamorphosed Gipsies.

157–9. *base . . . baser . . . basest*] This

her shoe, which is baser, guided by her foot, which
is basest, doth tread. I shall be forsworn, which is
a great argument of falsehood, if I love. And how   160
can that be true love which is falsely attempted?
Love is a familiar; Love is a devil: there is no evil
angel but Love. Yet was Samson so tempted, and
he had an excellent strength; yet was Solomon so
seduced, and he had a very good wit. Cupid's butt-   165
shaft is too hard for Hercules' club, and therefore
too much odds for a Spaniard's rapier. The first and

163. was Samson] was Sampson *Q1;* Sampson was *Ff,Q2.*

toying with a word is a characteristic
of Sir Philip Sidney's *Arcadia,* rather
than of Lyly, who repeats the letter
and the sound, not the word itself.
Hart quotes one or two passages from
bk iii: 'so terrible was his force, and yet
was his quicknes more forcible then his
force, and his judgement more quick
then his quicknes'; 'and yet did the
ones strength excel in nimblenes, and
the others nimblenes excel in strength
but now strength and nimblenes were
both gone'; 'exceedingly sory for
Pamela, but exceedingly exceeding
that exceedingnes in feare for Philo-
clea'. See again Armado's letter, IV. i.
63–4; and cf. Puttenham, p. 213:
'Then have ye a figure which the
Latines call *Traductio,* and I the tran-
lacer: which is when ye turne and tran-
lace a word into many sundry shapes
as the Tailor doth his garment, and
after that sort to play with him in your
dittie.' This is Arcadianism exactly,
but Armado does not go the whole
length.

160. *argument*] proof.

162. *familiar*] an attendant spirit; as
in *1H6,* III. ii. 122, and *2H6,* IV. iii. 114.
'Behold, there is a woman that hath a
familiar spirit at Endor' (1 Sam.,
xxviii. 7).

165–6. *Cupid's butt-shaft*] 'strong un-
barbed arrows used in the field exercises of the day' (Gifford). They hit
hard but were easily extracted, so that
they were suitable for Cupid's quiver.

Cf. *Rom.,* II. iv. 15: 'The very pin of his
heart cleft with the blind bow-boy's
butt-shaft.' No other example has been
adduced by the authorities, save
Hart's from Jonson's *Cynthia's Revels,* V.
iii (again in Cupid's possession): 'I
fear thou hast not arrows for the purpose. *Cupid.* O yes, here be of all sorts—
flights, rovers and butt-shafts.' See
note at 'bird-bolt', IV. iii. 23.

167. *Spaniard's rapier*] See note on
l. 70 above.

167–8. *first and second cause*] Cf.
AYL., v. iv. 52, 69, and *Rom.,* II. iv. 26.
Halliwell quoted Vincentio Saviolo's
Practise, (*Of . . . honorable Quarrels,*
1594): 'I will onely treate of that which
I shall judge meetest by a generall rule
to be observed, and include all com-
bats under two heads. First, then, I
judge it not meet that a man should
hazard himselfe in the perill of death,
but for such a cause as deserveth it, so
as if a man be accused of such a defect
as deserve to be punished with death,
in this case combate might bee
graunted. Againe, because that in an
honourable person, his honor ought to
be preferred before his life, if it happen
him to have such a defect laid against
him, as in respect thereof he were by
lawe to be accounted dishonorable,
and should therefore be disgraced before the tribunall seate, upon such a
quarrell my opinion is that hee be not
able by lawe to clere himself thereof.'
Later critics have felt that some other

second cause will not serve my turn; the passado he
respects not, the duello he regards not: his disgrace
is to be called boy, but his glory is to subdue men.   170
Adieu, valour! rust, rapier! be still, drum! for your
manager is in love; yea, he loveth. Assist me, some
extemporal god of rhyme, for I am sure I shall turn

169. duello] duella *Q1*.   172. manager] Armiger *Collier MS.*(*!*)

source must be sought, giving the two
causes more definitely and concisely,
and in *M.L.R.*, xii. 76, H. B. Charlton
claimed to have found it in a passage
from *The Book of Honor and Armes*,
attributed to Sir William Segar (1590),
which is clearly the germ of Saviolo's
dissertation: 'I say then that the
causes of all quarrell whereupon it be-
houeth to use the triall of Armes, may
be reduced into two: for it seemeth to
me not reasonable, that any man
should expose himselfe to the perill of
death, save onelie for such occasions as
doo deserue death. Wherefore when-
soeuer one man doth accuse another
of such a crime as meriteth death, in
that case the Combat ought to be
graunted. The second cause of Combat
is Honor, because among persons of
reputation, Honor is preferred before
life.' Yet Armado speaks of the 'causes'
not precisely, as the reasons for em-
barking on a quarrel, but generally, as
part of the regulations for its conduct.
Unlike Touchstone, Cupid will not
fight 'by the book'. I think, despite
Charlton's discovery, that the reference is not a particular one to Segar
but a general one to Saviolo and
Caranza (*De la Filosofia de las Armas*,
1569) whose prescription of an exact
etiquette of duelling is constantly ridiculed by Jonson as well as by Shakespeare. A better parallel is Jonson's *Alchemist*, IV. i (1610): Subtle instructs
Kastrill on the 'grammar and logic and
rhetoric of quarrelling', and tells him
'You must render causes, child, Your
first and second intentions, know your
causes.'

168. *passado*] See *Rom.*, II. iv. 26 and

III. i. 88. 'A forward thrust with the
sword one foot being advanced at the
same time' (*N.E.D.*). From the Spanish *pasada*. Jonson gives it *passada* in
Every Man in his Humour. Howell's
Vocabulary (1659) gives the different
forms: 'To make a pass, *Far' una
passata*; *Faire une passade*; *Hazer
passada*', in Italian, French, and
Spanish. Marston, quoting from
Saviolo apparently, has 'sly passatas,
Stramazones, resolute stocatas' (*Scourge
of Villainy*, Sat. xi [1598]).

169. *duello*] the correct practice of
duelling. Both this word and 'duellist'
(Harvey's *Pierce's Supererogation*, 1592)
preceded 'duel' in English use. Jonson
has it in *Cynthia's Revels*, I. i (1600): 'one
that . . . was your first that ever enriched his country with the true laws of
the duello'. Cf. *Gesta Grayorum*, 1594
(Malone Soc., ed. Greg, p. 28): 'Item,
no Knight of this Order shall, in point
of Honour, resort to any Grammar-
rules out of the Books *De Du[e]llo*, or
such like.' This is perhaps a direct
reference to Caranza's work.

172. *manager*] the earliest example
of this word in *N.E.D.* Cf. Jonson,
Every Man in His Humour, I. iv (1598):
'You do not manage your weapon
with any facility or grace to invite me.'
'Manage arms' occurs five times in
Marlowe's *Tamburlaine*, pt 1. Armado's mock-dignity here becomes the
true thing in *Oth.*, III. iii. 350–4.

173. *extemporal*] Cf. G. Harvey
(Grosart, i. 111), 1579: 'To his very
unfriendly frende that procurid the
edition of his so slender and extem-
porall devises'.

173–4. *turn sonnet*] It is odd that

sonnet. Devise, wit; write, pen; for I am for whole
volumes in folio.   [*Exit.*   175

174. sonnet] *Ff,Qq;* sonneteer *or* sonneter *Hanmer, etc.;* a sonnet *Amyot;* sonnets
Verplanck, Halliwell; sonnet-maker, sonnet-monger, sonnetist *various mod. edd.*

editors have boggled at the absence of
article here, while remaining un-
moved by IV. iii. 131—'did never
sonnet for her sake compile'. For *turn* in
this sense, cf. 'turn his merry note
Unto the sweet bird's throat' (*AYL.*,
II. v. 3). Furness thinks that Armado
means he will become an abstract
sonnet, he is so saturated with love.
Hart is surely wrong to take as a
parallel the 'turn a song' in Thos.
Brewer's (prose) *Merry Devil of Edmon-*
ton, 1608 (1631 text ed. Abrams, p.
263): 'M. Parson turned his song', and
'they turned it to his mind' (*ibid.*)
where the word means 'changed'. At
IV. i. 89 we find the sonnet Armado
turns. The expression in *AYL.* occurs
earlier in Hall's *Satires,* VI. i (1598):
'Whiles threadbare Martiall turns his
merry note'.

174–5. *Devise . . . in folio*] Cf. G.
Harvey, *Foure Letters* (Grosart, i. 200),
1592: 'a famous deviser in folio'.

ACT II

SCENE I

Enter the PRINCESS *of France,* MARIA, KATHARINE, ROSALINE,
BOYET, *Lords, and other Attendants.*

Boyet. Now, madam, summon up your dearest spirits:
    Consider who the king your father sends,
    To whom he sends, and what's his embassy:
    Yourself, held precious in the world's esteem,
    To parley with the sole inheritor   5
    Of all perfections that a man may owe,
    Matchless Navarre; the plea of no less weight
    Than Aquitaine, a dowry for a queen.
    Be now as prodigal of all dear grace
    As Nature was in making graces dear   10
    When she did starve the general world beside,
    And prodigally gave them all to you.
Prin. Good Lord Boyet, my beauty, though but mean,
    Needs not the painted flourish of your praise:
    Beauty is bought by judgment of the eye,   15
    Not utter'd by base sale of chapmen's tongues.
    I am less proud to hear you tell my worth
    Than you much willing to be counted wise

ACT II

Scene i

S.D. *Enter . . .*] *Rowe; Enter the Princesse of France with three attending Ladies and three
Lordes Qq,Ff.*   13. *Prin.*] *Ff2,3,4; Queene Qq,F1.*   Lord] L. *Qq,Ff.*

1. *summon up your dearest spirits*] bring
forward your best wits. Cf. 'muster
your wits', v. ii. 85; an expression used
by Dekker (Grosart, ii. 95).

5. *inheritor*] owner. Cf. Dekker,
Belman of London (Grosart, iii. 74):
'The admiration of these Bewties
made mee so enamoured, and so

really in love with the inheritor of
them'.

6. *owe*] own; as at i. ii. 99; and
commonly.

7. *plea*] that which is pleaded for.

14. *flourish*] ornamentation.

16. *chapmen*] merchants, dealers. See
Intro., 5.23.

In spending your wit in the praise of mine.
But now to task the tasker: good Boyet,   20
You are not ignorant all-telling fame
Doth noise abroad Navarre hath made a vow,
Till painful study shall outwear three years,
No woman may approach his silent court:
Therefore to's seemeth it a needful course,   25
Before we enter his forbidden gates,
To know his pleasure; and in that behalf,
Bold of your worthiness, we single you
As our best-moving fair solicitor.
Tell him the daughter of the King of France,   30
On serious business craving quick dispatch,
Importunes personal conference with his grace.
Haste, signify so much; while we attend,
Like humble-visag'd suitors, his high will.
Boyet. Proud of employment, willingly I go.   35
Prin. All pride is willing pride, and yours is so.   [*Exit Boyet.*
Who are the votaries, my loving lords,
That are vow-fellows with this virtuous duke?
First Lord. Lord Longaville is one.
Prin.   Know you the man?
Mar. I know him, madam: at a marriage-feast,   40
Between Lord Perigort and the beauteous heir
Of Jaques Falconbridge, solemnized

---

19. your wit in the praise] *Qq,F1;* thus your wit in praise, *Ff2,3,4.*   21. You . . .]
Princ. You . . . *F1,Q2.*   32. Importunes] Importuous *Q1.*   34. visag'd]
visage *Q1;* visaged *Ff,Q2.*   36. [*Exit Boyet*] *Dyce; Exit Qq,Ff (after previous
line).*   37–8.] *Prose in Qq,Ff; verse Rowe (ed. 2) et seq.*   39. *First Lord.*
Longaville] *Capell; Lor.* Longavill *Qq,Ff.*   40. *Mar.] Rowe; 1 Lady.
Qq,Ff.*   40–3. madam: at . . . solemnized In] *Capell;* madame at . . .
solemnized. In *Qq,Ff.*

---

20. *task the tasker*] task him who
tasks; like the old 'the guiler is beguiled' in Gower.

23. *outwear*] wear away, pass (the
time). Cf. Spenser, *Faerie Queene*
(1590), III. xii. 29: 'All that day she
outwore in wandering.'

28. *Bold*] confident.

29. *fair*] just, equitable.

34. *humble-visag'd*] Elsewhere Shake-

speare has *grim-visaged, pale-visaged,
tripe-visaged*. 'Sable-visaged night' occurs in the Prologue to *The Merry Devil
of Edmonton (c.* 1600); Jonson speaks of
the 'brass-visaged monster Barbarism'
(*Every Man in his Humour*). The Q 'visage' may be due to e : d confusion, so
easy in English script (see Intro., 2.4).

42. *solemnized*] The second syllable
bears the accent.

In Normandy, saw I this Longaville:
A man of sovereign parts he is esteem'd,
Well fitted in arts, glorious in arms;   45
Nothing becomes him ill that he would well.
The only soil of his fair virtue's gloss,
If virtue's gloss will stain with any soil,
Is a sharp wit match'd with too blunt a will;
Whose edge hath power to cut, whose will still wills   50
It should none spare that come within his power.

Prin. Some merry mocking lord, belike; is't so?

Mar. They say so most that most his humours know.

Prin. Such short-liv'd wits do wither as they grow.
Who are the rest?   55

Kath. The young Dumain, a well accomplish'd youth,
Of all that virtue love for virtue lov'd:
Most power to do most harm, least knowing ill,
For he hath wit to make an ill shape good,
And shape to win grace though he had no wit.   60
I saw him at the Duke Alençon's once;
And much too little of that good I saw
Is my report to his great worthiness.

---

44. of sovereign parts] *Ff,Q2;* of sovereign peerelsse *Q1.*   45. in arts] *Qq,F1;*
in the arts *Ff2,3,4.*   47, 48. gloss] glose *Q1.*   56. *Kath.*] *Rowe; 2. Lad. Qq,Ff.*
60. he] she *F1,Q2.*   61. Alençon's] Alansoes *Qq,F1.*

44. *sovereign parts*] Dover Wilson says the Q1 'peerelsse' is probably 'pertes' misread as 'perles'; taken in isolation it looks like a simple misprint for 'peerlesse' (one letter transposed). This suggests that Shakespeare wrote 'sovereign', crossed it out and substituted 'peerless' with a noun following; and that the compositor, who we know from iv. iii. 313 and v. ii. 809 was apt to blunder over erasures, did so here. The missing noun may well have been the 'parts' of F; certainly we cannot now make any better guess.

46. *would well*] intends kindly. His intention is too often malicious.

54. *short-liv'd wits*] Ascham, in *The Scholemaster* (Arber, pp. 32–4), has much about quick wits: 'Quicke wittes commonlie be apte to take, unapte to keepe . . . like over sharpe tooles, whose edges be verie soone turned. . . . In youthe also they be readie scoffers, privie mockers, and ever over light and merry. . . . They be like trees that shewe forth faire blossoms . . . but bring out small and not long lasting fruite . . . amongst a number of quicke wittes in youthe, fewe be found in the end . . . but decay and vanish, men know not which way.' Cf. Harvey's *Foure Letters* (Grosart, i. 193): 'Flourishing M. Greene is most wofully faded, and whilest I am bemoaning his over-piteous decay; and discoursing the usuall success of such ranke wittes, loe, his sworne brother, M. Pierce Penni-lesse (still more paltery)', etc.

Ros. Another of these students at that time
    Was there with him, if I have heard a truth,   65
    Berowne they call him; but a merrier man,
    Within the limit of becoming mirth,
    I never spent an hour's talk withal.
    His eye begets occasion for his wit;
    For every object that the one doth catch   70
    The other turns to a mirth-moving jest,
    Which his fair tongue (conceit's expositor)
    Delivers in such apt and gracious words
    That aged ears play truant at his tales,
    And younger hearings are quite ravished;   75
    So sweet and voluble is his discourse.
Prin. God bless my ladies! are they all in love,
    That every one her own hath garnished
    With such bedecking ornaments of praise?
First Lord. Here comes Boyet.

Re-enter BOYET.

Prin.   Now, what admittance, lord?
Boyet. Navarre had notice of your fair approach;   81
    And he and his competitors in oath
    Were all address'd to meet you, gentle lady,
    Before I came. Marry, thus much I have learnt;
    He rather means to lodge you in the field,   85
    Like one that comes here to besiege his court,
    Than seek a dispensation for his oath,

64. *Ros.*] *Rowe; 3 Lad. Qq,Ff.*   65. if] *Q1; as Ff,Q2.*   80. *First Lord*] *Lord Q1;*
Ma. Ff,Q2.   84. much] *not in Ff2,3,4.*

66. *Berowne . . . but a merrier*] Is there a pun on *brown*, meaning sombre?

74. *play truant*] leave their work, in order to listen.

76. *voluble*] fluent. See again III. i. 63; *Err.*, II. i. 92; and *Oth.*, II. i. 242. In Cotgrave, 1611. Dekker uses it in his *Lanthorne and Candle-Light* (Grosart, iii. 188), 1609: 'the high and ratling Dutch; the unfruitfull crabbed Irish, and the voluble significant Welch'. Puttenham, in his *Arte of English Poesie* (published 1589), says 'The utterance in prose is not of so great efficacie, because . . . not so voluble and slipper on the tongue' (p. 24); and at p. 156: 'a broad and voluble tong, thinne and movable lippes, teeth even'. And p. 111, speaking of the sphere: 'he is even and smooth . . . most voluble and apt to turne'. These last examples suffice to illustrate III. i. 63.

80. *admittance*] permission to enter.

82. *competitors*] associates, partners. Cf. *Gent.*, II. vi. 35.

83. *address'd*] made ready.

To let you enter his unpeopled house.
Here comes Navarre.

Enter KING, LONGAVILLE, DUMAIN, BEROWNE, *and*
Attendants.

King. Fair princess, welcome to the court of Navarre.   90
Prin. Fair I give you back again; and welcome I have
    not yet: the roof of this court is too high to be yours,
    and welcome to the wide fields too base to be mine.
King. You shall be welcome, madam, to my court.
Prin. I will be welcome then: conduct me thither.   95
King. Hear me, dear lady; I have sworn an oath.
Prin. Our Lady help my lord! he'll be forsworn.
King. Not for the world, fair madam, by my will.
Prin. Why, will shall break it will, and nothing else.
King. Your ladyship is ignorant what it is.   100
Prin. Were my lord so, his ignorance were wise,
    Where now his knowledge must prove ignorance.
    I hear your grace hath sworn out house-keeping:
    'Tis deadly sin to keep that oath, my lord,
    And sin to break it.   105

88. unpeopled] *Ff,Q2;* unpeeled *Q1, Cambridge (1863).*   89.] [*The Ladies*
mask] Capell.   90. *King.] Navar. Qq,Ff.*   99. it will] *Qq,Ff;* it; will *Capell*
et seq.   105–6. And . . . sudden-bold] *one line Q1.*   105. And] Not *Hanmer,*
Dyce.

88. *unpeopled*] Dover Wilson takes
the unique 'unpeeled' of Q1 as a misprint for 'unpeepled'. I agree. Cf.
AYL., III. ii. 134: 'Why should this a
desert be? For is it unpeopled?' and
R2, I. ii. 69: 'empty lodgings and un-
furnish'd walls, Unpeopled offices'.
The term here has the sense of without
servants or attendance suitable for
such guests. 'People', meaning retinue,
servants, is very commonly found in
Shakespeare, and the King has forsworn hospitality and womankind.

98. *by my will*] willingly.

99. *it will*] The Q1 punctuation is
far from infallible; Capell's version
makes good sense (that making and
breaking an oath are actions equally
arbitrary) and echoes Berowne's

speech on necessity (I. i. 148). But 'it
will' is good Shakespearean baby-talk
(see *Lr.,* I. iv. 239 and, for the tone,
Troil., IV. ii. 30). The Princess treats
the King as a wilful child—cf. the
'Don't-care was *made* to care' of
nurseries.

103. *sworn out house-keeping*] sworn
house-keeping at an end, sworn it
away, outsworn it, as in I. ii. 60. The
Princess is alluding to the deadly sin of
forgoing and banishing hospitality, another sense of the word 'house-keeping'. This was one of the cries of the
people, especially the 'poor players',
against the rich at the time.

105. *And sin*] Hanmer's emendation
is quite unwarranted. The King is in a
quandary: he must commit one or

But pardon me, I am too sudden-bold:
To teach a teacher ill beseemeth me.
Vouchsafe to read the purpose of my coming,
And suddenly resolve me in my suit.

King. Madam, I will, if suddenly I may.   110

Prin. You will the sooner that I were away,
    For you'll prove perjur'd if you make me stay.

[*Ber.* Did not I dance with you in Brabant once?

Ros. Did not I dance with you in Brabant once?

Ber. I know you did.   115

Ros. How needless was it then to ask the question!

Ber. You must not be so quick.

Ros. 'Tis long of you that spur me with such questions.

Ber. Your wit's too hot, it speeds too fast, 'twill tire.

Ros. Not till it leave the rider in the mire.   120

Ber. What time o' day?

Ros. The hour that fools should ask.

Ber. Now fair befall your mask!

Ros. Fair fall the face it covers!

Ber. And send you many lovers!   125

Ros. Amen, so you be none.

Ber. Nay, then will I be gone.]

109.] *Gives a paper. Collier MS.*   114, 116, *etc., to* 126. *Ros.*] *Kather. Q1.*   115–
17.] *Two lines ending* then, quick. *Capell.*

---

other deadly sin—against charity if he
keeps his oath, against good faith if he
breaks it.

109. *suddenly*] immediately.

113–27. *Did not I . . . be gone*] The
reasons for considering this, and the
parallel interchange at 179–93 below,
as accidental survivals from an early
draft are given in Intro., 2.52. The
omission of the passage, however, does
not leave much time for the King to
study the paper setting out the French
claim.

117. *quick*] sharp.

118. *long of you*] owing to you. Common provincially. Cf. Palsgrave, 1530:
'I am longe of this strife: *je suis en cause
de cest estrif.*'

spur . . . questions] 'Spur' puns on the

northern word 'speer', to put a question. The complete phrase occurs in
J. Rainoldes, *Overthrow of State Plays*
(ed. 1629, p. 60), 1593: 'You were disposed to spurre him idle questions.'

118, 119. *spur . . . wit's . . . speeds*] *spur*
and *speed* come together naturally—
both are frequently applied to wit. As
'Fresh wits need no spur' (Jonson, *Case
is Altered*, II. iii [1598]); and 'fooled
you up In a new suit with the best wits
in being, And kept their speed'.

123. *fair befall*] a very old phrase
occurring in Langland's *Piers the Plowman* (1377), and a favourite with
Shakespeare. Craig refers to Burns's
Lines to a Haggis: 'Fair fa' your honest
sonsy face'. For the *mask* see Intro.,
2.52.

King. Madam, your father here doth intimate
          The payment of a hundred thousand crowns;
          Being but the one half of an entire sum   130
          Disbursed by my father in his wars.
          But say that he, or we, as neither have,
          Receiv'd that sum, yet there remains unpaid
          A hundred thousand more; in surety of the which,
          One part of Aquitaine is bound to us,   135
          Although not valued to the money's worth.
          If then the king your father will restore
          But that one half of which is unsatisfied,
          We will give up our right in Aquitaine,
          And hold fair friendship with his majesty.   140
          But that, it seems, he little purposeth,
          For here he doth demand to have repaid
          A hundred thousand crowns; and not demands
          On payment of a hundred thousand crowns
          To have his title live in Aquitaine;   145
          Which we much rather had depart withal,
          And have the money by our father lent,
          Than Aquitaine, so gelded as it is.
          Dear princess, were not his requests so far
          From reason's yielding, your fair self should make   150

128. *King.*] *Ff; Ferd. Q1. The heading persists until the business discussion is concluded* (*it last appears before line 166*).   134. A] *Q1;* An *Ff,Q2.*   142. repaid] repaie *F1,Q2.*   144. On] *Theobald;* One *Qq,Ff.*

128. *intimate*] informs us of. Joseph Hunter (*New Illustrations*, 1845) was the first to claim an historical basis for this incident. He referred it to an engagement by Charles VI, about 1420, to pay Charles of Aragon, King of Navarre, 200,000 crowns. Sidney Lee suggested the more nearly contemporary negotiations (1586) between Catharine de Médicis and Henri of Navarre which partly concerned Aquitaine. An even more exact parallel has been traced by Abel Lefranc (*Sous le Masque de Shakespeare*, II, p. 90) with the embassy of Marguerite de Valois to her husband, Henri, in 1579, to settle disputes that had arisen over her dowry. See Intro., 5.21.

146. *depart withal*] part with, surrender.

148. *gelded*] impaired, reduced in power or value. The term was commonly applied to livings where the patron put in the incumbent, pocketing most of the income himself. Nashe says that 'he that first gelt religion of Church-livings . . . was Cardinal Wolsey' (*Unfortunate Traveller* [McKerrow, ii. 238]), 1594. 'A vicarige . . . gelded' is in *Return from Parnassus* (ed. W. D. Macray, p. 98), 1602; 'gelded chapel' in Hall's *Satires*, IV. ii (1598); 'gelded vicarage' in Marston and Shirley; and 'gelded bishoprick' in Sir John Harington (*Nugae Antiquae*, i. 101).

A yielding 'gainst some reason in my breast,
And go well satisfied to France again.
Prin. You do the king my father too much wrong,
And wrong the reputation of your name,
In so unseeming to confess receipt   155
Of that which hath so faithfully been paid.
King. I do protest I never heard of it;
And if you prove it I'll repay it back,
Or yield up Aquitaine.
Prin.   We arrest your word:
Boyet, you can produce acquittances   160
For such a sum from special officers
Of Charles his father.
King.   Satisfy me so.
Boyet. So please your grace, the packet is not come
Where that and other specialties are bound:
To-morrow you shall have a sight of them.   165
King. It shall suffice me: at which interview
All liberal reason I will yield unto.
Meantime, receive such welcome at my hand
As honour, without breach of honour, may
Make tender of to thy true worthiness.   170
You may not come fair princess, within my gates;
But here without you shall be so receiv'd
As you shall deem your self lodg'd in my heart,
Though so denied fair harbour in my house.
Your own good thoughts excuse me, and farewell: 175

---

167. I will] *Q1;* would I *Ff,Q2.*   171. within] *Q1;* in *Ff,Q2.*   174. fair] *Q1;*
farther *Ff,Q2.*

---

159. *arrest your word*] seize your word
as security. The expression occurs
again in *Meas.*, II. iv. 134. The *N.E.D.*
has these two and no other instances.
Shakespeare may have found this uncommon expression in Sidney's *Arcadia*, bk I (Feuillerat, i. 99), *ante* 1586:
'She tooke the advauntage one daye,
uppon Phalantus unconscionable
praysinges of her, and certaine cast-
awaie vows, howe much he would doo
for her sake, to arrest his woord
assoone as it was out of his mouth, and

by the vertue thereof to charge him to
goe with her.'
171. *fair princess, within*] Dover
Wilson suspects that 'queen' stood
for 'princess' in the first draft and
that Shakespeare corrected the word
without adjusting the metre. If
to write smoothly was really an aim
of Shakespeare's at this date, such
carelessness would be more than
Shakespearean; if not, need we boggle
at such roughnesses here or elsewhere?

To-morrow shall we visit you again.

Prin. Sweet health and fair desires consort your grace!

King. Thy own wish wish I thee in every place!   [*Exit.*

[*Ber.* Lady, I will commend you to mine own heart.

Ros. Pray you do my commendations; I would be glad   180
to see it.

Ber. I would you heard it groan.

Ros. Is the fool sick?

Ber. Sick at the heart.

Ros. Alack! let it blood.   185

Ber. Would that do it good?

Ros. My physic says, ay.

Ber. Will you prick't with your eye?

Ros. No point, with my knife.

Ber. Now God save thy life!   190

Ros. And yours, from long living!

Ber. I cannot stay thanksgiving.]   [*Retiring.*

Dum. Sir, I pray you, a word: what lady is that same?

Boyet. The heir of Alençon, Katharine her name.

Dum. A gallant lady. Monsieur, fare you well.   [*Exit.*   195

Long. I beseech you a word: what is she in the white?

Boyet. A woman sometimes, an you saw her in the light.

Long. Perchance light in the light. I desire her name.

176. shall we] *Q1;* we shall *Ff,Q2.*   179. mine own] *Q2;* my none *Q1;* my
own *Ff.*   179, 182, 184, 186, 188, 190, 192. Ber.] *Q1; Boy. Ff,Q2.*   183.
fool] *Q1;* soul *Ff,Q2.*   189. No point] *No poynt Qq,Ff.*   192. [*Retiring*]
Capell; [*Exit. Enter Dumain Qq,Ff.*   194. Katharine] *Singer (Capell conj.);*
Rosaline *Qq,Ff.*   197. an] and *Q1;* if *Ff,Q2.*

183. *fool*] The word is a favourite
with Shakespeare, who uses the phrase
'poor fool' where we should say 'poor
thing'. Cf. the Nurse's use of 'pretty
fool' in *Rom.*, I. iii. 31; and *Ado*, II. i.
328.

185. *let it blood*] bleed him. An expression of the time, as in Lyly's
Mydas, II. i: 'Hee is the man, that
being let blood, carries his arme in a
scarfe of his mistresse favour.'

189. *No point*] (i) it's blunt, (ii) not at
all. Florio (*World of Words*, 1598) has:
'*Punto*, . . . never a whit, no jot, no
point as the frenchmen say'. Stock

repartee, used even by Journeyman
Firk (Dekker, *Shoemaker's Holiday*, IV.
iv. 96). The repetition of both tag and
pun at V. ii. 277 supports the view that
the present passage is an early draft
left uncancelled.

192. *I cannot stay thanksgiving*] This
appears to trouble commentators.
Berowne's rejoinder to Rosaline's unkind wishes is that he cannot spare
the time to return proper thanks for
them.

194. *Katharine*] See Intro. 2.52.

197. *light*] wanton, quibblingly. A
very common sense in Shakespeare.

Boyet. She hath but one for herself; to desire that were a
　　　shame.
Long. Pray you, sir, whose daughter?　　　　　　　　　　　200
Boyet. Her mother's, I have heard.
Long. God's blessing on your beard!
Boyet. Good sir, be not offended.
　　　She is an heir of Falconbridge.
Long. Nay, my choler is ended.　　　　　　　　　　　　205
　　　She is a most sweet lady.
Boyet. Not unlike, sir; that may be.　　　　　　　[*Exit Long.*
Ber. What's her name in the cap?
Boyet. Rosaline, by good hap.
Ber. Is she wedded or no?　　　　　　　　　　　　　210
Boyet. To her will sir, or so.
Ber. O you are welcome, sir. Adieu.
Boyet. Farewell to me, sir, and welcome to you.　　[*Exit Ber.*
Mar. That last is Berowne, the merry mad-cap lord:
　　　Not a word with him but a jest.
Boyet.　　　　　　　　　　　　And every jest but a word.
Prin. It was well done of you to take him at his word.　216

---

202. on] *Qq*, a *Ff*.　209. Rosaline] *Singer;* Katharine *Qq,Ff*.　212. O you]
Q1; You *Ff,Q2*.　213. [*Exit Ber.*] *Q1; Exit. Ff,Q2*.

---

202. *blessing on your beard*] Longaville,
serious before, shows his irritation in
mocking the waggish Boyet. Satirical
references to one's beard were very
common forms of chaff, and were
generally summed up in the phrase 'to
play with one's beard', i.e. to insult,
belittle. It occurs in Jonson's *Bartholomew Fair*, IV. iii. Johnson says: 'may
you have sense more proportionate to
your beard', but he often takes gibes
too seriously.

211. *or so*] 'a mere expletive'
(Schmidt, who collects ten examples in
Shakespeare). Rather, as Craig says,
'or something of that sort'. See again
v. i. 143. Cf. Lyly's *Mother Bombie*, iv.
2: 'He would never tire—it may be he
would be so weary hee would goe no
further, or so.'

212. *O you*] See III. i. 142, n.

213. *Farewell . . . and welcome*] You
are welcome to go. Hardly obsolete.

214. *mad cap*] the earliest example of
the word in the *N.E.D.* Cf. 'mad
wenches', l. 256 below, and again at
v. ii. 264. I reject the always violent
senses of 'mad' in this place as given in
the *N.E.D.* The word has a playful
use, nearly our 'droll'. Greene has
'crue of Popish madcaps' in *The
Spanish Masquerado* (Grosart, v. 265),
which is probably earlier. There, and
again in his *Orlando Furioso*, the word
means madman, but not here. The
word 'mad-cap' occurs in Lyly's
Endymion, v. ii: 'O *lepidum caput*, O
mad-cap master! You were worthy
to winne Dipsas were she as olde
againe.'

216. *take him at his word*] take him up,
or talk to him in his own strain. Not
our sense of adopting a suggestion,
which occurs in *Err.*, I. ii. 17.

Boyet. I was as willing to grapple as he was to board.
Kath. Two hot sheeps, marry!
Boyet.   And wherefore not ships?
    No sheep, sweet lamb, unless we feed on your lips.
Kath. You sheep, and I pasture: shall that finish the jest? 220
Boyet. So you grant pasture for me.
Kath.   Not so, gentle beast:
    My lips are no common, though several they be.
Boyet. Belonging to whom?
Kath.   To my fortunes and me.
Prin. Good wits will be jangling; but, gentles, agree:
    This civil war of wits were much better us'd   225
    On Navarre and his book-men, for here 'tis abus'd.
Boyet. If my observation, which very seldom lies,
    By the heart's still rhetoric disclosed with eyes
    Deceive me not now, Navarre is infected.
Prin. With what?   230

218. *Kath.*] *La. Ka. Q1; La. Ma. F1.*   221.] [*Offering to kiss her*] *Capell.*

218. *ships*] pronounced like 'sheeps'
at this time, and affording quibbling
again in *Gent.*, I. i. 73, and in *Err.*, IV. i.
94, two of Shakespeare's earliest plays.
So engrained was this pun that the saying 'lose not the sheep for a ha'p'orth
of tar' was sometimes written 'ship',
which serves as well.

219. *feed on your lips*] Malone appro-
priately cites *Ven.*: 'Feed where thou
wilt, on mountain or on dale; Graze on
my lips' (Steevens, 1793).

222. *common, though several*] 'fields
that were enclosed were called severals,
in opposition to commons; the former
belonging to individuals, the latter to
the inhabitants generally' (Halliwell).
Katharine says: 'no doubt my lips are
good pasturing, but they are private
and reserved', with quibbling on
'several'. Boyet immediately sees her
meaning and asks for whom. Nares
and Steevens give several examples,
but the best is Johnson's: 'Of a lord
that was newly married, one observed
that he grew fat; "Yes," said Sir
Walter Raleigh, "any beast will grow
fat, if you take him from the common

and graze him in the several."'
Malone, Nares and others make a
difficulty out of the use of 'though'
here quite needlessly. But should they
insist upon it, the reply is easy: Shakespeare, like other writers of the time,
gave 'though' the meaning 'since',
'inasmuch as'. See *Oth.*, I. i. 70 and
III. iii. 146.

224. *Good wits*, etc.] Lyly has 'Good
wits will apply' (*Sapho and Phao*, III. ii
[1581]). Dekker put in 'Good wits love
good wine' (*The Honest Whore*, pt ii);
and 'Good wits jump' became proverbial later (*Wits Recreations*, 1640).

226. *book-men*] scholars. See below,
IV. ii. 33, for the only other use of the
word in Shakespeare. Cf. Greene's
Looking-Glass for London, 1143–4 (Grosart, xiv. 53): 'And though the Sailer
is no booke-man held, He knowes
more Art than ever booke-men read.'
Nashe uses the expression in *Summer's
Last Will*, l. 1421 (McKerrow, III. 278).

228. *still rhetoric*] Malone compares
Daniel, *Complaint of Rosalind* (1594):
'Sweet silent rhetorick of persuading
eyes; Dumb eloquence'.

Boyet. With that which we lovers entitle affected.
Prin. Your reason?
Boyet. Why, all his behaviours did make their retire
    To the court of his eye, peeping thorough desire:
    His heart, like an agate, with your print impress'd,   235
    Proud with his form, in his eye pride express'd:
    His tongue, all impatient to speak and not see,
    Did stumble with haste in his eyesight to be;
    All senses to that sense did make their repair,
    To feel only looking on fairest of fair: 240
    Methought all his senses were lock'd in his eye,
    As jewels in crystal for some prince to buy;
    Who, tend'ring their own worth from where they were
        glass'd,
    Did point you to buy them, along as you pass'd:

233. did] *Q1;* doe *Ff,Q2.*   243. where] *Q1;* whence *Ff,Q2.*   244. point you] *Q1;* point out *Ff,Q2.*

233. *all his behaviours*] all his powers of expression were concentrated in his eye, and shared in the longing look he gave you.

234. *thorough*] an old form of 'through', as in *thoroughfare.*

235. *like an agate*] Figures and mottoes were commonly cut in agate and worn as rings, the lineal descendants of the engraved gems of the ancients. Cf. *Doctor Dodypoll* (Bullen's *Old Plays,* iii. 111): 'See there (my Lord) this agget that contaynes The image of that Goddesse and her sonne Whom auncients held the sovereignes of Love'; and in Nichols's *Progresses,* ii. 52, a New Year's gift of 1576-7 is 'an agathe of Neptune sett with 6 very small rubyes', etc.

236. *his form*] the form impressed on the heart—the Princess's image.

237. *His tongue . . .*] 'His tongue, not able to endure the having merely the power of speaking without that of seeing' (Dyce).

240. *feel*] here used generally for the functions of all the senses. Each and every sense receives full satisfaction from the eye's contemplation of the Princess.

242. *jewels in crystal for some prince*] One of the New Year's gifts presented to Queen Elizabeth in 1573-4 is described as 'a juell, being a cristall garnished with golde; Adam and Eve enamuled white, and a cristole pendante garnished with golde, and four small perles pendaunte'; and in 1575-6: 'a juell, being a cristall sett in golde with two storyes appearing on both sides with a small pendaunte' (Nichols, i. 380; ii. 1).

243. *tend'ring*] offering, proffering for acceptance. So Gabriel Harvey, *An Advertisement for Papp-hatchett* (1589): 'fayre offer of preferment handsomely tendered unto some'.

from where] In his defence of the F 'from whence', Hart noted that the expression occurs at least nine times in Shakespeare's early plays and poems. 'From where' seems to be 'absent'.

glass'd] enclosed in glass, referring to the crystal glass the jewels were placed in.

244. *point*] direct, with a hint of urging. This is nearest to sense 12 in *N.E.D.,* which quotes Andrew Boorde's *Fyrst boke of the Introduction of Knowledge* (? 1550), ch. xxxii (oddly enough an

His face's own margent did quote such amazes,   245
That all eyes saw his eyes enchanted with gazes.
I'll give you Aquitaine, and all that is his,
An you give him for my sake but one loving kiss.
Prin. Come to our pavilion: Boyet is dispos'd.
Boyet. But to speak that in words which his eye hath disclos'd.
    I only have made a mouth of his eye,   251
    By adding a tongue which I know will not lie.
Mar. Thou art an old love-monger, and speak'st skilfully.
Kath. He is Cupid's grandfather and learns news of him.
Ros. Then was Venus like her mother, for her father is but
        grim.   255
Boyet. Do you hear, my mad wenches?
Mar.   No.
Boyet.   What then, do you see?
Mar. Ay, our way to be gone.
Boyet.   You are too hard for me.
                                        [*Exeunt.*

253. *Mar.*] *Lad. Q1; Lad. Ro. F1.*   254. *Kath.*] *Lad. 2. Q1; Lad. Mar. F.*   255.
Ros.] *Lad. 3. Q1; Lad. 2. F1.*   256. *Mar.*] *Lad. Q1; La. 1 F1.*   257. *Mar.*] *Lad.
Q1; Lad 3 F1.*

account of Navarre): 'I hauynge pitie
they [some pilgrims] should be cast
away poynted them to my hostage [i.e.
lodgings].' Cf. *Ham.*, I. v. 129: 'as your
business and desire shall point you';
and *Wint.*, IV. iv. 524. The concentrated interest in Navarre's face cries
out to be noticed.

    245. *margent*] Parallel passages, re-
ferences, and comments were commonly printed in the margins of books
at this time. Cf. *Rom.*, I. iii. 86, and
Lucr., 102. The amazement in
Navarre's face draws attention to the
love in his eyes.

    249. *dispos'd*] inclined to be playful
or merry. It occurs in Peele: 'I pray let
go, Ye are disposed I think' (*Edward I*,
Bullen's *Peele*, i. 135). See below, v. ii.
466.

    253. *love-monger*] Shakespeare has an
even dozen of these compounds with
monger. Nashe has a few others: news-
monger, star-monger, devil-monger,
metre-monger, complement-monger.

skilfully] knowledgeably.

    256. *Do you hear*] a common phrase
for claiming the hearer's attention—as
we today say 'listen'. Cf. *Troil.*, v. iii.
97.

    mad wenches] occurs again at v. ii.
264. See note at 'mad-cap' above, l.
214. Cf. Lodge, *Euphues Golden Legacie*
(*Shakes. Lib.*, 1875, p. 40): 'Why then
doth my Rosalynd grieve at the froune
of Torismond ... and more (mad lasse)
to be melancholy, when thou hast with
thee Alinda.' Cf. also 'mad-man', v. ii.
338. A phrase of Lyly's, *Sapho and Phao*,
I. iv (1581): 'Wee are mad wenches, if
men marke our words: for when ... we
cry away, doe wee not presently say go
to.' And in *Mother Bombie*, II. iii.

    257. *too hard for me*] See again, IV. i.
139, and *AYL.*, I. ii. 51. More than I
can manage (Sense 7 in *N.E.D.*). Cf.
Jonson, *The Magnetic Lady*, III. iv.
(Chorus): 'The boy is too hard for you,
brother Damplay; best mark the play
and let him alone.'

ACT III

SCENE I

Enter ARMADO *and* MOTH.

Arm. Warble, child: make passionate my sense of hearing.
Moth. [*sings*]. Concolinel.
Arm. Sweet air! Go, tenderness of years; take this key,
give enlargement to the swain, bring him festinately
hither; I must employ him in a letter to my love.   5

ACT III

Scene 1

S.D. *Enter* ARMADO *and* MOTH] *Enter Braggart and his boy* Q*1; Enter Braggart and Boys. Song Ff,*Q*2.*

1. *make passionate my sense of hearing*] Puttenham, speaking 'Of proportion by situation' (chap. x), says: 'This proportion consisteth in placing of every verse in a staffe or ditty by such reasonable distaunces as may best serve the eare for delight . . . which maner of situation, even without respect of the rime, doth alter the nature of the Poesie, and make it either lighter or graver, or more merry, or mournfull, and many wayes passionate to the eare and heart of the hearer' (Arber, pp. 97–8).

2. *Concolinel*] F informs us a song opens this Act, but it does not imply that this word is part of it, or even that the song is sung by Moth. Q has only *Concolinel*, which perhaps has no more sense that *tirra-lirra*, etc., and merely means that Moth exercised his notes in a warble. 'Warble' was the technical term for such utterances of melody. Cf. Laneham's *Letter* (Furnivall's *Cox*, p. 41), 1575: 'cleered his vois . . . wiped hiz lips . . . temperd a string or too with his wrast; and after a littl warbling on

hiz harp for a prelude, came foorth with a sollem song'. More probably *Concolinel* represents the title of Moth's song: and it was plausibly suggested by a correspondent to *N. & Q.* (ii. xi. 214, 1861) that it stands for *Can cailin gheal* (pronounced 'Con colleen yal'), meaning 'Sing, maiden fair'. Cf. Pistol's corruption of Irish song words in *H5*, iv. iv. 3. Collier would have it that 'Con Colinel' are the first two words of a lost Italian song.

4. *enlargement*] freedom. See *1H4*, iii. i. 31.

festinately] in a hurry. The adjective appears in *Lr.*, iii. vii. 10; and for both uses Shakespeare is the earliest authority in *N.E.D.* The word was not so rare perhaps. Nashe has it as a verb in *Have With You to Saffron Walden* (McKerrow, iii. 91): 'he would accelerate and festinate his procrastinating ministers' (1596); and Jonson uses it in *The Silent Woman*, iii. ii (1609): 'Gentlemen, my princess says, you shall have all her silver dishes, festinate.'

43

Moth. Master, will you win your love with a French
    brawl?

Arm. How meanest thou? brawling in French?

Moth. No, my complete master; but to jig off a tune at the
    tongue's end, canary to it with your feet, humour it   10
    with turning up your eyelids, sigh a note and sing a
    note, sometime through the throat as if you swal-
    lowed love with singing love, sometime through the
    nose, as if you snuffed up love by smelling love; with
    your hat penthouse-like o'er the shop of your eyes; with   15

6. Master, will you] *Q1;* Will you *Ff,Q2.*   10. your feet] *Q1;* the feet *Ff,Q2.*
11. eyelids] *Q1;* eye *Ff,Q2;* eyes *Dyce* (*2*), *Hudson.*   12. as if] *Theobald;* if *Qq,Ff.*
13. singing love, sometime] *Theobald;* singing love sometime *Q1;* singing, love
sometime *Ff,Q2.*   13–14. through the nose] *Ff2,3,4;* through: nose *Qq,F1.*

6–7. *French brawl*] a French dance
(the *bransle*) that became popular in
England during the second half of the
sixteenth century. In *Ancient Ballads
and Broadsides* (p. 221) there is a ballad
of date 1569 (or earlier) which begins:
'Good fellowes must go learne to
daunce, The brydeall is full nere a;
There is a brall come out of Fraunce,
The tryxt [trickiest] ye harde this
yeare a: For I must leape, and thou
must hoppe, And we must turne all
three a; The fourth must bounce it
lyke a toppe, And so we shall agree a.
I praye thee, mynstrell, make no
stoppe For we wyll merye be a.' In
Marston's *Pasquil and Katherine* (Act v),
1600, one says, 'what, gallants, have
you ne'er a Page can entertain the
pleasing time with some French
brawle or song?'—which recalls
Moth's position very plainly. The
same dramatist describes a brawl at
length in *The Malcontent*, iv. i (1604),
quoted by Steevens: 'music!—we will
dance. *Guer.* . . . . Passa regis, or Bianca's
brawl? *Aur.* We have forgot the brawl.
Fer. So soon? 'tis wonder! *Guer.* Why,
'tis but two singles on the left, two on
the right, three doubles forward, a tra-
verse of six round: do this twice, three
singles side, galliard trick-of-twenty
corantopace; a figure of eight, three
singles broken down, come up, meet,

two doubles, fall back, and then
honour.' The distinctly forced introduction of the phrase here is explained
by Miss F. A. Yates as a reference to the
1593 riots against Protestant refugees
(Huguenots from France especially),
satire of whom, in their capacity of
foreign language teachers, she finds
to be a major element in the topi-
cality of the play. See Intro., 3.222,
5.24.

9. *jig off a tune*] jerk off a tune, in the
manner of a jig. The earliest use of the
verb in *N.E.D.*

10. *canary*] dance, as if dancing the
canaries. See *All's W.*, ii. i. 79. To
'dance the canaries' became a common expression for dancing in a lively
fashion, as in Beaumont and Fletcher's
Rollo, ii. ii; Middleton's *Spanish Gipsy*,
iv. iii, and see Nares for more. Cf.
Dekker, *The Wonderfull Yeare* (Grosart,
i. 136), 1603: 'a drunkard, who no
sooner smelt the winde, but he thought
the ground under him danced the
canaries'. The passage in the text is the
earliest reference we have to the dance,
which appears to have been derived
from the aborigines of the 'Fortunate
Isles' by the Spaniards. It is described
by Arbeau, *Orchesographie* (1589),
quoted by Furness.

15. *penthouse-like*] like an overhang-
ing shed or projecting roof. Cf. *Mac.,*

your arms crossed on your thin-belly doublet like a
rabbit on a spit; or your hands in your pocket, like a
man after the old painting; and keep not too long in
one tune, but a snip and away. These are complements, these are humours, these betray nice wenches,   20
that would be betrayed without these; and make
them men of note (do you note, men?) that most are
affected to these.

Arm. How hast thou purchased this experience?
Moth. By my penny of observation.   25

16. thin-belly doublet] *Ff3,4;* thinbellies doblet *Q1;* thin belly doublet *Ff1,2,Q2;*
thin belly-doublet *Steevens, Schmidt, Craig;* thin belly's doublet *Collier.*   22. men
of note, (do you note, men?) that] *Steevens;* men of note: do you note men that
Qq,Ff; men of note—do you note me?—that *Hanmer, Cambridge.*   25. penny]
Hanmer et seq.; pen (*or* penne) *Qq,Ff, New.*

1. iii. 20, and *Ado,* iii. iii. 100. The hat
over the eyes, penthouse-like, was the
correct wear for a lover, or a critic.
The image is not new; see Sir T. Elyot,
Pasquil the Plaine (1540) A3: 'the tirfe
of the cappe tourned downe afore like
a pentise'.

16. *arms crossed*] Cf. iii. i. 178; iv. iii.
132; and *Gent.,* ii. i. 20. So also Jonson,
Cynthia's Revels, iii. ii: 'anon, doth seem
As he would kiss away his hand in
kindness; Then walks off melancholie,
and stands wreathed, As he were
pinned up to the arras'. And in Sidney's *Arcadia,* bk iii: 'the onely ods was
that when others tooke breath, he
sighed; and when others rested, he
crost his armes. For Love . . . still made
him remember'. And Lodge, *Euphues
Golden Legacie* (*Shakes. Lib.,* 1875, p.
66), 1590: 'they saw the sodaine
change of his lookes, his folded armes,
his passionate sighes, they heard him
often abruptly cal on Rosalynd.'

thin-belly doublet] The reading of the
earliest texts agrees here and is correct.
'Belly-doublet' is, in fact, nonsense, as
Staunton says. Some doublets were
stuffed, others were not; but the reference here is to the thinness of the belly,
like a spitted rabbit's. Cf. Dekker, *A
Strange Horse-race* (Grosart, iii. 335),

1613: 'The third that came sneaking in
was a leane, ill-faced, shotten-herring-
bellied rascall.'

17–18. *like a man after the old painting*] It is not known whether Moth is
referring to a particular old painting.

19. *snip*] a scrap or shred. The common phrase in Shakespeare's time was
'a snatch and away', which Dekker
varies to 'a licke at all sorts of learning,
and away' (*Gull's Horn Book* [Grosart,
ii. 258], 1609). Cf. Higgins, *Nomenclator* (1584): '*Prandium statarium . . .*
manger de bout en pied. A standing
dinner which is eaten in haste. . . . A
snatch and away.' And G. Harvey,
Foure Letters (Grosart, i. 230), 1592: 'A
snatch and away, with Neoptolemus,
and the common sort of students'.
Travellers reported that the dogs of
Egypt drank this way along the Nile
on account of the crocodiles.

22. (*do you note, men?*)] I believe with
Hart that Moth is here addressing the
male members *of the audience* and that,
in accordance with the regular clown's
tradition, he is giving them a tip on
how to be successful in love.

25. *penny of observation*] Cf. the similar
expression in the title of Greene's
Groatsworth of Wit bought with a million

Arm. But O, but O,—

Moth. The hobby-horse is forgot.

Arm. Call'st thou my love hobby-horse?

Moth. No, master; the hobby-horse is but a colt,—and
　　　　your love perhaps a hackney [*aside*]. But have you　　30
　　　　forgot your love?

Arm. Almost I had.

Moth. Negligent student! learn her by heart.

Arm. By heart, and in heart, boy.

Moth. And out of heart, master: all those three I will　　35
　　　　prove.

Arm. What wilt thou prove?

---

of repentance. Dover Wilson supports the reading 'pen' as peculiarly appropriate to a Moth who is the pamphleteer Nashe in disguise; but 'penny' (for which the Q 'penne' may well be a Shakespearean spelling) is even more suitable to the author of *Pierce Penilesse* who was being exhorted by Harvey to publish next his *Penniworth of Discretion*. 'A pennyworth of wit' is an ancient expression, and gave its name to a chapbook mentioned in Laneham's *Letter*, 1575, as *The Chapman of a peniwoorth of Wit* (Furnivall's *Cox*, p. 30). The expression occurs in *How a Merchande dyd hys Wyfe betray* (Hazlitt's *Early Popular Poetry*, i. 198), *c.* 1500: 'As thou art my trewe weddyd fere: Bye ye me a penyworth of wytt, And in youre hert kepe well hyt.'

26-7. *But O, but O,—The hobbyhorse is forgot*] a frequent lament, of which this is perhaps the earliest example. Perhaps the words are a fragment of a popular song. The hobby-horse went out of fashion before the Puritanical movement against sports in general became rancorous. It was a popular adjunct of the morris-dance and other May-games, and is mentioned as early as 1557 (*N.E.D.*) as a recognized village May-day sport. The words in the text occur again in *Ham.*, III. ii. 126. See also Kemp's *Nine Daies Wonder* (Bodley Head Quarto, p. 12), 1600: 'With hey and ho, through thicke and

thin, The hobby horse quite forgotten, I follow'd, as I did begin, Although the way were rotten.' The lament occurs also in Jonson's *Bartholomew's Fair*, v. iii, and in his *Masque of the Metamorphosed Gipsies*, and again in his *Satyr*. It is dwelt upon in Beaumont and Fletcher's *Woman Pleased* at some length. See also Cooke's *Greene's Tu Quoque* (quoted by Steevens). But the hobby-horse was by no means forgotten—it survives today in Cornwall —so that these words are most likely a quotation.

28. *Call'st thou my love hobby-horse?*] i.e. drudge, hackney. Jonson uses this as a term of abuse in *Cynthia's Revels*, v. ii (1600): '*Amorphys.* Make your play still upon the answer, sir. *Anaides.* Hold your peace, you are a hobby-horse.' And of a foolish lecherous person in *The Silent Woman*, IV. ii (1609): 'here be in presence have tasted of her favours. *Clerimont.* What a neighing hobby-horse is this!' In the latter passage it is equivalent to 'colt' of l. 29. In *Oth.*, IV. i. 157, it bluntly means 'prostitute'.

30. *hackney*] prostitute. Cf. Nashe, *Christ's Teares* (McKerrow, ii. 184), 1593: 'dormative potions to procure deadly sleepe, that when the hackney he hath payde for lyes by hym, hee may have no power to deale wyth her, but shee may steale from hym'.

Moth. A man, if I live; and this, by, in, and without, upon
     the instant: by heart you love her, because your heart
     cannot come by her; in heart you love her, because   40
     your heart is in love with her; and out of heart you
     love her, being out of heart that you cannot enjoy
     her.

Arm. I am all these three.

Moth. And three times as much more, and yet nothing at   45
     all.

Arm. Fetch hither the swain: he must carry me a letter.

Moth. A message well sympathized: a horse to be ambas-
     sador for an ass.

Arm. Ha? ha? what sayest thou?   50

Moth. Marry, sir, you must send the ass upon the horse,
     for he is very slow-gaited. But I go.

Arm. The way is but short: away!

Moth. As swift as lead, sir.

Arm. The meaning, pretty ingenious?   55
     Is not lead a metal heavy, dull, and slow?

Moth. *Minime*, honest master; or rather, master, no.

Arm. I say lead is slow.

---

38. and this, by] *Theobald;* (and this) by *Qq,Ff.*   55. The] *Q1;* Thy *Ff,Q2.*

---

48. *well sympathized*] in good harmony. Lyly seems to have introduced
the words 'sympathia' and 'sympathy'
(Arber's *Euphues*, pp. 46, 236, etc.),
which were both at once adopted by
Greene (Grosart's *Greene*, iv. 219, vii.
41, and ix. 179). Lyly seems also first
with verbs in -*ize*. The word 'sympa-
thize' is perhaps due to Shakespeare.
It is in Cotgrave, 1611. The minting of
words in '-ize' proceeded at a great
rate at this time. Nashe is eloquent
upon the subject in his To the Reader,
Christ's Teares (McKerrow, ii. 184),
1594: 'To the second rancke of repre-
henders that complain of my boy-
strous compound wordes, and ending
my Italionate coyned verbes all in *Ize*,
thus I replie. . . . Our English tongue
of all languages most swarmeth with
the single money of monasillables,
which are the onely scandall of it.

Bookes written in them and no other
seeme like Shop-keepers boxes, that
containe nothing else save halfpence,
three-farthings,   and   two-pences.
Therefore what did me I, but having a
huge heape of those worthlesse shreds
of small English . . . had them to the
compounders immediately . . . they
carrie farre more state with them
than any other, and are not halfe
so harsh in their desinence as the
old hobling English verbes ending in
R.'

50. *Ha? ha?*] Armado only half
hears Moth's insult. This joke is peren-
nial; cf. W. H. Auden, *Paid on Both
Sides (Poems,* 1930, p. 24).

57. Minime] Latin, by no means.
Moth gives us more evidence of his
Latin in v. i. 62. It was proper for
pages to know Latin. Cf. Sir Thopas's
attendants in Lyly's *Endymion*.

Moth.   You are too swift, sir, to say so:
    Is that lead slow which is fir'd from a gun?
Arm. Sweet smoke of rhetoric!   60
    He reputes me a cannon, and the bullet, that's he—
    I shoot thee at the swain.
Moth.   Thump then, and I flee. [*Exit.*
Arm. A most acute juvenal; voluble and free of grace!
    By thy favour, sweet welkin, I must sigh in thy face:
    Most rude melancholy, valour gives thee place.   65
    My herald is return'd.

Re-enter MOTH *with* COSTARD.

Moth. A wonder, master! here's a costard broken in a shin.
Arm. Some enigma, some riddle: come, thy l'envoy; begin.

63. voluble] *Ff,Q2;* volable *Q1, New.*   65. Most rude] Moist-eyed *Collier
MS. (!).*   67–124. A wonder ... let me loose] *Put in the margin by Pope.*   68.
come, thy] *Qq,F1;* no *Ff2,3,4.*   l'envoy; begin] *Capell;* lenvoy begin *Qq,Ff.*

62. *Thump*] represents the sound of
the cannon. Sometimes early writers
used 'dub a dub' for this purpose, as in
Peele's *Old Wives Tale* (Bullen, i. 333)
and in the ballad *Winning of Cales*
(Percy Folio, iii. 454). 'Bounce' was for
smaller fire-arms. Halliwell says
'thump' refers to the stroke of the
bullet (as in IV. iii. 22) but the bullet is
still on its way to the mark. The word
may be noun or verb, and Moth means
either 'Bang, I'm off' or 'Make a noise
like a gun and I'll go.'

63. *acute*] applied to the intellect.
This is the earliest example in the
N.E.D. See below again at IV. ii. 70.
The adverb occurs in *All's W.,* I. i. 221.
Jonson has early parallels for both
uses: 'the most divine and acute lady
in court' (*Every Man in his Humour,* III.
i [1598]); and 'she has the most acute
ready and facetious wit' (*Every Man
out of his Humour,* IV. vi [1599]).

juvenal] See note on I. ii. 8 above.

voluble] Dover Wilson retains the Q
reading 'volable', interpreted as
'quick-witted'. It might be better explained as a coinage of Armado's to
express Moth's quickness of movement, his bullet-swiftness in *flying* on an

errand. But the word is not found elsewhere, and 'voluble' is a term particularly appropriate to Moth. See
note on II. i. 76 above.

64. *welkin*] See below, IV. ii. 5: '*coelo,*
the sky, the welkin, the heaven'.

67. *costard*] apple, or head: 'here's
a head broken in the shin.'

broken in a shin] Hart wrote: 'References to the breaking of shins are so
abundant at this time that one is in-
clined to think they must have been
even more susceptible than nowadays.'
The probable explanation, for which I
am indebted to Mr John Crow, is that
a 'broken shin' had for the Elizabethans a metaphorical as well as a
literal sense, and was in fact slang for a
sexual disappointment. This is clearly
what it means in '*A merry new Song how
a Bruer meant to make a Cooper cuckold, and
how deere the Bruer paid for the bargaine*',
reprinted in Henry Huth's *Ancient
Ballads and Broadsides* (1867). The
same sense doubtless hovers at the
back of the present dialogue, which
never misses a pun where one is
possible.

68. *enigma*] Cf. Greene, *Tritameron,*
pt ii (Grosart, iii. 145), 1587: 'she

Cost. No egma, no riddle, no l'envoy; no salve in the mail,
    sir. O, sir, plantain, a plain plantain! no l'envoy, no   70
    l'envoy: no salve, sir, but a plantain!
Arm. By virtue, thou enforcest laughter; thy silly thought
    my spleen; the heaving of my lungs provokes me to

69. the mail] thee male *Qq,F1*; the male *Ff2,3,4*; the vale *Johnson conj.*; them all
Knight (*Tyrwhitt conj.*).   70. O] *Q1,Ff3,4*; Or *Q2,Ff1,2*.   plain] pline *Q1*.
71. no salve] *Qq,F1*; or salve *Ff2,3,4*.

tooke it either for some propheticall
Ænigma or els for a bare jest.' A rare
word at this time.

l'envoy] an address or send-off, usually placed at the end of a prose or
poetical composition; often taking the
form of a concise or obscure commendation to the readers. Common in
early writers as Lydgate, etc. Gabriel
Harvey places a L'Envoy at the end of
his poetical *Theme upon Vertue* of which
he was so proud (Grosart, i. 79), 1580.
He has another at the close of his
Gorgon Sonnett against Nashe (Grosart,
i. 297), 1592; and his use of the word in
this trivial manner was expressly
singled out for reprehension and ridicule by Nashe in *Have With You to
Saffron Walden* in his coarsest and wit-
tiest way. See McKerrow's edition, ii,
pp. 11, 113, 133, 135. Nashe makes a
verb of it: 'we shall l'envoy him', give
him farewell. Harvey's theme, to
which he appends a L'Envoy, is '*In
Commendation of three most precious Acci-
dentes, Virtue, Fame and Wealth*: and
finally of the fourth, *A good tongue*'.
The parallelism is striking, the goose
being 'the good tongue'.

69. *no l'envoy; no salve*] Costard mistakes the word 'salve' (as in the old
salve for a sore) for *salvé*, a salute. Since
the latter word was used as a verb
(Chaucer, Spenser), possibly the latter
syllable was occasionally slurred, but
in any case the orthography warranted
the pun. Greene at any rate thought so.
Cf. *Mamillia* (Grosart, ii. 22), 1583: 'so
his sodaine sore had a new salve . . . he
espied Mamillia . . . and after he had
curteously given her the Salve'. One
word suggests the other. See again pp.

196, 197. Both senses are very common
in Greene, and often, as in 'give one a
salve', only determinable by context.
To an ignoramus the pun was unavoidable, when puns were desiderata.
Steevens quoted the same quibble
from *Aristippus, or The Jovial Philoso-
pher*, 1630.

mail] wallet, budget. No ointment or
plaster in the bag. Cf. *Narcissus* (ed.
M. L. Lee, pp. 9, 10), 1602: 'wee may
provide a plaster Of holsome hearbes
to cure this dire disaster. *Tyresias*. If I
should tell you, you amisse would
iudge it: I have one salve, one mede-
cine in my budgett.' *Narcissus* has
several echoes of Shakespeare. See
'keel the pot', v. ii. 912 below, n.

70. *plantain*] Costard wants no high-
class remedy with a foreign name, but
the well-known simple, always required for the head or for the shin. Cf.
Tomkis, *Albumazar*, iv. 11 (1614):
'Help, Armellina, help: I'm fall'n in
the cellar: Bring a fresh plantane leaf,
I have broke my shin'; and Jonson,
The Case is Altered, ii. iv (1598):
'[*Martino breaks his head. Onion.* Foh,
tis nothing, a fillip, a device: fellow
Juniper get me a plantain; I had rather
play with one that had skill by half.'
According to Hart plantain leaves are
still used in the north of Ireland, because of their cooling properties, to
apply to bruises.

72–3. *laughter . . . spleen*] The excesses
of mirth or anger were controlled, it
was held, by the spleen. Cf. *Meas.*, ii.
ii. 122; and below, v. ii. 117; and Lyly,
Mother Bombie, iv. 2: 'for wee should
laugh heartily, and without laughing
my spleene would split'.

ridiculous smiling: O, pardon me, my stars! Doth
the inconsiderate take salve for l'envoy, and the word   75
l'envoy for a salve?

Moth. Do the wise think them other? is not l'envoy a
salve?

Arm. No, page: it is an epilogue or discourse to make plain
Some obscure precedence that hath tofore been sain.   80
I will example it:

   The fox, the ape, and the humble-bee,
   Were still at odds, being but three.
There's the moral: now the l'envoy.

Moth. I will add the l'envoy. Say the moral again.   85

Arm.   The fox, the ape, and the humble-bee,
   Were still at odds, being but three.

Moth.   Until the goose came out of door,
   And stay'd the odds by adding four.
Now will I begin your moral, and do you follow with   90
my l'envoy.

   The fox, the ape, and the humble-bee,
   Were still at odds, being but three.

Arm.   Until the goose came out of door,
   Staying the odds by adding four.   95

Moth. A good l'envoy, ending in the goose: would you
desire more?

Cost. The boy hath sold him a bargain, a goose, that's flat.

79. page] Moth *Rowe* (*ed. 1*). 80. sain] *Q1;* fain *Q2,Ff.* 81–9. I will . . .
four] *not in Ff,Q2.*

74–6. *Doth the inconsiderate,* etc.] The
whole point of this trifling is here; and
the answer, of course, is 'yes'. The
muddle which arises in the minds of
those who will not understand this may
be seen in pages of notes in Steevens
and in Furness.

75. *inconsiderate*] a thoughtless, ignorant person. Cf. Harvey's *New Letter,*
etc. (Grosart, i. 286): 'the shallow
breast of inconsiderate youth'.

80. *precedence*] that which has preceded. Walker (*Crit.,* iii. 36) suggests
that these two lines may be a quotation
from some old treatise on composition
(Furness).

82. *The fox, the ape*] For a guess at the
meaning, see Intro., 5.22.

89. *adding four*] adding a fourth.
There are so many fox and goose apo-
logues that the latter was bound to
appear. 'The Courtier, after travaile,
tells his Lady a better tale than of a fox
and a goose' (N. Breton, *An Old Man's
Lesson,* 1605) i.e. homely stuff.

98. *sold him a bargain, a goose*] made a
fool of him. Cf. *Rom.,* II. iv. 75 (with the
same pun on goose meaning prostitute
as at l. 119 below): 'was I there with
you for the goose? *Rom.* Thou wast
never with me for anything when thou
wast not there for the goose.' Similar

Sir, your pennyworth is good an your goose be fat.
To sell a bargain well is as cunning as fast and loose: 100
Let me see; a fat l'envoy; ay, that's a fat goose.

Arm. Come hither, come hither. How did this argument
begin?

Moth. By saying that a costard was broken in a shin.
Then call'd you for the l'envoy.   104

Cost. True, and I for a plantain: thus came your argument in;
Then the boy's fat l'envoy, the goose that you bought;
And he ended the market.

Arm. But tell me; how was there a costard broken in a
shin?

Moth. I will tell you sensibly.   110

Cost. Thou hast no feeling of it, Moth: I will speak that
l'envoy.
I, Costard, running out, that was safely within,
Fell over the threshold and broke my shin.

Arm. We will talk no more of this matter.   115

Cost. Till there be more matter in the shin.

Arm. Sirrah Costard, I will enfranchise thee.

Cost. O! marry me to one Frances—I smell some l'envoy, some goose in this.

Arm. By my sweet soul, I mean setting thee at liberty, 120
enfreedoming thy person: thou wert immured, re-
strained, captivated, bound.

Cost. True, true, and now you will be my purgation and
let me loose.

Arm. I give thee thy liberty, set thee from durance; and, 125
in lieu thereof, impose on thee nothing but this:
bear this significant to the country maid Jaquenetta.

121. immured] *Ff2,3,4;* emured *Qq,F1.*

expressions, by which the speaker points out that the other is a goose, as here, are numerous. 'To sell one a goose for a bargain', shortened to 'sell one a bargain' later, has not been earlier found than here. Taylor, in *The Goose*, puts it: 'take my goose amongst you, gentlemen' (*Works*, 1630, p. 111).

100. *fast and loose*] See I. ii. 147, n.

118. *Frances*] Nashe gives this name to the prostitute in his *Choise of Valen-*tines. McKerrow writes: 'Possibly a typical name for women of the class; cf. S. Rowlands' *Letting of Humorous Blood*, B5ᵛ, "*Francke* in name, and Francke by nature, Frauncis is a most kinde creature", and the same author's *Whole Crew of Kind Gossips*, E2, where a similar person is called "*Franke*" and "Mistris *Francis*".'

127. *significant*] sign, intimation, and so letter. Cf. *1H6*, II. iv. 25: 'Since you

There is remuneration; for the best ward of mine
honour is rewarding my dependents. Moth, follow.
                                                      [*Exit.*

Moth. Like the sequel, I. Signior Costard, adieu.   130
Cost. My sweet ounce of man's flesh! my incony Jew!
                                                      [*Exit Moth.*
Now will I look to his remuneration. Remunera-
tion! O that's the Latin word for three farthings:
three farthings, remuneration. 'What's the price of
this inkle?' 'One penny': 'No, I'll give you a remu-   135
neration': why, it carries it. Remuneration! why

---

129. honour] *Q1;* honours *Ff,Q2.*   130. adieu] adew *Q1,F1.*   131. Jew]
jewel *Warburton.*   135. inkle] yncle *Qq,Ff.*   One penny] i. d *Qq,Ff1,2;* i. de.
Ff3,4.   136. carries it. Remuneration!] *Theobald;* carries it remuneration
Qq,Ff1,2; carries it's remuneration *Ff3,4.*

---

are tongue-tied. . . . In dumb signi-
ficants proclaim your thoughts.'

128. *ward*] guard.

130. *sequel*] that which follows in a
story or book. Moth continues the tone
of illustration his master adopted with
the *l'envoy.* Cf. Nashe, *Foure Letters Confuted* (McKerrow, i. 268), 1593: 'he
mist the Oratorship of the Universitie,
of which, in the sequele of his booke, he
most slanderously complaineth'.

131. *incony*] 'darling'. The earliest
use of this slang term, the origin of
which is only guessed at. See Murray's
N.E.D. Jonson, in the latest example
found (1633), accents the word on the
second syllable and rhymes it with
'money' (*Tale of a Tub*, IV. i). The
N.E.D. says: 'rare, fine, delicate,
pretty, nice'. It must be connected
with 'cony' (also spelt and pronounced
'cunny') which was used as a term of
endearment for a woman (*N.E.D.*
cony, sense 5a & b). In Dekker's *Shoemaker's Holiday* (Pearson, i. 60) 'incony'
takes on a more active sense, almost
Shakespeare's 'honeying'—'There' (in
the Church) 'they shall be knit like a
paire of stockings in matrimony, there
theyle be incony'. Other examples of
its occurrence are *Doctor Dodypoll* (Bullen's *Old Plays*, iii. 117) and Brome's

Northern Lass, iii. The first of these is
noted in Steevens's *Shakespeare.* In the
early editions of Marlowe's *Jew of
Malta*, Act IV, the reading is 'Whilst I
in thy incoomy lap do tumble'.

Jew] Hart surmised that the word
'Jew' might have been suggested by
the Shylock association of 'ounce of
man's flesh'; but it is again used as a
term of endearment in *MND.*, III. i. 97:
'most brisky Juvenal and eke most
lovely Jew'. That it occurs there in
company with 'Juvenal' (of which
Dover Wilson conjectures it may be a
'playful diminutive') is significant.

133. *three farthings*] A three-farthing
coin, six grains, hammered, was issued
at various dates from 1561 to 1581. On
the obverse it bears the crowned bust,
with rose behind the head. See *John*,
I. i. 143.

135. *inkle*] a kind of linen tape; or, as
in *Per.*, v. 8 (Gower), the yarn it was
made from. See also *Wint.*, IV. iv. 208.
It is spelt 'yncle' in Cunningham's
Revels Accounts (Shakes. Soc., p. 119),
1576.

136. *it carries it*] it bears the prize, it
wins. See *Wiv.*, III. ii. 70; *All's W.*, IV.i
30, etc.; 'Tis not thy words proud
Queene shall carry it' (*The Troublesome Raigne of King John*, 1591).

it is a fairer name than French crown. I will never
buy and sell out of this word.

Enter BEROWNE.

Ber. O my good knave Costard! exceedingly well met.
Cost. Pray you, sir, how much carnation ribbon may a   140
man buy for a remuneration?
Ber. O what is a remuneration?
Cost. Marry, sir, halfpenny farthing.
Ber. O! why then, three-farthing worth of silk.
Cost. I thank your worship. God be wi' you!   145
Ber. O stay, slave! I must employ thee:
As thou wilt win my favour, good my knave,
Do one thing for me that I shall entreat.
Cost. When would you have it done, sir?

---

137. French] *Q1;* a French *Ff,Q2.*   142. O what] *Q1;* What *Ff,Q2.*   144,
146, 150, 152, 168. O] *Qq,Ff;* om. *Cambridge, New.*   144. three-farthing
worth] *Q1;* three farthings worth *Ff,Q2.*

---

137. *French crown*] a pun on the coin
and on the bald crown produced by
the 'French disease'. See *Meas.,* I. ii. 52.

138. *out of this word*] using any other
word but this.

139. *exceedingly well met*] so in Jonson's *Bartholomew's Fair,* v. iii: 'Master
Cokes! you are exceedingly well met.'

140. *carnation ribbon*] flesh-coloured
ribbon. The colour of a man's skin or
flesh. A very popular colour. Cf.
Dekker's *Honest Whore* (Pearson, ii.
49), 1604: 'Sweetest properest gallant
. . . flame-coloured doublet, red satin
hose, carnation silk stockings'; and
Heywood's *If you know not me,* etc.,
pt ii (Pearson, p. 259), *ante* 1605: 'carnation girdles and busk-point suitable,
as common as coales from Newcastle:
you shall not have a kitchen maid
scrape trenchers without her washt
gloves'; and in *A Warning for Faire
Women* (Simpson's *School of Shakespeare,*
ii. 277), Act II (*c.* 1599): 'Pray ye
bestow a groat, or sixpence, of Carnation ribbon to tie my smock sleeves;
they flap about my hands'. It appears

several times in the costumes of Jonson's masques at court.

142. *O what*] The 'O' with which
Berowne's lines so frequently begin
was explained by the Cambridge editors as having crept into the text from
the speech-heading 'Bero.', which still
occurs at many points in Q. Two facts
give some slight support to this theory:
the 'O' is never found beginning a
speech where the heading 'Bero.' is
retained; and it often throws out the
metre. It does, however, begin lines in
the middle of speeches where there can
be no question of an intrusion from a
heading; and metrical irregularities
need not be taken too seriously (see
note on II. i. 171). Hart's conclusion
was that ' "O" is an affectation of
Berowne's, inserted purposely here
and elsewhere for reasons known to the
author.' Whether or not we accept the
view that Shakespeare is here carica-
turing the mannerism of a real person,
it is wiser, when in doubt, to preserve
the Q reading. There is another heavy
crop of 'O's' in IV. iii.

Ber. O this afternoon.   150

Cost. Well, I will do it, sir. Fare you well.

Ber. O thou knowest not what it is.

Cost. I shall know, sir, when I have done it.

Ber. Why, villain, thou must know first.

Cost. I will come to your worship to-morrow morning.   155

Ber. It must be done this afternoon. Hark, slave, it is but
          this:

          The princess comes to hunt here in the park,
          And in her train there is a gentle lady;
          When tongues speak sweetly, then they name her
               name,   160
          And Rosaline they call her: ask for her,
          And to her white hand see thou do commend
          This seal'd-up counsel. There's thy guerdon: go.

Cost. Gardon, O sweet gardon! better than remunera-
          tion; a'leven-pence farthing better. Most sweet   165
          gardon! I will do it, sir, in print. Gardon! Remu-
          neration!   [*Exit.*

Ber. O! and I forsooth in love!
          I, that have been love's whip;
          A very beadle to a humorous sigh;   170

---

163. go] [*Gives him money (or shilling)*] *inserted by some edd.*   165. a'leven-pence]
a levenpence *Qq,Ff.*   168–73.] *Q1 prints as three lines, ending* whip, constable,
magnificent*; Ff as six, ending* love, whip, criticke, constable, boy, magnificent.

---

162. *white hand*] The commentators,
obsessed by Rosaline's 'blackness',
have jibbed unnecessarily at this, the
traditional attribute of a lady-love
whatever her complexion.

163. *guerdon*] When Costard devotes
a speech to explaining that Berowne has given him a guerdon of a
shilling, surely a stage-direction 'gives
him a shilling' is a useless excre-
cence? Johnson put it in first. 'Guerdon' was a common word at this time
and earlier. Cf. Cotgrave (1611):
'*Guerdon* guerdon, recompence, meed,
remuneration, reward; also as *Gardon*'.

166. *in print*] exactly, most carefully.
See *Gent.*, II. i. 175, and *AYL.*, v. iv. 92.

Greene uses this expression several
times, as in *Farewell to Follie* (Grosart,
ix. 308), 1591: 'Setting hir husbande
therefore foorth in print, he tooke his
waye unto the Court'; *Mamillia* (ii.
219), 1583; and see earlier in Harvey
(Grosart, i. 84), 1580: 'Every one A
per se A, his termes and braveries in
print'.

168–200. *I forsooth in love*, etc.]
Furnivall points out in *The Centurie of
Prayse* that Golding's speech in Heywood's *Faire Maide of the Exchange*
(Pearson, ii. 20) is an imitation of this.
'With that face?' (I. ii. 131) has occurred on p. 11 in the same play which,
besides being weak twaddle, is full of
plagiarism.

A critic, nay, a night-watch constable,
A domineering pedant o'er the boy,
Than whom no mortal so magnificent!
This wimpled, whining, purblind, wayward boy,
This signor junior, giant-dwarf, dan Cupid;   175
Regent of love rhymes, lord of folded arms,
The anointed sovereign of sighs and groans,

175. signor junior] senior junior *Hanmer;* Signior Junios *Qq,Ff;* Signior Junio
Pope; Signior Julio's *Upton conj.*   dan] *Q1;* Don *Ff,Q2.*

173. *magnificent*] proud, arrogantly
ambitious (*N.E.D.*). Cf. Knolles, *History of the Turks* (1621), p. 732: 'This
Perenus was one of the greatest peeres
of Hungarie, but of a most haughtie
and magnificent mind.' The line as a
whole may be read either as referring
to Berowne, whose pride in scorning
love led to his fall; or to imperious
Cupid, avenging such slights in the
high-handed manner of a tyrant. Of
the two, the second perhaps best fits
the humour of the speech as a whole:
'magnificent boy' is another paradox
to match 'giant-dwarf'.

174. *wimpled*] blindfold, muffled.
The 'wimple' was a kind of hood or
tippet, used as a muffler in the Shakespearean sense. Cf. *Appius and Virginia*
(Malone Soc., ed. McKerrow, 969),
1575: 'Let first my wimple bind my
eyes, and then thy blow assaile. Now
father worke thy will on me . . . [*Here
tye a handcarcher aboute hir eyes, and then
strike of hir heade*]'; and Lyly, *Mydas*,
I. i: 'Justice herselfe, that sitteth
wimpled about the eyes'.

175. *signor junior*] Hanmer's ingenious reading is widely accepted but
there is no reason why this half of the
pun should be brought out rather than
the other. Hart's suggestion 'Signior
junior' is almost exactly the old reading, the idea being to give a title to the
boy Cupid. This passage is recalled by
Heywood in *Love's Mistress* (Pearson,
v. 112–14): '*Clowne.* What might you
call that yong gentleman that rules
and raignes, revells and roares in these
walkes of Arcadia. . . . *2 Swain.* It is the
god of Love they call him Cupid. . . .

Clowne. Can any of you all give me his
true title. . . . I give you his stile in
Folio: Hee is King of cares, cogitations,
and coxcombes; Vice-roy of vowes
and vanities; Prince of passions,
prate-apaces and pickled lovers; Duke
of disasters, dissemblers, and drown'd
eyes; Marquesse of melancholly and
mad-folks, grand Signior of griefes and
grones, Heroe of hie-hoes, Admirall of
ay-mees, and Mounsieur of mutton-laced.' Laneham has an exordium to
Neptune on the same lines in his *Letter*
(1575): 'the great god of the swelling seas, Prins of profundities, and
soverain Segnior of al Lakes, freshwaters, Rivers, Creeks and Goolphs'.
These passages bear out the reading
signor.

dan Cupid] a variant of 'don,' a contraction of *dominus* (or its first syllable),
master, sir. A title of honour formerly.
Spenser applies 'dan' to Chaucer. 'Dan
Cupid' occurs earlier in T. Howell's
Devises (ed. Raleigh, p. 70), 1581:
'Then you that fayne Dan Cupide is a
God, Recante in tyme'; and in lines
prefixed to Greene's *Mamillia* (1583)
by 'Roger Portington Esquier, in
Commendation of this Booke' (Grosart, ii. 11, 12). For similar raillery
upon Cupid, see Sidney's *Arcadia*,
Eclogues concluding bk i (1593
Folio): '*Cupid* the wagg that lately
conquer'd had Wise Counsellors,
stout Captaines puissant Kings, And
ti'de them fast to leade his triumph
badd.'

176–8. *folded arms . . . malcontents*] Cf.
Gent., II. i. 20, and in the present play,
IV. iii. 132.

Liege of all loiterers and malcontents,
Dread prince of plackets, king of codpieces,
Sole imperator and great general   180
Of trotting paritors: O my little heart!
And I to be a corporal of his field,
And wear his colours like a tumbler's hoop!
What! I love! I sue! I seek a wife!
A woman that is like a German clock,   185

184. What! I love!] What? I! I love *Malone, Steevens (Tyrwhitt), New.* 185.
clock] *Ff2,3,4;* cloak *Qq,F1.*

179. *plackets . . . codpieces*] Both terms
occur several times in Shakespeare.
The former was used of a petticoat, or
the opening in it leading to a pocket,
and hence a pocket itself, as in *Lr.*, III.
iv. 100. The latter was 'a bagged
appendage to the front of the close-
fitting hose or breeches worn by men
from the fifteenth to the seventeenth
century; often conspicuous and ornamental' (*N.E.D.*). As distinctive por-
tions of female and male attire they
came to stand for 'women' and 'men',
especially in a flippant or bawdy sense,
as 'skirt' is used today. Nashe sets these
two terms in similar conjunction in his
fiercest raillery upon Gabriel Harvey
in *Have With You to Saffron Walden*
(McKerrow, iii. 129), 1596.

181. *paritors*] officers of the Ecclesiastical Courts, who served citations.
Johnson says these were most frequently issued for fornication and
such-like breaches. This statement is
borne out by a passage in Greene's *Art
of Conny-catching* (Grosart, x. 45), 1592:
'shifters and coosners, who learning
some insight in the civill law, walke
abrode like parators, sumners and in-
formers, being none at all either in
office or credit, and they go spying
about where any marchant, or mar-
chants prentice, . . . either accompany
with anie woman familiarly, or else
hath gotten some maide with childe
. . . they send for him . . . telling him he
must be presented to the Arches, and
the scitation shal be peremptorily
served in his parish church. The partie

afraid to have his credit crackt . . .
takes composition with this cosner for
some twentie markes.' They were a
class much hated by the people. 'Belike thou art the Divels paritor, The
basest officer that lives in Hell' (*Wily
Beguiled* [Malone Soc., ed. Greg,
2002]).

182. *corporal of his field*] 'A superior
officer of the army in the sixteenth and
seventeenth century, who acted as an
assistant or a kind of aide-de-camp to
the sergeant-major' (*N.E.D.*). He is
mentioned in Gerrard, *Art of Warre*,
1591. A field-officer to a general.

183. *wear his colours like a tumbler's
hoop*] a hoop decorated with ribbons,
twisted round it, or coloured silks.
With this the tumbler performed feats
with his juggling sticks, and other
buffoonery. See Chettle's account of
William Cuckoe (whose hoop is not
mentioned) in *King-Hartes Dream*
(Bodley Head Quarto, 12), 1592; and
see a picture of fourteenth-century
tumbling in Strutt's *Sports and Pastimes*.
It was not a hoop for jumping through
—which seems to be a later accom-
plishment. Tumbling was very popular and courtly at this time. See Laneham's *Letter* (Furnivall's *Cox*, p. 18) for
'the feats of agilitiee, in goinges, turn-
inges, tumblinges', etc., shown by an
Italian before Queen Elizabeth at
Kenilworth (1575).

185. *woman that is like a German clock*]
There can be no doubt the later Folios
correct 'cloak' rightly here, since this
simile was at once adopted by Shake-

Still a-repairing, ever out of frame,
And never going aright, being a watch,
But being watch'd that it may still go right!
Nay to be perjur'd, which is worst of all;
And among three, to love the worst of all;   190
A whitely wanton with a velvet brow,
With two pitch-balls stuck in her face for eyes;
Ay and by heaven, one that will do the deed
Though Argus were her eunuch and her guard:
And I to sigh for her! to watch for her!   195
To pray for her! Go to; it is a plague
That Cupid will impose for my neglect
Of his almighty dreadful little might.

191. whitely] *Ff3,4;* whitly *Qq,Ff1,2;* wightly *Cambridge;* witty *Collier.*

speare's successors. It is made use of by
Jonson, *The Silent Woman,* iv. ii; Webster, *Westward Hoe,* i. i; Middleton, *A
Mad World my Masters,* iv. i; Beaumont
and Fletcher ('Dutch watches'), *Wit
Without Money,* iii; and Cartwright,
Ordinary. Dekker has a variant in
Newes from Hell, 1606 (Grosart, ii.
106): 'their wits (like wheeles in
Brunswick clocks) being all wound up
so far as they could stretch, were all
going, but not one going truly'. There
is an earlier mention of a 'faire Ger-
maine clocke' in *The Travels of Sir
Jerome Horsey* (Hakluyt Soc. ed., p.
192). The work was never printed by
Horsey, but the incident of the clock is
dated 1580. It is surely a mere coincidence that Horsey's book is also the
source of our knowledge of Ivan the
Terrible's wooing (by proxy) of Lady
Mary Hastings, which, it has been
suggested, may lie behind the masque
of Muscovites in Act v. See Intro.,
3.227.

191. *whitely*] pale, sallow. Furness
gives a passage cited by Arrowsmith,
Shakespeare's Commentators, etc., p. 4)
from Heywood's *Troja Britannica,* cant.
5, st. 74: 'That hath a whitely face and
a long nose, And for them both I won-
derous well esteeme her' (1609). Fur-

ness also cites Walker (*Critical Examination,* ii. 349): 'In North's *Plutarch*
(*Life of Brutus*) Cassius and Brutus are
called by Cæsar "lean and whitely-
faced fellows".' These contemporary
parallels are ample confirmation of
Shakespeare's text, if confirmation be
needed. The word has been disputed
solely on the ground that Rosaline was
dark. See iv. iii. 243–73. How can this
be a difficulty? There is nothing (except perhaps l. 3 of Sonnet 130) to suggest that Rosaline or the Dark Lady of
the Sonnets was swarthy, though both
had black eyes and hair. The word
'whiteley' is in Johnson and several
other dictionaries of recent date; and
see Cotgrave in v. *blanchastre.* For the
connection with *Sonn.* see Intro., 3.21.

192. *pitch-balls . . . eyes*] paralleled by
the modern 'eyes like two burnt holes
in a blanket'; and cf. *2H4,* ii ii. 88.

193. *do the deed*] the act of love, as
Mer.V., i. iii. 86, and commonly.

194. *Argus*] For the tale of Cyllenius
(Mercury) closing the eyes of Argus,
whom Juno had set to 'duely watch
and warde' Io, see Golding's Ovid's
Metamorphoses, i. 770–900.

196. *Go to*] to business. 'Come now'
is, curiously enough, the modern
equivalent.

Well, I will love, write, sigh, pray, sue, and groan:
Some men must love my lady, and some Joan.   [*Exit.*

199. sue, and groan] sue and groan *Ff2,3,4;* shue, grone *Q1,F1.*

199. *sue and groan*] Some 'restoration' seems necessary here, and the best we can do now is to accept the 'and' supplied by F2; but the missing word may equally well be another verb.

200. *lady . . . Joan*] remembering the proverbial saying 'Joan's as good as my lady.' Cf. Munday's *Downfall of Robert Earl of Huntington* (Hazlitt's *Dodsley,* viii. 157): 'He is our lady's chaplain, but serves Joan. *Don.* Then from the Friar's fault perchance it may be The proverb grew, Joan's taken for a lady.' Joan was a common name in all royal families at a much earlier period, but in Shakespeare's time it had (as Praed says) descended to the cottage and kitchen. See the last line of the closing song in this play (v. ii. 921): 'While greasy Joan doth keel the pot'.

ACT IV

SCENE I

Enter the PRINCESS, MARIA, KATHARINE, ROSALINE, BOYET, *Lords, Attendants, and a Forester.*

Prin. Was that the king, that spurr'd his horse so hard
         Against the steep-up rising of the hill?
For.   I know not; but I think it was not he.
Prin. Whoe'er a' was, a' show'd a mounting mind.
         Well, lords, to-day we shall have our despatch;   5
         On Saturday we will return to France.
         Then, forester, my friend, where is the bush
         That we must stand and play the murderer in?

ACT IV

Scene I

S.D. *Enter . . .] Enter the Princesse, a Forrester, her Ladyes, and her Lordes Qq,Ff.*
1. *Prin.] Ff,Q2; Quee. Q1 throughout the scene.*   2. steep-up rising] steep up
rising *Qq;* steep uprising *F1;* steep unrising *Ff2,3,4.*   3. *For.] Forr. Q1; Boy.*
Ff,Q2.

---

2. *steep-up*] Cf. *Sonn.*, vii. 5: 'having
climbed the steep-up heavenly hill';
and *Pilgr.*: 'Her stand she takes upon
a steep-up hill'. 'Steep-down' occurs
in *Oth.*, v. ii. 280.

rising of the hill] Cf. *Gent.*, v. ii. 46:
'meet with me Upon the rising of the
mountain-foot'. Sidney has 'embushed
his footmen in the falling of a hill,
which was over-shadowed with a
wood' (*Arcadia*, iii [Feuillerat, i. 386]).
But the best parallel is in Golding's
Ovid's *Metamorphoses* (vii. 873, 4):
'They lagged slowly after with theyr
staves, and labored sore Ageinst the
rysing of the hill.'

4. *mounting mind*] Cf. Peele, *Edward I*,
i. i (Dramatic Works, ed. Bullen, i. 93),
ante 1593: 'Sweet Nell, thou shouldst

not be thyself, did not, with thy mounting mind, thy gift surmount the rest.'
This parallel was observed by Dyce.
See earlier in Whetstone's *Remem-
braunce of Gascoigne* (Arber, p. 18),
1577: 'and begging sutes from dunghill thoughts proceed: the mounting
minde had rather sterve in need.' It is
found also in *The Troublesome Raigne of
King John*, 1591.

8. *stand and play the murderer in*] The
shooting of driven deer, with cross-
bows, from a specially erected 'stand'
was a popular amusement for formal
occasions. See the account of the
Queen's Entertainment at Cowdray (1591),
and the German narrative (1602) of
the visit of Frederick, Duke of Wirtem-
berg, to Windsor in 1592. A common

59

For. Hereby, upon the edge of yonder coppice;
    A stand where you may make the fairest shoot.   10
Prin. I thank my beauty, I am fair that shoot,
    And thereupon thou speak'st the fairest shoot.
For. Pardon me, madam, for I meant not so.
Prin. What, what? first praise me, and again say no?
    O short-liv'd pride! Not fair? alack for woe!   15
For. Yes, madam, fair.
Prin.   Nay, never paint me now:
    Where fair is not, praise cannot mend the brow.
    Here, good my glass, take this for telling true:
    Fair payment for foul words is more than due.
For. Nothing but fair is that which you inherit.   20
Prin. See, see! my beauty will be saved by merit.
    O heresy in fair, fit for these days!

11–40. I thank . . . lord] *Consigned to the margin by Pope.*   14. and again] *Q1;* and then again *F1,Q2;* then again *Ff2,3,4.*   18.] [*giving him money*] *Johnson.* 22. fair] faith *Collier MS.*

practice was to set greyhounds to pull down the deer that were wounded but not killed—clearly a large proportion of the bag. Cf. Holofernes at IV. ii. 57 below, from which it appears that hounds were being used on the present occasion.

18. *good my glass*] The forester is the mirror that shows the Princess her face at its true value. For the order, cf. I. ii. 64 and III. i. 147.

20. *inherit*] own, possess; as in I. i. 73. A common use.

21. *saved by merit*] saved by that for which a person deserves recompense (as in *1H4,* I. ii. 121); but there is also a quibble upon the meaning of 'merit', reward, recompense. See *R2,* I. iii. 156, for another example of the substantive. The Princess is referring to her 'tip' to the forester, and likening it to the good works which the Catholics held would alone procure salvation, whereas the Protestants believed faith only was necessary. 'Justification by faith' became one of the standard tests by which Protestant orthodoxy was tried —hence 'heresy' of l. 22. 'Merits' may

also have a more concrete sense. Hart quotes Barnabe Googe's translation of Naogeorgus, *The Popish Kingdome,* 1570 (Chiswick, 1880): 'They go and buy of other men, that commonly have more. But specially of Monkes that have the merites chiefe to sell, Sufficient both to keepe themselves and other men from hell' (fol. 40, The Third Booke). And on the following page, 'All such as are not Monkes or saved by their merites heare, . . . and this makes fooles to buy their merites deare'. 'Merits' appears to mean certificates bought from the monks.

22. *fit for these days*] The passage may allude to what Elizabeth called the 'abominable act', whereby Henri of Navarre, a champion of protestantism and her ally, bought the Catholic powers' recognition of his right to the throne of France by conversion to Rome. He was formally absolved and attended public mass on 25 July 1593. The Princess's moralizings (ll. 30–3 below) must, on this assumption, be also aimed at Henri.

A giving hand, though foul, shall have fair praise.
But come, the bow: now mercy goes to kill,
And shooting well is then accounted ill.   25
Thus will I save my credit in the shoot:
Not wounding, pity would not let me do't;
If wounding, then it was to show my skill,
That more for praise than purpose meant to kill.
And out of question so it is sometimes,   30
Glory grows guilty of detested crimes,
When, for fame's sake, for praise, an outward part,
We bend to that the working of the heart;
As I for praise alone now seek to spill
The poor deer's blood, that my heart means no ill.   35
Boyet. Do not curst wives hold that self-sovereignty
Only for praise' sake, when they strive to be
Lords o'er their lords?
Prin. Only for praise; and praise we may afford
To any lady that subdues a lord.   40

Enter COSTARD.

Boyet. Here comes a member of the commonwealth.
Cost. God dig-you-den all! Pray you, which is the head
        lady?
Prin. Thou shalt know her, fellow, by the rest that have
        no heads.   45
Cost. Which is the greatest lady, the highest?

32. for praise] *Q1,F1;* to praise *Ff2,3,4.*   35. that] tho' *Warburton conj.*   42–
53.] *Put in the margin by Pope.*

30. *out of question*] beyond question, certainly.

31. *glory*] vainglory, or the desire for glory.

36. *curst*] shrewish, cross-grained. Usually applied to women, but cf. Ascham, *The Scholemaster* (Arber, p. 18), 1570: 'the shrewde touches of many curste boyes'.

41. *a member of the commonwealth*] Hart takes this (applied to Holofernes also at IV. ii. 74) as equivalent to a member of the *academe*, i.e. one of the study-group founded by the King.

Costard can hardly be said to have been more than an affiliated member (see I. i. 178); and the phrase was common jargon—cf. *Mer.V.*, III. v. 37. Here presumably jocular, meaning 'one of the lower orders'.

42. *God dig-you-den*] a mutilated form of 'God give you good even'. 'God deven' occurs in *Gammer Gurton's Needle*, 1575. F has '*Godgigoden*' in *Rom.*, I. ii. 59. See the *N.E.D.* for other varieties. Jonson has 'God you good morrow' in *Bartholomew Fair*, I. i.

Prin. The thickest and the tallest.

Cost. The thickest and the tallest! it is so; truth is truth.
  An your waist, mistress, were as slender as my wit,
  One o' these maids' girdles for your waist should be fit.
  Are not you the chief woman? you are the thickest   51
  here.

Prin. What's your will, sir? What's your will?

Cost. I have a letter from Monsieur Berowne to one Lady
    Rosaline.

Prin. O! thy letter, thy letter; he's a good friend of mine.   55
  Stand aside, good bearer. Boyet, you can carve;
  Break up this capon.

Boyet.   I am bound to serve.
  This letter is mistook; it importeth none here:

49. my wit] your wit *Johnson conj.*

48. *truth is truth*] proverbial. Cf.
Nashe, *Have With You to Saffron Walden*,
1596 (McKerrow, iii. 64): 'Yet in
truth (as truth is, and will out at
one time or other, and shame the
divell)'; and Gascoigne, *The Steel Glas*
(Arber, p. 103), 1576: 'I speake against
my sex, So have I done before, But
truth is truth, and muste be tolde,
Though daunger kepe the dore.'

49. *slender . . . wit*] Cf. Lyly, *Sapho and
Phao*, I. iii: '*Molus*. You are grosse
witted, master courtier. *Cryti*. And you
master scholler slender witted.'

53. *What's your will, sir?*] Obviously
the Princess is snubbing Costard for
his impertinence. Furness makes a
doubt of it.

56–7. *carve; Break up*] a technical
term, originally for carving a deer, but
subsequently of extended use. Cf.
Florio's Montaigne's *Essays*, i. 51.
Montaigne quotes from Juvenal *Sat.*,
v. 127: '*Nec minimo sane discrimine refert,
Quo gestu lepores, et quo gallina secetur.
What grace we use, it makes small difference, when We carve a Hare, or
else breake up a Hen*' ('decouper un
lievre ou un poulet'). In *Wint.*, III. ii.
132, the expression occurs of a letter:
'Break up the seals and read'. The
words 'you can carve' are addressed to

Boyet with a quibble on the sense
'court affectedly' (used also of Boyet at
v. ii. 323). Cf. Gascoigne, *Glasse of
Government*, 1575: 'Oh how this com-
forteth my hart; thys letter com-
meth from my younger sonne: I
will break it up.' See also *Mer.V.*,
II. iv. 10.

57. *capon*] Theobald pointed out
that 'capon is here used like the French
poulet'. Cotgrave has: '*Poulet:* a
chicken', also a love-letter or love-
message'. Thackeray uses the term:
'sate down to pen a poulet . . . to
Mademoiselle' (*Vanity Fair*, chap.
xxiv). French was so commonly spoken
I suppose the joke did not seem far-
fetched, especially as we are supposed
to be in France. Furness refers to Laneham's *Letter* (1575) for a similar expression, 'colld pigeon' (Feuillerat,
Cox, 59), but it is a bad parallel. The
expression there is equivalent to 'cold
pie', a rebuke or reprimand, and there
is no mention of a letter.

58. *mistook*] Cf. *Speeches to the Queen at
Rycot*, 1592 (Nichols, iii. 170): 'a
French Page came with three other
letters: the one written to the Lady
Squemish, which being mistaken by a
wrong superscription, was read before
her Majestie.'

It is writ to Jaquenetta.

Prin.   We will read it, I swear.

Break the neck of the wax, and every one give ear.   60

Boyet. [*reads*]. By heaven, that thou art fair, is most infallible; true, that thou art beauteous; truth itself,
that thou art lovely. More fairer than fair, beautiful
than beauteous, truer than truth itself, have com-
miseration on thy heroical vassal! The magnani-   65
mous and most illustrate king Cophetua set eye upon
the pernicious and indubitate beggar Zenelophon,

66. illustrate] illustrious *Q2*.   67. Zenelophon] Penelophon *Collier*.

60. *Break the neck*] still alluding to the
capon (Johnson).

63–4. *More fairer than fair . . . truer
than truth*, etc.] See note at I. ii. 157–9.
Cf. Sidney's *Arcadia*, bk i (ed. Fueil-
lerat, i. 32), *ante* 1586: 'That which
made her fairenesse much the fayrer,
was, that it was but a faire embassa-
dour of a most faire minde', and often
elsewhere.

66. *illustrate*] illustrous. See again
v. i. 113. The word also had the sense
resplendent, illuminated, as in Chapman's *Phyllis and Flora* (*Minor Poems*,
etc., 1875, p. 48), 1595: 'bright in blee
As stars illustrate bodies be'. The
N.E.D. has examples as early as 1526
in good English writers.

66–7. *king Cophetua . . . beggar Zenelophon*] We have already had a reference
to the ballad of the King and the
Beggar (without names) 'which the
world was very guilty of some three
ages since; but I think 'tis not now to
be found; or, if it were, it would
neither serve for the writing nor the
tune'. It is only reasonable to identify
Armado's first ballad with the reference he makes to the King and the
Beggar here. Shakespeare refers to the
story again in *Rom.*, II. i. 54: 'Young
Adam Cupid, he that shot so trim
When *King Cophetua* loved the beggar
maid'; and the name 'King Cophetua'
is mentioned (apparently a quotation)
in a ranting passage in *2H4*, v. iii. 106;
and again the title is recalled in *R2*, v.

iii. 80. Jonson also has 'as rich as King
Cophetua' in *Every Man in his Humour*,
III. iv. There is a ballad on 'King
Cophetua and the Beggar-maid' in
Percy's *Reliques*, 1st series, bk ii. 6,
from Johnson's *Crown Garland of
Goulden Roses*, 1612, where its title is
'A Song of a Beggar and a King'. But
the language of this ballad, as Capell
says, 'most certainly has not the age
that Moth speaks of'. One line in it
seems to me more likely to be a quotation from *Rom.* than *vice versa*. In this
ballad the name of the beggar is cor-
rupted to 'Penelophon'. But, on
Moth's authority, the early ballad was
very different from the dainty and de-
corously-worded song in Percy. There
is a passage in Marston's *Scourge of
Villainy* (Bullen's *Marston*, iii. 302),
1598, which alludes to something more
in keeping with Moth's reminiscences:
'Go buy some ballad of the Fairy
King, And of the Beggar-wench, some
roguy thing. Which thou mayst chant
unto the chamber-maid To some vile
tune.' Moth finds fault also with the
tune. There seems also to have been a
drama on the subject, which is referred to probably in *2H4*, and in
D'Avenant's *Wits*, II. i (1636): 'spoke
like the bold Cophetua's son!'

67. *indubitate*] certain. Not elsewhere
in Shakespeare, but a long-used (Cax-
ton, 1480) sound word. Schmidt suggests that Armado blunders, but he
does not. An unmistakable beggar is

and he it was that might rightly say, *veni, vidi, vici*;
which to annothanize in the vulgar (O base and obscure vulgar!) *videlicet*, he came, saw, and overcame: 70
he came, one; saw, two; overcame, three. Who
came? the king: why did he come? to see: why did
he see? to overcome. To whom came he? to the

69. annothanize] *Qq,F1;* anatomize *Ff2,3,4.*   70. saw] *Ff2,3,4;* see *Qq,F1.*
71. saw] *Rowe;* see *Qq,Ff.*   overcame] *Q2,Ff3,4;* covercame *Q1,Ff1,2.*

set antithetically against a most illustrious king. In a letter to *T.L.S.* of
26 Apr. 1947, Alan Keen pointed out
that 'indubitate' again appears with
'illustrate' (actually 'illustre') on the
title (1548) of Edward Hall's *The
Unoin of the two noble and illustre famelies
of Lancastre and Yorke,—proceeding to the
reigne of the High and prudent Prince King
Henry the eighth, the indubitate and very
heire of the said linages.* Shakespeare
clearly studied Hall deeply in pre-
paring *H4* and *H5.* If this letter is part
of the 'revision' of the play (see note on
l. 88 below) it might have been written
in 1597, at the very time when Shakespeare was steeped in Hall.

68–70. *say* veni, vidi, vici . . . *came,
saw, and overcame*] The original source
of this famous quotation is North's
Plutarch (Julius Caesar), 1570: 'Caesar
. . . fought a great battell with King
Pharnaces. . . . And because he would
advertise one of his friends of the suddenness of this victory, he only wrote
three words unto Anicius at Rome:
Veni, Vidi, Vici: to wit, I came, saw, and
overcome. These three words ending
all with like sound and letters in the
Latin, have a certain short grace, more
pleasant to the ear, than can be well
expressed in any other tongue' (Temple
Classics, vii. 187). This passage, in
North's words (from 'three words' to
'overcame'), is quoted earlier than by
Shakespeare in T. Bowes's translation
of De la Primaudaye's *French Academy*
(1586), in chap. xii, 'Of Speech and
Speaking'; and from thence into
Greene's prose-tracts (Grosart, v. 206,
276), in *Penelope's Web* (1587), and
The Spanish Masquerado (1589), but

without 'came, saw, and overcame'.

69. *annothanize*] usually taken as an
old spelling of *anatomize.* But Alan
Keen, in the letter quoted at l. 67
n. above, suggests it is a mock-latin
coinage meaning 'annotate', 'gloss'.

69–70. *vulgar (O base . . . vulgar)*]
This is another Arcadianism. Cf. bk ii
(Feuillerat, i. 238): 'Which when this
good old woman perceived—O the
good wold woman!' and again: 'her
body (O sweet body!) covered', etc.;
and again: 'One day (O day that
shined to make them dark!'). Lyly has
the same trick (later than *Arcadia*) in
Endymion, i. i: 'his person (ah sweet
person) . . . his sharpe wit (ah wit too
sharpe)', etc.

vulgar (O base and obscure vulgar!)]
'Vulgar', meaning vernacular tongue),
occurs again in *AYL,* v. i. 33, in a
similar strain: 'abandon, which is in
the vulgar, leave'. In i. ii. 45 above,
we have had 'the vulgar' used absolutely for the common people. Cf.
Puttenham, *Arte of English Poesie,* 1589
(but written earlier): 'Offices of service and love towards the dead . . .
called Obsequies in our vulgar' (p. 63);
'such maner of Poesie is called in our
vulgar ryme dogrell' (p. 89). 'In theyr
vulgar tongue', the full expression, is in
'Publike Baptisme', in *The First Prayer
Book of King Edward VI,* 1549.

73–7. *To whom came he? to the beggar
. . . on whose side? the beggar's*] This is
Gabriel Harvey's favourite style. Cf.
Pierce's Supererogation (Grosart, ii. 176):
'What the saluation of David Gorge?
a nullitie: what the deification of
N. H.? a nullitie: what the sanctifi-
cation of Browne? a nullitie; what the

beggar: what saw he? the beggar: who overcame
he? the beggar. The conclusion is victory: on whose   75
side? the king's. The captive is enriched: on whose
side? the beggar's. The catastrophe is a nuptial: on
whose side? the king's; no, on both in one, or one in
both. I am the king, for so stands the comparison;
thou the beggar, for so witnesseth thy lowliness. Shall   80
I command thy love? I may. Shall I enforce thy
love? I could. Shall I entreat thy love? I will. What
shalt thou exchange for rags? robes: for tittles? titles:

76. the king's] *Q2,Ff3,4;* the king *Q1,F1.*

communitie of Barrow? a nullitie:
what the plausibilitie of Marten? a
nullitie'. In scene iii of *Pedantius*
(levelled at G. Harvey), *c.* 1581, there
is a parallel noticed by Moore Smith
(*Materialien zur kunde des älteren Eng-
lischen Dramas,* Band viii, p. xlvii):
'Quis in Grammatica Congruus?
Nonne Pedantius? Quis in Poetarum
hortis floridus? Nonne Pedantius?
Quis in Rhetorum pompa potens?
Nonne Pedantius?' For Harvey see
Intro., 5.22.

80–1. *Shall I command . . . Shall I
enforce thy love*] from Lyly: 'I will not
enforce marriage where I cannot com-
pell love' (*Campaspe,* v. 4 [1581]); and
'Well Semele, I will not command
love, for it cannot be enforced: let me
entreat it' (*Endymion,* v. 3 [?1586]);
and *Sapho and Phao,* iv. 1 (1581):
'Yeeld to me, Phao; I intreat where I
may command; command thou,
where thou shouldst intreat.'

83. *exchange for*] obtain in exchange
for. *N.E.D.* refers this 'obsolete' sense
to Spenser, *Faerie Queene,* vii. vi. 6.

for rags? robes] 'Cupid is blinde and
shooteth at random, as soone hitting a
ragge as a robe, and piercing as soone
the bosome of a Captive as the brest of
a Libertine' (Lodge, *Euphues Golden
Legacie* [Hazlitt's *Shakes. Lib.,* p. 33],
1590); and again: 'Cupid shootes at a
ragge as soone as at a roabe' (p. 68):
and again: 'Venus jettes in Roabes not
ragges' (p. 100); and 'Will Venus

joyne roabes and ragges together?'
(p. 117). Thackeray perhaps remembered this: 'Lady Bareacres . . . a
toothless bald old woman now—a
mere rag of a former robe of state'
(*Vanity Fair,* chap. xlix).

tittles] jots, particles, points, or small
lines. Commonly used in the 'criss-
cross row'. An early example occurs in
The Two Italian Gentlemen (a translation of L. Pasqualigo's *Il Fedele,*
Malone Soc., ed. P. Simpson, l. 1704),
1584: 'I ipse tipse tittle tittle este
amen'. A standard ending, quoted by
Nashe in *Have With You,* etc. (Mc-
Kerrow, iii. 46): 'a per se, con per se,
tittle, est, Amen! . . . he comes upon
thee with a whole Hornbooke'; and in
How a Man may Chuse a Good Wife
(Hazlitt's *Dodsley,* ix. 42), *c.* 1600: 'I
was five years learning to crish-cross
from great A . . . so in process of time I
came to e per se e and com per se, and
tittle', etc. This was probably the most
familiar meaning.

for tittles? titles] a quibble of Harvey's: 'I am alwayes marvellously be-
holding unto you, for your bountifull
Titles. . . . But to let Titles and Tittles
passe, and come to the very point in
deede' (*Letter to Spenser* [Grosart, i. 25],
1579). This is pre-euphuist, but it is a
favourite mode of Lyly's and copied by
many writers: for example, Drayton in
his dedications to *The Harmonie of the
Church* (1591): 'not as poems of poets,
but praiers of prophets; and vouchsafe

for thyself? me. Thus, expecting thy reply, I profane
my lips on thy foot, my eyes on thy picture, and my   85
heart on thy every part.
  Thine in the dearest design of industry,
     Don Adriano de Armado.

Thus dost thou hear the Nemean lion roar
'Gainst thee, thou lamb, that standest as his prey;
Submissive fall his princely feet before,   91
And he from forage will incline to play.
But if thou strive, poor soul, what art thou then?
Food for his rage, repasture for his den.

Prin. What plume of feathers is he that indited this letter?   95
  What vane? what weathercock? did you ever hear
  better?

---

88. Adriano] *Q2; Adriana Q1,Ff.* Armado] *Ff2,3,4; Armatho Qq,F1.*

---

to be their gracious patronesse against
any gracelesse parasite'; and 'I speak
. . . not of toyes in Mount Ida, but of
triumphes in Mount Sion: not of
vanitie, but of veritie; not of tales, but
of truethes'.

 84–5. *profane my lips*] 'I kiss thy hand'
was a common, respectful ending to a
letter, especially from a lover or suitor.
Cf. *The Shepherdess Felismena* (Hazlitt's
Shakes. Lib., p. 284): 'all is mine doth
wholly consist in your hands, the
which, with all reverence and dutifull
affection, a thousand times I kisse';
and Nashe (mockingly), Ded. to
Lenten Stuffe (McKerrow, iii. 150): 'and
so I kisse the shadow of your feetes
shadow'.

 87. *industry*] assiduity in ladies' service. In *The Queen's Entertainment at
Cowdray*, 1591 (Nichols, iii. 109), industry is described as 'careful and kind
diligence'. This word was used widely
and affectedly. Gabriel Harvey has it
several times while bestowing lavish
praise on his friend Sidney and his
'Countess of Pembroke's Arcadia' in
Pierce's Supererogation (Grosart, ii. 99–
102): 'Lord, what would himselfe have
prooved in fine, that was the gentleman of Curtesy, the Esquier of Indus-

try, and the Knight of Valour at those
yeeres? Live ever sweete Booke.' Our
'gallantry'.

 88. *Adriano de Armado*] Dover Wilson
takes the unusual form of the name
found here in the early texts and the
setting of the letter in roman (as against
the elaborate italic of that in I. i) as
evidences that the two belong to different drafts of Shakespeare's manuscript. See Intro., 2.56.

 89. *Nemean lion*] so accented in *Ham.*,
I. iv. 83. The reference is to the first of
Hercules' labours, which Shakespeare
recalled from Golding's *Ovid*, ix. 242:
'The Nemean Lyon by theis armes
lyes dead upon the ground' (1567).
Here it was he found his pronunciation
of Nemean, an alternative in both the
Greek and the Latin. This is the sonnet
Armado promises us at I. ii. 173–4, so
we must be content. We have here too
the Armado of 'high-born words', fore-
shadowed and foregone, of I. i. 171.

 92. *from forage will incline*] will turn
from his first intentions, which are
naturally to prey.

 96. *vane*] 'vane' naturally suggests
weathercock, but it should more
properly be written here 'fane', an
obsolete word signifying 'flag, ban-

Boyet. I am much deceiv'd but I remember the style.
Prin. Else your memory is bad, going o'er it erewhile.   98
Boyet. This Armado is a Spaniard, that keeps here in court;
   A phantasime, a Monarcho, and one that makes sport
   To the prince and his book-mates.
Prin.   Thou, fellow, a word.
   Who gave thee this letter?
Cost.   I told you; my lord.   102

100. phantasime] *Qq,F1;* phantasm *Ff2,3,4;* phantasma *Capell conj.*
Monarcho] monarcho *Q2.*

ner, pendant' (*N.E.D.*), also written 'fan' as in Chapman's *Two Wise Men,* etc., iv. iii (1619): 'I could devise them a crest as fit as a fan for a forehorse'. There is a good illustrative passage in *The Feast of St George observed at Utrecht,* 1586 (Nichols's *Progresses,* ii. 457): 'Then began the trumpets to sound in the service, which was most prince-like and aboundant, served on the knee, carved and tasted to her Majesties trencher; . . . sundry sortes of musickes continued the entring of the first course; which done and avoyded, the trumpets sounded in for the second, which was all baked meats of beasts and fowles; the beasts, as lions, dragons, leopards, and such like bearing phaines or arms; and the fowles, as peacocks, swans, pheasants, turkie cocks, and others in their natural feathers, spread in their greatest pride, which sight was both rare and magnificent.'

weathercock] taken as a type of showiness, as in *Wiv.,* iii. ii. 18. So Sidney, *Arcadia,* bk iii (Feuillerat, i. 419): 'woulde . . . proclayme his blasphemies against womankinde; that namely that sex was . . . the shops of vanities, the guilded wethercocks'.

97–8. *style . . . going o'er it*] the same pun as in i. i. 197.

100. *phantasime*] This word, on which Q and F1 agree, is not found elsewhere, though 'phantasims' of v. i. 18 is presumably the same. The sense required is something distinct from 'phantasm'; not a creature of the fancy, but one full of fancies.

Monarcho] a real fantastical character of the time. He appears to have been a crazy hanger-on to the Court, whose vaingloriousness made him a butt. Thomas Churchyard wrote a tedious epitaph to *The Phantasticall Monarke,* printed in a collection called his *Chance* (1580) which is given at length by Steevens. Steevens also quotes from *A briefe Discourse of the Spanish State, with a Dialogue annexed, intituled Philobasilis* (1590), p. 39: 'The actors were that Bergamasco (for his phantastick humours) named Monarcho, and two of the Spanish embassadours retinue, who being about foure and twentie yeares past, in Paules Church in London, contended who was soveraigne of the world: the Monarcho maintained himself to be he, and named their king to be but his viceroy for Spaine, the other two with great fury denying it', etc. He is honoured by other references in writers of the time. Farmer quotes from Meres's *Wits Commonweatlh* (p. 178): 'Peter Shakerlye of Paules, and Monarcho that lived about the court'. Steevens refers also to Nashe's *Have With You to Saffron Walden* (McKerrow, iii. 76), 1596: 'an insulting monarch above Monarcha the Italian, that ware crownes in his shooes' while Douce cites from Scot's *Discoverie of Witchcraft,* 1584, to the effect that, like Thrasibulus, he was 'sore oppressed with the like spirit or conceipt' (ed. B. Nicholson, 1886, p. 42).

Prin. To whom should'st thou give it?
Cost.   From my lord to my lady.
Prin. From which lord to which lady?
Cost. From my lord Berowne, a good master of mine,   105
    To a lady of France that he call'd Rosaline.
Prin. Thou hast mistaken his letter. Come, lords, away.
    Here, sweet, put up this: 'twill be thine another day.
                    [Exeunt Princess and train.
Boyet. Who is the suitor? who is the suitor?
Ros.   Shall I teach you to know?
Boyet. Ay, my continent of beauty.
Ros.   Why, she that bears the bow.
    Finely put off!   111
Boyet. My lady goes to kill horns; but if thou marry,
    Hang me by the neck if horns that year miscarry.
    Finely put on!
Ros. Well, then I am the shooter.
Boyet.   And who is your deer?   115

---

107. lords] ladies *Johnson conj.*   109. suitor . . . suitor] *Steevens (Farmer);*
shooter *Qq,Ff.*   *109 to end of scene.*] *Put in margin by Pope.*

---

107. *mistaken*] taken to the wrong person, miscarried. See above, l. 58.

108. *be thine another day*] In *N. & Q.* for 26 Feb. 1910 (p. 164), and again for 4 Jan. 1914 (p. 7), 'M.P.T.' quoted a number of parallel passages to show, convincingly, that this phrase does not mean, as Daniel suggested, 'it will be of use to you hereafter,' but 'your turn will come one day.' The best is perhaps from Dekker, *Gul's Horn Booke* (ed. O. Smeaton, p. 52): 'Marry, when silver comes in, remember to pay treble their [the watermen's] fare, and it will make your Flounder-catchers to send more thanks after you, when you do not draw, then when you doe; for they know, *It will be their owne another daie.*' Evidently proverbial, though it does not occur again in Shakespeare.

109. *suitor*] formerly, and still provincially, pronounced 'shooter'. Hence the quibble. There are three closely written pages on this in Furness. He cites a good example from Lyly's *Euphues* (Arber, p. 293): 'There was a

Lady in Spaine . . . hadde three sutors (and yet never a good Archer).'

110. *continent*] that which contains; the sum. Cf. Greene, *Never Too Late* (Grosart, viii. 50): 'they be women and therefore the continents of all excellence' (1590); and his *Alcida* (ix. 208), 1588: 'women, the painted continents of flattery, of deceit', etc.

111, 117. *put off . . . put on*] These terms occur in antithesis in Gascoigne's *Hermit's Tale* (Works, ed. Cunliffe, ii. 480), 1576: 'charged . . . to weare this punyshment with paciens, which necessyty did putt on, and destyny wold putt off.' Perhaps military or fencing terms, to hit or strike at, and to guard, ward off or parry. Lyly has similar ejaculations of encouragement to punsters in *Mother Bombie*: 'well brought about', 'excellently applied'.

115. *who is your deer?*] so in Lyly's *Gallathea*, ii. i (1585): 'Saw you not the deere come this way . . . whose dear was it. . . . I saw none but mine own dear.'

Ros. If we choose by the horns, yourself come not near.
    Finely put on, indeed!
Mar. You still wrangle with her, Boyet, and she strikes at the
    brow.
Boyet. But she herself is hit lower: have I hit her now?
Ros. Shall I come upon thee with an old saying, that was   120
    a man when King Pepin of France was a little boy,
    as touching the hit it?
Boyet. So I may answer thee with one as old, that was a
    woman when Queen Guinever of Britain was a little
    wench, as touching the hit it.   125
Ros.   Thou canst not hit it, hit it, hit it,
               Thou canst not hit it, my good man.   [*Exit.*
Boyet.   An I cannot, cannot, cannot,
               An I cannot, another can.
Cost. By my troth, most pleasant: how both did fit it!   130

116. horns, yourself come] *Qq,Ff, Cambridge, Furness;* horns, yourself: come
Rowe, Steevens et seq.   128. An] And *Q1; not in Ff,Q2.*

116. *yourself come not near*] Boyet is
warned to keep off for fear of being
shot—he is such a temptingly good
'head'. Or perhaps Rowe's punctuation may be right, and the meaning
is that Rosaline gives Boyet 'the horns',
as common chaff, and then cries 'come
not near', as he threatens active
reprisals.

120. *come upon thee with*] attack thee
with (as in Gen., xxiv. 25). Cf. *Shr.*, I.
ii. 42: 'O heavens! Spake you not
these words plain, "Sirrah, Knock me
here" . . .? And come you now with
"Knocking at the gate"?'

121. *King Pepin*] the founder of the
Carlovingian dynasty, died 768. As a
representative of ancient times we
meet him again in *All's W.*, II. i. 79.

124. *Queen Guinever*] The name was
used in contempt. See Nashe, *Have
With You to Saffron Walden* (McKerrow,
iii. 102), 1596: 'Since the raigne of
Queen Gueniver was there never seene
worse'; and Dekker, *A Strange Horse-
Race* (Grosart, iii. 358), 1613: 'the
Divell . . . had no sooner touched his
old Laplandian Guenevora, but shee

as speedily quickened'. See also
Dekker's *Satiromastix* (Pearson, i. 219),
and Beaumont and Fletcher, *The
Scornful Lady*, v. i.

126. *Thou canst not hit it*] The tune of
this song, or catch, is given in Chappell's *Popular Music of the Olden Time*
(1859), i. 239, from a MS. at Oxford
bearing date 1620. It was a dance-
tune; and the dance is mentioned in
Wily Beguiled (Malone Soc., l. 2451),
1606: 'Thou art mine own sweetheart,
From thee Ile ne'er depart; Thou art
my Ciperlillie And I thy Trangdi-
downedilly, And sing hey ding a ding
ding: And do the tother thing, And
when tis done not misse, To give my
wench a kisse: And then dance canst
thou not hit it? Ho, brave William
Cricket!' Gosson refers to it as a dance
in his *Quips for Upstart New-fangled
Gentlewomen*, 1595: '*Can you hit it* is oft
their daunce.' The song is referred to in
Rowley's *Match at Midnight*, I. i (Hazlitt's *Dodsley*, xiii. 23): 'A widow witty
—Is pastime pretty . . . an old man—
Sim. Then will she answer, *If you cannot,
a younger can.*'

Mar. A mark marvellous well shot, for they both did hit it.
Boyet. A mark! O! mark but that mark; a mark, says my lady.
      Let the mark have a prick in't, to mete at, if it may be.
Mar. Wide o' the bow-hand! i' faith, your hand is out.
Cost. Indeed, a' must shoot nearer, or he'll ne'er hit the clout.
Boyet. An if my hand be out, then belike your hand is in.   136
Cost. Then will she get the upshoot by cleaving the pin.
Mar. Come, come, you talk greasily; your lips grow foul.

131. hit it] *F4;* hit *Qq,Ff1,2,3.*   137. pin] *Ff2,3,4;* is in *Qq,F1.*

133. *mark . . . prick . . . mete at*] Minshew's *Guide into the Tongues* (ed. 1627)
has: 'a *Marke,* white or pricke to
shoote at . . . L(atin), *Meta, à metendo,*
quod posita sit in dimenso spatio'.
      prick] This word had a variety of
derivative senses in archery, which are
dealt with by Furnivall at considerable
length in a note prefixed to *The Babees
Book,* pp. c–ciii, where many references
will be found, including, of course,
Ascham's *Toxophilus.* We are only concerned here with the primary meaning
of 'mark'. But it is quite possible that
this sense arose from the use of peeled
wands (cf. butchers' *pricks*) as a mark.
Cf. *Guye of Gisborne,* one of the earliest
Robin Hood ballads (Percy Folio, ii.
232): 'they cutt them downe the summer shroggs Which grew both under a
Bryar, And sett them 3 score rood in
twinn To shoote the prickes full neare'.
See l. 139 below, n.
      to mete at] to measure, to aim or level
at.
      134. *Wide o' the bow-hand*] far from
the mark; literally, on the left or bow-
hand side. An instruction from the
butts called out to the archer, by those
who gave aim. This is the earliest example of the expression in *N.E.D.* It
became common later in the dramatists. Cf. Sir J. Harington, *A Brief View,*
etc. (*Nugae Antiquae,* ed. 1779, i. 28),
1608: 'wide of the right way, upon the
sinister or bow-hand, many miles'.
      135. *hit the clout*] The target was
fixed by a pin or clout (Fr. *clou*), the
head of which was painted white and
marked the centre. Cf. Jonson, Epi-

logue to *The Staple of News*: 'our hope
Is though the clout we do not always
hit, It will not be imputed to his wit.'
See also Marlowe's *Tamburlaine* (pt ii),
iv. 8: 'For kings are clouts that every
man shoots at.' The derivation here
given (supported by 'clout-nail') may
be doutbful; it comes from Gifford,
but is not quoted in *N.E.D.* A 'white
rag' is possibly the true origin.
      137. *upshoot*] upshot. It is so written
in Bullen's *Old Plays,* iv. 137; and in
Masques Performed before the Queen, 1592
(Nichols, iii. 208). Cf. Nashe, *Anatomie
of Absurditie* (McKerrow, i. 7), 1589:
'every man shotte his bolte, but this
was the upshut'; *How a Man may Chuse
a Good Wife* (Hazlitt's *Dodsley,* ix. 23):
'who could miss the clout Having so
fair a white, such steady aim; This is
the upshot: now bid for the game'; and
Middleton's *Family of Love,* v. iii: 'an
arrow that sticks for the upshot against
all comers'. Not necessarily the decid-
ing shot, but the best shot in, till it is
beaten.
      cleaving the pin] This expression
occurs in *Guye of Gisborne* quoted
above: 'he clove the good pricke
wand'; and in Middleton's *No Wit no
Help like a Woman's,* ii. 1: 'I'll cleave the
black pin i' the midst of the white.' See
also *Rom.,* II. iv. 15; and G. Harvey's
Three Proper Letters (Grosart, i. 65),
1580: 'The second more speciall, as it
were, hitting the white indeede, and
cleaving the Pinne in sunder'.
      138. *greasily*] indecently, in a
'smutty' way. Marston speaks of
'greasie Aretine' (Bullen's ed., iii.

Cost. She's too hard for you at pricks, sir: challenge her to
    bowl.
Boyet. I fear too much rubbing. Good night, my good owl.
                [*Exeunt Boyet, Maria, and Katharine.*
Cost. By my soul, a swain! a most simple clown!   141
    Lord, Lord, how the ladies and I have put him down!
    O' my troth, most sweet jests! most incony vulgar wit;
    When it comes so smoothly off, so obscenely as it were,
      so fit.
    Armado to th'one side, O! a most dainty man,   145
    To see him walk before a lady, and to bear her fan!

140. *Exeunt*] *Theobald; not in Qq,Ff.*   145. Armado to th'one] *New;* Armatho
ath toothen *Q1;* Armathor ath to the *F1;* Armado ath to *Ff2,3,4;* Armado a'th
to *Rowe;* Armado o' the one *Dyce, Cambridge;* Armado a th' t'other *Keightley.*

320); and Jonson, *Bartholomew Fair,* II.
i: 'her language grows greasier than
her pigs.'

139. *at pricks*] Cf. *Gesta Grayorum,*
1594 (Malone Soc., ed. Greg, p. 17):
'any forbidden manner of Shooting; as
at Pricks in common Highways'.

140. *rubbing*] 'Rub' was a technical
term in the game of bowls. It was
definitely used of the touches of the
bowl against others on its passage to
the jack or mistress. But it was em-
ployed generally of the course of the
bowl. Sir J. Harington says Martin
Marprelate took 'this taunting scoffe
that the Bishop would cry Rub, rub,
rub, to his bowle, and when it was
gone too farre say, The Divell goe with
it' (*A Brief View,* etc., 1608 [*Nugae
Antiquae,* i. 21, ed. 1779]). Shadwell, in
Epsom Wells, Act iii, has 'Rub, rub,
narrow, short, gone a thousand yards,
and such like words of Bowlers'.

owl] rhymes with *bowl,* which was
evidently pronounced as *owl* now is.
See for the word in its other sense, v. ii.
917, rhyming again with *owl.* Jonson
makes a point of this rhyme in a passage about 'Crambo! another of the
devil's games' in *The Devil is an Ass,*
v. v (1616): 'Yes, wis, knight, shite,
Poul, joul, owl, foul, troul, boul.' The
word is still heard so 'in the vulgar'.

144. *obscenely*] Costard's word is apt,

whether he intends it or not. Maria's
rebuke (l. 138) might well have come
ten lines earlier.

145. *to th'one*] To explain the Q
reading Dover Wilson supposes that
the compositor expanded 'Armath',
carelessly written, with a break between syllables, into 'Armath ath'.

145–8. *Armado . . . his page*] What are
they doing in this scene? We must suppose that they took some part in it in an
earlier draft. See note on l. 88 above
for possible evidence of revision. The
vagueness of the directions, in Q and F,
for the characters leaving the stage,
may also be due to careless redrafting.

146. *bear her fan*] a correct attention,
presumably, from a gallant of the time.
Henry Hutton satirizing a gallant in
Folies Anatomie (1616), says: 'I durst
not use my mistres' fan Or walk
attended with a hackneyman.' These
gentlemen would purloin a feather as a
keepsake: 'this feather grew in her
sweet fan sometimes' (Jonson, *Every
Man out of his Humour,* II. i); and 'A
third . . . Will spend his patrimony for
a garter Or the least feather in her
bounteous fan' (*Cynthia's Revels,* III. ii).
We come from the sublime to the ridiculous when the Nurse in *Rom.,* II. iv.
232, says: 'Peter take my fanne and
goe before and apace' (Q1, Cambridge ed.). Farmer quotes from *The*

To see him kiss his hand! and how most sweetly a' will
    swear!
And his page o' t' other side, that handful of wit!
Ah! heavens, it is a most pathetical nit.
Sola, sola!   [*Shout within.*   150
                                               [*Exit Costard.*

SCENE II

Enter HOLOFERNES, *Sir* NATHANIEL, *and* DULL.

Nath. Very reverend sport, truly: and done in the testimony of a good conscience.
Hol. The deer was, as you know, *sanguis*, in blood; ripe

147.] *Collier inserted a line of his own here:* 'Looking babies in her eyes his passion to
declare.'   148. o' t' other] atother *Q1,F1;* at other *Q2,Ff2,3,4.*   149. a] *not in
Qq,F1.*   150. Sola] Sowla *Qq,Ff.*   [*Shout within*] *F4; Shoot within Q1; Shoote
within F1; Showte within F2.*   [*Exit . . .*] *Capell; Exeunt Qq,Ff.*

Scene II
S.D. HOLOFERNES] *Holofernos, the Pedant Qq,Ff.*   3. *Hol.*] *Ped. Qq,Ff.*

Serving Man's Comfort, 1598: 'The mistress must have one to carry her cloake
and hood, another her fanne.'
    147. *To see him kiss his hand*] See also
v. ii. 324. Malone believed a line
was lost after l. 147. Hence Collier's
amazing insertion which gave rise to
some entertaining notes.
    149. *pathetical*] See I. ii. 90.
    nit] anything very small, as in *Shr.,*
IV. iii. 110. A speck. Properly the word
means the egg (lens) of any small
insect, especially a louse. Florio has:
'*Lendini,* nits before they be lice, chits'.
Also a gnat, a fly, a fairy.
    150. *Sola*] Cf. Lancelot's 'Sola, sola:
wo ha ho, sola, sola' (*Mer.V.,* v. i. 49).
This is given as a hunting halloo in *A
Twelfe Night Merriment* (*Narcissus*),
1602.
    Shout within] As this is a hunting
scene (and 'Sola' a hunting cry) the
'Shot' or 'Shoot' of early texts may
conceivably be correct. But 'shouting'
is printed as 'shooting' in *Cor.,* I. i. 218

(F1); and it would be difficult to produce an effective 'noise off' from the
twang or thud of a crossbow.

Scene II
    Enter Holofernes] The name was
probably borrowed from Rabelais's
Gargantua (1535), whose hero was
taught Latin by 'un grand docteur
sophiste, nommé Maistre Thubal
Holoferne'.
    1–2. *in the testimony of a good conscience*]
with the approbation or warrant of a
good conscience. Cf. 2 Cor., i. 12.
    3. sanguis, *in blood*] Dover Wilson
quotes a suggestion of W. W. Greg that
Shakespeare wrote 'sanguĩe', a recognized abbreviation for 'sanguine', but
the S may as easily be Holofernes'
blunder as the compositor's. See also
note on *coelo,* l. 5. These Latin words
are devoid of any special force excepting that they are the emblems of the
pedant's (schoolmaster's) trade, for
testimony of which they are dragged

as the pomewater, who now hangeth like a jewel in
the ear of *coelo*, the sky, the welkin, the heaven; and   5
anon falleth like a crab on the face of *terra*, the soil,
the land, the earth.

Nath. Truly, Master Holofernes, the epithets are sweetly
varied, like a scholar at the least: but, sir, I assure
ye, it was a buck of the first head.   10

Hol. Sir Nathaniel, *haud credo*.

4. the] *Qq1,2; a Ff.*   5. *coelo*] celo *Qq,Ff1,2.*

in. 'In blood, a term of the chase, in a
state of perfect health and vigour'
(Schmidt). Cf. *1H6*, IV. ii. 48; *Cor.*, I.
i. 163 and IV. v. 225. No satisfactory
parallel has been given outside Shakespeare. But cf. Jonson, *The Sad Shepherd*, I. ii: '*Robin*. What head? *John*.
Forked: a heart of ten. *Marian*. He is
good venison, According to the season
in the blood.'

4. *pomewater*] once a popular apple,
but long forgotten. Parkinson (1627)
figures it in his *Paradisus*: 'The *Pome-
water* is an excellent good and great
whitish apple, full of sap or moisture,
somewhat pleasant sharp, but a little
bitter withal: it will not last long, the
winter frosts soone causing it to rot and
perish.' It was evidently in much
demand since it was cried by the Irish
costermongers. See Jonson's *Irish
Masque at Court*, 1613: 'I sherve ti
majesties owne cashtermonger, be me
trote; and cry peepsh [pippins] and
pomwatersh in ti majesties shervice,
tis five year now'; and Dekker, *Old
Fortunatus*, 1600: 'Enter *Andelocia* and
Shadowe, like Irish costarmongers . . .
peeps of Tamasco, feene peeps: I fat
'tis de sweetest apple in de world, 'tis
better den Pome-water, or apple
John'.

5. coelo] '*Cielo*. The heaven, the
skie, the firmament or welkin' (Florio,
New World of Words, 1611); '*Terra*.
The element called earth. . . . Also, any
land . . . or soile' (*ibid.* 1598). These
definitions are given here because they
support Dr Warburton's conjecture
that Holofernes stood for Florio, in

which he was supported by Farmer
and others. But the date of Florio's
Italian Dictionary upsets that slight
argument. Marshall altered *sanguis* to
an Italian form (*sanguino*), probably
according to the same theory.

10. *buck of the first head*] a fully grown
buck. Steevens quotes here from the
Return from Parnassus (1602), where the
names of the 'speciall beasts for chase'
are given as in the text (ed. W. D.
Macray, pp. 107, 108), and see Harrison's *Description of England*, bk III, chap.
iv, 1577 (New Shakes. Soc., p. 26):
'The yoong males which our fallow
deere doo bring foorth, are commonlie
named according to their severall
ages: for the first yeere it is a fawne, the
second a puckot [pricket], the third
a serell, the fourth a soare, the fift a
bucke of the first head; not bearing the
name of a bucke till he be five yeers
old: and from henceefoorth his age is
commonlie knowne by his head or
horns.' The form *prekette* dates back to
1503 (Eden's *Translation of Verto-
mannus*).

11. *Sir*] the normal title for a priest.
Marprelate even gives it to Saint Peter,
to show how Catholics would make an
ecclesiastic of him.

haud credo] This occurs in *The
Troublesome Raigne of King John* (Hazlitt's ed. of *Shakes. Lib.*, p. 264), *ante*
1591: '*Haud credo* Laurentius, that
thou shouldst be pend thus In the
presse of a Nun we are all undone'.
A. L. Rowse, in a letter to the *T.L.S.*
of 18 July 1952, suggested that Dull
hears this as awd (old) grey doe. He

Dull. 'Twas not a *haud credo*, 'twas a pricket.

Hol. Most barbarous intimation! yet a kind of insinuation, as it were *in via*, in way of explication; *facere*,
as it were replication, or, rather, *ostentare*, to show,   15
as it were, his inclination,—after his undressed,
unpolished, uneducated, unpruned, untrained, or
rather unlettered, or ratherest, unconfirmed fashion
—to insert again my *haud credo* for a deer.

Dull. I said the deer was not a *huad credo*; 'twas a pricket.   20

Hol. Twice-sod simplicity, *bis coctus!*

insists it is not a doe of any sort, but a
young buck.

12. *pricket*] a two-year-old red-deer.
See Cotgrave in v. *Brocart.* Cf. Greene,
Carde of Fancie (Grosart, iv. 68), 1584:
'the Lion seldome lodgeth with the
Mouse, the Hart seldome feedeth with
the Pricket.' See note at l. 10, and
Gesta Grayorum, 1594 (ed. Greg, p. 18):
'young Deer, Prickets or any other
game'.

13. *intimation*] I owe the following
note to Professor J. A. K. Thomson:
'Holofernes, like pedants in all ages,
loves to use words in their *original*
sense, because it shows their learning.
I think that 'intimation' probably
means "thrusting into the very inside"—*intima*. He says it is "a kind of
insinuation"—*insinuare*, "to insert"
("insert my haud credo for a deer").
Then "explication" means "unfold-
ing", "replication" is "folding back",
so as to reveal. Thus the general sense
of the whole sentence would be "Most
ignorant interruption by an uneducated person offering his foolish
explanation".'

13–14. *insinuation*] Cf. T. Wilson,
Art of Rhetorique, 1553: 'A privy
begynnyng, or crepyng in, otherwyse
called Insinuation, must then and not
els be used, when the iudge is greaved
with us, and our cause hated of the
hearers' (ed. 1562, fol. 53). Probably
Holofernes has Wilson's or Cox's
earlier treatise on the same subject in
his mind. Sir Philip Sidney has a

similar passage in *Arcadia*, bk i: 'his
insinuation being of blushinge, and his
division of sighes, his whole oration
stood upon a short narration.'

14–15. *explication . . . replication*]
Nashe uses the verbs *explicate, replicate,*
in *Lenten Stuffe.* '*Replication . . .* a confirmation of one's saying with new
allegations' (Blount, *Glossographia,*
1670).

18. *unconfirmed*] Unless there be a
reference to the religious rite, and the
word have the sense of 'irreligious',
'heathen', it is difficult to find a climax
in 'unconfirmed'. The word occurs
again in *Ado*, III. iii. 124. Schmidt interprets it 'inexperienced, raw'. The expression *bis coctus* below expressly forbids that meaning here. 'Unratified'
'unconsolidated', 'unavouched', might
be suggested, but each seems feeble as
a superlatively strong qualification.

21. *Twice-sod . . .* bis coctus!] probably a reference to the old proverb or
aphorism about twice-sodden coleworts, used of a tale twice told, or a
sentence twice uttered, like Dull's.
The Greek form, Δὶς κράμβη θάνατος,
is of remote antiquity; and Pliny (xx.
9) says: 'Coleworts . . . twice sodden, it
bindeth the bellie' (Holland's trans.
1601). The proverbial use occurs in
Lyly's *Euphues* (Arber, p. 391): 'they
fell to the whole discourse of Philautus
love, who left out nothing that before I
put in, which I must omitte, least I set
before you Coleworts twise sodden.'
In Laurence Humphrey's *Oration to*

O! thou monster Ignorance, how deform'd dost thou
    look.

Nath. Sir, he hath never fed of the dainties that are bred in
    a book.

He hath not eat paper, as it were; he hath not drunk
ink: his intellect is not replenished; he is only an   25
animal, only sensible in the duller parts;

And such barren plants are set before us, that we
    thankful should be,

Which we of taste and feeling are, for those parts that
    do fructify in us more than he;

For as it would ill become me to be vain, indiscreet, or
    a fool,

So were there a patch set on learning, to see him in a
    school: 30

But, *omne bene*, say I; being of an old father's mind,

Many can brook the weather that love not the wind.

Dull. You two are book-men: can you tell me by your wit
    What was a month old at Cain's birth, that's not five
    weeks old as yet?

27–8.] *Prose Qq,Ff; verse Hanmer et seq.*   28. of] *Tyrwhitt; not in Qq,Ff.*   do]
Q1,Ff; not in Q2.   33. me] *Q1;not in Ff,Q2.*

Queen Elizabeth at Woodstock, 1575
(Nichols, i. 589), it occurs in Latin:
'*Cramben qui bis coctam apponit minister,
mortem apponit, et qui eadem oberrat chorda
citharædus, ridetur, et . . . coccysmus seu
cuculi cantilena audienti insuavis est*', etc.
Perhaps it will be found in some of
the school-books of the time, like
several others of the pedant's tags. It is
in Burton's *Anatomy of Melancholy*
(Democritus to the Reader): 'an unnecessary work, *cramben bis coctam
apponere*, the same again and again in
other words'.

30. *So were there a patch set on learning*]
It would be setting a fool to learn.
'Patch' was a common word for a fool.
Or we may take it 'a fool intent on
learning'. I prefer the more active
construction.

patch] fool. There has been much
written upon this signification of the

word, which occurs again in *Tp.*, III. ii.
71; *Err.*, III. i. 32; and *Mer.V.*, II. v. 46;
and see the *N.E.D.* There is no occasion to seek for derivations such as
Wolsey's fool named 'Patch' and the
Italian *pazzo* (Florio). The word was
used as a synonym for 'pied-coat',
from the fool's dress. Cf. Rider's *Bibliotheca Scholastica*, 1589: 'Pied coate or
Patch, *Sticte*'.

31. *old father's*] Lodge has the same
expression: 'For tragedies and comedies Donate the Grammarian sayth,
they wer invented by lerned fathers of
the old time to no other purpose, but to
yeelde prayse unto God' (*Reply to
Gosson*, 1579, 1580); and see Golding's
Ovid (vii. 449): 'Here men (so auncient
fathers said that were as then alive) did
breede of deawie Mushrommes.' The
precise author of this particular
aphorism has not been traced.

Hol. Dictynna, goodman Dull; Dictynna, goodman Dull.   35
Dull. What is Dictynna?
Nath. A title to Phoebe, to Luna, to the moon.
Hol. The moon was a month old when Adam was no more;
      And raught not to five weeks when he came to five-score.
      The allusion holds in the exchange.   40
Dull. 'Tis true indeed: the collusion holds in the exchange.
Hol. God comfort thy capacity! I say the allusion holds
      in the exchange.
Dull. And I say the pollution holds in the exchange, for
      the moon is never but a month old; and I say beside   45
      that, 'twas a pricket that the princess killed.
Hol. Sir Nathaniel, will you hear an extemporal epitaph

35. Dictynna] *Rowe;* Dictisima *Q1,Ff1,2,3;* Dictissima *Q2,F4.*   36. Dictynna]
Dictima *Qq,F1;* Dictinna *Ff2,3,4.*   39. raught] rought *Q1;* wrought *Ff,*
Q2.

35. *Dictynna*] Steevens says Shakespeare might have found this uncommon title for Diana in the second book
of Golding's translation of Ovid's
Metamorphoses: 'Dictynna garded with
her traine and proud of killing deere'.
It occurs earlier in one of N. Grimald's
songs in *Tottel's Miscellany* (Arber, p.
97), *ante* 1557: 'Acteon may teach thee
Dictynnaes ire'. The Q and F spelling
is a corruption that might easily arise
from a misreading of *manuscript* (y
taken for i long s, and the nn minims
wrongly divided). See Intro., 2.4. It is
doubtful if it is really necessary to correct the 'Dictima' of l. 37; it may be
just Dull's blunder. See notes on i. i.
283 and l. 90 below.
      39. *raught*] reached.
      40. *The allusion holds in the exchange*]
i.e. 'the riddle is as good when I use the
name of Adam, as when you use the
name of Cain' (Warburton). 'Allusion'
meant more in Shakespeare's time
than now. Cf. Cotgrave: '*Allusion:* an
allusion or likening; an alluding or
applying of one thing unto another'.
Blount (1670) in *Glossographia* is more
explicit: '*Allusion:* a likening or applying of one thing to another, and it is as
it were a dalliance or playing with

words like in sound', etc.—in fact a
pun.
      44. *pollution*] This modernizing of
the Q spelling 'polusion' is justified by
a parallel example in *Lucr.*, l. 1157.
The word remains an instance of
Dull's 'mistaking'. See 'reprehend',
i. i. 182. In a note to this passage Furness quotes from 'Courthope, iv. 86'
(*History of English Poetry*, London,
1903), to the effect that we owe Shakespeare's stage-representation of Dull
to Lyly's 'Master Constable and the
Watch' in *Endymion*, characters further
developed in *Ado* and elsewhere. *Endymion* bears the date of 1591, but the
similarities do not go deep, except for
the introduction of Latin tags which
characterizes both plays. Moreover
Lyly's Watch, although they have
rusty wits and no wise words, do not
'mistake words'. See note at v. ii. 488
and 499, 500.
      47–8. *epitaph on the death of*] Capell
said this should be 'epigram' (adopted
into the text by Rann). Furness says
'of course, right—there cannot be an
epitaph on the death of anything'.
Why? Is it not a perfectly common use
of the word? For Shakespearean times,
see *N.E.D.*: 'An Epitaphe made upon

on the death of the deer? and, to humour the ignorant, I have call'd the deer the princess killed, a
pricket.   50

Nath. *Perge,* good Master Holofernes, *perge;* so it shall
please you to abrogate scurrility.

Hol. I will something affect the letter; for it argues facility.

> The preyful princess pierc'd and prick'd a pretty
>   pleasing pricket;   55
> Some say a sore; but not a sore, till now made sore
>   with shooting.

49. I have] call'd *Rowe;* cald *Q1;* call'd *Ff;* I will call *Singer;* call't *Furness;*
call I *Cambridge.*   52. scurrility] squirilitie *Q1.*   55. preyful] prayfull *Qq,F1;*
praysfull *F2, Malone.*   55–60.] *Printed as twelve lines in Qq,Ff.*

the dethe of Frenche' (1532); 'A Book
of Epitaphes made upon the Deathe of
Sir William Buttes' (1583), etc.

48–9. *to humour the ignorant*] to satisfy
Dull. But Holofernes has already given
his decided opinion that the Princess's
bag was a two-year-old pricket, and
not a buck of antler, in his *haud credo.*
Evidently they are introduced arguing
the point at the opening of the scene,
just as Shallow, Sir Hugh, and Slender
open *Wiv.* They were bystanders.

49. *I have call'd*] Rowe's emendation
is as good as any, since it preserves the
one surviving word of the early texts.
Q has also a misprint 'ignorault',
which may indicate a clumsy attempt
to reinsert letters that had come loose
from the chase. See Intro. 2.2.

52. *abrogate scurrility*] abolish coarse-
ness. Puttenham gives examples of
'pleasant speeches favouring some
skurrility' in this sense (pp. 274–5).
'Scurrility' had the sense of foulness of
speech. Gabriel Harvey has 'fie on
grosse scurility and impudent
calumny' (*Foure Letters* [Grosart, i.
204]); and cf. Webster's *Westward Hoe,*
II. i: 'ha ha! I must talk merrily, sir.
Justiniano [a Pedant]. Sir, so long as
your mirth be void of all squirrilitie,
'tis not unfit for your calling.' This
spelling (as in Q1) was not rare.

'Scullery' was spelt 'squillery' likewise.

53. *affect the letter*] resort to allitera-
tion. Cf. E. Kirke, Ep. Ded. (to G.
Harvey) to Spenser's *Shepheard's Calendar,* 1579: 'I scorne and spue out the
rakehellye route of our ragged rymers
(for so themselves use to hunt the
letter)' (Oxford ed., p. 417). In a letter
of Gabriel Harvey's, 'To my verie
friende, M. Immerito' (Spenser),
dated Oct. 1579, this passage occurs
(Grosart, i. 18): 'your gentle Master-
ships long, large, lavish, Luxurious,
laxative letters withall (now a God's
name, when did I ever in my life, hunt
the Letter before? but belike there's no
remedie, I must needes be even with
you once in my dayes).'

56–7. *sore . . . sorel*] See note on l. 10.
The term *Sorell,* for 'a young buck', is
in Palsgrave's *Lesclaircissement,* 1530.
To explain the logical connection of
Holofernes' lines may be a piece of
pedantry worthy the man himself; but
they are not pure nonsense, and ll. 59
and 60 follow the actual course of the
shoot—the baying of the hounds that
starts the game moving, and the jeers
of the bystanders when an archer
misses, and fails even to wound. I am
not sure whether in the next line a
second yell greets a successful shot, or

> The dogs did yell; put 'ell to sore, then sorel jumps
>   from thicket;
> Or pricket sore, or else sore'll the people fall a-hooting.
> If sore be sore, then 'ell to sore makes fifty sores—O—
>   sorel!
> Of one sore I an hundred make, by adding but one
>   more l.   60

Nath. A rare talent!

Dull. If a talent be a claw, look how he claws him with a
talent.

Hol. This is a gift that I have, simple, simple; a foolish extravagant spirit, full of forms, figures, shapes, objects,   65
ideas, apprehensions, motions, revolutions: these are
begot in the ventricle of memory, nourished in the

57. 'ell] ell *Ff*; l *Q 1*.   59. O—sorel!] o sorell *Q 1*; O sorell *Ff*; O sore L! *Capell;*
of sorel *Warburton;* o' sorel *New;* one sorel *Cambridge, Globe.*   64. *Hol.*] *Nath.*
Qq,Ff (see line 71).

whether Holofernes has by this time
fallen to quibbles merely of mathematical typography. 'O—Sorel!' I
take to be complacent mock-surprise
at the new position to which his punning has carried him. The Warburton
reading and its derivatives lack just
that logic so unrelentingly pursued by
Holofernes; he is making not fifty
sores out of sorel, but sorel out of fifty
sores.

57. *dogs did yell*] See *Ven.*, 688, for
'yell' applied to the cry of hounds. The
dogs here do not apparently agree
with the 'sport' at Cowdray or Windsor, 1591–2. But they may have been
used to wake up the unfortunate
animals in the paddock. See note at
'stand', IV. i. 8.

62. *talent*] 'Talon' was commonly
written 'talent'. 'The greedie talents
of the Eagles' (Grosart's *Harvey*, iii.
20). The pun is unavoidable.

claw] quibbling on the word's two
meanings, to scratch, and to flatter.

65. *figures*, etc.] Puttenham dwells
upon this style: 'a stile to be lift up and
advaunced by choice of wordes,
phrases, sentences, and figures, high,
loftie, eloquent and magnifik in pro-

portion' (Arber, p. 164). And again:
'When so ever we multiply our speech
by many words or clauses of one sence,
the Greekes call it *Sinonimia.* . . . Ye see
that all these words, face, looks, favour,
features, visage, countenance, are in
sence all but one. Which store, never-
thelesse, doeth much beautifie and in-
large the matter' (p. 223). Armado
and Holofernes share this affectation,
which is very prevalent in Gabriel
Harvey's letters; also in Lyly's plays,
as: 'How canst thou thus divine,
divide, define, dispute, and all on the
sodaine? *Manes.* Wit will have his
swing; I am bewitcht, inspired, in-
flamed, infected' (*Campaspe*, iii. 2
[1581]); and in many writers of this
period. See v. i. 58 for a different use of
the word 'figure'. Here we may equate
it with our idea, imagination.

66. *revolutions*] applied to the gifts of
the intellect, may mean any turning of
the thoughts. Florio has '*Riuolgment:* a
revolving, a revolution, a turning and
tossing up and downe. Also a winding
or crankling in and out. Also a cunning
tricke or winding shift. Also a revolt
. . . or rebellion.'

67. *ventricle of memory*] Furness quotes

womb of *pia mater*, and delivered upon the mellowing
of occasion. But the gift is good in those in whom it is
acute, and I am thankful for it.   70

Nath. Sir, I praise the Lord for you, and so may my
parishioners; for their sons are well tutored by you,
and their daughters profit very greatly under you:
you are a good member of the commonwealth.

Hol. Mehercle! if their sons be ingenious, they shall want   75
no instruction; if their daughters be capable, I will
put it to them. But *vir sapit qui pauca loquitur.* A soul
feminine saluteth us.

Enter JAQUENETTA *and* COSTARD.

Jaq. God give you good morrow, master Person.
Hol. Master Person, *quasi* pierce-one. An if one should be   80
pierced, which is the one?

68. *pia mater*] *Rowe; primater Qq,Ff.*   69. in whom] whom *Q1.*   71. *Nath.*]
Hol. Qq,Ff (see line 64).   75. *Hol.*] *Nath. Qq,Ff.*   ingenious] *Capell;* ingenous
Q1; ingennous *F1;* ingenuous *Q2,Ff3,4.*   77. *sapit*] *sapis Q1,F1.*   80. *Hol.*]
Nath. Qq,Ff.   pierce-one] *Hall;* Person *Q1,F1;* Persone *Ff2,3.*   80–6.] *Put
in the margin by Pope.*

here from Vicary, *The Anatomie of the
Bodie of Man* (E.E.T.S., p. 31), 1548:
'Next is the Brayne, of which it is mar-
veylous to be considered and noted,
how this Piamater devideth the sub-
staunce . . . into three partes or ven-
trikles. . . . In the thirde Ventrikle, and
last, there is founded and ordeyned the
vertue Memorative: in this place is
registred and kept those things that are
done or spoken with the senses and
keepeth them in his treasurie.'

68. pia mater] 'the fine membrane
or pellicle called *Pia Mater*, which
immediately lappeth and enfoldeth
the braine' (Pliny's *Natural History*
[trans. P. Holland, xxiv. 8], 1601). In
the *Stanford Dictionary* (Cambridge,
1892) there is a quotation from
Jerome of Brunswick's Surgery, 1525:
'than the panne, than within be ij
small fleces named dura mater and pia
mater, than the substance of the
braynes'. And cf. Nashe's *Christ's
Teares*, Epistle to Reader (McKerrow,

ii. 184), 1593: 'having a huge heape
of those worthlesse shreds of small
English in my *Pia mater's* purse'.

70. *acute*] See III. i. 63.

76. *capable*] The audience doubtless
enjoyed the double meaning, pointed
by 'under you' of l. 73, and Holofernes' unwitting admission of mis-
conduct.

77. vir . . . loquitur] 'with few words
a wise man will compass much' (*Proverbs of Alfred* [Morris, *Specimens of
Early Eng.*, i. 329], *c.* 1250). The Latin
form is in various collections.

80–4. *pierce-one . . . piercing a hogshead*]
'Hogshead' was not uncommonly
applied to a thick-witted person,
especially in the old phrase 'couch a
hogshead', occurring as early as *Cock
Lorel's Bote*. This explains Costard's
impertinence. Cf. Dekker's *Wonderfull
Yeare* (Grosart, i. 142): 'after they had
laid their hogsheads togither, to draw
out some holesome counsell'. Hart was
certain that this dialogue ('with its

Cost. Marry, master schoolmaster, he that is likest to a
    hogshead.
Hol. Of piercing a hogshead! a good lustre of conceit in
    a turf of earth; fire enough for a flint, pearl enough   85
    for a swine: 'tis pretty; it is well.
Jaq. Good master Person, be so good as read me this
    letter: it was given me by Costard, and sent me from
    Don Armado: I beseech you, read it.

84. *Hol.*] *Nath. Qq,Ff.*

emphatic "of"") was an echo of the
passage in Gabriel Harvey's *Pierce's
Supererogation* (1593) in which he
quotes a certain gentlewoman's strictures on Nashe's *Pierce Penilesse*. 'She
knew what she said that intituled
Pierce, the hoggeshead of witt: Pen-
niles, the tosspot of eloquence: &
Nashe the very inventor of Asses. She
it is that must broach the barrell of thy
frisking conceite, and canonise the[e]
Patriarke of newe writers.' This
'parallel' is rendered less certain by
a discovery of Mr John Crow's, that
'piercing a hogshead' was sixteenth to
seventeenth century slang for getting
drunk. He draws my attention to an
epigram in *Witt's Recreations*, 1640
(repr. J. C. Hotten, No. 239). It is
entitled 'On a Drawer Drunk', and
runs: 'Drawer with thee now even is
thy wine, For thou hast pierc'd his
hogs-head, and he thine.' There would
therefore be some point in the interchange without bringing in Harvey
and Nashe. But see Intro., 5.22.

80. *pierce-one*] Hall's emendation,
which an Elizabethan might conceivably have spelt 'Pers-on', is the
simplest that will give Holofernes a
clear meaning. The alternative is to
read 'Master *Parson*' in both lines and
assume that Holofernes begins by
deriving it correctly from 'person'
(persona); his imagination then takes
wing, and he proceeds to suggest
a more remote derivation from
'pierce'.

81. *pierced*] This word was pro-

nounced as it is spelt in Qq,Ff (*perst*).
See the quibble in *1H4*, v. iii. 59: 'If
Percy be alive I'll pierce him.' For the
spelling cf. Puttenham *Arte of English
Poesie* (Arber, p. 176): 'Her beautie
perst mine eye, her speach mine wofull
hart.' Ellis (*Early English Pronunciation*)
says 'Pierce, the family name, is pronounced Perse in America.' This is to
be noted in connection with Nashe's
tract, *Pierce Penilesse.*

one] See Q reading at 1. i. 165. Commonly pronounced *on* or *un* provincially. In Gabriel Harvey's early
letters 'one' is constantly written 'on'
(Grosart, i. 112, etc.). It seems to have
been an affectation of Harvey's: 'on of
my standinge' (pp. 114-17), etc.

84. *Of piercing a hogshead*] Cambridge
edd. suggest that 'Of', which com-
mences this line in the old edition was
part of the stage-direction, 'Holof.',
which crept into the text. They make
a similar guess at 'O' (from 'Bero.') at
III. i. 142, etc. But it is odd that the
form 'Holof.', which we should have to
assume underlies the careless 'Nath.'
of Q, never occurs elsewhere. The 'Of',
a sort of savouring of the expression, is
not impossible.

85. *turf of earth*] clod of earth. Cf.
Jonson, *Every Man out of his Humour*, 1. i
(1599): 'Who can endure to see blind
fortune dote thus? To be enamoured
on this dusty turf, This clod, a whoreson puck-fist!' And again in *Tale of a
Tub*, 1. iii: 'Whereas the father of her is
a Turfe, A very superficies of the
earth.'

Hol. Facile precor gelida quando pecus omne sub umbra Ruminat, 90
 and so forth. Ah! good old Mantuan. I may speak of
 thee as the traveller doth of Venice:

Venetia, Venetia,
Chi non ti vede, non ti pretia.

Old Mantuan! old Mantuan! who understandeth 95
thee not, loves thee not. *Ut, re, sol, la, mi, fa.* Under

90. *Facile*] *Facile precor gellida quando pecas omnia Q1,F1; Fauste precor gelida quando pecus omne Ff2,3,4.* 93–4. *Venetia . . . pretia*] *Cambridge; Venchie vencha, que non le unde, que non te perreche Q1,F1 (more corrupt in Q2,Ff2,3,4).* 96. loves thee not] *Q1; not in Ff,Q2.*

90. Facile . . . Ruminat] The quotation is not given its strictly correct form in any text earlier than F2. It is the beginning of the first eclogue of Mantuanus. Battista Spagnuoli, surnamed Mantuanus from the place of his birth, was a writer of pastoral poems, who flourished towards the latter end of the fifteenth century. He died in 1516. A translation by George Turberville appeared in 1567. Mantuan's eclogues were in regular use as a school-book. The quotation had recently been a centre of skirmishing in the battles between Harvey and Nashe; and it should be noted how the combatants treat the quotation. In Gabriel Harvey's *Foure Letters* (Grosart, i. 195), he attacks *M. Pierce Penilesse* (p. 194) in these words: 'The summe of summes is, He lost his imagination a thousand waies, and I belieue searched every corner of Grammar-Schoole witte (for his margine is as deeplie learned, as *Fauste precor gelida*) to see if he could finde anie meanes to relieue his estate.' Nashe, in his reply in *Foure Letters Confuted* (McKerrow's *Nashe*, i. 306), singles out this passage thus: 'With the first and second leafe hee plaies verie pretilie, and in ordinarie termes of extenuating, verdits Pierce Penilesse for an Grammer Schoole wit: saies his Margine is as deepelie learnd as *Fauste præcor gelida*, that his Muse sobbeth and groneth verie piteouslie', etc. Here we have the words classified, by two of the

chief writers before the public, as the one tag that even the worst of Grammar School dunces might be expected to remember. A line so well known and so recently notorious could hardly be misquoted by Shakespeare. Surely the blunder is Holofernes'; and this raises the question of how far the other quotations from foreign languages are intentionally corrupt. The 'sapis' of l. 77 is most probably a misprint; but how much of the chaos, to which e.g. Florio's proverb (see next note) is reduced in Q, is genuine Holofernes? Unfortunately, we cannot now distinguish, but must restore all or nothing.

93–4. Venetia . . . pretia] This proverb is given by Malone from Florio's *Second Fruites* (1591): '*Venetia*, etc., with a tag, *Ma chi ti vede, ben gli costa*'. Theobald was the first to correct the old text. Furness states it is in Florio's *First Fruites* (1578) with translation: 'Venise who seeth thee not, praiseth thee not, but who seeth thee, it costeth hym well.' It has also been discovered by Wolfgang Keller in *The Garden of Pleasure*, translated by James Sandford from the Italian, in 1573. The English version is in *The Book of Riddels*, mentioned by Captain Cox in 1575. See Furnivall's *Captain Cox* (Ballad Soc., 1871), p. cxiii. Howell has a very different conclusion in his *Italian Proverbs*, 1659.

96. Ut . . . fa] He hums the notes of the gamut as Edmund does in *Lr.*, I. ii

pardon, sir, what are the contents? or, rather, as
Horace says in his—what, my soul! verses?
Nath. Ay, sir, and very learned.
Hol. Let me hear a staff, a stanze, a verse: *lege, domine.*   100
Nath. If love make me forsworn, how shall I swear to love?
   Ah! never faith could hold, if not to beauty vow'd;
   Though to myself forsworn, to thee I'll faithful prove:
   Those thoughts to me were oaks, to thee like osiers
     bow'd.
   Study his bias leaves and makes his book thine eyes,
   Where all those pleasures live that art would
     comprehend.   106

100. stanze] *F1,Q2;* stauze *Q1;* stanza *Ff2,3,4.*   102. Ah!] O! *Pilgr.*   103.
faithful] constant *Pilgr.*   104. were] like *Pilgr.*   106. would] can *Pilgr.*

—and gets them wrong. See Chappell's *Popular Music,* pp. 14–15, where the Latin hymn (about 774) for St John Baptist's Day, from which they are taken, will be found. SI for B was not settled till nearly the end of the seventeenth century, and DO replaced UT about the same time, but the French retained UT. See again *Shr.,* III. i. 70–80. Jonson uses this in a transferred sense in *Cynthia's Revels,* II. i: 'your courtier elementary is one but newly entered, or as it were in the alphabet, or ut-re-mi-fa-sol-la of courtship'. Nashe has it where we should say 'ding dong': '*Summer.* Will Sol come before us? *Vertumnus.* Sol, sol; ut, re, mi, fa, sol. Come to church while the bell toll' (for the sake of a quibble) in *Summer's Last Will,* 1592. Holofernes is airing one part of his acquirements; the instruction of children in singing, whether for chapel or theatre, was of the first importance. A schoolmaster was a singing-master.

98. *what, my soul! verses?*] This sounds like a quotation, but its source has not been discovered. Holofernes' excitement, as he at last gets a sight of the letter over Nathaniel's shoulder, is too much for him, and his pose, of being too deeply absorbed in high thoughts to have time for vulgar curiosity, is shattered on the instant.

100. *a staff, a stanze*] equivalent terms. The form 'stanze' occurs in Armin's *Two Maides of Moreclacke* (Grosart, p. 110, 1609). Puttenham says: 'the meetre Heroicall of *Troilus and Cresseid* is very grave and stately, keeping the staffe of seven [lines] and the verse of ten [feet]' (Arber, p. 76); and a little later: '*Staffe* in our vulgare Poesie I know not why it should be so called. . . . The Italian called it *stanza,* as if we should say a resting place . . . a certaine number of verses allowed to go altogether and joyne.' Florio has: '*Stanza* . . . properly a stanzo or stance or stave of eight or six verses'.

101–14. *If love,* etc.] This sonnet was appropriated by William Jaggard in the collection he published in 1599: '*The Passionate Pilgrim,* by W. Shakespeare'. It contains pieces by Barnfield, Bartholomew Griffin, Weelkes, Marlowe, and others besides Shakespeare.

105. *bias*] tendency, bent.
his book thine eyes] See below, IV. iii. 298–300; and *MND.,* II. ii. 126. So in Nashe's *Tragedie of Dido* (McKerrow, ii. 363), 1594: 'His glistering eyes shall be my looking glasse; . . . His lookes shall be my only Librarie.' 'And folly's all they taught me,' adds Thomas Moore.

If knowledge be the mark, to know thee shall suffice;
　Well learned is that tongue that well can thee
　　commend;
All ignorant that soul that sees thee without wonder;
　Which is to me some praise that I thy parts admire.
Thy eye Jove's lightning bears, thy voice his dreadful
　　thunder,　　　　　　　　　　　　　　　　　　　　　111
　Which, not to anger bent, is music and sweet fire.
Celestial as thou art, O! pardon love this wrong,
That sings heaven's praise with such an earthly
　　tongue.

Hol. You find not the apostrophus, and so miss the ac-　115

111. Thy] Thine *Pilgr.*　　bears] seems *Pilgr.*　　113. pardon love this] do not
love that *Pilgr.*　　114. That sings] To sing *Pilgr.;* That sings the *S. Walker conj.*
115. apostrophus] *N.E.D. conj.;* apostraphas *Q1,Ff1,2, Globe;* apostrophas *Q2,
Cambridge;* apostrophes *Ff3,4.*

113. *pardon love this wrong*] wrongly
punctuated in several modern editions
(Rowe, Steevens, etc.) *pardon, love, this
wrong.*

114. *That sings heaven's praise*] The
last line of the canzonet appears to be
a foot short; although Q prints
'singes', and it has been suggested that
this and 'heaven' must each be given
two syllables. Critics have even taken
this possibility of a catch for the un-
wary reader as the ground for an explanation of Holofernes' comment on
the poem, which many have found
puzzling. In his notes on the play in the
Temple edition Sir Israel Gollancz
wrote: 'Does not Holofernes' criticism
bear directly on the last line of the
canzonet? Nathaniel should have
read:—That singës heaven's praise
with such an earthly tongue. It was
usual to mark e's with two dots when
sounded. Holofernes may mean by
"apostrophas", "diaereses".' The editors of the New Cambridge Shakespeare agree: 'Nathaniel should have
said "sing s" and Holofernes should
have said "diaeresis" (*N.E.D.* quotes
the word from Cotgrave, 1611) but
Holofernes blunders as usual, and employs a term which implies contraction

rather than expansion.' But Shakespeare, whose mind was always fixed
on stage effect, could hardly have
planned such a joke, which no one in
the audience would be likely to grasp
without a printed text before him. It is
surely all much simpler: Holofernes,
who has a reputation for learning to
keep up, is bound to find fault with
Nathaniel's reading. Any term, provided it *sounds* learned, will do to con-
found the poor curate, but should not
bluff us into the belief that the sonnet
(or even Nathaniel's reading of it) is
necessarily faulty. The editor of *Pilgr.*,
far from attempting to mend the line,
presents it in a form which no diæresis
can eke out.

115. *apostrophus*] Furness calls Murray's suggestion in the *N.E.D.* 'an
emendatio certissima', but the form
'apostrophes' of F3 would sound just as
technical at this date. There were but
the two forms of the word, *apostrophe* or
apostrophus, meaning the sign (') indi-
cating the omission of one or more
letters. Jonson gives a careful definition
(overlooked in the *N.E.D.*) in *The
Second Book of the English Grammar (ante
1637)*: '*Apostrophus* is the rejecting of a
vowel from the beginning or end of a

cent: let me supervise the canzonet. Here are only
numbers ratified; but, for the elegancy, facility, and
golden cadence of poesy, *caret*. Ovidius Naso was
the man: and why, indeed, *Naso*, but for smelling
out the odoriferous flowers of fancy, the jerks of in-   120
vention? *Imitari* is nothing; so doth the hound his
master, the ape his keeper, the tired horse his rider.
But, damosella virgin, was this directed to you?

116. canzonet] *Theobald;* cangenet *Qq,Ff.*   116–23. Here are . . . to you?]
Spoken by Hol., Theobald; Qq,Ff give to Nath.   120–1. invention? *Imitari*]
Theobald; invention *imitarie Qq,Ff.*   122. tired] tyred *Qq,Ff;* try'd *Theobald;*
'tired *Capell.*

word. The note whereof, though it
many times through the negligence of
writers and printers, is quite omitted,
yet by right . . . hath his mark, which is
such a semi-circle (') placed in the
top.' It is this negligence the pedant
complains of as misleading Nathaniel.
Jonson confirms the reading I give.

116. *supervise*] Again Holofernes
uses a word in its root sense 'look over'.
See note on l. 13 above.

canzonet] T. Morley (1593) is the
earliest use given in the *N.E.D.* of this
term, the present example, I suppose,
being somewhat uncertain. Florio has:
'Canzonetta, a canzonet or dittie.'
Jonson uses the word early: 'I will
have a canzonet made with nothing in
it but Sirrah' (*Cynthia's Revels*, IV. i
[1600]). 'Cangenet' of Q may be
Holofernes' error.

117. *numbers ratified*] verses brought
into proportion or rate. From the context this appears to be the speaker's
meaning.

elegancy] a frequent form of 'ele-
gance'. It occurs in Gabriel Harvey
and Jonson (*Every Man out*, etc.).

facility] fluency. Puttenham advises
'makers' to use 'this or that kind of
figure, according to the facilitie of each
man's utterance' (Arber, p. 304).

118. *cadence*] not elsewhere in Shakespeare. In the sense of rhythmical
measure the term is in Chaucer. Puttenham uses it: 'there can not be in a

maker a fowler fault, then to falsifie his
accent to serve his cadence, or by
untrue orthographie to wrench his
words to helpe his rime . . . such a
maker is not . . . his craft's master'
(p. 94).

119. Naso . . . *for smelling*] Cf. Har-
vey's *Letters* (Grosart, i. 85), 1580:
'Eyed, like to Argus, Earde, like to
Midas, Nosd, like to Naso'.

120–1. *jerks of invention*] strokes or
sallies of wit. A very proper figure for a
schoolmaster's use, since 'jerking' was
equivalent to whipping. In Greene's
Never Too Late (Grosart, viii. 193),
1590, there is a good example: 'if they
have childrens malladies, twere good
to use childrens medicines, and that's a
rod: for be they never so froward, a
jerck or two will make them forward'.
Shakespeare has not 'jerk' again,
although he uses the verb 'yerk'
twice.

122. *the tired horse*] Furness explained
this as dull-spirited, or with the independent spirit broken in him. This
may be so, but the passage he quoted
in support from Gervase Markham's
Masterpeece—the chapter 'Of Tyred
Horses' (the first of two numbered
LXII in the 1703 revised edition)—suggests no such meaning. Markham expressly says that as a technical term
'tired horse' implies one that '*refuseth*
reasonable Labour' and will not obey
his rider.

Jaq. Ay, sir, from one Monsieur Berowne, one of the
strange queen's lords.   125
Hol. I will overglance the superscript. 'To the snow-
white hand of the most beauteous Lady Rosaline.'
I will look again on the intellect of the letter, for the
nomination of the party writing to the person written unto: 'Your ladyship's in all desired employ-   130
ment, Berowne.' Sir Nathaniel, this Berowne is one
of the votaries with the king; and here he hath
framed a letter to a sequent of the stranger queen's,
which, accidentally, or by the way of progression,
hath miscarried. Trip and go, my sweet; deliver   135
this paper into the royal hand of the king; it may

126–31. I will . . . Berowne] *Given to Nath. Qq,Ff.*   129. writing] *Rowe;* written
Qq,Ff.   131. Berowne.' Sir Nathaniel] *See collation at* IV. ii. 126–31; Berowne.
Ped. Sir Holofernes *Qq;* Berowne. *Per.* Sir Holofernes *Ff;* Biron. Sir Nathaniel
Capell.   136. royal] *Q1; not in Ff,Q2.*

124–5. *Berowne . . . queen's lords*] It is
odd that Jaquenetta, who at l. 89
thought her letter came from Armado,
now knows it is Berowne's; odder that
she takes him for one of the *Princess's*
suite. Dover Wilson reads 'Boyet' and
assumes an original intrigue lost in
revision; the blunder may be more
simply put down to 'pure ignorance'
on the part of the author.

126. *superscript*] superscription, address. See Greene's *Third Parte of
Conney-catching* (Grosart, x. 150): 'and
sewed an old card upon it, whereupon
he wrote a superscription unto the
Maister of the Maide, and at what
signe it was to be delivered'. See note
at IV. i. 58.

128. *intellect*] intelligence conveyed
or meaning. Furness quotes from
Baynes (*Shakespeare Studies*) a reference
to Wilson's *Arte of Rhetorique* where the
figure *Synecdoche* (Puttenham's 'Figure
of quick conceite') is rendered by
'intellection'. The writer parallels
Holofernes' use of 'superscript' above
for 'superscription', and suggests
this as the source of his far-fetched
term.

129. *party*] person. Several times in

Shakespeare. Cf. Lodge, *Euphues
Golden Legacie* (*Shakes. Lib.* 1875, p. 52):
'the party beloved is froward, and
having curtsie in her lookes, holdeth
disdaine in her tongues ende.'

133. *sequent*] follower.

135. *Trip and go*] Chappell says this
was 'one of the favourite Morris-
dances of the sixteenth and seventeenth centuries'. The expression became proverbial and is often made use
of. 'O how she scudded! O sweet scud
how she tripped! O delicate trip and
go!' (Jonson, *The Case is Altered*, IV. iv
[1598]); and in Nashe's *Summer's Last
Will* (McKerrow, iii. 240), 1592, a
morris-dance is introduced, with
'three clowns and three maids singing
this song, dancing': 'Trip and goe,
heave and hoe, Up and downe, to and
fro. . . . A Maying, a playing; Love
hath no gainsaying, So merrily trip
and goe.' Chappell gives the music.
Nashe refers to it again in *Foure Letters
Confuted* (McKerrow, i. 276), in the
same manner as Holofernes does:
'Thou shalt not breath a whit, trip and
goe.' See also Gosson, *Schoole of Abuse*
(Arber, p. 25), 1579: 'Trip and goe, for
I dare not tarry.'

concern much. Stay not thy compliment; I forgive
thy duty: adieu.

Jaq. Good Costard, go with me. Sir, God save your life!

Cost. Have with thee, my girl.   [*Exeunt Costard and Jaquenetta.*

Nath. Sir, you have done this in the fear of God, very   141
religiously; and, as a certain father saith,—

Hol. Sir, tell not me of the father; I do fear colourable
colours. But to return to the verses: did they please
you, Sir Nathaniel?   145

Nath. Marvellous well for the pen.

Hol. I do dine to-day at the father's of a certain pupil of
mine; where, if (before repast) it shall please you
to gratify the table with a grace, I will, on my privi-
lege I have with the parents of the foresaid child or   150
pupil, undertake your *ben venuto*; where I will prove
those verses to be very unlearned, neither savouring
of poetry, wit, nor invention. I beseech your society.

Nath. And thank you too; for society, saith the text, is
the happiness of life.   155

Hol. And, certes, the text most infallibly concludes it.

---

137. compliment] complement *Qq,Ff*.   148. before] *Q1;* being *Ff,Q2, Hart*.
151. ben venuto] Rowe; bien venuto *Q1, Ff2,3,4;* bien vonuto *F1,Q2*.

138. *duty*] She is excused a curtsy.
For 'compliment' see note on I. i.
167.

143-4. *colourable colours*] plausible
pretexts. The substantive is common,
but the adjective not elsewhere in
Shakespeare. It is used in the same
sense in Sidney's *Arcadia*, bk ii: 'If my
soul could have been polluted with
treachery, it would likewise have
provided for itself colourable answers.' Holofernes is quibbling on the
stock phrase 'I fear no colours.' On
its occurrence in *Tw.N.*, I. v. 6, this
is said by Maria to be a saying
'born in the wars'. Presumably
it means 'I do not fear the enemy's
standards,' and so 'I fear no foe.'

146. *Marvellous well for the pen*] See
below, v. ii. 39, 40. Lodge has the same
retort in *Euphues Golden Legacie* (*Shakes.
Lib.*, 1875, p. 80), 1590: 'How like you

this sonnet? quoth Rosader. Marry,
quoth Ganimede, for the pen well, for
the passion ill.'

148. (*before repast*)] As Dover Wilson
points out, Holofernes takes care to
emphasize that he is offering a free
dinner, not merely the honour of saying grace and hearing the conversation
after it.

151. *undertake your* ben venuto] act as
your sponsor, introduce you to the
host, and ensure your welcome. Hor-
tensio makes the same promise to
Petruchio at the end of the first act of
Shr. The French form *bien venue* was
anglicized much earlier, and occurs in
Peele and Nashe.

154. *saith the text*] The text has not
yet been identified. A similar passage
occurs in *Damon and Pithias* (Hazlitt's
Dodsley, iv. 8): ' "*Amicitia inter bonos*",
saith a learned man.'

[*To Dull*] Sir, I do invite you too: you shall not say
me nay: *pauca verba*. Away! the gentles are at their
game, and we will to our recreation.   [*Exeunt.*

SCENE III

Enter BEROWNE, *with a paper.*

Ber. The king he is hunting the deer; I am coursing myself: they have pitched a toil; I am toiling in a pitch,
—pitch that defiles: defile! a foul word. Well, set
thee down, sorrow! for so they say the fool said, and
so say I, and I the fool: well proved, wit! By the Lord,   5
this love is as mad as Ajax: it kills sheep, it kills me,

Scene III

3. set] *Qq,Ff*; sit *Hanmer*.

158. pauca verba] Nym has 'pauca,
pauca', in *Wiv.*, I. i. 123. No use earlier
than the present is known, the next
being Jonson's *Every Man in his
Humour*, 1598, where it is labelled 'the
bencher's phrase' (IV. i. 40).

Scene III

2. *pitched a toil*] set a snare. 'The
hay's a pitching' [hay=rabbit-net]
(Jonson, *Alchemist*, II. i). Jonson in his
translation of Horace ('*Beatus ille*',
etc. [Odes, v. ii]) has: 'Or hence, or
thence, he drives with many a hound
Wild boars into his toils pitched
round' (*ante* 1619). And Beaumont and
Fletcher's *Woman's Prize*, IV. iv: 'How
daintily and cunningly you drive me
up like a deer to the toil.' 'The Master
of the Toyles and Tents' is an office at
Court mentioned in Powell's *Plaine
Pathway to Preferment* (New Shakes.
Soc., p. 168). And in an *Account of the
Queen's Purse from 1559 to 1569*
(Nichol's *Progresses* [1823], i. 269),
'The Toyle' appears amongst necessary charges for the queen's horses and
deer: 'maiking and fynishing 75
clothes for the Toyle'.

toiling in a pitch] Is not Berowne re-
calling the deep black of Rosaline's
eyes to which he refers as 'two pitch-
balls'? (III. i. 192) (Furness). Jonson
said 'alluding to lady Rosaline's complexion, who is through the whole play
represented as a black beauty', although we are distinctly told (III. i.
191) she was a 'whitely wanton'
(with snow-white hands). Berowne
shows at once (ll. 9, 10) it is her
eyes he means. He is careful to
correct 'her eye' (a pitch) to 'her
two eyes'.

3–4. *set thee down, sorrow!*] Costard's
remark at I. i. 305–6.

6. *love is as mad as Ajax: it kills
sheep*] 'so it kills me' is added by
Thomas Fuller, M.D., in his *Gnomologia*, 1732 (No. 3287). See again note
at 'He's a god', v. ii. 636; and at l. 87
of this scene.

mad as Ajax: it kills sheep] This occurs
again in *2H6*, v. i. 26: 'like Ajax Tela-
monius, On sheep or oxen could I
spend my fury'. There were at least
two plays concerning Ajax acted, one
at Court and one at Cambridge, before
this time.

I a sheep: well proved again o' my side! I will not
love; if I do, hang me; i' faith, I will not. O! but her
eye,—by this light, but for her eye, I would not love
her; yes, for her two eyes. Well, I do nothing in the   10
world but lie, and lie in my throat. By heaven, I do
love, and it hath taught me to rhyme, and to be
melancholy; and here is part of my rhyme, and here
my melancholy. Well, she hath one o' my sonnets
already: the clown bore it, the fool sent it, and the   15
lady hath it: sweet clown, sweeter fool, sweetest lady!
By the world, I would not care a pin if the other three
were in. Here comes one with a paper: God give him
grace to groan!   [*Stands aside.*

Enter the KING, *with a paper.*

King. Ay me!   20
Ber. Shot, by heaven! Proceed, sweet Cupid: thou hast
   thumped him with thy bird-bolt under the left pap.
   In faith, secrets!

---

13. melancholy] mallichollie *Qq,Ff.*   19. [*Stands aside*] *Gets up into a tree*
Capell.

---

11. *lie in my throat*] occurs several
times in Shakespeare, e.g. *2H4*, I. ii. 93,
Oth., IV. iv. 13. A very deep lie.
Berowne refers here to the perjury of
his loving. A lie, not of the tongue or
lips, but coming from the heart. Sidney
has it: 'Thou lyest in thy throate (said
Zelmarie)' (Feuillerat, i. 506), *ante*
1586, and Gabriel Harvey, *Three
Proper Letters* (Grosart, ii. 73) *ante* 1580:
'Out lyar out, thou lyest abhominably
in thy throat.'

16. *sweet . . . sweeter . . . sweetest*] See
note at I. ii. 157–9.

17. *By the world*] used twice by
Armado, V. i. 93–4 and 97; and *Shr.*,
II. i. 161.

22. *thumped*] Greene has 'fro mine
eyes I gave her such a thump on the
brest that she would scarce say no'
(*Never Too Late* [Grosart, viii. 198]).

bird-bolt] a kind of blunt-headed
arrow used for shooting birds with.

Steevens says in a note to *Ado*, I. i:
'Such are to this day in use to kill
rooks with, shot from a cross-bow'.
Marston has 'gross-knobbed birdbolt'
in *What You Will*. Playfully applied to
Cupid's arrows, which are presumably
of the sharpest and most piercing
description, probably because used by
a boy. Nares refers to Cooke's *Greene's
Tu Quoque*, and Steevens to Shirley's *Love in a Maze*. Often spelt
'burbolt'.

left pap] Cf. *MND.*, V. i. 305: 'left
pap Where heart doth hop'. And see
The Shepherdess Felismena (from B.
Yonge's translation of Montemayor's
Diana) (*Shakes. Lib.*, 1875, p. 306), *ante*
1598: 'But Felismena helped him out
of that trouble, by putting another
arrow into her bow, the which trans-
piercing his armour, she left under his
left pap, and so iustly smote his heart
that this knight also followed his tow

King [*Reads.*]

　　So sweet a kiss the golden sun gives not
　　　　To those fresh morning drops upon the rose,　　25
　　As thy eye-beams when their fresh rays have smote
　　　　The night of dew that on my cheeks down flows:
　　Nor shines the silver moon one half so bright
　　　　Through the transparent bosom of the deep,
　　As doth thy face through tears of mine give light　　30
　　　　Thou shin'st in every tear that I do weep:
　　No drop but as a coach doth carry thee;
　　　　So ridest thou triumphing in my woe.
　　Do but behold the tears that swell in me,
　　　　And they thy glory through my grief will show:　　35
　　But do not love thyself; then thou will keep
　　My tears for glasses, and still make me weep.
　　O queen of queens! how far dost thou excel,
　　No thought can think, nor tongue of mortal tell.

　　How shall she know my griefs? I'll drop the paper:　　40
　　Sweet leaves, shade folly. Who is he comes here?

　　　　　　　　　　　　　　　　　　　　[*Steps aside.*

　　What, Longaville! and reading! listen, ear.

Enter LONGAVILLE, *with several papers.*

Ber. Now, in thy likeness, one more fool appear!

26. smote] smot *Qq,Ff.*　　27. night of dew] *Qq,Ff;* dew of night *Singer.*　　36.
will] *Q1;* wilt *Ff.*

companions.' The expression is also in
Speed's *History of Great Britain* (ed.
1632), at the year 1585: 'Henry Percy,
Earle of Northumberland . . . being
upon suspicion of treason committed
to the Tower of London, he laid violent
hands upon his owne life, by dis-
charging a Dag, charged with three
bullets, under his left pappe, wherewith he pierced his heart.'

24. *kiss the golden sun*] Cf. *Sonn.*,
xxxiii: 'a glorious morning . . . kissing
with golden face', etc. For the connection between this play and the *Sonn.*
see Intro., 3.21.

27. *night of dew*] night's allowance of

tears; or tears as many as there are
drops of dew produced in a night.

32. *coach*] See below, l. 152.

43. *in thy likeness . . . appear*] in thy
shape, thyself. Cf. *Rom.*, II. i. 21, and
Tp., III. ii. 138. Dekker uses this expression very violently to our ears, meaning in person, in the flesh: 'At last the
wise Gentleman appeared in his like-
nesse: Are you the Constable saies the
player; yes that I am for fault of a
better, quoth he' (*Iests to make you
Merrie* [Grosart, ii. 279], 1607); 'No
sooner were their backes turned, but I
that all this while had stood in a corner
(like a watching candle) appeared in

Long. Ay me! I am forsworn.
Ber. Why, he comes in like a perjure, wearing papers.   45
King. In love, I hope: sweet fellowship in shame!
Ber. One drunkard loves another of the name.
Long. Am I the first that have been perjur'd so?
Ber. I could put thee in comfort: not by two that I know.
      Thou mak'st the triumviry, the corner-cap of society,   50
      The shape of love's Tyburn, that hangs up simplicity.
Long. I fear these stubborn lines lack power to move.
      O sweet Maria, empress of my love!
      These numbers will I tear, and write in prose.

45. perjure] perjured *F2*.   46. *King.*] *Rowe; Long Q1.*   50. triumviry] *Rowe (ed. 2); triumphery Qq, Ff1,2; triumphry Ff3,4; triumvirate Rowe (ed. 1).*

my likeness' (*Belman of London* [Grosart, iii. 91], 1608). See also *Martins Months Minde* (Grosart's Nashe, i. 173), 1589: 'Martin dares not land in his likenes at Lambeth staiers.'

45. *perjure*] perjurer. 'But now blackspotted Perjure as he is, He takes a truce with Elnor's damned brat' (*Troublesome Raigne of King John*, pt i [*Shakes. Lib.*, 1875, p. 351], 1591).

wearing papers] 'To sette openly with a paper on his hed to be mocked in perjury for forging of evidences, or such like. *Catamidio*' (J. Rider, *Bibliotheca Scholastica*, 1589). And cf. Chettle, *Kind-Hartes Dreame* (Bodley Head Quarto, p. 54), 1592: 'an odd Atturney, was not long since disgraded of his place by pitching over the Barre, yet promoted to looke out of a wodden window, cut after the Dove hole fashion, with a paper on his suttle pate, containing the iugling before shewed.' Steevens gives references to Holinshed (p. 838 [1587]), which ascribes the penance to Cardinal Wolsey's invention, and to *Leicester's Commonwealth*. In Harrison's *England* the punishment was the pillory and the letter P branded in the forehead. Longaville has presumably a spare sonnet tucked into his hatband.

50. *corner-cap*] Was the college-cap or mortar-board ever three-cornered?

In the *Queen's Entertainment*, 1591, Nereus is described as 'having a cornerd cappe on his curled heade', and the picture shows it to be square (Nichol's *Progresses*, iii. 101, 110). The corner-cap is mentioned in *New Custom* (Hazlitt's *Dodsley*, iii. 11), *ante* 1573, cited in *N.E.D.*, Furness quotes from Stubbes's *Anatomie of Abuses* (New Shakes. Soc., p. 69), 1583: 'Cappes with three hornes, three corners I should saie, like the forked cappes of Popishe Priestes'. As the emblem of the Bishops, it was more commonly referred to, by both Marprelate and his opponents, as 'cater-cap' which, with its derivation from 'quatre', plainly implies *four* corners.

51. *The shape of . . . Tyburn*] References to the triangular shape of the gallows are abundant, and cuts of this form of gibbet are frequent, as in Holinshed's *Chronicle* (Halliwell). The 'tripple tree' is a name for the gallows in Harman's *Caveat*. Others were—three trees, tripple trestle, ride the three-legged mare, the three foote crosse (Chettle); three-cornered tree (N. Breton). Dekker has a parallel allusion: 'Well, suppose the sessions past, our dreamer awake, and caried in a cart to have a corner of Doctor Stories cap' (*Iests to make you Merrie* [Grosart, ii. 309], 1607). Doctor Story was a 'Romish canonical Doctor' who

Ber. O! rhymes are guards on wanton Cupid's hose :   55
   Disfigure not his shop.

Long.   This same shall go. [*Reads the Sonnet*

   Did not the heavenly rhetoric of thine eye,
      'Gainst whom the world cannot hold argument,
   Persuade my heart to this false perjury?
   Vows for thee broke deserve not punishment.   60
   A woman I forswore; but I will prove,
      Thou being a goddess, I forswore not thee :
   My vow was earthly, thou a heavenly love;
      Thy grace being gain'd cures all disgrace in me.
   Vows are but breath, and breath a vapour is :   65
      Then thou, fair sun, which on my earth dost shine,
   Exhal'st this vapour-vow; in thee it is :
      If broken then, it is no fault of mine :
   If by me broke, what fool is not so wise
      To lose an oath to win a paradise?   70

Ber. This is the liver vein, which makes flesh a deity;
   A green goose a goddess; pure, pure idolatry.
   God amend us, God amend! we are much out o' th' way.

---

56. shop] *Qq,Ff;* slop *Theobald;* shape *Collier MS.*   58. cannot] could not *Pilgr.*
60. deserve] deserves *Q2.*   63. earthly] earthy *Ff3,4.*   65. Vows are but
breath] My vow was breath *Pilgr.*   67. which on my earth dost] that on this
earth doth *Pilgr.*   67. Exhal'st] Exhale *Pilgr.*   70. lose] break *Pilgr.*
72. idolatry] ydotarie *Q1.*

was hanged at Tyburn for high treason
(1 June 1571). His cap became proverbial.

55. *guards*] embroideries.

56. *shop*] I follow Dover Wilson in
retaining the Q reading, which makes
sense (the organ of generation, and
hence codpiece). See note on III. i.
179).

57. *Did not*, etc.] This sonnet is in
Pilgr. See note above, IV. ii. 101.

64. *grace*] favour.

67. *Exhal'st*] Exhale, 'of the sun
drawing up vapours and thus causing
meteors' (Schmidt), is used several
times by Shakespeare, as in *Lucr.*,
779; *1H4*, v. i. 19; *Rom.*, III. v. 13.
To absorb. So in *The Troublesome
Raigne of King John* (Hazlitt's *Shakes.
Lib.*, p. 301): 'And when their

vertue is exhaled drie, I'll hang them.'

70. *lose*] The Q spelling *loose* was
used for either meaning.

71. *liver vein*] vein or style of love.
The liver was held to be the seat of
passionate love. 'In Aprile and May,
the liuer veine must be lette bloudde'
(Paynel, *Salarnes Regim.*, 1538
[*N.E.D.*]). See *Wiv.*, II. i. 121; *Ado*,
IV. i. 233; *AYL.*, III. ii. 449. Dowden
noted the following: 'But when the
whole body aboundeth with melan-
cholike bloud, it is best to begin the
cure with letting of bloud, and you
must cut the liver vaine on the arme'
(Philip Barrough, *The Method of
Physick*, lib. i, ch. xxviii, p. 46 [1590]).

72. *green goose*] See note I. i. 97.

73. *out o' the way*] gone wrong. Cf.
Oth., I. iii. 365.

Long. By whom shall I send this?—Company! stay.

[*Steps aside.*

Ber. All hid, all hid; an old infant play.   75
    Like a demi-god here sit I in the sky,
    And wretched fools' secrets heedfully o'er-eye.
    More sacks to the mill! O heavens! I have my wish:

Enter DUMAIN, *with a paper.*

    Dumain transform'd: four woodcocks in a dish!
Dum. O most divine Kate!   80
Ber. O most profane coxcomb!
Dum. By heaven, the wonder in a mortal eye!
Ber. By earth, she is not, corporal; there you lie.
Dum. Her amber hairs for foul have amber quoted.
Ber. An amber-coloured raven was well noted.   85
Dum. As upright as the cedar.
Ber.   Stoop, I say;

78. S.D. *Enter . . . paper*] *Dyce.*   82. in] *Q1;* of *Ff,Q2.*   83. not, corporal] but
corporal *Theobald.*   86. Stoop] *Qq,Ff;* —stoup *New.*

75. *All hid*] '*Cline-mucette:* The game
called Hodman-blind; Harry-racket;
or are you all-hid' (Cotgrave, 1611). It
is mentioned in Jonson's *Epicene,* iv. ii:
'*Truewit* [*binds his eyes*]. Come, sir
[*leads him forward*]. All-hid, Sir John!'
Truewit is here master of the ceremonies and arranging a sport for
others to play at. Berowne is in the
same position of supervisor.

78. *More sacks to the mill*] plenty of
drudgery to do; lots more to come. A
proverbial expression. Cf. Skelton,
Why Come Ye not to Courte? (Dyce, ii.
30): 'Good reason and good skyll,
They may garlycke pyll, Cary sackes
to the myll, Or pescoddes they may
shyll, Or elles go rost a stone: Ther is
no man but one That hathe the strokes
alone'; and *Pasquil's Apologie* (Mc-
Kerrow's *Nashe,* i. 123), 1590: 'To the
next, to the next, more sacks to the
Myll'.

79. *woodcocks*] simpletons. The word
was in common use for a fool from
Stephen Gosson (1579) down to
Motteux's *Rabelais* (1708); it is a

favourite of both Jonson and Shakespeare. The bird had not the wit to
keep its neck out of the noose. 'Snipe'
was often used in the same sense. Cf.
especially Heywood's parallel, 'two
snights to a dish' (*Fair Maid of the
Exchange* [Pearson, p. 69]).

83. *she is not, corporal*] a much disputed passage. Many editors follow
Theobald, 'she is but corporal', using
'corporal' in the sense of corporeal as
elsewhere in Shakespeare. Berowne,
however, has already applied the
name ('corporal of his field', III. i. 182)
to himself when he discovered he was
in love. And why not now to Dumain?
Berowne means to contradict Dumain
emphatically; it is Rosaline, not Kate,
who is the wonder.

85. *raven*] as a type of foul (fowl), in
opposition to fair or amber.

86. *Stoop*] Berowne merely contra-
dicts Dumain's 'upright', concisely
and ungrammatically. 'Stoop' signified a bow or to bow. Cf. *H5,* v. ii. 168:
'a straight back will stoop'; and
Nashe, *The Unfortunate Traveller* (Mc-

Her shoulder is with child.

Dum.   As fair as day.

Ber. Ay, as some days; but then no sun must shine.

Dum. O! that I had my wish.

Long.   And I had mine!

King. And I mine too, good Lord!   90

Ber. Amen, so I had mine. Is not that a good word?

Dum. I would forget her; but a fever she

    Reigns in my blood, and will remember'd be.

Ber. A fever in your blood! why, then incision

    Would let her out in saucers: sweet misprision!   95

Dum. Once more I'll read the ode that I have writ.

Ber. Once more I'll mark how love can vary wit.

Dum. [*reads his sonnet*].

        On a day, alack the day!

        Love, whose month is ever May,

91. I] *Johnson; not in Qq,Ff.*   96. ode] Odo *Q1 (Devon copy).*   98. [*reads his sonnet*] *Qq,Ff.*   99. month is ever May] *Q1;* month was ever May *E.H.;* month is every May *Ff,Q2.*

Kerrow, ii. 222): 'all feare you, love you, stoup to you. Therefore, good sir, be ruld by mee, stoup your fortune so low, as to', etc. Berowne's word implies an injunction to Dumain to come down from his stately images.

87. *shoulder . . . child*] The worthy Thomas Fuller, M.D. (not Thomas Fuller, D.D., of *The Worthies*), has this vulgarism in his *Gnomologia*, No. 2493. He had evidently the good sense to study Shakespeare when making his collection. See note above at 'Ajax', l. 6.

91. *Is not that a good word*] Is not that kind of me? 'Good word' is commonly used meaning an expression of kindness in Shakespeare.

94. *incision*] blood-letting. A favourite word with Shakespeare in this sense. Nashe speaks of a doctor's 'incision-knife' (lancet) in *The Unfortunate Traveller* (McKerrow, ii. 306); and see *Captain Smith* (Arber, p. 74), 1607-9: 'to scarifie or make incision, their best instruments are some splinted stone'.

95. *saucers*] Furness quotes here from Halliwell: 'The practise of bleeding in fevers was very common in Shakespeare's time, and it was not unusual for the barber-chirurgions to exhibit their saucers with blood in them as signs of their profession. . . .' Amongst the MSS. of the Company of Barbers in London is the following order under the date 1606: 'Item, it is ordeyned that no person usinge flebothomy or bloudlettinge within London . . . shall at any tyme hereafter set to open shewe any (of) his or their porrengers, saucers, or measures with bloud, upon peyne to forfeyt', etc. These saucers seem to be of the rarest mention; perhaps the custom of exhibiting them was short-lived. 'Bleeding basin' was the accepted name a little later for the vessel used to receive the blood.

98. *On a day,* etc.] This poem is in *Pilgr.* See note above, IV. ii. 101. It is also in *E.H.,* 1600. There is a pretty little pastoral poem of twenty-six lines, by Nicholas Breton, in *The*

Spied a blossom passing fair   100
Playing in the wanton air:
Through the velvet leaves the wind,
All unseen can passage find;
That the lover, sick to death,
Wish'd himself the heaven's breath.   105
Air, quoth he, thy cheeks may blow;
Air, would I might triumph so!
But alack! my hand is sworn
Ne'er to pluck thee from thy thorn:
Vow, alack! for youth unmeet,   110
Youth so apt to pluck a sweet.
Do not call it sin in me,
That I am forsworn for thee;
Thou for whom Jove would swear
Juno but an Ethiop were;   115
And deny himself for Jove,
Turning mortal for thy love.

This will I send, and something else more plain,
That shall express my true love's fasting pain.
O! would the king, Berowne, and Longaville,   120
Were lovers too. Ill, to example ill,
Would from my forehead wipe a perjur'd note;
For none offend where all alike do dote.
Long. [*advancing*]. Dumain, thy love is far from charity,

102. velvet leaves the] Velvet, leaves the *Qq,Ff1,2,3;* velvet leaves, the *F4.*
103. can] 'gan *Theobald;* gan *Pilgr. and E.H.*   104. lover] shepheard *E.H.*
105. Wish'd] *Ff2,3,4, Pilgr.;* Wish *Qq,F1.*   108. alack] alas *Pilgr. and E.H.*
is] hath *Pilgr. and E.H.*   109. thorn] *E.H., Rowe (ed. 2);* throne *Qq,Ff, Pilgr.*
112-13. Do . . . thee] *not in Pilgr. and E.H.*   114. whom Jove] whom ev'n Jove
Rowe (ed. 2) et seq.   119. fasting] fest'ring *Theobald conj.;* lasting *Capell.*

Queen's Entertainment at the Earl of Hertford's, 1591 (Nichols's *Progresses,* iii. 117), which bears a family likeness to this piece. It begins: 'In the merrie moneth of May, In a morne by breake of day, Forth I walked', etc. And compare with these two the song in *Pilgr.,* by Richard Barnfield (1595), beginning 'As it fell upon a day, In the merrie month of May, Sitting in a pleasant shade', etc. (Oxford Book of English Verse, no. 203).

115. *Ethiop*] blackamoor; as a type of ugliness. See *Ado,* v. iv. 38. Jonson uses this form as a noun, Nashe as an adjective. 'It is a dowry, Me thinkes should make that sun-burnt proverbe false, *And wash the Ethiop white*' (Webster, *White Devil* [Lucas, i. 179]).

119. *fasting*] hungry, 'hunger-starved', pain of abstinence.

122. *perjur'd note*] See notes at 'perjure' and 'wearing papers', l. 45 above.

That in love's grief desir'st society: 125
You may look pale, but I should blush, I know,
To be o'erheard and taken napping so.
King [*advancing*]. Come, sir, you blush; as his your case is such;
You chide at him, offending twice as much:
You do not love Maria! Longaville   130
Did never sonnet for her sake compile,
Nor never lay his wreathed arms athwart
His loving bosom to keep down his heart.
I have been closely shrouded in this bush,
And mark'd you both, and for you both did blush.   135
I heard your guilty rhymes, observed your fashion,
Saw sighs reek from you, noted well your passion:
Ay me! says one: O Jove! the other cries;
One, her hairs were gold, crystal the other's eyes:
You would for paradise break faith and troth;   140
                                                    [*to Long.*]
And Jove, for your love would infringe an oath.
                                                    [*to Dum.*]
What will Berowne say when that he shall hear

127. o'er-heard] ore-hard *Q1*.   128. you blush] do, blush *Capell conj.;* blush
you *Collier MS.;* your blush *S. Walker conj,*   130. Maria!] Maria? *Qq,Ff1,2;*
Maria, *Ff3,4;* Maria; *Cambridge.*   139. One, her] *Q1;* On her *F1,Q2;* Her
Ff2,3,4; One's *S. Walker conj.*   140, 141. [*to Long.*], [*to Dum.*]] *Johnson.*

125. *grief desir'st society*] referring to
the commonly used proverb 'Solamen
miseris socios habuisse dolores'; or as
Chaucer writes: 'Men seyn, to
wrecche is consolacioun, To have
another felawe in his peyne.'

127. *taken napping*] Oliphant (*New
English*) says this occurs in Bishop
Pilkington's *Sermons* (Parker Society)
about 1560. Harington (*Orlando Furioso*, xxxix. 58) has 'At last he said, as
erst Sileno said, To those that took him
napping in the cave'. 'Taken napping
as Moss caught his mare' was a common version, arising out of the title of
a ballad (1569, 1570), according to
Hazlitt. See Cotgrave in v. *Desprouven.*
In Ebbsworth's notes to *Westminster
Drollery* it appears that the mare was
caught up a tree. How unlucky it is
that the words are not addressed to

Berowne, where Capell placed him
(l. 19).

132. *wreathed arms*] See III. i. 176,
'folded arms', and again, 'arms
crossed', III. i. 16.

137. *sighs reek from you*] 'love is a
smoke made with the fume of sighs'
(*Rom.*, I. i. 196).

140. *faith and troth*] so in Lodge's
Euphues Golden Legacie (*Shakes. Lib.*,
1875, p. 113), 1590: 'we know fewe
subtilties, and litle eloquence for
that we lightly account of flattery:
onely faith and troth thats shepheards
wooing.' And in Nicholas Breton's *In
the Merrie Moneth of May* (Nichols's
Progresses of Queen Elizabeth [1823], iii.
117): 'Thus with many a pretie Oath,
Yea and nay and faith and troth Such
as silly shepheards use, When they
will not love abuse' (1591).

A faith infringed, which such zeal did swear?
How will he scorn! how will he spend his wit!
How will he triumph, leap, and laugh at it!   145
For all the wealth that ever I did see,
I would not have him know so much by me.
Ber. Now step I forth to whip hypocrisy.   [*Advancing.*
Ah! good my liege, I pray thee, pardon me:
Good heart! what grace hast thou, thus to reprove   150
These worms for loving, that art most in love?
Your eyes do make no coaches; in your tears
There is no certain princess that appears:
You'll not be perjur'd, 'tis a hateful thing:
Tush! none but minstrels like of sonneting.   155
But are you not asham'd? nay, are you not,
All three of you, to be thus much o'ershot?
You found his mote; the king your mote did see;

143. A faith] *Ff2,3,4;* Faith *Qq,F1;* Of faith, Faith so, Such faith, Faiths *various conj.* zeal] a zeal *F2.* 145. leap] geap *Warburton.* 146. I] eye *Capell conj.* 148. [*Advancing*] *Coming from his tree Capell.* 152. coaches; in] *Hanmer;* couches in *Qq,Ff;* coaches in *Rowe (ed. 2).* 158. mote . . . mote] *Rowe;* moth . . . moth *Qq,Ff.*

145. *leap, and laugh at it*] 'That heavy Saturn laugh'd and leap'd with him' (*Sonn.*, xcviii). 'We should certainly read *geap,* i.e. jeer, ridicule' (Warburton). Warburton, who 'wrote for Warburton and not for Shakespeare', meant 'jape'. Jonson has 'To sit and clap my hands, and laugh and leap, knocking my head against my roof with joy' (*Every Man out of his Humour,* i. 1). Cf. below, v. ii. 291.

147. *by me*] concerning me. Cf. *Mer.V.,* i. ii. 60: 'How say you by the French lord?'; and 1 Cor., 4.

151. *worms*] here applied to lovers, as in *Tp.,* iii. i. 31. Cf. Lyly, *Campaspe,* v. 4: 'Two loving wormes'; and *Mother Bombie,* ii. 2: 'the loving worme my daughter'.

152. *coaches*] referring to the King's sonnet above, l. 32. Rowe (ed. 2, 1714) first corrected the misreading 'couches', according to Furness, and was followed by Pope, etc. The same

misprint occurs in *Euphues Golden Legacie* (by Lodge), 1590 (*Shakes. Lib.,* 1875, p. 131), where the text reads: 'No sooner did Phoebus Henchman appear in the skie, to give warning that his maisters horses should be trapt in his glorious couch'.

155. *sonneting*] For this contemptuous reference to 'sonneting' see *Gent.,* iii. ii. 68, and *Rom.,* ii. iv. 41–4. The word 'sonnet' had originally a musical connotation—hence 'minstrels'. Byrd published more than one set of 'Psalms, Songs and Sonnets'.

157. *o'ershot*] astray in your aim; gone wrong, as in 'out of the way' above, l. 73. Cf. *Cæs.,* iii. ii. 155; and Jonson, *Silent Woman,* iv. ii: 'You shall not overshoot yourself to send him that word by me.' See *N.E.D.* (*overshoot*) for a minute analysis of the general sense, 'fall into error'.

158. *mote*] There is constant confusion between the words *moth* and

But I a beam do find in each of three.
O! what a scene of foolery have I seen,   160
Of sighs, of groans, of sorrow, and of teen;
O! me with what strict patience have I sat,
To see a king transformed to a gnat;
To see a great Hercules whipping a gig,

163. gnat] knot *Theobald;* sot *Johnson conj.*

mote. See *Oth.*, I. iii. 257 and *Per.*, IV. iv. 21. Apparently they were often used synonymously and spelt at haphazard. Cf. *John*, IV. i. 92. 'Mote', in our sense, was spelt 'moth', as it is twice in this line in the old editions; and 'moth' seems to have been pronounced 'mote'. R. G. White and Ellis agree that 'Moth' (the name) was pronounced 'Mote'; but the probability is it was unfixed. There is here an undoubted allusion to the figure of the mote and the beam (Matt., vii. 3–5; Luke, vi. 41–2); cf. 'festu (straw) or a litil mote' and 'festu other a mot' (Wyclif). But where is the line to be drawn in the quibbling between moth and mote, beam of the sun and chip or fescue of wood? It may not have been in Wyclif, but it is in the A.V.; and as 'Rabbi Zeal-of-the-Land Busy, a Banbury man', says in his confusion: 'that remains, as I may say, a beam, a very beam, not a beam of the sun, not a beam of the moon, nor a beam of the balance, neither a house-beam, nor a weaver's beam, but a beam in the eye, in the eye of the brethren, a very great beam, an exceeding great beam' (Jonson, *Bartholomew Fair*, v. iii).

161. *teen*] grief. A common word from Chaucer downwards, especially with rhymers. See *Tp.*, I. ii. 64. In *Rom.*, I. iii. 13, it is used non-rhymingly for the sake of a 'vile pun'.

163. *gnat*] an insignificant insect; a 'worm'. The editors have searched for a further meaning here, and to assist them have imagined that the text needed alteration; 'knot', 'sot', and 'quat' having been proposed or adopted. Hart thought 'gnat' was suggested by the moth above, and (like

'coaches') by the eye-beams that smote the King's cheek in his sonnet. The King is a gnat playing, like the other moths or motes, in the beams of love. Jonson has the same expression: 'They that before, like gnats, played in his beams, And thronged to circumscribe him, now not seen' (*Sejanus*, v. 10 [1603]). There is no commoner simile from Chaucer downwards than 'as thick as motes in the sun-beam'. But it is the later emblem or proverb of the moth or gnat singeing in the flames that illuminates this passage. Whitney's emblem, *In amore tormentum* (edited H. Green, p. 219), 1586, gives the King's position: 'Even as the gnattes, that flie into the blaze, Doe burne their wings and fall into the fire; So, those too muche on gallant showes that gaze, Are captives caught and burne in their desire.'

164, 165, 166, 167. *Hercules, Solomon, Nestor, Timon*] Cf. Webster, *White Devil* (ed. F. L. Lucas, i. 187): '*Flamineo.* Whither shall I go now? O Lucian thy ridiculous purgatory— to finde Alexander the great cobling shooes, Pompey tagging points, and Julius Caesar making haire buttons, Haniball selling blacking, and Augustus crying garlike', etc. And see Rabelais, ii. 30.

164. *whipping a gig*] whipping a top. See v. i. 60. Gabriel Harvey uses the word: 'I may chance rattle him like a baby of parchment, or kneade him like a cake of dowe, or chearne him like a dish of butter, or girke him like a hobling gig' (*New Letter* [Grosart, i. 283]). 'Whirligig' preserves this word. According to Halliwell, a gig was a special kind of top. He says: 'It is

And profound Solomon to tune a jig,   165
And Nestor play at push-pin with the boys,
And critic Timon laugh at idle toys!
Where lies thy grief? O! tell me, good Dumain,
And, gentle Longaville, where lies thy pain?
And where my liege's? all about the breast: 170
A caudle, ho!

King.   Too bitter is thy jest.

165. to tune] *Q1;* tuning *Ff,Q2.*   167. toys] toyles *Q2.*   171. caudle] *Q1,*
Rowe, Theobald, Johnson; candle *Ff,Q2.*

described by an aged person as having
been generally made of the tip of a
horn, hollow, but with a small ballast
at the bottom of the inside.' Its connection with a horn is referred to at
v. i. 60 below.

165. *jig*] a dance, or the music to it.
See Greene, *James the Fourth* (*ante* 1592)
(Grosart, xiii. 209–10): 'I have two
sonnes, that with one Scottish gigge
shall breake the necke of thy Antiques
. . . gather uppe your legges and
daunce me forthwith a gigge worth the
sight.'

166. *play at push-pin*] more com-
monly 'put-pin'. Halliwell quotes from
the MS. play of *Misogonus* (*ante* 1577)
(Hazlitt): 'That can play at put-pin,
Blow-poynte and near [ne'er] lin'. In
Nashe's *Foure Letters Confuted* (Mc-
Kerrow, i. 303) it is again 'put-pin':
'I will play at put-pinne with thee for
all that thou art woorth.' And also in
Marston's *Scourge of Villainy*, Satire
viii: 'Playing at put-pin, doting on
some glass. . . . Toying with babies'.
Later, in Beaumont and Fletcher, in
Massinger, and in Herrick, it is 'push-
pin'. The earliest definition appears to
be that in John Ash's *New and Complete
Dictionary of the English Language*
(1775): '*Push-pin*, a child's play in
which pins are pushed with an endeavour to cross them'. From a reference in *N.E.D.*, it seems that the
game was familiar at least as late as
1825.

167. *critic*] critical, censorious. 'Sitting like a looker-on Of this worldes

stage, doest note, with critique pen,
The sharpe dislikes of each condition'
(*Edmund Spenser to Gabriel Harvey:*
'Dublin: this xviii. of July: 1586'
[Oxford Spenser, p. 603].

critic Timon laugh at idle toys] Greene
refers to Timon earlier: 'Now hote now
could, first as courteous as Traian, and
then as currish as Tymon, one while a
defender of lust, and an other time a
contemner of love' (*Tritameron* [Gro-
sart, iii. 79], 1584) and 'Tymonlike to
condemne those heavenlie creatures
whose onlie sight is a sufficient salve
against all hellish sorrowes' (*Carde of
Fancie* [iv. 40], 1587). See Plutarch's
Life of Mark Anthony. Timon the mis-
anthropist was a snarler at everything,
and the force of this line would seem to
be that he became as good-humoured
and cheerful as a sportive kid. But 'idle
toys', or 'toys of an idle head', had a
definite sense of foolish mental or
literary efforts; and it is possible that
the meaning of the line is that the
academics, professedly as severe on
human follies as Timon, have now
been caught taking a delight in mere
idle sonneteering. At l. 198 below
Berowne shows what he means by 'a
toy'; his own sonnet to Rosaline is 'a
toy, my liege, a toy'.

171. *caudle*] occurs (as noun) only
once again in Shakespeare (in *2H6*),
and there as well as here Ff read
candle. A warm, thin drink of gruel and
ale or wine, with sugar, etc., given to
women, children, and especially
invalids.

Are we betray'd thus to thy over-view?
Ber. Not you by me, but I betray'd to you:
I, that am honest; I, that hold it sin
To break the vow I am engaged in;   175
I am betray'd, by keeping company
With moon-like men, men of inconstancy.
When shall you see me write a thing in rhyme?
Or groan for Joan? or spend a minute's time
In pruning me? When shall you hear that I   180
Will praise a hand, a foot, a face, an eye,
A gait, a state, a brow, a breast, a waist,
A leg, a limb—?
King.   Soft! whither away so fast?
A true man or a thief that gallops so?

173. by me ... to you] *Qq,Ff;* by me ... by you *Theobald;* to me ... by you *Capell.*
177. moon-like men, men of inconstancy] *Steevens;* men like men of inconstancy
Qq,F1; men like men of strange inconstancy *Ff2,3,4.*   179. Joan] Ione *Q1;*
Loue *Q1 (Devon copy).*   180–3.] *Q1 prints as prose.*

177. *men of inconstancy*] The line is
clearly corrupt, and the insertion of
'strange' in the later Ff an attempt at
a cure that is earlier, but no more
worthy of acceptance, than any other.
Of many ingenious suggestions Steevens's is perhaps the happiest; of all
words that might have been dropped
from the middle of the line a repeated
'men' is likeliest, and 'moon' in English script might easily be misread as
'men', especially if, as Dover Wilson
suggests, Shakespeare spelt it 'mon'.
And the moon is a standard symbol of
inconstancy in Shakespeare; cf. 'the
inconstant moon' of *Rom.,* II. ii. 109,
and the quibbles on the moon's
changes in the present play, v. ii. 212 ff.

179. *Joan*] The reading 'Loue' is a
fine illustration of the additional corruptions to be found in the copy of
Q that formerly belonged to the Duke
of Devonshire and is now in the Huntington Library. Dover Wilson took
them as evidence that this copy was
one of the last copies printed, when the
compositor's original blunders had
been extended by disturbance of the
type in the course of printing and the

'machine-minder's' attempts to repair
the damage. See Intro., 2.2. Mr John
Crow has, however, shown me that the
state at least of the present sheet (sig.
E) is better explained if the Devonshire Q is regarded rather as an *early*
copy, lacking the corrections that were
later to be made while the book was
printing (a common Elizabethan
practice).

180. *pruning*] preening, or pryning,
as birds do their feathers; trimming.
Jonson has 'prunes his mustaccio', and
'pruning his clothes', in *Cynthia's Revels*
(Induction, and III. ii), 1600.

182. *state*] an 'act of standing' as
opposed to gait (Steevens). A pose.

brow] the countenance; as above at
IV. i. 17, and often in Shakespeare.

183. *whither away so fast*] This expression occurs four times in Shakespeare.
Cf. *King Leir* (Malone Soc., ed. Greg,
991) 1593: 'My honest friend, whither
away so fast?'

184. *true man*] honest man. Very
commonly set in opposition to a thief,
as in *1H4,* II. ii. 105, and Chaucer's
Squire's Tale: 'A true wight and a thief
thinkest not one.' Nashe has 'One true

Ber. I post from love; good lover, let me go.   185

Enter JAQUENETTA *and* COSTARD.

Jaq. God bless the king!
King.   What present hast thou there?
Cost. Some certain treason.
King.   What makes treason here?
Cost. Nay, it makes nothing, sir.
King.   If it mar nothing neither,
    The treason and you go in peace away together.
Jaq. I beseech your grace, let this letter be read: 190
    Our Person misdoubts it; 'twas treason, he said.
King. Berowne, read it over.   [*Berowne reads the letter.*
    Where hadst thou it?
Jaq. Of Costard.
King. Where hadst thou it?   195
Cost. Of Dun Adramadio, Dun Adramadio.
King. How now! what is in you? why dost thou tear it?
Ber. A toy, my liege, a toy: your grace needs not fear it.
Long. It did move him to passion, and therefore let's hear it.
Dum. [*gathers up the pieces*]. It is Berowne's writing, and here
    is his name.   200
Ber. [*to Costard*]. Ah! you whoreson loggerhead, you were
    born to do me shame.

---

189. away] *not in Ff2,3,4.*   191. 'twas] it was *Ff,Q2.*   197. is in] *Qq,Ff1,2;*
mean *Ff3,4.*   200. [*gathers up the pieces*]] *Capell.*

---

man is stronger than two theeves'
(*Foure Letters Confuted* [McKerrow, i.
298]); and Heywood (ed. Sharman,
p. 158), 1546: 'When thieves fall out
true men come to their good.' In *The
Famous Victories of Henry V* (*Shakes. Lib.*,
1875, p. 329) occurs: '*Theafe.* It is not
too late for true men to walke.
[*Dericke.*] We know thee not to be a
true man.'

185. *post*] ride with urgency.
186. *present*] writing, presentment.
Cf. *AYL.*, I. ii. 132; and Jonson,
Cynthia's Revels, v. ii: 'Be it known to all
that profess courtship, by these presents, that we' (*per has literas presentes*,

legal). Very unusual in the singular.
188. *makes* ... *mar*] 'To make or mar'
is a proverbial expression traced back
in *N.E.D.* to Lydgate's *Assembly of
Gods* (*c.* 1420). This and its parallel,
'mend or mar', were very common in
Shakespeare's time. See *Mac.*, II. iii.
26; *Lr.*, I. i. 97, etc. Tusser has it in
Verses (1573): 'to disagree Is ventring
all to make or mar' (Eng. Dial. Soc.,
p. 204).
191. *misdoubts*] suspects, mistrusts.
198. *toy*] For the 'toy' see IV. ii. 101–
14; and see note at 'idle toys', l. 167
above.
201. *loggerhead*] blockhead. The

Guilty, my lord, guilty! I confess, I confess.

King. What?

Ber.   That you three fools lack'd me, fool, to make
up the mess;

He, he, and you, and you, my liege, and I,

Are pick-purses in love, and we deserve to die.   205

O! dismiss this audience, and I shall tell you more.

Dum. Now the number is even.

Ber.   True, true; we are four.
Will these turtles be gone?

King.   Hence, Sirs; away!

Cost. Walk aside the true folk, and let the traitors stay.

            [*Exeunt Costard and Jaquenetta.*

Ber. Sweet lords, sweet lovers, O! let us embrace.   210

As true we are as flesh and blood can be:

The sea will ebb and flow, heaven show his face;

Young blood doth not obey an old decree:

We cannot cross the cause why we were born;

Therefore, of all hands must we be forsworn.   215

King. What! did these rent lines show some love of thine?

Ber. Did they? quoth you. Who sees the heavenly Rosaline,

That, like a rude and savage man of Inde,

At the first opening of the gorgeous east,

---

212. show] shew *Q1;* will shew *Ff,Q2.*   214. were] *Q1,Ff3,4;* are *Ff1,2,Q2.*
217. quoth you] *om. Capell.*

earliest example in *N.E.D.* It is used again in *1H4,* II. iv. 4. Nashe makes an adjective of it: 'This loggerhead Legend of lyes' (*Have With You to Saffron Walden* [McKerrow, iii. 71], 1596).

203. *make up the mess*] make up the party of four. 'At great dinners and feasts the company was usually arranged into fours, which were called messes' (Nares), who gives plenty of examples of the common expression, as: 'Foure makes a messe, and we have a messe of masters that must be coozened' (Lyly, *Mother Bombie,* II. i). See below, v. ii. 361, and *3H6,* I. iv. 73. A good example occurs in Lodge's *Euphues Golden Legacie*

(*Shakes. Lib.,* 1875, p. 118), 1590: 'which Ganimede espying thinking hee [Saladyne] had had his Mistresse long inough at shrift, sayd: what, a match or no? A match (quoth Aliena) or els it were an ill market. I am glad (quoth Ganimede), I would Rosader were wel here to make up a messe.'

204. *and you, and you*] both referring to 'my liege'. Reed omitted one 'and you'.

215. *of all hands*] on every side.

218. *man of Inde*] Craig quotes from Ascham's *Toxophilus* (Arber, p. 212): 'The men of Inde had theyr bowes made of a rede.' Inde was a common early name for India, abundantly illustrated in *N.E.D.*

Bows not his vassal head, and strooken blind,   220
Kisses the base ground with obedient breast?
What peremptory eagle-sighted eye
Dares look upon the heaven of her brow,
That is not blinded by her majesty?

King. What zeal, what fury hath inspir'd thee now?   225
My love, her mistress, is a gracious moon;
She an attending star, scarce seen a light.

Ber. My eyes are then no eyes, nor I Berowne:
O! but for my love, day would turn to night.
Of all complexions the cull'd sovereignty   230
Do meet, as at a fair, in her fair cheek;
Where several worthies make one dignity,
Where nothing wants that want itself doth seek.
Lend me the flourish of all gentle tongues,—
Fie, painted rhetoric! O! she needs it not: 235

220. strooken] *Qq,Ff1,2,3;* strucken *F4, Cambridge.*

222. *peremptory*] originally a law term meaning 'decisive', 'final'; hence 'determined'. 'obstinately resolute'. See *John,* II. i. 454: 'Not death himself In mortal fury half so peremptory As we to keep this city.'

eagle-sighted] a reference to the eagle's supposed power, alone of all birds, of looking at the sun. It is mentioned in Chaucer's *Assembly of Foules.* See Pliny, I. xxvii (Holland's translation, p. 160); and Greene, *Menaphon* (Grosart, vi. 105), 1589: 'Pardon me, faire shepheardesse, . . . for I cannot chuse, being Eagle-sighted, but gaze on the Sunne the first time I see it'; and in his *Mourning Garment* (ix. 157): 'I am not Eagle-sighted, and therefore feare to flie too nigh the Sunne.'

226–7. *moon . . . scarce seen a light*] Cf. *Gesta Grayorum,* 1594 (ed. Greg, p. 68): 'at the Royal Presence of Her Majesty, it appeared as an obscured Shadow: in this, not unlike unto the Morning-star, which looketh very chearfully on the World, so long as the Sun looketh not on it.' Perhaps from Horace, *Odes,* 1, 12. Cf. *Entertainment of Ambassador to Landgrave of Hesse,* 1596: 'There was

the Lady Anna . . . and many that waited on the Princess. And she herselfe, as Horace says of Julium Sidus, stood by her bedside, *velut inter ignes luna minores*' (Nichols's *Progresses,* iii. 388–9).

227. *attending star*] Staunton says: 'It was a prevailing notion formerly that the moon had an attending star. . . . Sir Richard Hawkins, in his *Observations on a Voyage to the South Seas in 1593,* remarks: 'Some I have heard say, and others write, that there is a starre which never separateth itself from the moon, but a small distance.' Lodge mentions Hawkins's star in *Euphues Golden Legacie (Shakes. Lib.,* 1875, p. 79), 1590: 'for as the Moone never goes without the starre Lunisequa, so a lover never goeth without the unrest of his thoughts.' I doubt if Shakespeare refers to it here.

229, 235, 242, 246, 279, 283, 285, etc. *O*] For Berowne's ejaculation 'O!' see above, III. i. 142, n.

232. *worthies*] excellencies, things of worth.

235. *painted rhetoric*] Cf. Lodge, *Euphues Golden Legacie (Shakes. Lib.,*

To things of sale a seller's praise belongs;
She passes praise; then praise too short doth blot.
A wither'd hermit, five-score winters worn,
Might shake off fifty, looking in her eye:
Beauty doth varnish age, as if new-born,   240
And gives the crutch the cradle's infancy.
O! 'tis the sun that maketh all things shine.
King.   By heaven, thy love is black as ebony.
Ber.   Is ebony like her? O wood divine!
A wife of such wood were felicity.   245
O! who can give an oath? where is a book?
That I may swear beauty doth beauty lack,
If that she learn not of her eye to look:
No face is fair that is not full so black.
King.   O paradox! Black is the badge of hell,   250
The hue of dungeons and the school of night;

---

245. wood] *Rowe (ed. 1)*; word *Qq,Ff.*   251. school] schoole *Qq,Ff*; scowl
Theobald; stole *Hanmer*; soul, soil, shade, scroll, shroud, seal, *and* suit, *various conjectures and lections.*

1875, p. 18): 'A painted tongue may
shroud a subtle heart'; and R.
Edwards, *Damon and Pithias* (Hazlitt's
Dodsley, iv. 88), *ante* 1566: 'these need
no subtle sleight, No painted speech
the matter to convey.'

236. *a seller's praise*] Cf. above, II. i.
16, *Sonn.*, 21, and (for the whole passage) *Sonn.* 82.

241. *crutch ... cradle*] 'From cradle to
crutch, from infancy to old age', was a
symbolical expression used several
times by Greene, e.g. 'from the cradle
to the crouch, and from the crouch had
one legge in the grave' (*Penelope's Web*
[Grosart, v. 224], 1587).

249. *No face ... black*] See Sidney's
Astrophel and Stella, vii: 'whereas blacke
seemes Beauties contrarie, Shee even
in blacke doth make all Beauties flowe.'
Stella, however, combined black eyes
with a pink-and-white complexion
and golden hair. See Intro., 5.24.

251. *school of night*] Almost all the
editors were agreed on the need for
emending this phrase (but not on the

emendation) until Arthur Acheson
suggested, in his *Shakespeare and the
Rival Poet* (1903), that there was a real
'Schoole of Night' existing at this time,
and that it was synonymous with the
'Schoole of Atheism' of which Sir
Walter Ralegh was reputed by contemporaries to be the chief patron.
See Intro., 5.23. E. A. Strathmann, in
*The Textual Evidence for 'The School of
Night'* (*M.L.N.*, LVI, March 1941),
insists that this is historically unproven
and textually impossible. I find the
second part of his argument unconvincing, since it rests on two false
assumptions—that the chaotic punctuation of Q, including the comma
after 'dungeons', is as likely to be
Shakespeare's as its oddities of spelling;
and that Shakespeare habitually took
care to balance his clauses. Strathmann would substitute for 'schoole'
some word more closely corresponding
to the 'badge' and 'hue' of the other
comparisons, and suggests 'suit', which
Shakespeare (who used 'shue' for 'sue'

And beauty's crest becomes the heavens well.
Ber. Devils soonest tempt, resembling spirits of light.
   O ! if in black my lady's brows be deck'd,
   It mourns that painting and usurping hair   255
   Should ravish doters with a false aspect;
   And therefore is she born to make black fair.
   Her favour turns the fashion of the days,
   For native blood is counted painting now:
   And therefore red, that would avoid dispraise,   260
   Paints itself black, to imitate her brow.
Dum. To look like her are chimney-sweepers black.
Long. And since her time are colliers counted bright.
King. And Ethiops of their sweet complexion crack.
Dum. Dark needs no candles now, for dark is light.   265
Ber. Your mistresses dare never come in rain,
   For fear their colours should be wash'd away.
King. 'Twere good, yours did; for, sir, to tell you plain,
   I'll find a fairer face not wash'd to-day.
Ber. I'll prove her fair, or talk till doomsday here.   270
King. No devil will fright thee then so much as she.
Dum. I never knew man hold vile stuff so dear.

---

252. crest] dress, crete, craye, cresset, *and* best, *various conjectures and lections.*
255. and] *F4; not in Qq,F1;* an *Ff2,3.*   262. black] blake *Q1.*   264. sweet]
swart *anonymous conj.*   crack] *Q2,Ff3,4;* crake *Q1,Ff1,2.*   267. their] her *Q2.*

---

at III. i. 201) may well have spelt 'shoote'. (Indeed, the man who wrote 'scilens' for 'silence' may easily have written 'schoote' for 'suit'). To drop the comma seems to me the simpler solution.

252. *beauty's crest*] There have been many explanations and emendations of this passage, but none of them very convincing. The explainers can be broadly divided into two schools. One takes the last line as ironical, and construes the King's speech: 'black is the badge of *hell*; you make it the badge of beauty—a fine emblem for what is usually regarded as a *heavenly* quality!' The other sees the line as a straight rejoinder to Berowne's claim (l. 242) that his black beauty is a sun. It would

mean 'true (i.e. fair) beauty, not that which Berowne admires, is the proper subject for such heavenly comparisons', and it aptly provokes the reply that this conventional beauty is often a screen for evil deeds. The first interpretation better suits the drift of the King's speech, the second that of the dialogue as a whole.

253. *Devils . . . spirits of light*] Cf. 2 Cor., xi. 14.

257–8. *black . . . turns the fashion*] Lyly has the same thought: 'such a common thing is it amongst you to commend, that oftentimes for fashion's sake you call them beautiful whom you know blacke' (*Campaspe*, iv. 2 [1581]).

264. *crack*] boast.

Long. Look, here's thy love: my foot and her face see.

               [*Showing his shoe.*

Ber. O! if the streets were paved with thine eyes,

 Her feet were much too dainty for such tread.   275

Dum. O vile! then, as she goes, what upward lies

 The street should see as she walk'd overhead.

King. But what of this? Are we not all in love?

Ber. O! nothing so sure; and thereby all forsworn.

King. Then leave this chat; and, good Berowne, now prove

 Our loving lawful, and our faith not torn.   281

Dum. Ay, marry, there; some flattery for this evil.

Long. O! some authority how to proceed;

 Some tricks, some quillets, how to cheat the devil.

Dum. Some salve for perjury.

Ber.   O! 'tis more than need. 285

 Have at you then, affection's men-at-arms:

 Consider what you first did swear unto,

 To fast, to study, and to see no woman;

 Flat treason 'gainst the kingly state of youth.

 Say, can you fast? your stomachs are too young, 290

 And abstinence engenders maladies.

 [And where that you have vow'd to study, lords,

 In that each of you have forsworn his book,

 Can you still dream and pore and thereon look?

 For when would you, my lord, or you, or you, 295

---

273. [*Showing his shoe*] *Johnson, Steevens, Craig, etc.* 279. O! nothing] *Qq,F1;* Nothing *Ff2,3,4, Cambridge.* 285. O! 'tis] O tis *Qq,Ff2;* 'Tis *Cambridge.*

---

273. [*Showing his shoe*] Furness writes: 'It is almost humiliating to have to record that a large majority of editors, following Johnson, have deemed it necessary to add a stage-direction here.' I like it. Even so the point is generally missed when the play is staged, for designers do not choose that Longaville should be shod, as he must be, in black.

284. *quillets*] subtleties. Cf. *2H6*, III. i. 261: 'do not stand on quillets how to slay him: Be it by gins, by snares, by subtlety, sleeping or waking, 'tis no matter how.' The use in the text is the earliest in *N.E.D.* Origin obscure, but perhaps a variant of 'quiddit'. Gabriel Harvey has 'quillity' earlier. Cf. also Holland's *Plinie*, xi. 3 (1601): 'to judge and determine of these doubtful quillets and their causes'. Shakespeare uses the word several times later.

288. *To fast . . . no woman*] So Lucio says in *Meas.*, I. iv. 60–1: 'Blunt his natural edge with profits of the mind, study and fast.'

295–300. *For when would you . . . true Promethean fire*] Dyce omits these lines, also ll. 308–15, on account of their repetition either verbally or in substance elsewhere in the speech. Capell notices this, and attributes it to the

Have found the ground of study's excellence
Without the beauty of a woman's face?
From women's eyes this doctrine I derive:
They are the ground, the books, the academes,
From whence doth spring the true Promethean fire.   300
Why, universal plodding poisons up
The nimble spirits in the arteries,
As motion and long-during action tires
The sinewy vigour of the traveller.
Now, for not looking on a woman's face,   305
You have in that forsworn the use of eyes,
And study too, the causer of your vow;
For where is any author in the world
Teaches such beauty as a woman's eye?
Learning is but an adjunct to ourself,   310
And where we are our learning likewise is:
Then when ourselves we see in ladies' eyes,
Do we not likewise see our learning there?]
O! we have made a vow to study, lords,

---

301. poisons] poysons *Qq,Ff*; prisons *Theobald et seq.*   304. sinewy] sinnowy
Qq,Ff.   309. beauty] duty *Warburton;* leaving *Collier MS.*   312–13. eyes,
Do] *Ff2,3,4;* eyes, With our selves. Do *Qq,F1 (insertion of half line).*

intermingling of two different drafts of
MSS. Dover Wilson defines the early
draft more probably than Dyce, as
running from l. 292 to l. 313. The new
draft begins at l. 314; its first six lines
are a close rendering of ll. 292–7, the
next three a much freer one of 301–4.
At 323 begins a rhapsody of twenty-
four lines that is entirely new; but ll.
346–50 return to take up ll. 298–300,
hitherto passed over, and the final
eleven lines are an expansion of ll.
305–13. See Intro., 2.51.

296. *ground*] base, foundation.

299. *academes*] See note, I. i. 13.

300. *Promethean fire*] Chapman has
this expression about the same date:
'Therefore Promethean poets with the
coals Of their most genial, more than
human souls, In living verse created
men like these' (*The Shadow of Night*,
1594). See Intro., 5.23.

301. *poisons up*] Dyce pointed out
that F misprints *poison'd* for *prison'd* in
1H6, v. iv. 120. Halliwell and Furnivall retain 'poisons'. Furnivall says:
'You don't want the metaphor of
nimble spirits struggling to burst their
prison: you want them dulled and
numbed by poison.' But if these lines
were redrafted as 320–2 below, only
'prisons' can have suggested 'keep the
brain', and 'immured' (l. 324). Much
may be said on both sides, but it is
better to adhere to the originals.

304. *sinewy*] The old spelling 'sinnowy' is of interest here, since it has led
to the quaint misprint in Marlowe's
Tamburlaine (pt I, II. i): 'His arms and
fingers long and snowy'.

312. *eyes*] The additional fragment
preserved in the early texts is again
evidence that two drafts overlap
here.

And in that vow we have forsworn our books: 315
For when would you, my liege, or you, or you,
In leaden contemplation have found out
Such fiery numbers as the prompting eyes
Of beauty's tutors have enrich'd you with?
Other slow arts entirely keep the brain,   320
And therefore, finding barren practisers,
Scarce show a harvest of their heavy toil;
But love, first learned in a lady's eyes,
Lives not alone immured in the brain,
But, with the motion of all elements,   325
Courses as swift as thought in every power,
And gives to every power a double power,
Above their functions and their offices.
It adds a precious seeing to the eye;
A lover's eyes will gaze an eagle blind;   330
A lover's ear will hear the lowest sound,
When the suspicious head of theft is stopp'd:
Love's feeling is more soft and sensible
Than are the tender horns of cockled snails:
Love's tongue proves dainty Bacchus gross in taste.   335
For valour, is not Love a Hercules,
Still climbing trees in the Hesperides?

335. dainty Bacchus] *Ff2,3,4;* dainty, Bacchus *Qq,F1.*

318. *fiery numbers*] referring to the sonnets and 'toys' of the lovers.

320. *keep*] inhabit, remain in.

332. *suspicious head of theft*] Farmer says 'the head suspicious of theft', supporting this by 'to watch like one that fears robbing', in *Gent.,* II. i. 26. From which slight and accidental assistance Furness declares that this interpretation carries conviction. The obvious meaning is surely the correct one. Cf. *3H6,* V. vi. 11–12: 'Suspicion always haunts the guilty mind: the thief doth fear each bush an officer.' Nashe implies that the thought was proverbial: 'Wee, carelesse of these mischances, helde on our flight, and saw no man come after us but we thought had pursued us. A theefe, they saie, mistakes everie bush for a true man; the winde ratled not in any bush by the way as I rode, but I straight drew my rapier' (*The Unfortunate Traveller* [McKerrow, ii. 319], 1594). It occurs again in *Time's Whistle,* Satire 7, 3485 (1615). Sir E. Maunde Thompson suggested 'th' eft', which pairs, in my opinion too well, with the cockled snail two lines later.

334. *cockled*] 'inshell'd like the fish called a cockle' (Steevens). I incline rather to the meaning puckered, folded, wrinkled. See the figure of 'The Snail Mount' in Nichols, iii. 101, of date 1591, where the shell is forgotten when the horns are prominent.

337. *Hesperides*] frequently used as the name of the garden in which the golden apples grew, watched by the daughters of Hesperus, the Hesperides

Subtle as Sphinx; as sweet and musical
As bright Apollo's lute, strung with his hair;
And when Love speaks, the voice of all the gods   340
Make heaven drowsy with the harmony.
Never durst poet touch a pen to write
Until his ink were temper'd with Love's sighs;
O! then his lines would ravish savage ears,
And plant in tyrants mild humility.   345

340–1. the voice . . . heaven] the voice makes all the gods of heaven *Farmer conj.*
345. humility] humanity *Mrs Griffith, Walker, Dyce.*

of Grecian mythology. The final 'labour' that Hercules was called upon to perform was to enter the garden, overcome a guardian dragon, and pick the apples from the tree. Peter Martyr's *Decades of the Ocean* (1516) (translated by M. Lok, Hakluyt [1587], ed. 1812, vol. v, p. 206) identifies the islands with the Fortunate Isles: 'the Islands of Hesparides, now called Caboverde'.

338. *Subtle as Sphinx*] 'and if I coulde have found a Sphinx to have expounded ther ridel' (*Letters of Elizabeth to James* (Camden Soc., p. 173), *ante* 1586. The Sphinx of Greek mythology *posed* the riddle; it was Oedipus who expounded it. The passage in the text is the earliest cited in this sense in the *Stanford Dictionary*.

339. *Apollo's . . . hair*] Apollo's hair is often mentioned by Greene, not as lute-strings, but as a type of sunshiny loveliness. In *Menaphon* (Grosart, vi. 126), 1587, he writes: 'Apollo, when my Mistres first was borne, Cut off his lockes and left them on her head, And said: I plant these wires in Naturis scorne, Whose beauties shall appeare when Time is dead.' And in *Tullies Love*, 1589 (Grosart, vii. 105): 'His haire was like the shine of Apollo, when shaking his glorious tresses, he makes the world beauteous.' Steevens quotes from *How a Man may Chuse a Good Wife from a Bad* (Hazlitt's *Dodsley*, ix. 77), 1602: 'Hath he not torn those gold wires from your head, Wherewith Apollo would have strung

his harp, And kept them to play music to the gods?' This seems to be a somewhat incoherent echo of the passage in the text. Lyly makes Pan say to Apollo: 'Tell mee, Apollo, is there any instrument so sweete to play on as one's mistresse? Had thy lute beene of laurell and the strings of Daphne's haire thy tunes might have been compared to my notes' (*Mydas*, iv. 1 [?1589]).

340–1. *Love speaks . . . Make heaven drowsy*] Tyrwhitt remarked, about a century and a half ago, that 'Few passages have been more canvassed than this'; and a long list of subsequent comments is given by Furness. Tyrwhitt alters the pointing; Farmer transposes words: Warburton changes them (*Mark!* for *Make*), which Heath reprints, saying Warburton's note is 'one of the completest pieces of nonsense extant'. Furness finishes with Knight's words as the most satisfactory. He says: 'The meaning appears to us so clear amidst the blaze of poetic beauty, that an explanation is hardly wanted. When love speaks, the responsive harmony of the voice of all the gods makes heaven drowsy.' Cf. Shirley's *Love Tricks*, iv. 2 (*c.* 1625): 'The tongue that's able to rock Heaven asleep And make the music of the spheres stand still'. The power of harmony to make the hearers drowsy is commonly referred to by Shakespeare. All the gods are mouth-pieces of the musical eloquence of Love.

345. *humility*] Halliwell quotes Huloet's *Abecedarium*, 1552: '*Humilitie*

From women's eyes this doctrine I derive:
They sparkle still the right Promethean fire;
They are the books, the arts, the academes,
That show, contain, and nourish all the world;
Else none at all in aught proves excellent.   350
Then fools you were these women to forswear,
Or, keeping what is sworn, you will prove fools.
For wisdom's sake, a word that all men love,
Or for love's sake, a word that loves all men,
Or for men's sake, the authors of these women,   355
Or women's sake, by whom we men are men,
Let us once lose our oaths to find ourselves,
Or else we lose ourselves to keep our oaths.
It is religion to be thus forsworn;
For charity itself fulfils the law;   360
And who can sever love from charity?
King. Saint Cupid, then! and, soldiers, to the field!
Ber. Advance your standards, and upon them, lords!
Pell-mell, down with them! but be first advis'd,
In conflict that you get the sun of them.   365
Long. Now to plain-dealing; lay these glozes by:

354. loves] moves *Hanmer;* leads *Mason;* joyes *Heath;* learns *Bailey.*   355.
authors] *Capell;* author *Qq,Ff.*

is a gentlenes of the mynde, or a gentle
patience withoute all angre or wrathe',
as a protest against the necessity of
adopting 'humanity', as several editors took upon themselves to do.
Schmidt gives the sense of 'bene-
volence, kindness, humanity', to
humility; an interpretation not recognized by *N.E.D.* though supported by
the use of 'humble' in v. ii. 621 and 727
below. Humility in the sense of meek-
ness is very reasonably placed in opposition to the pride that characterizes a
tyrant.

346–8. *From women's eyes ... academes*]
See notes above, ll. 295–300.

354. *love ... a word that loves all men*]
love that impresses itself, or inspires its
being into all men—makes them
lovers. The verb seems to be given an
unique sense. Cf. the old 'to meat', to
supply with meat; and Ralegh's use of

the verb 'scorn' in his earliest known
verses, prefixed to Gascoigne's *Steel
Glas* (1576): 'this medicine may suffyse
To scorne the rest and seke to please
the wise'. 'Scorn' seems perforce to
mean here 'to make subject to scorn'.
Capell explained *loves* 'is a friend to',
or, as Malone put it, 'is pleasing to',
used as the verb 'like'; but that seems
too mild a sense for the antithesis.

360. *charity ... law*] The 'Bishops''
Bible, 1568, has (Rom. xii. 8): '(For he
that loveth another, hath fulfylled the
lawe).'

364. *Pell-mell*] confusedly, with
violence. Greene has 'least love entering pell mell with war' (*Tullies Love*
[Grosart, vii. 135]).

366. *Now to plain-dealing ... glozes by*]
This may be interpreted in two ways:
'Now to business, mere verbal flour-
ishes achieve nothing' and 'Now for

Shall we resolve to woo these girls of France?

King. And win them too: therefore let us devise
Some entertainment for them in their tents.

Ber. First, from the park let us conduct them thither;   370
Then homeward every man attach the hand
Of his fair mistress: in the afternoon
We will with some strange pastime solace them,
Such as the shortness of the time can shape;
For revels, dances, masks, and merry hours,   375
Forerun fair Love, strewing her way with flowers.

King. Away, away! no time shall be omitted
That will be time, and may by us be fitted.

Ber. *Allons! allons!* Sow'd cockle reap'd no corn;
And justice always whirls in equal measure: 380
Light wenches may prove plagues to men forsworn;
If so, our copper buys no better treasure.   [*Exeunt.*

376. her] his *Capell conj.*   378. be time] *Qq,Ff;* betime *Rowe* (*ed. 2*), *Cambridge.*
379. *Allons! allons!*] *Theobald* (*Warburton*); Alone, alone *Qq,Ff.*

honest plain sense; enough of bawdy double-meanings, such as those with which Berowne has just crammed his speech'.

glozes] marginal comment, or superficial word-play. Shakespeare does not have the noun elsewhere but the sense 'empty verbal dexterity' is reflected in his use of the verb in *R2*, II. i. 10.

375. *revels, dances, masks, and merry hours*] This line is found in *England's Parnassus*, 1600.

379. Allons! allons!] At the last words of Act II of *Wiv.*, the Quarto of 1602 reads: 'Alon, alon, alon.' Nashe has the expression in *Have With You to Saffron Walden* (McKerrow, iii. 110). It occurs also in Marston's *What You Will*, III. 1 ('aloun, aloun'); and in Day's *Parliament of Bees*, chap. iv ('all oone'). 'Alone' for '*allons*' occurs again in the present play, v. i. 142.

cockle . . . corn] The name 'cockle' was often used by early writers—incorrectly, and much to the annoyance of such botanical precisians as William Turner (*The Names of herbes*, 1548)—for 'darnel', a grass whose seed might be mistaken for corn. In Wyclif's Bible, and in some other editions later, in Matt., xiii. 25, cockel is used instead of tares or darnel. See also Skeat's Chaucer's *Canterbury Tales* (T. 14403): 'or springen [sprinkle] cokkel in our clene corn'. Abundant references are to be found in *N.E.D.* Berowne's note of warning here comes in rather inharmoniously after his magnificent address of loyalty to Love. What he says amounts to: 'we are forsworn, we must look out for squalls, these girls may bring us the punishment we deserve'.

ACT V

SCENE I

Enter HOLOFERNES, *Sir* NATHANIEL, *and* DULL.

Hol. Satis quid sufficit.

Nath. I praise God for you, sir: your reasons at dinner
have been sharp and sententious; pleasant without
scurrility, witty without affection, audacious without

ACT V

Scene I

1. *quid*] Qq,Ff; quod Rowe et seq.   4. affection] Qq,F1; affectation Ff2,3,4.

1. Satis quid sufficit] correctly *'satis est quod sufficit'*, according to some lists. Cf. Lodge, *Euphues Golden Legacie* (*Shakes. Lib.*, 1875, p. 51), 1590: 'Mistresse I have so much Latin, *Satis est quod sufficit.*' It occurs also in *A Twelfe Night Merriment (Narcissus)*, 1602 (ed. M. L. Lee): 'It is a most condolent tragedye wee shall move. *Porter. Dictum puta; satis est quod suffocat. Sec.* In faith, I tickle them for a good voice. *Porter. Sufficiente quantitate,* a woord is enough to the wise' (p. 5). The English extension 'enough is as good as a feast' is in Heywood's *Proverbs*, 1546.

2, 4, 5. *reasons . . . audacious . . . opinion*] 'It may be proper just to note, that reason here, and in many other places, signifies discourse; and that audacious is used in a good sense for spirited, animated, confident. Opinion is the same with obstinacy or opiniâtreté' (Johnson). Johnson says further: 'I know not well what degree of respect Shakespeare intends to obtain for this vicar, but he has here put into his mouth a finished representation of colloquial excellence.'

3. *sententious*] pithy. Puttenham has a chapter (xix) 'Of Figures sententious, otherwise called Rhetoricall'. On p. 207 he speaks of words 'pithie or sententious'.

3–6. *pleasant . . . heresy*] Furness quotes from Chalmers, *Supplemental Apologie*, 1799 (p. 281), to the effect that 'the original of these lines' is in Sidney's *Arcadia* (p. 17, ed. 1598). The words that are somewhat parallel to those in the text are: 'her speach being as rare as pretious, her silence without sullennesse; her modestie without affectation; her shamefastnesse without ignorance' (*Works*, ed. A. Feuillerat, i. 32). There is a structural resemblance. Gabriel Harvey delighted in this method of apposition when he waxed eloquent. See his 'Earthquake Letter' (Grosart, pp. 69–72); and again in his *Letters*, p. 72 (1580). Later, as in his *Foure Letters* (1592), he cannot proceed without it.

4. *affection*] the act of affecting; affectation. See again v. ii. 407, and *Ham.*, II. ii. 473 (Q reading).

audacious] See note at l. 2 above. Steevens quotes from Jonson's *Epicene,*

impudency, learned without opinion, and strange   5
without heresy. I did converse this quondam day
with a companion of the king's, who is intituled,
nominated, or called, Don Adriano de Armado.

Hol. *Novi hominem tanquam te:* his humour is lofty, his discourse peremptory, his tongue filed, his eye ambi-   10
tious, his gait majestical, and his general behaviour
vain, ridiculous, and thrasonical. He is too picked,

---

9. *hominem*] *Ff3,4; hominum Qq, Ff1,2.*

---

11. iii: 'She that shall be my wife must
be accomplished, with courtly and
audacious ornaments.'

5. *opinion*] self-conceit (*N.E.D.*),
over-confidence in the rightness of
one's own opinion. *N.E.D.* parallels
1H4, 111. i. 185, and *Troil.,* 1. iii. 353.

7. *intituled*] Dover Wilson declares
that this is merely 'entitled' in a common Elizabethan spelling.

9. Novi . . . te] I know the man as
well as I know you. This phrase is
given in 'Lyly's Grammar' (*Brevissima
Institutio,* 1549, etc.) as an example of
the use of *tamquam* (Syntaxis: Adverbii
constructio, under *Quasi*). It may have
become a catchword. Harvey has
similar expressions in his *Letters to
Spenser* (Grosart, i. 74), 1580: 'With as
many gentle goodnights as be Letters
in this tedious Letter. *Nosti manum
tanquam tuam*'; and p. 84: '*nosti homines,
tanquam tuam ipsius cutem*'. See Intro.,
5.22.

10. *peremptory*] See note on IV. iii.
222.

his tongue filed] polished. 'Filed
tongue' was an old and common expression. The first example of the verb
'to file', in the figurative sense of 'to
smooth, to polish' in *N.E.D.*, is from
Romaunt of the Rose, c. 1400 (381/2):
'His tunge was fyled sharpe & square'.
The phrase is in Spenser's *Colin Cloutes
Come Home Again,* 701–2 ('a filed
toung furnisht with tearmes of art'),
several times in Lyly's plays, and in
Beaumont and Fletcher's *Loyal Subject,*
III. ii.

11. *majestical*] grand, stately, as in
H5, IV. i. 284. Cf. Lyly's *Endymion,* v.
ii: 'O sir your chinne is but a quyller
yet, you will be most majesticall when
it is full fledge'. An earlier form than
'majestic', and apparently introduced
by Lyly.

12. *thrasonical*] boastful, from
Thraso, the braggart soldier in
Terence's play *Eunuchus.* Though Furness gives a 1578 reference from
Richard Tarlton, the adjective was
probably the invention of Stanyhurst
who had begun to write in 1570 the
Conceits printed in 1582. This volume
contains the famous epigram (in English hexameters) on a 'loftye Thrasonical huf snuffe' so scoffed at by
Nashe in the Epistle Dedicatory prefixed to Greene's *Menaphon,* 1589
(McKerrow, iii. 320). Greene uses the
word elsewhere, as does also Gabriel
Harvey a couple of times.

picked] neat, elaborate, over-
refined. Cf. Nashe, *Foure Letters Confuted* (McKerrow, i. 286): 'Shrouded a
picked effeminate Carpet Knight
under the fictionate person of Herma-
phroditus'. Furness refers to Grosart's
Green's *Works* (xi. 72), where the passage 'certayne quaint, pickt and neate
companions' occurs in the *Defence of
Conny-catching* 1592 (author unknown;
an attack on Greene). See also Rider's
Bibliotheca Scholastica, 1589: 'Picked or
curious. *Argutus, elegans, accuratus,
eximius, exquisitus*'. Ainsworth's seventh sense of *argutus* is 'short, neat,
picked'.

too spruce, too affected, too odd, as it were, too peregrinate, as I may call it.

Nath. A most singular and choice epithet.   15
                    [*Draws out his table-book.*

Hol. He draweth out the thread of his verbosity finer than
the staple of his argument. I abhor such fanatical
phantasimes, such insociable and point-devise companions; such rackers of orthography, as to speak

15. [*Draws*] *Ff3,4; Draw . . . Qq,Ff1,2.*   18. phantasimes] *Cambridge, Globe;*
phantasims *Qq,Ff1,2,3;* phantasms *F4.*   19. orthography] ortagriphie, orto-
graphie, ortagriphy, ortagraphy *early edd.*

13. *spruce*] here means *over*-elegant,
affected. Cf. v. ii. 407, and Nashe,
Terrors of the Night (McKerrow, i. 366),
1594: 'Whose names if you aske, hee
claps you in the mouth with halfe a
dozen spruce titles, never til he invented them heard of by any Christ-
ian'.

13–14. *peregrinate*] having the air of a
traveller or foreigner—like 'Italianate'. No other example in *N.E.D.*,
excepting in Lytton's *My Novel*, taken
from here.

15. *singular*] unparalleled, excellent.
Ascham uses the word frequently in
this sense: 'So singular in wisedome (in
their owne opinion) as scarse they
count the best Counsellor the Prince
hath comparable with them' (*The
Scholemaster* [Arber, p. 85], 1568.

[*Draws out his table-book*] The direction is given as an imperative in early
texts, a sign that they derive from an
original that had at least been used as
a prompt-book. 'Tables', a book in
which to jot down anything noteworthy either read or overheard, were
standard equipment for any Elizabethan with pretensions to learning or
fashion. Cf. *Ham.*, i. v. 107: 'My tables!
meet it is I set it down.'

17. *staple*] thread, pile, or texture of
wool or flax. An early use of this technical word, which is perhaps implied
in the following passage: 'flockes
Yeelding forth fleeces stapled with
such woole, As Lecester cannot yeelde
more finer stuffe' (Greene [Grosart,

xiii. 71], *Friar Bacon and Friar Bungay*).

fanatical] frantic, extravagant. Applied to persons this use has escaped
the *N.E.D.*, being considerably earlier
than its first example. The meaning
of the word was hardly fixed. Nashe
speaks of 'phanatical strange hiero-
gliphicks' where he means puns and
ciphers (McKerrow, ii. 182); and in
another place (*Foure Letters Confuted* [i.
321]) he calls Harvey 'the foresaid
fanatical Phobetor, geremumble, tir-
leriwhisco, or what you will'. For
'phantasime' see note on IV. i. 100
above.

18. *insociable*] impossible to associate
with, intolerable. In the sense of 'in-
compatible' the *N.E.D.* has one earlier
example from Savile's *Tacitus*, 1851;
the passage here is not dealt with.
'Insociable' occurs again in this play
(v. ii. 791) with the meaning un-
sociable, and is the earliest example in
the *N.E.D.* It does not occur elsewhere
in Shakespeare.

point-devise] precise, affectedly exact.
See *AYL.*, III. ii. 401. Generally used
adverbally with a preposition: 'Uprist
this jolly lover Absolon, and him aray-
eth gay at point devise.'

19. *orthography*] The spelling 'orto-
graphie' occurs several times in Puttenham (p. 127), but the omission of
the *h* would be abominable here.
Furness gives several extracts from
commentators, and notes, upon the
principles of pronunciation dealt with
in the text. But Holofernes gives much

dout, fine, when he should say doubt; det, when he   20
should pronounce debt,—d, e, b, t, not d, e, t; he
clepeth a calf, cauf; half, hauf; neighbour *vocatur* ne-
bour; neigh abbreviated ne. This is abhominable,
which he would call abominable, it insinuateth me of
insanie: *ne intelligis domine?* to make frantic, lunatic.   25

20. fine] *Qq,Ff; sine* b *New Temple.*   24. he] we *Ff3,4.*   abominable] *Ff3,4;*
abbominable *Q1;* abbominable*Ff1,2.*   25. insanie] *Theobald (Warburton conj.);*
infamie *Qq,Ff.*   ne] *nonne Johnson conj.;* anne *Porson conj.* MS.

more information than any of them,
and they are mainly conjectural. Furness refers to a communication which
appeared in the *New York Times Literary
Review* (July, 1899) by Mr Noyes, 'our
highest living authority on the subject
of Elizabethan pronunciation'. He
quotes from Baret's *Alvearie* (1573?),
where it is expressly stated that the *h*
was not sounded in 'abhominable',
and that 'negh' was pronounced 'nay'.
Apparently, therefore, Holofernes
would confute the Baret school? Puttenham says: 'I would as neare as I
could observe and keepe the lawes of
the Greeke and Latin versifiers, that is
to prolong the sillable which is written
with double consonants or by dip-
thong . . . and to shorten all sillables
that stand upon vowels if there were no
cause of *elision*, and single consonants,
and such of them as are most flowing
and slipper upon the tongue as n. r. t.
d. l. and for this purpose to take away
all aspirations'. Evidently Holofernes
is railing against such innovations as a
pedant should; but the trend of the
times was against him, and for simpli-
fication of pronunciation, as of spelling. In one of his *Letters to Spenser*
(Grosart, iii. 103–5), 1580, Gabriel
Harvey has a tirade against the pedantries of 'Orthography or rather Pseudo-
graphy'. Harvey's patron, Sir Thomas
Smith, was another eminent 'racker of
orthography'. See Intro., 5.22.
    21. *debt*] I owe to Mr John Crow an
example of the adoption of Holofernes'
recommended pronunciation as late
as 1625, when Hugh Holland, in his

A Cypres Garland (C³), could write:
'Then you great Lord, that were to me
so gracious, In twenty weekes (a time
not very spacious) To cause me thrice
to kisse (me thrice your depter) That
hand which bore the Lillybearing
Scepter.'
    22. *calf, cauf; half, hauf*] Holofernes
would sound the *l*s.
    23. *abhominable*] a common spelling
of the time, and earlier, arising from a
mistaken etymology, *ab homine* instead
of *ab omine*. It is found in early dictionaries: *Promptorium,* 1450, and
Levin's *Manipulus,* 1570. Minshew
(ed. 1627) has it 'Abominable, *vide
Abhominable*'. Cotgrave has it right in
1611, but Sherwood (1672) sets Cotgrave straight with the insertion of the
h he omitted. Nashe, Harvey, Greene,
and all writers of the time, as well as
every use in the Shakespeare Folio
(1st and 2nd) have the *h*, I believe.
Indeed, if we accept the Q1 'abbominable', it is apparently the earliest example of the omission of the aspirate
intentionally. The two *b*s in the Q
conform with the Italian of John
Florio's dictionary, *New World of
Words.*
    24–5. *insinuateth me of insanie*] Most
commentators construe 'suggests in-
sanity to me'. Professor J. A. K.
Thomson, however, has suggested
(privately) that Holofernes is giving an
English version of the Latin 'insinuat
in me insaniam' and means 'it introduces frenzy into me', i.e. 'drives me
frantic', as he explains in the next line.
Renaissance schoolmasters were al-

Nath. Laus Deo, bone intelligo.

Hol. Bone? Bon, fort bon; Priscian a little scratched: 'twill serve.

Enter ARMADO, MOTH, *and* COSTARD.

Nath. Videsne quis venit?

26. *bone*] Theobald; bene Qq,Ff.   27. *Bone? Bon, fort bon*; Priscian] New; Bome boon for boon prescian, Qq,Ff; Bome?— bone for bene; Priscian Theobald; Bon, bon, fort bon Priscian! Cambridge.

ways 'inculcating' or 'insinuating' knowledge into their pupils. See note on IV. ii. 13.

25. *insanie*] No other example of this word is known than that adduced by Steevens, and given in the *N.E.D.*, although Furness says: 'Unfortunately I cannot verify this quotation'. The dictionary dates it 1572. Steevens quotes from 'a book entitled, *The Fall and evil Successe of Rebellion from Time to Time*, by Wilfride Holme': 'In the days of sixth Henry Jack Cade made a brag, With a multitude of people; but in the consequence, After a little insanie they fled tag and rag, For Alexander Iden he did his diligence.'

27. Bone?... bon] 'Priscian a little scratched' points to a fault in Nathaniel's Latin and 'Bome' shows clearly where it lies; but 'boon' must represent a distinct word from 'bome'. 'Forboon' stands for 'fort bon' in Heywood's *If You Know not me you Know Nobody* and may well do so here. A similar corruption occurs in *Rom.*, II. iv. 37 ('bones' for 'bons') and note 'alone' of IV. iii. 379 above.

Priscian a little scratched] Priscian, the grammarian, who wrote about A.D. 525, and several of whose works have come down to us, gave rise to the proverb in English, 'to break Priscian's head', used to such as speak false Latin ('*diminuis Prisciani caput*'). Holofernes means 'your Latin is a little mutilated' (or wounded). The earliest example I have of the proverb is from Skelton's *Speke Parrot*, l. 176 (1515): 'Prisian's hed broken now handy dandy, And *Inter didascolos* is rekened for a fole.'

Puttenham has it (Arber, p. 258). Sir John Harington has an interesting passage in *The Metamorphosis of Ajax*, 1596 (Chiswick repr., p. 84): 'Yet least old Priscian should say I brake his head when I never came near him, I will keep me in this', with a marginal note: 'There is a Comedy called *Priscianus vapulans*; where if one should say *ignem hanc*, Priscian would cry, his head were broken.'

29. Videsne quis venit] Classical Latin would require 'veniat', but 'venit' is good enough colloquial usage and it is not necessary to assume a blunder on the part of either Holofernes or the compositor. Furness quotes from T. S. Baynes, *Shakespeare Studies* (1896, p. 181): 'These scraps of Latin dialogue exemplify the technical Latin intercourse between master and pupils in their work, as well as the formal colloquies the latter were required to prepare as exercises.' Baynes quotes *Familiares Colloquendi Formulae*: 'Who comes to meet us? *Quis obviam venit?* He speaks improperly, *Hic incongrue loquitur*; He speaks false Latin, *Diminuit Prisciani caput*; 'Tis barbarous Latin, *Olet barbariem*'. This particular book is a seventeenth-century work, but no doubt borrows from those contemporary with the play. As this was a standard method of teaching Latin, there were many manuals, the chief being the *Colloquies* of Erasmus and of Cordier, the *Sententiae Pueriles* of Leonhard Cullmann, and Vives's *Exercitatio*. In view of ll. 49–53 below (see note) the model here may be the last.

Hol. Video, et gaudeo.   30
Arm. Chirrah!
Hol. Quare chirrah, not sirrah?
Arm. Men of peace, well encountered.
Hol. Most military sir, salutation.
Moth. They have been at a great feast of languages, and   35
    stolen the scraps.
Cost. O, they have lived long on the alms-basket of words.
    I marvel thy master hath not eaten thee for a word;
    for thou art not so long by the head as *honorificabili-*

---

30. Video, et gaudeo] *Video & taceo*
was 'Her Maiesties poesie at the great
Lotterie in London 1568: and ende
1569' (Whitney's *Emblems* [ed. H.
Greene, p. 61], 1586).

31. *Chirrah*] 'Sirrah' was the correct
title from a master to his page. See
Wiv., i. iii. 88. The odd form, to which
Holofernes calls attention, must have a
special point, and M. C. Bradbrook
(*The School of Night*, 1936) has suggested that it is a take-off of Sir Walter
Ralegh's west-country accent. See
Intro., 5.25. An alternative solution
has been put forward by Professor
J. A. K. Thomson—that the word is
Armado's attempt at 'chaere' (χαῖρε),
one of the forms of salutation listed by
Erasmus in the first and most elementary section of his *Familiaria Colloquia*,
on which Elizabethan schoolboys cut
their teeth. This chimes well with the
pedantry and bungled learning on
which much of the fun of this scene
depends.

37. *alms-basket*] 'The refuse of the
table was collected by the attendants,
who used wooden knives for the purpose, and put into a large basket [or
tub], which was called the alms-
basket, the contents of which were
reserved for the poor' (Halliwell). It is
mentioned in Greene's *Quip for an
Upstart Courtier*: 'I sit and dine with the
Nobility, when thou art faine to waite
for the reversion of the almes basket'
(Grosart, xi. 224). The term is, it may
be noted, only relevant to feasts and
banquets. Jonson has a similar meta-

phor in his 'Ode to Himself' (*New Inn*):
'For who the relish of these guests will
fit Needs set them by the alms-basket
of wit.' And see Day, *Isle of Gulls*, i. i,
where 'alm's basket scraps' reminds
one of the present passage.

39–40. honorificabilitudinitatibus]
'often mentioned as the longest word
known' (Johnson). Steevens refers to
Marston's *Dutch Courtesan* and Nashe's
Lenten Stuffe; Grey gives Taylor's example, who adds a syllable in the
middle. See, too, Fletcher's *Mad Lover*
(Glover and Waller, ii. 10), i. i. These
are later than Shakespeare. Dyce
quoted Hunter, who found it scribbled
somewhere in a MS. of the reign of
Henry VI. Furness gives an exhaustive
and learned note from Hermann,
Euphorion, 1894, who traces the word
back, in the Latin schoolmaster vein,
to Dante's treatise, *De vulgari elo-
quentia* (*c.* 1300); and to *Excerpts* from
Petrus of Pisa, Charlemagne's teacher.
Hermann finds it in two old German
comedies of about 1580, both of which
place their action in the schoolroom.
He finds it derived from *Honorifica* in a
Liber derivationum of the twelfth century, and he gives several references to
its appearance in dictionaries from
1200 to 1500. Murray (*N.E.D.*) gives a
reference to *The Complaynt of Scotland*,
1548–9. The extract was quoted in
Notes and Queries (June 1902) by G.
Stronach; it concludes: 'There vas ane
uthir that writ in his verkis, [thir lang-
tailit vordis,] *gaudet honorificabilitudini-
tatibus.*' Hermann says this term en-

 tudinitatibus: thou art easier swallowed than a flap- 40
  dragon.
Moth. Peace! the peal begins.
Arm. [*To Hol.*] Monsieur, are you not lettered?
Moth. Yes, yes, he teaches boys the horn-book. What is
  a, b, spelt backward with the horn on his head? 45
Hol. Ba, *pueritia,* with a horn added.
Moth. Ba! most silly sheep with a horn. You hear his
  learning.
Hol. Quis, quis, thou consonant?

folds the names of Dante and Shake-speare; and reveals how a purely literary word can survive, by means of the schools (as he believes), for nine hundred years—a span of life to which neither by origin nor by form it had any title. It finds its way into *N.E.D.*, as an English word, *honorificabilitudinity* (a mere mouthful), given in Blount's *Glossographia,* and Philips's *New World of Words.* ⸪

40–1. *easier swallowed than a flap-dragon*] said to be the thing, usually a burning plum or raisin, floating and snapped at in our Christmas game of Snapdragon. 'Flapdragon', as a swaggering humour, is mentioned in Jonson's *Cynthia's Revels,* v. iii (1600). Like many other drinking expressions, it seems to have been of Dutch extraction. Cf. the following quotations: 'In the time a Fleming drinks a flapdragon' (Dekker, *The Wonder of a Kingdom,* Act 1 [1636]). 'My brother Swallows it with more ease than a Dutchman Does flapdragons' (Barry, *Ram Alley,* 1611; Hazlitt's *Dodsley,* vol. x, p. 298). 'swallow it like flapdragons, as if you had lived With chewing the cud after' (Webster, *Devil's Law Case,* II. i. [1623]). It seems to have been a lover's exploit, from the passage at the end of *Cynthia's Revels:* 'From stabbing of arms, flapdragons, healths, whiffs, and all such swaggering humours, [*Chorus*] Good Mercury, defend us.'

42. *the peal begins*] as of bells, not as Schmidt says, 'a mighty sound'. To

ring one a peal was a common expression for a torrent of words. 'I will go and ringe a peale through both his ears for this dishonest behaviour' (*Menechmus* [by W. W.], v. i [1595]).

44. *horn-book*] 'A leaf of paper containing the alphabet (often with the addition of the ten digits, some elements of spelling, and the Lord's Prayer), protected by a thin plate of translucent horn, and mounted on a tablet of wood with a projecting piece for a handle' (*N.E.D.*). 'The horn-book gradually gave way to the "battledore" and "primer"' (Chambers, *Book of Days*). In A. W. Tuer's *History of the Horn-book* it is recorded that the last order for them, as school-requisites, came from the country about 1799. From that time the demand wholly ceased. Specimens are now unobtainable of the early black-letter type. There is no earlier example than the one in the text of the use of the word in the *N.E.D.* The quotation therein from (Lyly's) *Pappe with a Hatchett* preceded *Love's Labour's Lost,* since Harvey wrote his answer to it in 1589. The earlier name for the primer, or alphabet-book, was the Christ's cross-row, or Cross-row.

49. *consonant*] Cf. with this a quotation in *N.E.D.* from Walkington's *Optic Glasse,* 1607: 'Like the foole, a consonant when hee should bee a Mute'. Apparently used derisively in the sense of that which has no existence alone; a nonentity, since it requires the vowel sound.

Moth. The last of the five vowels, if you repeat them; or   50
  the fifth, if I.

Hol. I will repeat them; a, e, i,—

Moth. The sheep: the other two concludes it; o, u.

Arm. Now, by the salt wave of the Mediterraneum, a
  sweet touch, a quick venue of wit! snip, snap, quick   55
  and home! it rejoiceth my intellect; true wit!

Moth. Offered by a child to an old man; which is wit-old.

Hol. What is the figure? what is the figure?

Moth. Horns.

Hol. Thou disputes like an infant: go, whip thy gig.   60

50. last] *Qq,F ;* third *Theobald et seq.*   54. wave] wane *Q1.*   55. venue] *Dyce,*
Cambridge, Globe; vene ve *Q1,F1;* venewe *F2;* venew *Ff3,4.*   60. disputes]
Qq,F1; disputes't *Ff2,3;* disputest *F4.*

50. *last*] Furness 'suggests that Moth
purposely framed his answer ambigu-
ously so as to lure the Pedant, to a
repetition of the vowels'. To Moth,
Holofernes remains 'you' (and so the
sheep) no matter who repeats the
vowels.

53. *concludes it*] both 'proves the pro-
position' and 'completes the list of
vowels'. F. A. Yates (*A Study of Love's
Labour's Lost,* 1936) draws attention to
a passage in Vives' *Exercitatio Linguae
Latinae* in which the pupil is exhorted
to remember the Spanish word 'oueia'
(sheep) as a mnemonic for the vowels.
Their mere repetition would therefore
suggest 'sheep' to any Elizabethan
schoolboy.

54. *salt*] suggested perhaps by the
sense of acutely witted, as in Gascoigne: 'unlesse the invention have in
it also *aliquid salis* . . . some good and
fine devise, shewing the quicke capa-
citie of a writer' (Arber, p. 31) (1575).
Jonson uses it.

Mediterraneum] Greene has this
form: 'resting himself on a hill that
over-peered the great Mediterraneum
noting how Phœbus fetched his
Lavaltos on the purple Plaines of
Neptunus . . . the Dolphines (the
sweete conceipters of Musicke) fetcht
their carreers on the calmed waves'
(*Menaphon* [Grosart, vi. 36], 1587).

55. *touch*] stroke, trick, taste of one's
'quality'. Cf. Ascham, *The Scholemaster*
(Arber, p. 18), 1570: 'Playing both
with the shrewde touches of many
courste boyes, and with the small discretion of many leude Scholemasters'.

venue of wit] assault of wit. See *Wiv.,*
I. i. 295. In fencing, the attack leading
to a hit. See Lodge, *Euphues Golden
Legacie* (*Shakes. Lib.,* p. 98), 1590:
'Love . . . seeing the parties at the gaze,
encountered them both with such a
veny, that the stroke . . . could never
after be raced out.'

snip, snap] See *Wiv.,* IV. v. 3.
Gabriel Harvey, in *Pierce's Supererogation* (Grosart, ii. 313) has: 'if any who-
soever will needes be offering abuse in
fact or snip-snapping in termes'; and
Nashe in his Epistle Dedicatorie to
Have With You, etc. (McKerrow, iii. 10)
has 'torment him, & deal as snip snap
snappishly with him as ever he was
dealt withall'. See above, III. i. 19.

57. *wit-old*] The word on which
Moth quibbles only occurs once in
Shakespeare, in *Wiv.,* II. ii. 314 (and
'wittolly' l. 284). It is a synonym of
'cuckold', also in Greene's *Philomela*
(Grosart, xi. 166), of about this date.

58. *figure*] our 'figure of speech'.

60. *disputes*] Shakespeare often has
this form of the second person singular.
There is another example at v. ii. 208.

Moth. Lend me your horn to make one, and I will whip
    about your infamy *manu cita*. A gig of a cuckold's
    horn!

Cost. An I had but one penny in the world, thou should'st
    have it to buy gingerbread. Hold, there is the very   65
    remuneration I had of thy master, thou halfpenny
    purse of wit, thou pigeon-egg of discretion. O, an
    the heavens were so pleased that thou wert but my
    bastard, what a joyful father wouldst thou make me.
    Go to; thou hast it *ad dunghill*, at the fingers' ends, as   70
    they say.

Hol. O, I smell false Latin: dunghill for *unguem*.

Arm. Arts-man, preambulate: we will be singled from the
    barbarous. Do you not educate youth at the charge-
    house on the top of the mountain?   75

62. *manu cita*] *Anon. conj., Cambridge;* unū cita *Q1;* unum cita *Ff; circum circa,
Theobald et seq.; unum cito! Furnivall.*   73. preambulate] *Cambridge;* preambulat
Qq,Ff; praeambulat *Theobald.*   singled] *Ff,Q2;* singuled *Q1, Cambridge.*
74–5. charge-house] church-house *Theobald conj.;* large house *Collier MS.*

gig] See note on IV. iii. 164. The
'infamy' at which Moth gibes in return
must be a topical hit; there is some
buried quibbling here I cannot reach.
Why should Holofernes be a cuckold?

62. manu cita] with ready, or ener-
getic hand. Theobald's emendation is
right in principle—the phrase must be
a schoolboy or benchers' tag—but it is
a pity to reject the one part of the Q
reading that sounds right. *Manu* is not
unquestionable, but "twill serve"; a
persevering reader of the Elizabethans'
Latin phrase-books and legal docu-
ments might well find something better.

66–7. *halfpenny purse*] These small
purses, probably for holding the little
silver halfpence of the time, are
mentioned again in *Wiv.,* III. v.
149; and Lyly, *Mother Bombie,* III. iv.
(1589).

67. *discretion*] This recalls Harvey's
jibe at Nashe. See note on III. i. 26.

70–2. ad . . . unguem] to the nail. A
common proverbial phrase, said to
be borrowed from sculpture (Horace,
Satires, I. v. 31–3). Cf. Jonson's translation of Horace, *De Arte Poetica* ('Per-

fectum decies non castigavit ad unguem') : 'Not ten times o'er corrected
to the nail'. It was used of a lesson
learnt perfectly: 'But, Sirra, see you
learne your lesson perfectlie, and have
it without booke *ad unguem*' (*Martins
Months Minde* [Grosart's *Nashe,* i. 203],
1589). And Webster, *Westward Hoe,* ii.
1 : 'She has her letters *ad unguem*'. Jonson has it several times. They are the
last words in Harvey's much laughed
at *Judgement on Earthquakes* (Grosart, i.
74), 1580.

72. *false Latin*] See note on l. 29
above.

73. *Arts-man*] scholar, learned person. *N.E.D.* gives an example from
Bacon's *Advancement of Learning.* The
word was commoner in the sense of
workman, as in Chapman's *Homer.* We
have elsewhere in this play 'man of
peace' and 'warman'.

singled] separated. Similarly in
Greene, *Alcida* (Grosart, ix. 73), 1588:
'When wee were in the greene meades,
Meribates and my daughter had
singled themselves.'

74–5. *charge-house*] school. Not

Hol. Or *mons*, the hill.

Arm. At your sweet pleasure, for the mountain.

Hol. I do, sans question.

Arm. Sir, it is the king's most sweet pleasure and affection
to congratulate the princess at her pavilion in the   80
posteriors of this day, which the rude multitude call
the afternoon.

Hol. The posterior of the day, most generous sir, is liable,
congruent, and measurable for the afternoon: the
word is well culled, chose; sweet and apt, I do assure   85
you, sir; I do assure.

Arm. Sir, the king is a noble gentleman, and my familiar,

79. most] *not in Q2.*   85. chose] *Qq,F1 ;* choise *F2 ;* choice *Ff3,4.*   86. you]
not in Q2.

known elsewhere. Probably one where
children were taught at the charge of
the parish, or else merely a house for
their charge or care. The commentators have worked hard to find topical
explanations of this passage, some of
which are discussed in the Intro., 5.21
and 5.23. The point may, however, be
much simpler. Professor J. A. K.
Thomson draws my attention to the
conversation that follows the *salutandi
formulae* at the outset of Erasmus'
Familiaria Colloquia. It is between
Georgius and Livinus, who has just
arrived from Paris. Georgius asks *unde
prodis*, 'where do you come from ?' and
Livinus replies *e collegio Montis acuti*,
'from the college of the Mountain with
the sharp crest'. G. *ergo ades nobis
onustus literis*, 'so you have come to us
laden with learning ?' L. *immo pediculis*,
'no, with lice.' It is easy to believe that
Elizabethan schoolboys would have
loved this passage, and that the
'charge-house on the Mountain'
would be a byword with them as a sort
of Dotheboys Hall. Erasmus was in
fact having his revenge on the Collège
de Mont Aigu in Paris, where he had
been unhappy in his own youth.

81. *posteriors*] The word occurs in the
Prologue to Harington's *Metamorphosis of Ajax*, 1596.

83. *liable*] suitable, apt. See *John*, IV.

ii. 226. In *N.E.D.* there is a quotation
from a letter dated 1570: 'To chewse
persons lyable to give good information'. This quotation is not satisfactory
per se. It may mean 'likely', which is
nearer Sense 3.

84. *congruent*] Armado has already
used this word (I. ii. 13), which is not
elsewhere in Shakespeare. *N.E.D.* has
an early reference to Higden, *Rolls*
(*ante* 1453). Craig quotes from Udall's
Erasmus (Roberts's repr., p. 93), 1542:
'He thought not the name of a manne
to bee a congruente or a right name for
such persones as lived not according to
reason.' A stilted and neglected word.
Sir Owen ap Meredith, the Welsh
knight in *Patient Grissel* (by Dekker and
Chettle) ridicules it in 1600 (Collier's
ed., pp. 21–2).

measurable] meet, competent. Cf.
Cor., II. ii. 127: 'He cannot but with
measure fit the honours which we
devise him.' Cotgrave has '*Moyen:*
mean, indifferent, moderate, measurable, competent, reasonable'.

85. *chose*] for 'chosen'. Holofernes'
synonyms may seem better balanced if
we accept the reading 'choice'. The
corruption is easy if Shakespeare used
the spelling 'choise', as in F2; it was
common at this time—cf. Nashe's MS.
poem *The Choise of Valentines*.

87. *familiar*] particular friend; as in

I do assure ye, very good friend. For what is inward
between us, let it pass; (I do beseech thee, remember thy courtesy—I beseech thee, apparel thy head)   90
and among other importunate and most serious de-
signs, and of great import indeed, too, but let that

89-90. remember] refrain *Capell;* remember not *Malone.*   91. importunate]
Ff,Q2; important *Q1;* important *Cambridge.*

2H4, II. i. 144. Cf. Lodge, *Euphues
Golden Legacie (Shakes. Lib.,* 1875, p.
30): 'Rosader . . . accompanyed with a
troupe of yoong gentlemen that were
desirous to be his familiars'.

88. *inward]* confidential, private.

89-90. *remember thy courtesy*] the
usual explanation ('don't forget your
head is uncovered') assumes Holofernes to have been bareheaded since
'salutation', at l. 34. Armado notices it
and tells him to apparel his head. Dyce
quoted as parallel the following from
Jonson's *Every Man in his Humour,* I. ii:
'*Servant.* . . . I was required . . . to
deliver you this letter, sir. *Knowell.* To
me, sir! What do you mean? Pray you
remember your courtesy. [*Reads.*] . . .
Nay, pray you be covered'; but the
meaning may well be the reverse.
Knowell is insulted when he says:
'What do you mean?' He bids the servant remove his hat by the expression,
he keeps him bareheaded while he
reads the letter, and not till he speaks
to him again does he bid him be
covered. We shall have then to take
opposite meanings from the two passages. Armado reminds Holofernes to
conclude his courtesy or salutation;
Knowell reminds his servant to begin
it. Parallels to the signification given
here have been adduced from *Lusty
Juventus* (Hazlitt's *Dodsley,* ii. 74), and
from Marlowe's *Doctor Faustus* (Case
ed., p. 156). The latter has nothing to
do with the text, excepting that the
words 'remember your courtesy'
(make a leg or bow) occur: the former
('be remembered and cover your
head') carries no weight one way or the
other. Hart provided an alternative

explanation that is most attractive.
His note runs: 'It was the custom to
uncover at the name of the king, or
during a conversation about the king.
This is the *courtesy* Armado claims for
his friend the King. In *Lusty Juventus*
there is so far a parallelism that Juventus may have uncovered at Hypocrisy's introduction of the Deity into
the conversation. As a mark of defer-
ence to the King's mention, a passage
in Beaumont and Fletcher's *Noble
Gentlemen* (Act III) drew my attention,
and be it remembered the scene is laid
also in France: '*Shatillion.* Can you
give me reason From whence this great
duke sprang that walks abroad? *Lady.*
E'en from the king himself. *Shat.* As
you're a woman, I think you may be
cover'd: Yet your prayer would do no
harm good woman. *Lady.* God preserve him! *Shat.* I say Amen, and so say
all good subjects.' If the mode was
French, no doubt other parallels will
be found, but this one is so exact as to
be conclusive. The hat was removed
as evidence that the wearer prays for
the king upon specific reference to
him; as we do at "God save the King!"
Holofernes may have been bare since
Armado began to talk of the King, and
be now released from his courtesy; or
he may be reminded of it by these
words.'

92-3. *but let that pass*] never mind
about that. A common colloquialism.
Dekker's Shoemaker's wife can hardly
open her lips without using the catch-
phrase. Sidney puts it into the mouth of
Miso, in that much abused but highly
entertaining part of *Arcadia* (Feuillerat,
i. 237) where he depicts the dialogue of

pass; for I must tell thee, it will please his grace, by
the world, sometime to lean upon my poor shoulder, and with his royal finger, thus, dally with my   95
excrement, with my mustachio: but, sweet heart,
let that pass. By the world, I recount no fable: some
certain special honours it pleaseth his greatness to
impart to Armado, a soldier, a man of travel, that
hath seen the world: but let that pass. The very all   100
of all is, but, sweet heart, I do implore secrecy, that
the king would have me present the princess, sweet
chuck, with some delightful ostentation, or show,
or pageant, or antic, or firework. Now, understanding that the curate and your sweet self are good at   105
such eruptions and sudden breaking out of mirth,
as it were, I have acquainted you withal, to the end
to crave your assistance.

Hol. Sir, you shall present before her the Nine Worthies.

101. secrecy] secretie *Q1.*

the people: 'I might have had an
other-gaines husband, then Dametas.
But let that passe, God amend him!
And yet I speake it not without good
cause' (bk ii). Jonson has it in his
Staple of News, I. vi (Herford and Simpson, vi. 300); and see *Gesta Grayorum*,
1594 (ed. Greg, p. 59): 'Well, let that
pass, and to the purpose now.'

93–4. *by the world*] See IV. iii. 17.

96. *excrement*] 'that which grows out
or forth' (*N.E.D.*). See *Mer.V.*, III. ii.
87, and *Wint.*, IV. iv. 733. The earliest
known use of the word in this sense
(hair, nails, feathers) is probably that
in *Solyman and Perseda*, I. iii. 136: 'whose
chin bears no impression of manhood.
Not an hayre, not an excrement'. The
play is attributed to Kyd, and dated
approximately 1592.

100–1. *all of all*] sum of everything.

103. *chuck*] chick, or chicken. A term
of endearment, used familiarly, occurring several times in Shakespeare. It is
in Jonson and Chapman's *Eastward
Hoe*, V. 1.

ostentation] No other example of this
use of the word (spectacular show) is

given in *N.E.D.* The following comes
near it: 'The lockes of haire with their
skinnes he hanged on a line unto two
trees. And thus he made ostentation as
of a great triumph at Werowocomoes'
(*Captain Smith* [Arber, p. 82], 1612).

104. *antic*] a grotesque pageant. Cf.
Captain Smith (Arber, p. 123), 1608:
'Being presently presented with this
anticke, 30 young women came naked
out of the woods (only covered behind
and before with a few greene leaves),
their bodies all painted . . . every one
different. . . . The leader had a faire
paire of stagges hornes on her head . . .
every one with their severall devises
. . . with most hellish cries and shouts.'
Fernando in Ford's *Love's Sacrifice*, III.
ii, speaks of 'an antic, a rare conceit he
saw in Brussels' performed by knights
and ladies of the Court. Jonson seems
to have foreseen the strictures of Nares,
Gifford, and others upon this word in
The Fox, III. vi: 'And my dwarf shall
dance, My eunuch sing, my fool make
up the antic, Whilst we, in changed
shapes, act Ovid's parts.'

109. *Nine Worthies*] They were,

Sir Nathaniel, as concerning some entertainment of   110
time, some show in the posterior of this day, to be
rendered by our assistance, the king's command,
and this most gallant, illustrate, and learned gentleman, before the princess; I say, none so fit as to present the Nine Worthies.   115

Nath. Where will you find men worthy enough to present them?

Hol. Joshua, yourself; [myself and] this gallant gentleman, Judas Maccabæus; this swain, because of his
 great limb or joint, shall pass Pompey the Great;   120
 the page, Hercules—

---

110. Sir Nathaniel] *Capell, Steevens, Craig;* Sir Holofernes *Qq,Ff;* Sir *Rowe.*
112. rendered] rended *Q1.*   assistance] *Hanmer;* assistants *Qq,Ff.*
Hart. the] at the *F2.* 118. [myself and]] *Cambridge;* myself, and
Qq,Ff; myself—, and *New;* myself or *Steevens (1793);* om. *Rowe.* 120. pass]
pass for *Capell.*

---

according to Gerard Legh, *Accedens of Armorye* (who gives all their blazons), Duke Josua, Hector, David, Alexander, Judas Machabeus, Julius Cesar, King Arthure, Charlemayne, Sir Guy (of Warwicke). But the latter was sometimes replaced amongst 'the learned and authentic fellows' (see Dyce's *Beaumont and Fletcher,* i. 143) by Godfrey of Bouillon. Douce says it has not been accounted for why Shakespeare includes Hercules and Pompey. In the second part of Whetstone's *Promos and Cassandra* (the source of *Measure for Measure*), 1578, the 'nyne worthyes' are to 'Be so instauld, as best may please the eye' (I. iv), amongst the shows and pageants welcoming the king upon his return. Two men 'apparalled like greene men at the Mayor feast, with clubbes of fyreworke' keep a passage clear. The only name given of those represented is Hercules conquering monsters, though it is not stated he was one of the Worthies. This may account for his inclusion here. The recognized Worthies were often trifled with. Nashe says: 'To Charles the fifte then Emperour, they reported how he shewed the nine

worthies, David, Salomon, Gedeon, and the rest, in that similitude and likenes that they lived upon earth' (*The Unfortunate Traveller* [McKerrow, ii. 253], 1594). And Greene: 'Which if I should obtaine, I would count it a more rich prize then ever Scipio or any of the nine Worthies wonne by conquest' (*Alcida* [Grosart, ix. 49], 1588). Ritson (*Remarks,* 38) gave a specimen of a 'Pageant of the Nine Worthies' from an original MS. of Edward IV's time, which is reprinted in Furness's Variorum edition. See Intro., 5.1(*h*).

 112. *assistance*] Hanmer's emendation (first suggested by Theobald) is supported by Armado's use of the word a few lines earlier. The 'assistants' of Q may be explained either as a misreading of manuscript or, possibly, as archaic spelling, though Hart's parallel from Nashe's *Christ's Teares* rests on a misinterpretation.

 113. *illustrate*] See note on IV. i. 66.

 118. [*myself and*] By the time the pageant appears, it has been largely recast, and we may take this passage to be an unrevised draft, with no part as yet assigned to Holofernes.

 120. *pass*] represent, perform. An

Arm. Pardon, sir; error: he is not quantity enough for
    that Worthy's thumb: he is not so big as the end of
    his club.

Hol. Shall I have audience? he shall present Hercules   125
    in minority: his enter and exit shall be strangling a
    snake; and I will have an apology for that purpose.

Moth. An excellent device! so if any of the audience hiss,
    you may cry 'Well done, Hercules! now thou crush-
    est the snake!' That is the way to make an offence   130
    gracious, though few have the grace to do it.

Arm. For the rest of the Worthies?

Hol. I will play three myself.

Moth. Thrice-worthy gentleman!

Arm. Shall I tell you a thing?   135

Hol. We attend.

Arm. We will have, if this fadge not, an antic. I beseech
    you, follow.

Hol. *Via*, goodman Dull! thou hast spoken no word all
    this while.   140

---

easy sense to give a verb of such wide
powers. The sense of execute, or complete, in Jonson's *Fox*, iii. vi: 'I told his
son, brought, hid him here, Where he
might see his father pass the deed',
comes near to it. It seems to me absurd
to suppose *pass* can mean surpass (a
common sense) here; as if Costard was
a real giant. He is not intended to excel
Pompey, only to reproduce him.
Malone (followed by Furness) is posi-
tive *pass* means surpass.

121–4. *Hercules . . . club*] See note at
l. 109. For the hero's exploit 'in
minority' cf. 'It is my Cradle game To
vanquish Snakes' (Golding's Ovid's
Metamorphoses, ix. 79–80 [1567]).

125. *have audience*] be heard. See
AYL., v. iv. 157, etc.

126. *enter*] *N.E.D.* has two other
examples, both earlier, of the substantive 'enter'; the act of entering.

137. *fadge*] suit, succeed, turn out
well. See *Tw.N.*, ii. ii. 34. The earliest
example of this verb in *N.E.D.* is from
Whetstone's *Promos and Cassandra*, pt i

(1578). The passage in the text would
probably be the next historically, but
it occurs again in the second part of the
same old play. The sixth scene of Act i
—to which the words ending 'clubbes
of fyre worke' (note above, l. 109) are
a stage instruction—begins '*Phallax.*
This geare fadgeth now, that these
fellowes peare.' Coupled with the
remaining allusions, and with the
exactly parallel use of *fadge* as referring
to a pageant, it amounts to a certainty
that Shakespeare recalled Whetstone's
play while writing this scene. For *antic*
see above, l. 104.

139. Via] 'An adverbe of encourag-
ing much used by commanders, as also
by riders to their horses, Goe on, forward, on, away, goe to, on quickly'
(Florio, *New World of Words*, 1611). It
seems here to mean rather 'buck up',
'what cheer'. It occurs several times in
Shakespeare, and his contemporaries,
Jonson, Fletcher, and Chapman. The
example in the text is the earliest yet
quoted.

Dull. Nor understand none neither, sir.

Hol. Allons! we will employ thee.

Dull. I'll make one in a dance, or so; or I will play on
the tabor to the Worthies, and let them dance the
hay.   145

Hol. Most dull, honest Dull. To our sport, away!   [*Exeunt.*

142. *Allons!*] Alone *Qq,Ff.*   142–5.] *Given as two lines verse ending* play, hay,
Halliwell, Dyce, Cambridge, Globe; as prose Steevens and old texts.

142. *Allons*] See IV. iii. 379.

143. *make one*] be of the party. See
Wiv., II. iii. 48, and *1H4*, I. ii. 113.
N.E.D. gives a reference to Udall's
Erasmus, 1542. The expression occurs
several times in Shakespeare.

or so] See II. i. 211.

144. *tabor*] a small drum played with
one hand; with the other the musician
held his pipe, playing the two instruments simultaneously. See *Wint.*, IV. iv.
183. When Kemp started on his *Nine
Daies Wonder Performed in a Morrice
from London to Norwich* on 'The first
Mondaye in Lent' (1600), he was
'attended by Thomas Slye, hys
Taberer'. On the title of his tract is a
figure of the pair, the tabor being held
apparently by a single band round the
left wrist, which hand also holds the
pipe to the mouth, the right using the
short stick. The tabor is about twice
the length of its diameter, covered
at each end alike. No doubt is here
also attached by a string round the
neck.

144–5. *dance the hay*] 'A country
dance, having a winding or serpentine
nature, or being of the nature of a reel'
(*N.E.D.*). 'To dance the hay became a
proverbial expression signifying to

twist about or wind in and out without
making any advance' (Chappell's
Popular Music [1859], ii. 629). There
were several varieties of hay. Furness
quotes from *Orchesographie*, 1588, already referred to in a note to 'brawl'
(III. i. 6). The French writer gives a
description of the *Braule de la Haye*,
which Furness quotes, and points out
its resemblance to the grand chain in a
quadrille. This may not be the English
hay, which is mentioned by Skelton in
1529. *N.E.D.* says '*haye d'allemaigne* is
used in 15 c. French by C. Marot.'
Marlowe has 'dance an antic hay' in
his *Edward II*, I. i (Chase ed., p. 73).
Hart took pleasure in pointing out that
there was a special variant called the
Irish hay which was unusually bois-
terous. Guilpin mentions it in *Skialetheia*, Satire iv (repr., p. 43), 1598:
'His head is like a windmils trunke so
bigge Wherein ten thousand thoughts
run whirlegigge, Play at barleybreake,
and daunce Irish hay, Civill and
peacefull like the Centaurs fray'; and
Day, *Law Tricks*, 1608: 'A company of
bottlenos'd devils dauncing the Irish
hay'; and Dekker, *Strange Horse-Race*
(Grosart, iii. 365), 1613: 'The Daunce
was an infernall Irish hay.'

SCENE II

Enter the PRINCESS, MARIA, KATHARINE, *and* ROSALINE.

Prin. Sweet hearts, we shall be rich ere we depart,
    If fairings come thus plentifully in:
    A lady wall'd about with diamonds!
    Look you what I have from the loving king.
Ros. Madam, came nothing else along with that? 5
Prin. Nothing but this! yes; as much love in rhyme
    As would be cramm'd up in a sheet of paper,
    Writ o' both sides the leaf, margent and all,
    That he was fain to seal on Cupid's name.
Ros. That was the way to make his godhead wax; 10
    For he hath been five thousand year a boy.
Kath. Ay, and a shrewd unhappy gallows too.

Scene II

S.D. *Enter . . . Rosaline*] *Enter the Ladyes Q1.* 1. *Prin.*] *Quee. Q1 throughout.*
3, 4.] *Transposed Hudson (S. Walker conj.), New.* 8. o'] *Cambridge*; a *Q1*; on
Ff,Q2. 11. year] yeare *Q1*, yeeres *F1.* 12. shrewd] shrowd *Q1.*

2. *fairings*] Cf. Greene's *Never Too Late* (Grosart, viii. 195), 1590: 'Oenone chose Paris . . . thinking the sweetest face the best fayring for a gentlewoman's eye.' In these days almost anything, or everything, was purchased at fairs.

3. *A lady . . . diamonds*] a favourite design of Elizabethan jewellers. For parallels see *Queen Elizabeth's New Year's Gifts* (reproduced in Nichols's *Progresses*, 1823). Here is an example dating from 1581–2: 'Item, a juell of golde, being the personage of a woman . . . garnished, with smale rubyes and dymondes, and a smale perle pendent geven by Thomas Howarde'. Plenty more occur. At ii. 72 (1577–8) there is 'a man of golde annamuled grene, hanging at a small cheyne'; at ii. 79 'a woman en-namuled . . . the bodye garneshed with sparks of diamunds and rubyes'; and at ii. 419 (1583–4) 'a juell of golde, being a personage of a woman of mother-of-perle, garnished on the one side with smale diamondes'. In view of

such evidence, it is hard to maintain, with Hart, that 'The Princess points to herself bedecked with the gems, probably she had others as well, and calls herself a lady enclosed in diamonds.' To make the passage quite clear Walker (followed by Hudson and Dover Wilson) would transpose this line to follow l. 4; and Dover Wilson supports the change by claiming that the Q printing of the lines as prose indicates corrected copy, of which the compositor could not make out either the order or the metrical form. I cannot, however, see that there is any real difficulty in the passage as it stands in Q.

10. *wax*] increase (with quibble).

11. *thousand year a boy*] Halliwell compares Sidney, *Arcadia* (p. 174, ed. 1590): 'This is thy worke, thou God for ever blinde; Though thousands old, a Boy entitled still.'

12. *shrewd*] curst, unlucky, evil. From Middle English *schrewe*, malicious.

gallows] gallows bird, one fit for the

Ros. You'll ne'er be friends with him: a' kill'd your sister.
Kath. He made her melancholy, sad, and heavy;
  And so she died: had she been light, like you,   15
  Of such a merry, nimble, stirring spirit,
  She might ha' been a grandam ere she died;
  And so may you, for a light heart lives long.
Ros. What's your dark meaning, mouse, of this light word?
Kath. A light condition in a beauty dark.   20
Ros. We need more light to find your meaning out.
Kath. You'll mar the light by taking it in snuff;
  Therefore I'll darkly end the argument.
Ros. Look what you do, you do it still i' the dark.
Kath. So do not you, for you are a light wench.   25
Ros. Indeed I weigh not you, and therefore light.

13. ne'er] neare *Q1.* 17. ha'] a *Qq,Ff1,2;* have *Ff3,4.* a grandam]
Grandam *Q1.*

hangman. Cf. *Tp.,* I. i. 32: 'his complexion is perfect gallows'; and *Meas.,* IV. ii. 35: 'hanging look'. Beaumont and Fletcher's *Knight of the Burning Pestle* gives an example: 'he be a notable gallows'. Shakespeare applies the equally uncomplimentary epithet of 'hangman' to Cupid in *Ado,* III. ii. 11, as an executioner of human hearts. This would have supported Furness in his incorrect conjecture that '*gallows*' here means 'hangman', based on an extract from *Arcadia.*

13–17.] Abel Lefranc's discoveries suggest that this story was developed later by Shakespeare, and its heroine christened Ophelia. See Intro., 4.2.

18. *a light heart lives long*] Udall's *Ralph Roister Doister* (1550) opens with '*Matthew Merrygreek.* [*He entereth singing.*] As long lyveth the mery man (they say), as doth the sory man, and longer by a day.' A frequent saying.

18, 19, 20, 21, 22, 25, 26. *light*] cheery or merry, casual or unimportant, frivolous or wanton, information, a candle, irresponsible, light in weight.

19. *mouse*] an endearing term. See *Ham.,* III. iv. 183. Craig gives a quota-tion from *The Triall of Treasure,* 1567 (Hazlitt's *Dodsley,* iii. 293). In *Speeches to the Queen at Bisham* (1592), Pan says to two virgins: 'be not agaste, sweet mice. . . . Can you love?' (Nichols, iii. 133); and Lyly (*Mother Bombie,* IV. ii): 'God save you, pretty mouse.'

22. *taking it in snuff*] a very common expression representing the expression of disgust at the smell of a snuffed candle. See *1H4,* I. iii. 41, for another example; and Greene, *Penelope's Web* (Grosart, v. 211), 1587: 'Calamus hearing this rough replye of his Tenant was driven into a marvellous choler, so that scarce affoording her a farewell, hee flung out of doores. . . . The goodwife glad that he took the matter so in snuffe, commanded', etc. The verb 'to snuff', to resent, be angry with, is older, and influenced this saying. Palsgrave (*Lesclaircissement,* 1530) has 'I snoffe, as a man doth or a horse, *Je reniffle.* This boye wyll be of a stubborn herte and he lyve, herke howe he snoffeth.'

24. *Look what you do*] whatever you do. An idiom; again in *Mer.V.,* III. iv. 51: 'look what notes and garments he doth give thee, Bring them.'

Kath. You weigh me not? O! that's you care not for me.
Ros. Great reason; for past care is still past cure.
Prin. Well bandied both; a set of wit well play'd.
>   But, Rosaline, you have a favour too: 30
>   Who sent it? and what is it?
Ros.   I would you knew:
>   An if my face were but as fair as yours,
>   My favour were as great; be witness this.
>   Nay, I have verses too, I thank Berowne:
>   The numbers true; and, were the numbering too,   35
>   I were the fairest goddess on the ground:
>   I am compar'd to twenty thousand fairs.
>   O! he hath drawn my picture in his letter.
Prin. Any thing like?
Ros. Much in the letters, nothing in the praise.   40
Prin. Beauteous as ink; a good conclusion.
Kath. Fair as a text B in a copy-book.
Ros. Ware pencils, ho! let me not die your debtor,

---

28. care . . . cure] *Qq,Ff;* cure . . . care *Theobald* (*Thirlby conj.*).   43. pencils]
Rowe; pensalls *Q1;* pensals *F1;* pensils (*the rest*).   ho!] *Hanmer;* How? *Qq,Ff.*

---

28. *past care . . . past cure*] Greene has: 'rather remember the olde proverbe, not so common as true: past cure, past care, without remedie, without remembrance' (*Mamillia* [Grosart, ii. 154], 1583). Theobald's reading gives the proverb its usual form and makes the neatest sense; but it is strange that the compositor should blunder over something so well known, and Shakespeare has it again in this odd inverted form, with almost a pun on 'care', in *Sonn.*, 147: 'Past cure I am, now reason is past care'—'without medical attention, without remedy'.

30, 33. *favour*] token of love, personal appearance.

37. *fairs*] beautiful women. The senses, a beautiful person or beauty itself, occur several times in this play, as they do in Lodge's *Euphues Golden Legacie.*

39–40. *Any thing like? Much in the letters*] Cf. IV. ii. 146.

41, 42.] Both lines taunt Rosaline on her dark colouring, compared to ink. 'Text' hand was a formal script.

43. *Ware*] take heed of, beware. Still in sporting use. Cf. 'Ware horns, ho!' (*Troil.*, v. vii. 12); and Greene's *Mamillia* (Grosart, ii. 91): 'if thou waver, ware dost not as the dogge, loose both bones'.

pencils] small, finely-pointed brushes for the insertion of spots or lines (not here for 'laying on colours', as Schmidt explains). Rosaline, with a transition from the writing-master's art to that of the painter, retaliates upon Katharine by calling her spotty-faced and flame-coloured. Cf. Greene, *Planetomachia* (Grosart, v. 75), 1585: 'Diana is painted kissing Vertue, and spotting beauties face with a Pensel.' Dover Wilson suggests that there is a quibble on 'pencel' (pennoncel), the pennon or streamer on a knight's lance, and that Rosaline's phrase is a battle-cry, 'Look out for cavalry!'

My red dominical, my golden letter:
O! that your face were not so full of O's.   45
Prin. A pox of that jest! and I beshrew all shrows!
　　But, Katharine, what was sent to you from fair Dumain?
Kath. Madam, this glove.
Prin.　　　　　　　　Did he not send you twain?
Kath. Yes, madam; and moreover,
　　Some thousand verses of a faithful lover;   50
　　A huge translation of hypocrisy,
　　Vilely compil'd, profound simplicity.
Mar. This, and these pearls to me sent Longaville:
　　The letter is too long by half a mile.
Prin. I think no less. Dost thou not wish in heart   55
　　The chain were longer and the letter short?
Mar. Ay, or I would these hands might never part.
Prin. We are wise girls to mock our lovers so.
Ros. They are worse fools to purchase mocking so.
　　That same Berowne I'll torture ere I go.   60
　　O! that I knew he were but in by the week.

45. not so] *Q1; not in Ff,Q2.*　　46. *Prin.] Qq,Ff; Kath. Theobald; Kath.* A pox
... jest! *Prin.* And I ... *New.*　　47. But] *Qq,Ff; Prin.* But *Theobald, Steevens,*
Cambridge.　　53. pearls] *Ff;* pearle *Q1.*

44. *My red dominical*] so in Sharp-ham's *Cupid's Whirligig*, Act II (1607): 'he lookes for all the world like the Dominicall Letter in his red Coate.' The red S for Sunday in the old almanacs.

　golden letter] the excellent, or Sunday letter, with a reference to Katharine's 'amber locks'.

45. *O's*] spots, pimples; pock-marks are implied perhaps by the next line. 'O' was used as a substantive of anything round, especially of spangles.

46–7. *A pox . . . Dumain?*] Dover Wilson divides l. 46 between Kathar-ine and the Princess, supposing that the unmetrical 'Katharine' is a scribbled speech-heading which the compositor bundled into the speech.

46. *I beshrew all shrows*] I condemn all shrews: my curse on them. Cf. Dods-ley's *Old Plays*, iv. 69: 'I beshrew . . . that great knave's heart.' A common

imprecation. The Princess desires to put an end to their wrangling and uses strong language. Her first expression in this speech was, it is said, often in Queen Elizabeth's mouth. Jonson says it was 'most courtly' (*Poetaster*, ii. 1 [1600]).

61. *in by the week*] caught, trapped. Cf. *Ralph Roister Doister*, I. ii (Malone Soc. ed. Greg, l. 72): 'I tolde you I, we should wowe an other wife. [*Aside*] *R. Roister.* Why did God make me suche a goodly person? *M. Merry.* He is in by the weke.' A passage in Web-ster's *White Devil* (ed. F. L. Lucas, i. 135) suggests imprisonment: '[*Enter* Flamineo *and* Marcello *guarded, and a lawyer.*] *Lawyer.* What, are you in by the weke? So—I will try now whether thy wit be close prisoner.' These examples and two or three others have been quoted, but the phrase is not common, nor satisfac-

How I would make him fawn, and beg, and seek,
And wait the season, and observe the times,
And spend his prodigal wits in bootless rimes,
And shape his service wholly to my hests   65
And make him proud to make me proud that jests!
So Pair-Taunt like would I o'ersway his state
That he should be my fool, and I his fate.

Prin. None are so surely caught, when they are catch'd,
As wit turn'd fool: folly, in wisdom hatch'd,   70
Hath wisdom's warrant and the help of school
And wit's own grace to grace a learned fool.

Ros. The blood of youth burns not with such excess
As gravity's revolt to wantonness.

65. wholly to my hests] *Dyce* (*Knight conj.*), *Cambridge, New;* wholly to my device *Qq,F1;* all to my behests *Ff2,3,4.*   66. that] *Qq,F1;* with *Ff2,3,4.*   67. Pair-Taunt like] perttaunt like *Q1;* pertaunt-like *Ff,Q2;* pedant-like *Theobald;* portent-like *Hanmer;* pageant-like *Capell.*   74. wantonness] *Ff3,4;* wantonesse *F2;* wantons *Qq,F1.*

torily explained. Taken in connection with the Princess's words, 'mockery merriment' (l. 139), it is evident Rosaline means caught in earnest.

65. *wholly to my hests*] It is rash to emend a Q reading merely on the grounds that it does not fit what an editor believes is Shakespeare's rhyme-scheme (collation, i. i. 106); but here the pattern is particularly rigid and metre as well as rhyme is broken. Knight's conjecture does the least violence to the original.

66. *make me proud*] There is no need to equate this with the 'flesh being proud' of *Lucr.*, 712. The line may be paraphrased: 'And deck himself out in order to make me proud of him—when all the time I am not taking the affair seriously.' The phrase 'proud array', and 'pride' in the sense of finery, are common in the literature of the period; and 'make him proud' is surely parallel to 'shape his device' rather than to 'make him fawn'.

67. *Pair-Taunt like*] The Q reading baffled every editor until 1945, when Dr Percy Simpson (in a letter to the *T.L.S.* of 24 Feb.) explained its mean-

ing. 'Paire-Taunt' is the winning hand in the obsolete card-game of Post and Pair. Simpson quoted the description on p. 74 of Randle Holme's *The Academy of Armory*, left in manuscript and printed only in 1905 (for the Roxburgh Club): 'A Paire is two cards of a sort, as 2 Kings, 2 Aces, 2 tens &c. A Paire Royall is three cards of a sort. A double Paire Royall, or a Paire-Taunt is foure cards of a sort'; and the last lines of an epigram ('Mortal Life compared to Post and Pare') from *Wittes Pilgrimage* (1605) in which John Davies of Hereford uses the term in much the same image as Shakespeare's: '*PUR Ceit* deceives the expectation Of him, perhaps, that took the stakes away; Then to *PUR Tant* he's in subjection, For Winners on the Losers oft do play.' Rosaline means that, whenever Berowne thinks he holds the winning cards, she will always produce a hand to beat them.

74. *wantonness*] See notes to i. i. 106 and l. 65 above. Here it is sense and metre that Q outrages, though the use of 'be' for 'is' and 'are' is Shakespearean ('Lord what fools these mortals

Mar. Folly in fools bears not so strong a note   75
     As foolery in the wise, when wit doth dote;
     Since all the power thereof it doth apply
     To prove, by wit, worth in simplicity.

Enter BOYET.

Prin. Here comes Boyet, and mirth is in his face.
Boyet. O! I am stabb'd with laughter. Where's her grace? 80
Prin. Thy news, Boyet?
Boyet.   Prepare, madam, prepare!
     Arm, wenches, arm! encounters mounted are
     Against your peace: Love doth approach disguis'd,
     Armed in arguments; you'll be surpris'd:
     Muster your wits; stand in your own defence;   85
     Or hide your heads like cowards, and fly hence.
Prin. Saint Denis to Saint Cupid! What are they
     That charge their breath against us? say, scout, say.
Boyet. Under the cool shade of a sycamore

---

79. is] *Q1; not in Ff,Q2.*   80. stabb'd] *F1;* stable *Q1;* stuff'd *Keightley conj.*
89. sycamore] siccamone *Q1.*

---

be.') Dover Wilson thinks Shakespeare
wrote 'wantones', taken as 'wantons'
by the compositor, who filled up an
apparently defective line as best he
could.

75. *bears not so strong a note*] *Note* has
here the sense of 'stigma'—as we say
'a black mark'. Elyot, *The Governor*
(1531), 80, has: 'Augustus ... only for
playing at dice, ... sustaineth in hys-
tories a note of reproche.' Derived
from the mark of censure made by the
Roman censors.

78. *simplicity*] foolishness. The wise
man turned to folly will devote all his
cleverness to proving that folly is more
valuable than wisdom.

80. *stabb'd with laughter*] F is clearly
right, in spite of Collier, who pronounced this 'an awkward and unusual expression'. Furness says dog-
matically: 'Barron Field (*Shakes. Soc.
Papers*, ii. 56) rightly interpreted the
word "*stabb'd*" by "the *stitch* in the

side, which is sometimes brought on by
laughter".' But 'that idiot, laughter,'
is not half the thing it used to be, at
least in 'good society'. In ll. 115–16
these characters, royal and noble, are
said to 'tumble on the ground with
zealous laughter'. And cf. Nashe, *The
Unfortunate Traveller* (McKerrow, ii.
219), 1594: 'If (I say) you had seene
but halfe the actions that he used ...
you wold have laught your face and
your knees together.' See note on l. 465
below.   In T.B.'s translation of
Primaudaye's *French Academy*, 1586,
occurs: 'Felt such a motion in them of
the spleene, that they were stifled with
laughter' (chap. iii).

82–8. *mounted ... charge*] raised in
readiness, as of cannon. Cf. *John*, II. i.
381: 'Mounted their battering cannon
charged to the mouths'.

85. *Muster your wits*] so Dekker,
News from Hell (Grosart, ii. 95): 'I
mustred all my wits about me.'

I thought to close mine eyes some half an hour,   90
When, lo! to interrupt my purpos'd rest,
Towards that shade I might behold addrest
The king and his companions: warily
I stole into a neighbour thicket by,
And overheard what you shall overhear: 95
That, by and by, disguis'd they will be here.
Their herald is a pretty knavish page,
That well by heart hath conn'd his embassage:
Action and accent did they teach him there;
'Thus must thou speak, and thus thy body bear':   100
And ever and anon they made a doubt
Presence majestical would put him out;
'For,' quoth the king, 'an angel shalt thou see;
Yet fear not thou, but speak audaciously.'
The boy replied, 'An angel is not evil;   105
I should have fear'd her had she been a devil.'
With that all laugh'd and clapp'd him on the shoulder,
Making the bold wag by their praises bolder.
One rubb'd his elbow thus, and fleer'd, and swore
A better speech was never spoke before;   110
Another, with his finger and his thumb,
Cry'd '*Via!* we will do't, come what will come';
The third he caper'd, and cried, 'All goes well';
The fourth turn'd on the toe, and down he fell.

93. companions: warily] companions warely *Q1*.   96. they] thy *Q1*.

102. *majestical*] See v. i. 11. Here
means 'princely'.

107. *clapp'd him on the shoulder*] patted
him on the back in approval. Cf. Lyly,
Campaspe, i. 2 (1581): 'He commendeth
one that is an excellent musition, then
stand I by and clap another on the
shoulder and say, this is a passing good
cooke.' Similarly used in *Much Ado
About Nothing*. It also had the sense of
'take into custody'.

109. *One rubb'd his elbow*] When the
elbows itched it was a sign of satisfaction. 'Their elbows itch for joy'
(Nashe, *Lenten Stuffe* [McKerrow, iii.
192]). Cf. *1H4*, v. i. 77: 'Gape and rub
the elbow at the news of hurly burly

innovation'; and Guilpin's *Skialetheia*
(repr., p. 22), 1598: 'He'll cry oh rare!
and scratch the elbow too To see two
butchers curres fight.'

fleer'd] grinned. Gascoigne speaks of
'Flearing Flattery' (*The Steel Glas*
[Arber, p. 51], 1576). The verb occurs
several times in Shakespeare. See
Oth., iv. i. 83, for his one use of the
noun 'fleer'.

111. *his finger and his thumb*] snaps his
fingers in exuberance of spirits.

112. Via] See note to l. 139 in the
previous scene.

114. *turn'd on the toe*] a light and airy
gesture of departing. Cf. Chettle's
Kind-Hartes Dreame, 1592, Bodley

With that, they all did tumble on the ground,   115
With such a zealous laughter, so profound,
That in this spleen ridiculous appears,
To check their folly, passion's solemn tears.
Prin. But what, but what, come they to visit us?
Boyet. They do, they do; and are apparell'd thus,   120
Like Muscovites, or Russians, as I guess.
Their purpose is to parle, to court and dance;

118. folly, passion's solemn] *Theobald;* follie pashions solembe *Q1;* folly passions solemne *F1,Q2;* folly passions, solemn *Ff2,3,4;* folly's passion, solemn *Staunton conj.* 120.] *S. Walker thinks a following line may be lost.* 121. as] *Qq,F1;* or *F2;* and *Ff3,4.* 122. parle, to] *Capell;* parlee, to *Qq,Ff1,2;* parlee *Ff3,4.*

Head Quarto, p. 44: 'So wishing the chearful, pleasaunce endlesse; and the wilful sullen, sorrow till they surfet; with a turn on the toe I take my leave. *Richard Tarleton.*' Here presumably a pirouette.

117. *spleen*] See III. i. 73, and note.

118. *passion's solemn tears*] Theobald compares *M.N.D.*, v. i. 69, 70: 'more merry tears The passion of loud laughter never shed.'

120.] Furness says 'Tiessen (*Eng. Studien*, ii. 189 [1878]) kindly supplies the [supposed] missing line: "Hats furr'd, bootes piked, in long and motley dress".' How grateful we should feel! Tiessen drew his archaisms from Ritson's extract (see next note).

121. *Muscovites, or Russians*] Ritson quotes from Hall (*Henry VIII*, p. 6) to prove that a mask of Muscovites had been previously shown. In the first year of Henry VIII, at a banquet for the foreign ambassadors at Westminster, 'came the lorde Henry, Earle of Wiltshire, and the lorde Fitzwater, in twoo long gounes of yellowe . . . after the fashion of *Russia* or *Ruslande*, with furred hattes of grey . . . and bootes with pykes turned up'. This is very ancient history. Lodge, in his *Reply to Gosson*, must be alluding to a more recent stage-show when he says: 'If I may speak my mind I think we shall find but few poets if it were exactly wayd what they oughte to be:

your Muscovian straungers, your Scithian monsters wonderful, by one Eurus brought upon one stage in ships made of Sheepeskins wyll not prove you a poet' (1579–80). A very close parallel, in the Gray's Inn Revels for 1594–5, was noted by Sir E. K. Chambers in his *William Shakespeare* and elaborated independently by R. Taylor (*The Date of Love's Labour's Lost*, 1932). These Revels, at which had already occurred a notorious performance of the *Comedy of Errors*, concluded with a pageant whose theme was the return of Knights from a campaign in Russia against 'Negro-Tartars'. They brought prisoners who were 'attired like Monsters and Miscreants' and may conceivably have been blackamoors. There followed a 'Russian ambassador', at whose request the 'Prince of Purpoole' (the benchers' master of ceremonies) made a state visit to Russia. His 'return' was made the occasion of a further pageant, when the Prince declared that he was only prevented from paying his respects to Elizabeth by the fact that his body 'by length of my Journey, and my sickness at Sea, is so weakened'. This has been taken as proof that the present scene at least could not have been written before 1595. But Muscovy was much in the news throughout the 'eighties and 'nineties. See Intro., 3.228.

122. *parle*] hold conference, discuss

And every one his love-feat will advance
Unto his several mistress, which they'll know
By favours several which they did bestow.   125
Prin. And will they so? the gallants shall be task'd;
For, ladies, we will every one be mask'd,
And not a man of them shall have the grace,
Despite of suit, to see a lady's face.
Hold, Rosaline, this favour thou shalt wear,   130
And then the king will court thee for his dear:
Hold, take thou this, my sweet, and give me thine,
So shall Berowne take me for Rosaline.
And change you favours too; so shall your loves
Woo contrary, deceiv'd by these removes.   135
Ros. Come on, then; wear the favours most in sight.
Kath. But in this changing what is your intent?
Prin. The effect of my intent is to cross theirs:
They do it but in mockery merriment;
And mock for mock is only my intent.   140
Their several counsels they unbosom shall
To loves mistook, and so be mock'd withal
Upon the next occasion that we meet,
With visages display'd, to talk and greet.
Ros. But shall we dance, if they desire us to't?   145
Prin. No; to the death we will not move a foot:

---

123. love-feat] *Q1,Ff;* love-seat *Q2;* love-suit *Dyce (S. Walker conj.).*   134. you]
Q1; your *Ff,Q2.*   too] *Ff;* two *Q1.*   139. mockery merriment] *Q1;* mocking
merriment *Ff,Q2.*

---

matters. Cf. Greene, *Carde of Fancie*
(Grosart, iv. 57): 'But Castania altogether unwilling to parle with her new
patient, kept herself out of his sight.'
The noun is common.

123. *love-feat*] exploit, deed, or effort
prompted by love, or in connection
with love; love-affair. The sense is
strained, but not impossible, and
is perhaps well in keeping with
that of 'advance', which in Shakespeare almost invariably implies ag-
gression rather than suggestion (but
'suit' of l. 129 supports Walker's
guess). We may give the expression a sarcastic touch, since the

purport of Boyet's speech, as well
as the Princess's, is to belittle the
'mockery merriments' of the King
and his party.

136. *most in sight*] conspicuously.

139. *mockery merriment*] These words
are to be noted; they rob the Princess's
plans of any ill-nature at once. See 'in
by the week', above, l. 61.

146. *No; to the death*] not as long as
we live; never. Equivalent here to our
'to death', with no suggestion of conflict. Cf. *R3,* III. ii. 55: 'I will not do it,
to the death' (I will never do it).
Schmidt wrongly equates this with the
sense mortally, fatally.

Nor to their penn'd speech render we no grace;
But while 'tis spoke each turn away her face.
Boyet. Why, that contempt will kill the speaker's heart,
    And quite divorce his memory from his part.   150
Prin. Therefore I do it; and I make no doubt
    The rest will ne'er come in, if he be out.
    There's no such sport as sport by sport o'erthrown,
    To make theirs ours and ours none but our own:
    So shall we stay, mocking intended game,   155
    And they, well mock'd, depart away with shame.
                                 [Sound trumpet.
Boyet. The trumpet sounds: be mask'd; the maskers come.

*Enter Blackamoors with music; MOTH with a speech; the KING and
the rest of the lords disguised like Russians, and visored.*

Moth. All hail, the richest beauties on the earth!
Boyet. Beauties no richer than rich taffeta.

148. her] *Ff2,3,4;* his *Qq,F1.*   149. speaker's] *Q1;* keepers *Ff,Q2.*   152. ne'er]
Ff2,3,4; ere *Qq,F1.*   156. *Sound trumpet*] *Q1; Sound Ff,Q2.*   157. S.D.
Enter . . .] *Enter Blackmores with musicke, the Boy with a speech, and the rest of the Lords
disguised. Qq,Ff; Enter Blackamoors with Music; Moth; the King, Berowne, Longaville,
and Dumain, in Russian habits and masked, Dyce, Cambridge; Enter Blackamoors
with music om. Craig.*   159. *Boyet.*] *Theobald; Berow. Q1; Ber. F1,Q2; Bir.
Ff2,3,4.*

147. *penn'd*] specially composed and
written out for the occasion.

149. *kill the speaker's heart*] utterly
dishearten him. Cf. *Wint.,* IV. iii. 88:
'offer me no money, I pray you; that
kills my heart.' It is an old expression,
as in Malory's *Morte d'Arthur* (Bk x,
chap. lviii): 'Fie upon treason, said
Sir Tristram, for it killeth my heart to
hear this tale.' 'Speaker' here refers
expressly to Moth.

151-2. *no doubt . . . will ne'er come
in*] The use of the negative after expressions of doubt is notoriously tricky,
so perhaps Shakespeare did write the
ungrammatical 'e'er'.

157. S.D. Blackamoors] African ne-
groes. They seem to have become very
popular on the stage. Jonson tells all
about them in his *Masque of Blackness*
(1605), saying it was 'her majesty's will

to have them (the masquers) black-
moors'. We cannot tell when this stage-
direction was inserted, or by whom,
but it is at least as old as 1597. Taylor
(see note on l. 121 above), thinks that
these blackamoors are a reflection of
the Negro-Tartars in the Gray's Inn
Revel; but the prisoners of the Gray's
Inn Knights are not clearly stated to
have been captured in their Negro-
Tartar campaign, nor is there much
connection between prisoners and
attendants with music. The visors,
mentioned often in this scene, were
necessary to a masque. Speaking of the
Mountebank's Masque (16 Feb. 1618),
Chamberlain says: 'their show, for I
cannot call it a masque, seeing they
were not disguised, nor had vizards'
(*Court and Times of James I,* ii. 66).

159. *Beauties . . . rich taffeta*] All their

Moth. A holy parcel of the fairest dames,   160
                    [*The Ladies turn their backs to him.*
    That ever turn'd their—backs—to mortal views!
Ber. 'Their eyes,' villain, 'their eyes.'
Moth. That ever turn'd their eyes to mortal views!
    Out—
Boyet. True; 'out' indeed.   165
Moth. Out of your favours, heavenly spirits, vouchsafe
    Not to behold—
Ber. 'Once to behold,' rogue.
Moth. Once to behold with your sun-beamed eyes,—
    with your sun-beamed eyes—   170
Boyet. They will not answer to that epithet;
    You were best call it 'daughter-beamed eyes.'
Moth. They do not mark me, and that brings me out.
Ber. Is this your perfectness? be gone, you rogue! [*Exit Moth.*
Ros. What would these strangers? know their minds, Boyet.
    If they do speak our language, 'tis our will   176
    That some plain man recount their purposes:
    Know what they would.
Boyet.   What would you with the princess?
Ber. Nothing but peace and gentle visitation.
Ros. What would they, say they?   180
Boyet. Nothing but peace and gentle visitation.
Ros. Why, that they have; and bid them so be gone.
Boyet. She says, you have it, and you may be gone.

160. *The Ladies . . .*] *after* views (*line 161*) *Qq,Ff.*   161. ever] *Ff;* even *Q1.*
165, 171. *Boyet.*] *Qq,F1; Ber. Ff2,3,4.*   166. spirits] *Qq,F1;* spirit *Ff2,3,4.*
174. [*Exit Moth*] *Cambridge;* [*Moth withdraws*] *Capell; not in Qq,Ff.*   175.
strangers] stranges *Q1.*   178. princess] Princes *Q1.*

visible beauty is that of their taffeta
masks. It is just possible that the play
on 'rich' has topical significance. See
Intro., 5.25.

169–72. *sun . . . daughter*] This grievous pun occurs about a dozen times in
Shakespeare, collected by Schmidt
in v. *Son.* There is one painful example (not mentioned by Schmidt
in that most beautiful of sonnets
(xxxiii).

173. *brings*] puts; as in the expression 'bring one on his way'.

out] Cf. 'out of countenance', below,
l. 272. Here the meaning is, 'out of my
part', as proved by l. 336 below. Cf.
Cynthia's Revels, Induction (1600):
'some satisfaction in your prologue, or,
I'll be sworne, we have marred all.
2 Child. Tut, fear not, child, this will
never distaste a true sense: be not out,
and good enough.'

179. *visitation*] visit. See *Meas.*, III. ii.
255. 'Visit' (substantive) does not
occur in this sense in Shakespeare. It is
in Jonson, *Underwoods,* xxxii.

King. Say to her, we have measur'd many miles
    To tread a measure with her on this grass.   185
Boyet. They say, that they have measur'd many a mile
    To tread a measure with you on this grass.
Ros. It is not so. Ask them how many inches
    Is in one mile: if they have measur'd many,
    The measure then of one is easily told.   190
Boyet. If, to come hither, you have measur'd miles,
    And many miles, the princess bids you tell
    How many inches doth fill up one mile.
Ber. Tell her we measure them by weary steps.
Boyet. She hears herself.
Ros.   How many weary steps,   195
    Of many weary miles you have o'ergone,
    Are numbered in the travel of one mile?
Ber. We number nothing that we spend for you:
    Our duty is so rich, so infinite,
    That we may do it still without account.   200
    Vouchsafe to show the sunshine of your face,
    That we, like savages, may worship it.
Ros. My face is but a moon, and clouded too.
King. Blessed are clouds, to do as such clouds do!

185. her on this] *Q1;* you on the *Ff,Q2.*

185. *tread a measure*] the proper expression to apply to this stately dance. It is in Lyly's *Campaspe,* IV. iii (1581): 'But let us draw in, to see how well it becomes them to tread the measures in a daunce, that were wont to set the order for a march.' An earlier use occurs in Gosson's *Schoole of Abuse* (Arber, p. 26), 1579: 'Terpandrus when he ended the brabbles at Lacedoemon, neyther pyped Rogero nor Turkelony, but . . . taught them to treade a better measure.'

200. *account*] The archaic 'accompt' is retained here, and in one or two other passages where it deals with a money reckoning, by several modern editors. In F1 'accompt' occurs thirteen times, and 'account' seventeen times in the sense of reckoning.

202. *like savages, may worship*] See

above, IV. iii. 218–21; and *Cym.,* III. iii.

203. *face . . . moon . . . clouded*] Rosaline refers here to her 'whitely' and dark colouring—perhaps; she may mean that she is in reality only a lesser light; or that her light is borrowed (Dover Wilson). Her clue is missed. The King thinks she is the Princess.

204. *Blessed are clouds*] blessed is the cloud, veil, or mask that does as yours does, kisses your face. 'These happy masks that kiss fair lady's brows' (*Rom.,* I. i. 236). The quibbling upon the cloud and mask here, and again at l. 297, was first noted by Hart, who wrote: 'It is perfectly necessary for the sense. A cloud in this material sense would be familiar to dramatists.' Cf. Cunningham's *Extracts from Revels Accounts* (Shakes. Soc., p. 147), 1579: 'For a hoop and blew lynnen to

Vouchsafe, bright moon, and these thy stars, to shine,
Those clouds remov'd, upon our watery eyne.   206
Ros. O vain petitioner! beg a greater matter;
Thou now requests but moonshine in the water.
King. Then, in our measure do but vouchsafe one change.
Thou bidd'st me beg; this begging is not strange.   210
Ros. Play, music, then! nay, you must do it soon.
Not yet?—no dance:—thus change I like the moon.
King. Will you not dance? How come you thus estranged?
Ros. You took the moon at full, but now she's changed.
King. Yet still she is the moon, and I the man.   215
The music plays; vouchsafe some motion to it.
Ros. Our ears vouchsafe it.
King.   But your legs should do it.

208. requests] *Qq,Ff;* request'st *Theobald.*   209. do but vouchsafe] *Q1;* vouchsafe but *Ff,Q2.*   212. Not yet?—no dance] *New;* Not yet no dance; *Qq,Ff;* Not yet? no dance? *Pope, Theobald;* Not yet; no dance: *Capell;* Not yet! no dance! *Cambridge.*   216.] *Given to Rosaline in Qq,Ff; corrected by Theobald.*

mend the clowde that was Borrowed and cut", etc.'

205. *bright moon, and these thy stars*] The King makes a similar remark at IV. iii. 226–7: 'gracious moon; She an attending star', which tends to show that Shakespeare was not referring to the supposed star Lunisequa but to any of the stars. Furness quotes Staunton: 'Lilly calls it Lunisequa' (no reference). It is mentioned by Lodge, *Euphues Golden Legacie* (*Shakes. Lib.*, 1875, p. 79), quoted already (IV. iii. 227).

208. *moonshine in the water*] a thing of naught, waste of time. An old proverbial expression. It is in *The Proverbs of John Heywood* (Sharman's ed., p. 77), 1546: 'Farewell he (quoth I), I will soon be hilt [held ?] As waite againe for the mooneshine in the watter. But is not this a pretie piked matter?' And in North's *Doni's Moral Philosophie* (Jacob's repr., p. 182), 1570: 'How they laboured and toyled for life about moone shine in the water'. It appears in Lyly's *Endymion*, II. ii (?1585) and is very common later, as in Burton's *Anatomy of Melancholy* (Democritus to

the Reader); Harington, *Epigrams*, ii. 56; Jonson, *Staple of News*, III. i. And see Cotgrave in v. *Debatre.* Hence our 'it's all moonshine.' Ellis notes that 'water' rhymes with 'matter' in *Lr.*, III. ii. 81, 82; Heywood (*ut supra*) gives an early instance.

209. *change*] The King puns on changes of the moon and 'changes' (distinct figures or rounds) in the dance.

210. *this begging is not strange*] The King means, although we are strangers (foreigners), you understand what begging means.

211. *do it soon*] Nonplussed by Rosaline's sudden consent the King is not quick enough to take advantage of it before she changes her mind and revokes it.

215. *Yet . . . man*] Theobald believed this verse about the man in the moon to be spurious, because it breaks in on the rhyme, and because 'the conceit of it is not pursued.' Capell omitted it. But the conceit *is* pursued. I am a partner for you, will you dance? Perhaps an alteration in punctuation would make this plainer.

Ros. Since you are strangers, and come here by chance,
      We'll not be nice: take hands:—we will not dance.
King. Why take we hands then?
Ros.   Only to part friends.   220
      Court'sy, sweet hearts; and so the measure ends.
King. More measure of this measure: be not nice.
Ros. We can afford no more at such a price.
King. Price you yourselves: what buys your company?
Ros. Your absence only.
King.   That can never be.   225
Ros. Then cannot we be bought: and so adieu;
      Twice to your visor, and half once to you!
King. If you deny to dance, lets hold more chat.
Ros. In private then.
King.   I am best pleased with that.
                              [*They converse apart.*
Ber. White-handed mistress, one sweet word with thee.   230
Prin. Honey, and milk, and sugar: there is three.
Ber. Nay then, two treys, an if you grow so nice,
      Metheglin, wort, and malmsey: well run, dice!

220. we] *Q1;* you *Ff,Q2.*   224. Price] *Rowe (ed. 1);* Prise *Qq,Ff1,2,3;* Prize *F4.*
you yourselves] *Q1;* yourselves *F1,Q2;* yourselves then *Ff2,3,4.*   229, 237, 241,
255. [*They converse apart*] *Capell;* [*They walk away chatting*] *Furnivall.*   232. an]
Q1,F1; and *Q2,Ff2,3,4.*

221. *Court'sy*] Cf. *Tp.,* I. ii. 443:
'Curtsied when you have, and kist'.
The curtsy and the kiss began the
dance. The King alludes to the kiss,
perhaps (l. 222).

224. *Price you*] seems to be preferable
to *Prize* in continuation of Rosaline's
remark. 'Price' was very commonly
written *prise.* So, however, was 'prize'.

227. *Twice . . . you*] Hart explains
this as 'two kisses for your mask
(identical with Berowne's), little for
the man behind it'—another doubtful
speech hinting at the speaker's not
being the Princess; but his interpretation is forced. Dover Wilson is probably right in deducing from this and
the 'Fair befall your mask' of II. i. 124
a contemporary joke about masks
which is now lost to us.

228. *deny*] refuse. Cf. *Wint.,* v. II.

139: 'You denied to fight with me the
other day because I was no gentleman
born.' This construction occurs several
times in Shakespeare ('deny to wed',
Shr., II. i. 180, etc.), but I have not
noted it elsewhere.

232. *treys*] threes, at dice. Not again
in Shakespeare, but frequently used.
Craig gives a quotation from Chaucer's *The Pardoner's Tale,* l. 19: 'Seuen
is my chaunce and thyn is cink and
treye.' Although the word does not
stand alone in Shakespeare again, it
probably forms the first part of 'tray-
trip', a game at dice, mentioned in
Tw.N., II. v. 207.

nice] subtle, sophistical (Schmidt).
Cf. *1H6,* II. iv. 7: 'These nice sharp
quillets of the law'; and *3H6,* IV. vii.
58. Our 'nice point'.

233. *Metheglin*] a Welsh drink of

There's half-a-dozen sweets.

Prin.   Seventh sweet, adieu.

Since you can cog, I'll play no more with you.   235

Ber. One word in secret.

Prin.   Let it not be sweet.

Ber. Thou griev'st my gall.

Prin.   Gall! bitter.

Ber.   Therefore meet.

[*They converse apart.*

Dum. Will you vouchsafe with me to change a word?

Mar. Name it.

Dum.   Fair lady,—

Mar.   Say you so? Fair lord,—

Take that for your fair lady.

Dum.   Please it you,   240

As much in private, and I'll bid adieu.

[*They converse apart.*

Kath. What! was your visor made without a tongue?

240. Take that] *Q1;* Take you that *Ff,Q2.*   242, 244, 247, 248, 249, 253, 255.
Kath.] *Rowe; Mar. Qq,Ff.*

honey and water, herbs and other ingredients. See *Wiv.*, v. v. 167, where
Sir Hugh Evans classes it with sack and
wine.

wort] unfermented beer; 'the sweet
infusion of malt' (Schmidt). It is mentioned in Chaucer's *Canterbury Tales*,
and in Holland's *Plinie* (xviii. 7, p. 560
[1601]): 'The skum or frothe that
gathereth aloft by the working of the
woort'.

malmsey] 'A strong sweet wine,
originally the product of the neigh-
bourhood of Monemvasia (Napoli di
Malvasia) in the Morea, but now
obtained from Spain, etc. . . . as well
as from Greece' (*N.E.D.*). It is called
malvesie in Chaucer. Greene speaks of a
cheater in a tavern at some market-
town who there 'tipled so much
malmesie that he had never a ready
woord in his mouth' (*Notable Discovery
of Coosnage*, 1591 [Grosart, x. 11]); so
that it appears to be rather a vulgar
drink at this time. Speaking of the ale

provided for Queen Elizabeth on her
way to Kenilworth in 1575, Lord
Leicester writes: 'We were fain to send
to London with bottels, to Kenelworth,
to divers other places where ale was.
Her own bere was such as that was no
man able to drink it; yt had been as
good to have drank malmsey' (Nichols,
i. 526).

235. *cog*] cheat. Expressly applied
to cheating with dice. Cf. Gabriel
Harvey, *An Advertisement for Papp-
hatchett* (Grosart, ii. 214), 1589: 'He'll
cogg with the dye of deceit'. This
is the oldest sense of the verb, and
is abundantly illustrated from 1532
downward in *N.E.D.* It was transferred to every sort of deceit. See
Lyly's *Sapho and Phao*, i. 3 (1581):
'We fall from cogging at dice to cogge
with states.'

238. *change a word*] Cf. *Ado*, iv. i. 185.
Interchange a word. Cf. *Rom.*, iii. v.
31: 'Some day the lark and loathed
toad changed eyes.'

Long. I know the reason, lady, why you ask.

Kath. O! for your reason; quickly, sir; I long.

Long. You have a double tongue within your mask,   245
    And would afford my speechless visor half.

Kath. Veal, quoth the Dutchman. Is not veal a calf?

Long. A calf, fair lady!

Kath.   No, a fair lord calf.

Long. Let's part the word.

Kath.   No, I'll not be your half:

Take all, and wean it: it may prove an ox.   250

Long. Look, how you butt yourself in these sharp mocks.

Will you give horns, chaste lady? do not so.

Kath. Then die a calf, before your horns do grow.

Long. One word in private with you ere I die.

Kath. Bleat softly then; the butcher hears you cry.   255
                       [*They converse apart.*

Boyet. The tongues of mocking wenches are as keen
    As is the razor's edge invisible,

Cutting a smaller hair than may be seen;

---

251. butt] but to *Ff2,3,4.*   257. invisible] invincible *Theobald.*

245. *double tongue . . . mask*] In a letter to *T.L.S.* (7 June 1923) W. J. Lawrence wrote: 'This deft passage-at-arms . . . is really witty. The old vizard was what the youngster of today calls "a false face".' Made of black velvet on a leather base, it covered the entire features and was kept in place by a tongue, or interior projection, held in the mouth. Of a surety all annotated editions of the play should have a note to this effect appended to the passage.' I concur and comply. Longaville's 'double' surely has a hint of 'ambiguous' or 'quibbling'; there may even be a suggestion of the supposedly venomous 'double tongue' of snakes.

247. *Veal, quoth the Dutchman*] Viel, plenty, answers Longaville's plea for half. The Dutch skipper in Dekker's *Shoemaker* (II. ii. 127) says 'Yaw, yaw, ic heb veale ge drunck.'

Is not veal a calf?] It is, and more:

'*Veau:* A calf or Veal; also a lozel, hoiden, dunce, jobbernol, doddipole' (Cotgrave). Boswell cites *Doctor Dody-poll* (1600): 'me be right glad for see veale. *Hans.* What, do you make a Calfe of me, M. Doctor? *Doct.* O no pardona moy; I say vell, be glad for see you vell, in good health.' In the present passage, however, the puns are four deep. Besides anticipating Doctor Dodypoll's ambiguity Katharine glances at Longaville's disguise, his visor or *veil* (often spelt 'veal' at this time; cf. Spenser's *Letter to Harvey* [Oxford *Spenser*, p. 611] 'his Moother with a Veale hath coovered his face'); and she also reveals by a quibble that she knows who is behind it. The last word of her previous speech was 'long'; with the first word of this she completes his name. She has indeed afforded him halves.

249. *your half*] your better-half, your wife. See *Cæs.,* II. i. 274.

Above the sense of sense; so sensible
Seemeth their conference; their conceits have wings   260
Fleeter than arrows, bullets, wind, thought, swifter
    things.
Ros. Not one word more, my maids: break off, break off.
Ber. By heaven, all dry-beaten with pure scoff!
King. Farewell, mad wenches: you have simple wits.
Prin. Twenty adieus, my frozen Muscovites.   265
                    [*Exeunt Lords and Blackamoors.*
Are these the breed of wits so wonder'd at?
Boyet. Tapers they are, with your sweet breaths puff'd out.
Ros. Well-liking wits they have; gross, gross; fat, fat.
Prin. O poverty in wit, kingly-poor flout!
Will they not, think you, hang themselves to-night?   270
Or ever, but in visors, show their faces?
This pert Berowne was out of countenance quite.

259. sense; so sensible] *Pope;* sence so sensible, *Q1;* sence so sensible; *Ff,Q2.*
261. bullets] *om. Capell.*   265. Exeunt . . .] *Exeunt F1 (after line 264); not in Q1.*
269. wit, kingly-poor] wit, kingly poor *Qq,Ff;* wit, kill'd by pure *Collier MS;*
wit, poor-liking *Staunton conj.*

261. *bullets*] Capell conjectures that 'bullets' was a prior word, changed for 'arrows', and left in the text through an oversight.

263. *dry-beaten*] literally, bruised without blood drawn. Occurs in the transferred sense, as here, in *Martins Months Minde* (Grosart's *Nashe*, i. 175), 1589: 'old Martin first drie beaten, & therby his bones broken . . . made a Maygame upon the Stage, and so bang'd both with prose and rime on everie side.' Greene has 'dry blows' similarly several times: 'these dry blowes could draw no blood' (*Mamillia* [Grosart, ii. 150]).

264. *mad wenches*] See II. i. 256.

268. *Well-liking*] in good condition. See *Wiv.*, II. i. 54 (for the noun); and *1H4*, III. iii. 6. Steevens refers to Job, xxxix. 4: 'Their young ones are in good liking.'

Well-liking . . . fat] Rosaline's 'flout' is equivalent to 'Fat paunches have lean pates' (I. i. 26: see note). Fatness and wit were held to disagree with one another. Cf. Udall's *Erasmus* (Roberts's repr., p. 128), 1542: 'For that sort of men are fedde up with the grosse kindes of meates, which in deed conferres to the body hard braune, and clene strength, but as for the witte, it maketh as grosse and dulle as can be thought.'

269.] The Princess retorts upon Rosaline's poverty in wit, in making such a grievous pun on 'king' in her 'well-li*king*'. She proves that is her thought by continuing it in '*king*ly-poor'. I do not believe there is any further profundity in her remark, which has been worked into many shapes from the supposition her words refer to the King's last speech. Her 'kingly-poor' is merely 'well-liking' with an inserted quibble, mocking Rosaline.

272. *out of countenance*] disconcerted. Hardly distinguishable from Moth's 'out' at l. 173 above. Cf. Puttenham, *Arte of English Poesie* (Arber, p. 149), 1582: 'These great Madames of

Ros. O, they were all in lamentable cases!
    The king was weeping-ripe for a good word.
Prin. Berowne did swear himself out of all suit.   275
Mar. Dumain was at my service, and his sword:
    No point, quoth I: my servant straight was mute.
Kath. Lord Longaville said, I came o'er his heart;
    And trow you what he call'd me?
Prin.   Qualm, perhaps.
Kath. Yes, in good faith.
Prin.   Go, sickness as thou art!   280
Ros. Well, better wits have worn plain statute-caps.

273. O] *Ff2,3,4; not in Qq,F1.*

honoure ... if they want their courtly habillements . . . would be halfe ashamed or greatly out of countenaunce.' *N.E.D.* has an example from a ballad (early sixteenth century).

274. *weeping-ripe*] See *3H6,* I. iv. 172. The expression occurs in Sidney's *Arcadia,* bk i (Feuillerat, i. 107), *ante* 1586: 'But Lalus (even weeping ripe) went among the rest, longing to see some bodie that would avenge Uranias wronge.' It occurs also in Heywood's *Rape of Lucrece* (Pearson, p. 193), 1608, and in Armin's *Italian Taylor* (Grosart, p. 180), 1609. Elsewhere Shakespeare has *reeling-ripe* and *sinking-ripe.* Beaumont and Fletcher give us *dropping-ripe, tumbling-ripe,* and *crying-ripe.* All seem to be built on the expression *rope-ripe* (fit for hanging, crack-halter), which occurs in Adlington's *Apuleius' Golden Asse,* chap. 30 (1566); and in Wilson's *Arte of Rhetorique* (according to Malone), 1553. *Dropping-ripe* is in Marlowe's *First Book of Lucan.*

275. *out of all suit*] out of fitness, agreement, or suitability. Cf. 'out of suits with fortune' (*AYL.,* I. ii. 258), where the plural is equivalent to the collective 'all'. Cotgrave, Florio, and Miege distinguish *suit* in this sense (*Quadrer*) with the spelling 'sute'. The Princess may allude to the love-suit Berowne was engaged in. 'All' was

similarly inserted for emphasis in several old expressions, as: '*out of all* ho', '*out of all* cry', '*out of all* nick', *out of all* count', '*out of all* scotch and notch'. These are all about the date of *Love's Labour's Lost,* excepting the first two, which are earlier.

276. *service*] again connected with 'suit' in ll. 831–2 below. Perhaps through the law term 'suit and service' (Feudal).

277. *No point*] See II. i. 189. Not at all.

279. *Qualm*] There must have been more similarity in the pronunciations of 'qualm' and 'came' than at present if this quibbling is to be recognized. Cf. Gabriel Harvey (Grosart, ii. 279), *Pierce's Supererogation*: 'to ravish the affections, and even to mealt the bowels of bravest mindes: see, see what a woundrous quaime'.

281. *better wits have worn plain statute-caps*] Johnson said this line was 'not universally understood because every reader does not know that a statute-cap is part of the academical habit'. Grey quoted from Strype's *Annals of Queen Elizabeth* (ii. 74) an Act of Parliament of 1571 'for continuance of making and wearing woollen caps in behalf of the trade of cappers; providing that all above the age of six years (except the nobility and some others) should on sabbath days and holy days, wear caps of wool, knit,

But will you hear? the king is my love sworn.
Prin. And quick Berowne hath plighted faith to me.
Kath. And Longaville was for my service born.
Mar. Dumain is mine, as sure as bark on tree.   285
Boyet. Madam, and pretty mistresses, give ear.
    Immediately they will again be here
    In their own shapes; for it can never be
    They will digest this harsh indignity.
Prin. Will they return?
Boyet.   They will, they will, God knows; 290
    And leap for joy, though they are lame with blows:
    Therefore change favours; and when they repair,

thicked and dressed in England, upon
penalty of ten groats'. Johnson, however, still stuck to his explanation.
Grey's is clearly nearer the truth,
though it does not explain the meaning
of 'plain', and it is too universal, applying as it did to the whole community
almost. Steevens quotes passages from
Marston, *Dutch Courtesan* (Bullen, ii.
60), 1605: 'though my husband be a
citizen, and his cap's made of wool, yet
I have wit'; and from Middleton's *The
Family of Love* (Bullen, iii. 102), 1608:
' 'Tis a law enacted by the common-
council of statute-caps.' It is obvious
that whatever explains these passages
is also the explanation of the line in the
text. But there is nothing of citizens in
the 1571 Act, nor is it an enactment of
the Common Council. The best solution is that of Hart, who showed that
in 1582 there were 'Regulations recommended for the Apparel of London Apprentices', and ' "Twas by the
Lord Mayor and Common Council
enacted. That from henceforth no
Apprentice should presume—1. To
wear any apparel but what he receives
from his Master. 2. To wear no hat
within the City and liberty thereof,
nor any thing instead thereof, but a
woollen cap, without any silk in or
about the same . . . [there are eight
more clauses, concluding with:] every
Apprentice offending . . . for the first
offence to be punished at the discretion

of his Master; for the second to be publicly whipped at the Hall of his Company', etc. (Nichols's *Progresses*, ii. 393,
394). The passage in the play appears
to refer directly to the prentice caps of
London. There were so many statutes
of apparel that Nashe says: 'Why they
[Harvey's *Letters*] are longer than the
Statutes of Clothing or the Charter of
London' (*Have With You*, 1596 [Mc-
Kerrow, iii. 34]).

285. *bark on tree*] inseparable, closely
united, hand and glove. Cf. J. Heywood *Proverbs* (Sharman, p. 98), 1562:
'It were a folly for me, To put my hand
betweene the barke and the tree. . . .
Between you' (*N.E.D.*); and Mar-
mion, *A Fine Companion* (near the end),
1633: 'Master Dotario and my
daughter *Æmilia*, hand in hand, and
married together . . . there they are,
bark and tree.'

291. *leap for joy*] See IV. iii. 145.

292. *favours*] some part of the presents (ribbons or gloves), or the presents themselves, given by the different
suitors to their mistresses, and worn, as
we are told, to confuse the donors. See
ll. 30, 130, 134. The masks are now
removed. See above, 'be masked'
(l. 157), where the editors usually insert a stage-direction, 'The ladies
mask.' Perhaps another, 'The ladies
dismask,' might be inserted at l. 296
for uniformity's sake. They are 'known'
now (l. 301) and no longer disguised:

Blow like sweet roses in this summer air.
Prin. How blow? how blow? speak to be understood.
Boyet. Fair ladies, mask'd, are roses in their bud: 295
　　　Dismask'd, their damask sweet commixture shown,
　　　Are angels vailing clouds, or roses blown.
Prin. Avaunt, perplexity! What shall we do
　　　If they return in their own shapes to woo?
Ros. Good madam, if by me you'll be advis'd,   300
　　　Let's mock them still, as well known as disguis'd.
　　　Let us complain to them what fools were here,
　　　Disguis'd like Muscovites, in shapeless gear;
　　　And wonder what they were, and to what end
　　　Their shallow shows and prologue vilely penn'd,   305
　　　And their rough carriage so ridiculous,
　　　Should be presented at our tent to us.
Boyet. Ladies, withdraw; the gallants are at hand.
Prin. Whip to our tents, as roes run o'er the land.
　　　　　[*Exeunt Princess, Rosaline, Katharine, and Maria.*

296–7. Dismask'd . . . blown] Or angel-vailing clouds: are roses blown, Dismaskt
. . . shewn *Theobald* (*Warburton conj.*).   297. Are . . . blown] Are angels (val'd
the clouds) . . . blown *Becket conj.*; Are angels veil'd in clouds of roses blown *Peck
conj.*   vailing] *Ff,Q2*; varling *Q1*.   309. roes run o'er the] *F4* (runs ore the
F3); roes runnes ore *Qq,Ff1,2, Cambridge*; roes run over *Steevens, Craig*.

Boyet expresses his approbation at l.
297. For *favours*, see, again, l. 455
below.

　296. *damask*] red and white, like the
Damascus rose. Cf. *AYL.*, III. v. 125
(quoted in *N.E.D.* as the earliest use
in this sense); and Holland's *Plinie*,
xii. 11 (1601): 'another tree . . . bearing
a blossom like to a damaske or incarnate rose' where 'incarnate' means
flesh-coloured. More punning.

　commixture] 'Commistura, a commixture, a blending' (Florio's *World of
Words*, 1611). Complexion. Shakespeare has the word in *3H6*, II. vi. 6, in
the sense of 'compound'.

　297. *vailing*] lowering, letting fall.
Commonly used in the nautical expression 'vail bonnet' which Greene
has twice (metaphorically) in *Arbasto*,
1584. Cf. *Ven.*, 956: 'She vailed her
eyelids', etc.

　angels vailing clouds] angels letting

down (or lowering) clouds or veils (or
masks) that hid their fairness. 'Vailing'
has the actual sense of unveiling. Johnson put it quite clearly: 'Ladies un-
masked are like angels vailing clouds,
or letting those clouds which obscured
their brightness sink from before
them.' This is obvious when we give
clouds the meaning of masks or disguises, which the word seems to bear
at l. 204 above.

　298. *Avaunt, perplexity*] 'Enough, you
riddler!' (to Boyet). Cf. *Rom.*, III. v.
171, 'hold your tongue, Good pru-
dence.'

　303. *shapeless gear*] uncouth dress.

　305. *vilely penn'd*] See l. 147.

　309. *Whip*] move quickly (to or from
a place). Cf. Greene's *Disputation betweene a Hee and a Shee Conney-Catcher*
(Grosart, x. 219), *ante* 1592: 'Why
then, quoth shee, steppe into this
closet: hee whipt in hastily and never

Re-enter the KING, BEROWNE, LONGAVILLE, *and* DUMAIN, *in their proper habits.*

King. Fair sir, God save you! Where's the princess?   310
Boyet. Gone to her tent. Please it your majesty,
  Command me any service to her thither?
King. That she vouchsafe me audience for one word.
Boyet. I will; and so will she, I know, my lord.   [*Exit.*
Ber. This fellow pecks up wit, as pigeons pease,   315
  And utters it again when God doth please.
  He is wit's pedlar, and retails his wares
  At wakes, and wassails, meetings, markets, fairs;
  And we that sell by gross, the Lord doth know,

309. S.D. *Re-enter . . .*] *Enter the King and the rest Qq,Ff.*   310. Where's] *Qq,Ff;* Where is *Steevens.*   312. thither] *Q1; not in Ff,Q2.*   315. pecks] *Q1;* picks *Ff,Q2.*   316. God] *Q1; Jove Ff,Q2.*

remembered his cloathes'; and Fenton's *Bandello*, 1567 (Henley, ii. 146): 'She whipped into the house and shoot the doare upon the nose of her amarus clyent.'

roes . . . land] 'fleeter than the roe' occurs in *Shr.*, Induction, ii. 50; and it is an odd coincidence that in the old *Taming of a Shrew* (*Shakes. Lib.*, 1875, p. 496) there is the same defect in the metre as here, from *over* and *o'er*, and the same obsolete form (a northern dialect plural) of the verb: 'Your hounds stands readie cuppeld at the doore. Who in running will oretake the Row', etc. Greene has the same simile: 'Never went roe bucke swifter on the downes Than I will trip it till I see my George' (Grosart, xiv. 151).

the land] i.e. the 'laund' (lawn) as in *3H6*, iii. i. 2: 'Through this laund anon the deer will come.' 'Laund' is properly an open space in a wood, or surrounded by trees. Cf. Lodge, *Euphues Golden Legacie* (*Shakes. Lib.*, 1875, p. 130): 'She tript alongst the Lawnes full of joy.'

310. *Where's the princess*] Steevens sought to restore verse-form to a line which, together with the next two, is printed in early texts as prose.

315. *This fellow pecks up wit*] The

whole simile later became proverbial as can be seen from Thomas Coriate, *Traveller for the English Wits*, 1616: 'He pickes up wit as pigeons pease, And utters it when God doth please.' It is in this debased form that it appears in F.

316. *utters*] issues, distributes, offers for sale. This, the original sense of the word as given in *N.E.D.*, is preserved in the legal phrase 'to forge and utter' bad coin.

318. *wakes*] Cf. Stubbes, *Anatomie of Abuses*, 1583: 'The manner of keeping wakesses and feasts in England . . . manie spend more at one of their wakesses than in all the whole year besides.' Every village had its annual 'wake-day'.

wassails] health-drinkings, revels. 'The jolly wassal walks the often round' (Jonson, *Forest*, iii). Usually applied to a special drink, or act of drinking. See *Ham.*, i. iv. 9.

319. *by gross*] by wholesale. Opposed to 'retail' in Gabriel Harvey, *Pierce's Supererogation* (Grosart, ii. 34), 1592: 'Some have called them knaves in grose: I have found them fooles in retayle.' And in William Covell [Dowden], *Polimanteia* (Grosart, p. 54), 1595: 'Compelled to retaile that which they had bought by grosse'.

Have not the grace to grace it with such show.   320
This gallant pins the wenches on his sleeve;
Had he been Adam, he had tempted Eve.
A' can carve too, and lisp: why, this is he
That kiss'd his hand away in courtesy;
This is the ape of form, monsieur the nice,   325
That, when he plays at tables, chides the dice
In honourable terms: nay, he can sing

323. A' can] *Q1;* He can *Ff,Q2.*   324. his hand away] *Q1;* away his hand
Ff,Q2.

321. *pins the wenches on his sleeve*] The
idea is probably from the wearing of
favours on the sleeve, with a pun on the
wenches' *penchant* for themselves hanging on their lovers' arm. Cf. *Err.,* II. ii.
177: 'Come, I will fasten on this sleeve
of thine: Thou art an elm, my husband, I a vine.' The expression is found
in Greene's *Mourning Garment* (Grosart, ix. 173), 1590: 'What it is for mee
to pinne a fayre meacocke and a witty
milksop on my sleeve, who dare not
answere with their swords in the face of
the enemy?' And again, in *Farewell to
Follie* (ix. 327), 1591: 'to avoide
iealousie, you may ever wear her
pinde on your sleeve.' And earlier, in
Lyly's *Sapho and Phao,* ii. 4 (1581):
'But bee not pinned alwayes on her
sleeves, strangers have green rushes,
when daily guests are not worth a
rush.'

323. *carve*] See *Wiv.,* I. iii. 49: 'she
carves, she gives the leer of invitation.'
'Carve' was a fashionable word of the
day, difficult of explanation, with
some such sense as 'show great courtesy and affability' (Schmidt), but
especially applying to courtship. An
early example of the noun was found
by Hart in Greene's *Philomela* (Grosart, xii. 117), printed in 1592 but
stated in the Epistle Dedicatory to be
one of 'the first frutes of my witts':
'Feeding upon this passion that knaw-
eth like envy upon hir owne flesh, he
called to minde to which of his friends
she shewed the most gratious lookes,
uppon whom she glaunst the most

smiling favours, whose carver she
would be at the table, to whom she
would drink, and who had most cur-
teus intertainment at hir hands.'

324. *kiss'd his hand away in courtesy*]
Cf. Jonson, *Cynthia's Revels,* iii. 11
(1600): 'Another swears His scene of
courtship over . . . anon, doth seem . . .
As he would kiss away his hand in
kindness.' Jonson's line is taken by
Hart as establishing the F against the
Q reading. For other references to the
kissing hands, or fingers, in courtesy,
see *AYL.,* III. ii. 50, *Oth.,* II. i. 173. The
'*fore-finger kiss*' is in Gabriel Harvey's
'Speculum Tuscanismi' (1580). The
courtesy was of French origin appropriate to Monsieur Boyet. Cf. Florio's
Montaigne, bk ii, chap. 12: 'to see them
ignorant of the French tongue, of our
kissing the hands, of our low-lowting
courtesies'.

325. *form*] observance of etiquette;
as in *Ham.,* III. i. 161: 'The glass of
fashion and the mould of form'. Our
'good form'.

326. *tables*] backgammon. The
oldest name for one of the oldest games
which is said to have been discovered
in the tenth century as a rival to chess
in order to combine chance and skill
to bring together players of unequal
talents. See Strutt's *Sports and Pastimes*
for a figure of players at tables of the
thirteenth century. It was always
played with dice on the folding boards
or tables used also for draughts. The
word is still used in the game, but not
usually of the game.

A mean most meanly, and, in ushering,
Mend him who can: the ladies call him sweet;
The stairs, as he treads on them, kiss his feet.   330
This is the flower that smiles on every one,
To show his teeth as white as whale his bone;
And consciences, that will not die in debt,
Pay him the due of honey-tongu'd Boyet.
King. A blister on his sweet tongue, with my heart,   335
That put Armado's page out of his part!

Re-enter the PRINCESS, *ushered by* BOYET; ROSALINE, MARIA,
KATHARINE, *and Attendants.*

Ber. See where it comes! Behaviour, what wert thou
Till this madman show'd thee? and what art thou now?

332. whale his] *Ff2,3,4, Rowe;* whales *Qq,F1, Steevens;* whale's *Cambridge;*
whales' *Halliwell.*   334. due] *Q1;* duty *Ff,Q2.*   338. madman] *Qq,Ff, Cambridge, Globe;* man *Theobald, New.*

328. *A mean*] a middle or 'fill up' part between treble and bass. The quibble is common. See Greene's *Farewell to Follie* (Grosart, ix. 279), 1591: 'The meane that grees with countrie musicke best'. Lyly has it in *Gallathea* (acted 1585?), v. 3: 'Can you sing? ... Basely.... And you? ... Meanly.... And what can you doe? ... If they double it I will treble it.'

328–30. *ushering ... he treads*] Similarly Jonson speaks of 'fine-paced huishers' (*Devil is an Ass,* II. iii). The gentleman-usher was specially selected with 'little legs of purpose' (Jonson, *Every Man out of his Humour,* iii. 1 (1599)) for the sake of his fine or delicate pacing.

332. *as white as whale his bone*] an old simile. It occurs in the romance *Eglamore* (Percy Folio, ed. Furnivall and Hales, ii. 342), *ante* 1400: 'The Erle had noe child but one a maiden as white as whalles bone.' And the Earl of Surrey in *Tottel's Miscellany* (Arber, p. 218), 1557: 'I might perceive a wolfe as white as whale bone.' And Greene, *Never Too Late* (Grosart, viii. 213): 'Legges as white as whales bone:

so white and chaste was never none.' The division into two words representing the old pronunciation seems a necessary modernization. Whalebone here probably meant the ivory of the walrus.

333–4. *die in debt, Pay*] Cf. *Rom.,* I. i. 244: 'I'll pay that doctrine or else die in debt.' See also l. 43 above.

334. *honey-tongu'd*] It is interesting to note here that Meres, who gives us the earliest reference to *Love's Labour's Lost* by name, and also the earliest tribute of praise to Shakespeare by name, applies this term to Shakespeare himself. The quotation is classical: 'As the soule of Euphorbus was thought to live in Pythagoras: so the sweete wittie soule of Ovid lives in mellifluous & honey-tongued Shakespeare, witnes his *Venus and Adonis,* his *Lucreece,* his sugred Sonnets among his private friends, &c.' (*Wits Treasurie,* 1598). These two are the only early examples in *N.E.D.*

336. *out of his part*] See l. 173.

338. *Till this madman*] Dover Wilson would drop the 'mad' as disturbing to the metre, and plausibly suggests that

King. All hail, sweet madam, and fair time of day!
Prin. Fair in all hail is foul, as I conceive.   340
King. Construe my speeches better, if you may.
Prin. Then wish me better: I will give you leave.
King. We came to visit you, and purpose now
    To lead you to our court: vouchsafe it then.
Prin. This field shall hold me, and so hold your vow: 345
    Nor God, nor I, delights in perjur'd men.
King. Rebuke me not for that which you provoke:
    The virtue of your eye must break my oath.
Prin. You nickname virtue; vice you should have spoke;
    For virtue's office never breaks men's troth.   350
    Now, by my maiden honour, yet as pure
    As the unsullied lily, I protest,
    A world of torments though I should endure,
    I would not yield to be your house's guest;
    So much I hate a breaking cause to be   355
    Of heavenly oaths, vow'd with integrity.
King. O! you have liv'd in desolation here,
    Unseen, unvisited, much to our shame.
Prin. Not so, my lord; it is not so, I swear:
    We have had pastimes here and pleasant game.   360
    A mess of Russians left us but of late.

---

350. men's *Ff3,4;* mens *Q1;* men *Ff1,2,Q2.*   352. unsullied] *Ff2,3,4;* unsallied *Qq,F1.*   356. oaths] oath *Q2.*

---

the compositor caught it from the 'madam' of the next line. But a mere roughness of metre should not damn the livelier reading.

madman] jester. See notes at 'madcap', II. i. 214; and at 'mad wenches', II. i. 256.

339. *All hail*] The quibble here occurs in *The Two Noble Kinsmen,* III. v; and in *The Faithful Friend,* III. ii; both have been ascribed to Beaumont and Fletcher, the second doubtfully, but Shakespeare himself may well have helped Fletcher with the first. So too, in Dekker's *Old Fortunatus* (Pearson, p. 113): 'Brother all haile. *Shadow.* There's a rattling salutation.'

348, 349. *virtue . . . virtue*] power . . . goodness.

349. *nickname*] 'To name by mistake: to assert wrongly to be something' (*N.E.D.*). Simply, to miscall.

352. *unsullied*] Some editors like to retain the obsolete alternative spelling *unsallied* of the first editions. This spelling (*sally* for *sully*) occurs again in the Q *Ham.,* II. i. 39, and possibly (*sallied* for *sullied*) at I. ii. 129 as well. The Princess may have the lily of France in her thoughts. At the beginning of Dekker and Chettle's *Patient Grissel,* 'sully not this morning' is spelt '*sally*'. See Collier's ed.

361. *mess*] See note on IV. iii. 203. A mess was a set of four.

King. How, madam! Russians!

Prin.   Ay, in truth, my lord;
    Trim gallants, full of courtship and of state.

Ros. Madam, speak true. It is not so, my lord:
    My lady, to the manner of the days,   365
    In courtesy gives undeserving praise.
    We four, indeed, confronted were with four
    In Russian habit: here they stay'd an hour,
    And talk'd apace; and in that hour, my lord,
    They did not bless us with one happy word.   370
    I dare not call them fools; but this I think,
    When they are thirsty, fools would fain have drink.

Ber. This jest is dry to me. My gentle sweet,
    Your wit makes wise things foolish: when we greet,
    With eyes best seeing, heaven's fiery eye,   375
    By light we lose light: your capacity
    Is of that nature that to your huge store
    Wise things seem foolish and rich things but poor.

Ros. This proves you wise and rich, for in my eye,—

Ber. I am a fool, and full of poverty.   380

Ros. But that you take what doth to you belong,
    It were a fault to snatch words from my tongue.

Ber. O! I am yours, and all that I possess.

Ros. All the fool mine?

Ber.   I cannot give you less.

Ros. Which of the visors was it that you wore?   385

368. Russian] Russia *F1,Q2.*   373. My] *Malone; not in Qq,F1;* Fair *Ff2,3,4.*
374. wit makes] *Ff2,3,4;* wits makes *Qq,F1.*   385. was it] what it *F1.*

365. *to the manner of the days*] according to the fashion of the times.

369. *talk'd apace*] chattered. Tibet Talkapace is the name of a chatterbox in *Ralph Roister Doister.* See *Meas.*, iii. ii. 116, where the form used is 'speak apace'.

372. *When . . . drink*] one of the numerous paraphrases for 'you're a fool.' Cf. *The Penniless Parliament of Threadbare Poets,* 1608 (*Harl. Misc.*, iii. 73): 'Some shall be so humorous in their walks as they cannot step one foot from a fool'. And Scotch 'When you're

served, a' the geese are watered.'

373. *My gentle sweet*] Malone's 'my' is the most likely word to have been dropped by the compositor after 'me'. But it is perhaps unnecessary to fill out the line at all.

375. *heaven's fiery eye*] Craig quotes Spenser, *Faerie Queene,* I. iii. 4: 'The great eye of heaven' (referring to the sun), and Marlowe's *Tamburlaine* (pt II), IV. iv. 7 (1586): 'The horse that guides the golden eye of Heaven'. It is also in *Ven.*, 178; *Sonn.*, xlix. 6, xviii. 5; *John*, III. i. 79, etc.

Ber. Where? when? what visor? why demand you this?

Ros. There, then, that visor; that superfluous case
      That hid the worse and show'd the better face.

King. We were descried: they'll mock us now downright.

Dum. Let us confess, and turn it to a jest.   390

Prin. Amaz'd, my lord? Why looks your highness sad?

Ros. Help! hold his brows! he'll swoon. Why look you pale?
      Sea-sick, I think, coming from Muscovy.

Ber. Thus pour the stars down plagues for perjury.
      Can any face of brass hold longer out?   395
      Here stand I, lady; dart thy skill at me;
      Bruise me with scorn, confound me with a flout;
      Thrust thy sharp wit quite through my ignorance;
      Cut me to pieces with thy keen conceit;
      And I will wish thee never more to dance,   400
      Nor never more in Russian habit wait.
      O! never will I trust to speeches penn'd,
      Nor to the motion of a school-boy's tongue,
      Nor never come in visor to my friend,
      Nor woo in rhyme, like a blind harper's song,   405

389. were] *Q1;* are *Ff,Q2.*   390. *Dum.*] *Duman. Q1; Du. F1,Q2; Duke Ff2,3,4.*
392. swoon] *Pope, Steevens;* sound *Qq,F1;* swound *Ff2,3,4.*   396. I, lady;]
I, Ladie *Qq,Ff;* I; lady, *Cambridge.*

392. *hold his brows*] Cf. *John,* iv. i. 41–
5: 'When your head did but ache,
I knit my handkercher about your
brows. . . . And with my hand at midnight held your head.'

393. *Sea-sick . . . coming from Muscovy*]
may be an echo of the Gray's Inn
Revels, 1594–5. See l. 121n.

395. *face of brass*] assurance, confident manner. This passage is given in
N.E.D. as the first example of the expression. The next use is from Fuller,
half a century later. Shakespeare may
have found it in Whetstone's *Promos
and Cassandra* (pt. II), III. i (1578): 'My
troubled hart with guiltynesse agrev'd
Lyke fyre doth make my eares and
cheekes to glow: . . . Well, I wyll set a
face of brasse on it.' 'Brazenface' is in
Wiv., IV. ii. 145.

397. *flout*] a mocking speech. 'Knowest thou not that a deniall at the first is

a graunt, and a gentle answere a flat-
tering floute?' (Greene, *Arbasto* [Gro-
sart, iii. 214], 1584).

400. *wish thee*] entreat thee.

401. *wait*] attend upon, do service.

404. *friend*] sweetheart. Cf. *Meas.,*
I. iv. 29; *Wiv.,* III. iii. 124, etc.

405. *like a blind harper's song*] Cf.
Lyly, *Sapho and Phao,* IV. iii: 'Harping
alwaies upon love, till you be as blind
as a harper'. Blind harpers were proverbial as early as John Heywood's
Proverbs (Sharman's edition, p. 137),
1542: 'Proface. Have among you,
blind harpers (say'd I); the mo the
merrier.' Hart noted that the race of
blind harpers and fiddlers is hardly yet
extinct in Ireland: they were the sur-
vivors of those (incapacitated by
blindness from smallpox) who were
unfitted for any profession save that of
music. Puttenham, *Arte of English*

Taffeta phrases, silken terms precise,
Three-pil'd hyperboles, spruce affection,
Figures pedantical; these summer flies
Have blown me full of maggot ostentation:
I do forswear them; and I here protest,   410
By this white glove (how white the hand, God knows),
Henceforth my wooing mind shall be express'd
In russet yeas and honest kersey noes:

---

407. affection] *Qq,Ff, Malone, Halliwell;* affectation *Rowe, Cambridge.*

Poesie (Arber, p. 97), 1589, has: 'Blind harpers or such like taverne minstrels that give a fit of mirth for a groat'.

406. *Taffeta phrases*] similarly used by Nashe in his Epistle to the Gentleman Students prefixed to Greene's *Menaphon* (McKerrow, iii. 323), 1589: 'Sundry other sweete Gentlemen I doe know, that have vaunted their pennes in private devices, and tricked up a companie of taffaty fooles with their feathers.' He refers to actors, whose stage-clothes are as little natural to them as the lines they speak. Berowne means that fine speech, like actors' dress, is put on for the occasion.

407. *Three-pil'd*] the best quality, as of the richest velvet. See *Meas.,* i. ii. 33, and *Wint.,* iv. iii. 14. Dekker has 'three-pil'd oaths' in *A Strange Horse-Race* (Grosart, iii. 354).

hyperboles] Shakespeare uses this expression elsewhere only in *Troil.,* i. iii. 161: 'Which from the tongue of roaring Typhon dropp'd, Would seem hyperboles; at this fusty stuff The large Achilles', etc. There, as here, the word is trisyllabic. Puttenham has a page or two (Arber, pp. 202–3) on the 'Hyperbole, Or the Over-reacher, otherwise called the loud lyer' (*Arte of English Poesie,* 1589). The word occurs in *Gesta Grayorum,* 1594: 'Such like hyperbolies' (Malone Soc., p. 29).

spruce] See note on v. i. 13.

affection] affectation. See above, v. i. 4. 'Affection' is quadrisyllabic here, as above, in i. i. 9. Malone said: 'The modern editors read *affectation.*

There is no need of change.' There is every reason against it, except a rigid adherence to rhyme, which is absolutely no argument. Shakespeare uses the shorter form again in *Ham.,* ii. ii. 473.

408. *Figures*] turns of rhetoric (Schmidt). See i. ii. 51n. and v. i. 58n.

pedantical] Cf. Gabriel Harvey, *An Advertisement for Papp-hatchett* (Grosart, ii. 129), 1589: 'He is no boddy, but a few pilfred Similes; a little Pedanticall Latin; and the highest pitch of his witt, Bulles motion, alias the hangman's apron.' Harvey's tract was written before *Love's Labour's Lost.*

408, 409. *flies . . . blown . . . maggot*] *N.E.D.* has this in v. *blow* (28) ('To fill with eggs') as the earliest example. Cf. 'fly-blown', which occurs in Gabriel Harvey, 1573.

409. *ostentation*] vanity, affection, 'pretentious parade' (*N.E.D.*). The word occurs above (v. i. 103) in a different use.

411. *By this white glove*] Slender burlesques this in *Wiv.* ('by these gloves', i. i. 156, 161, 168); Jonson has it in *Every Man Out of his Humour.*

413. *russet*] Fr. *rousset,* reddish-brown (Cotgrave); the colour of the peasants' cloth. Cf. *Ham.,* i. i. 166. 'Russet-coat' was a term for a rustic, as in Porter's *Two Angry Women of Abingdon* (Malone Soc., ed. Greg, l. 1369); and Jonson's *Tale of a Tub,* iii. v. Sometimes it was 'russeting'; 'Vile russetings Are matcht with monarchs and with

And, to begin: Wench,—so God help me, law!—
My love to thee is sound, sans crack or flaw.   415
Ros. Sans 'sans,' I pray you.
Ber.   Yet I have a trick
Of the old rage: bear with me, I am sick;
I'll leave it by degrees. Soft! let us see:
Write 'Lord have mercy on us' on those three;
They are infected, in their hearts it lies;   420
They have the plague, and caught it of your eyes:

---

414. to begin: Wench,—so] to begin Wench, so *Qq,Ff;* to begin, wench, so *Theobald et seq.*

---

mighty kings' (Hall, *Satires,* I. iii. [1598]).

kersey] coarse woollen cloth, a staple English export of the period. Plain, homely, unsophisticated.

414. *Wench*] This—to a lady-in-waiting—must mark the beginning of Berowne's new bluntness.

law] perhaps a corruption of *La,* an exclamation to call attention, occurring several times in *Merry Wives of Windsor.* 'Law', generally used as an asseveration, is now confounded with *Lor'* for Lord. See also *N.E.D.* (*La, Lo*). 'Law' occurs in Marston several times, as in *Eastward Hoe,* v. i. 'La' is in Jonson's *Every Man out of his Humour,* III. I.

416. *Sans 'sans', I pray you*] 'Sans' is a spruce 'affection'; 'give it up', Rosaline says. We have had it before (v. i. 78). Common in Lyly: 'The boy hath wit sance measure, more than needs' (*Mother Bombie,* II. i).

419. '*Lord have mercy on us*'] at first a name for an intestinal affliction known as the 'iliac passion'. See Higgins, *Nomenclator,* 1585: 'Ileus . . . the Iliake passion . . . which the homelier sort of Physicians doe call, *Lord have mercy upon me*'. Thence transferred to the plague. Halliwell says: 'This touching inscription was frequently a printed placard which was generally surmounted by a red cross. . . . In Shakespeare's time the inhabitants of every infected house were compelled to place some conspicuous mark upon it to denote the fact,' etc. Steevens gives several quotations, one of which is from *More Fools Yet,* by R(oger) S(harpe), 1610: 'A doore belonging to a house infected, Whereon was plac'd (as 'tis the custom still) *The Lord have mercy on us*: this sad bill The sot perus'd.' It is used by Nashe in *The Unfortunate Traveller* (McKerrow, ii. 286), 1594: '[Whilest I was in Rome] So it fel out that it being a vehement hot summer . . . there entred such a hot-spurd plague . . . it was but a word and a blowe, *Lord have mercie upon us* and he was gone.' And by Dekker, *The Dead Tearme* (Grosart, iv. 81), 1608: 'Two such Ravens (who preied uppon a dead body) flew that way, cryed presently out, *Lord have mercy uppon us,* clapping their hard handes on their country-breastes, and looking more pale than the sheete in which the man was buryed.' This suggests that the prayer was fixed upon the winding-sheet of the dead body passing to burial. F. P. Wilson (*The Plague in Shakespeare's London,* 1927, p. 61) has shown that the inscription was in use in 1568, if not earlier, and is therefore worthless for the dating of the play.

420. *infected*] Nashe refers to the great plague of 1592 as 'this last infection' (*Foure Letters Confuted* [McKerrow, i. 301], 1593).

These lords are visited; you are not free,
For the Lord's tokens on you do I see.
Prin. No, they are free that gave these tokens to us.
Ber. Our states are forfeit: seek not to undo us.   425
Ros. It is not so. For how can this be true,
That you stand forfeit, being those that sue?
Ber. Peace! for I will not have to do with you.
Ros. Nor shall not, if I do as I intend.
Ber. Speak for yourselves: my wit is at an end.   430
King. Teach us, sweet madam, for our rude transgression
Some fair excuse.
Prin.   The fairest is confession.
Were not you here, but even now, disguis'd?
King. Madam, I was.
Prin.   And were you well advis'd?
King. I was, fair madam.

433. not you] *Q1*; you not *Ff,Q2*.

422. *visited*] the technical term for attacked by plague. Cf. Dekker, *The Wonderfull Yeare* (Grosart, i. 115), 1603: 'let us therefore with bag and baggage march away from this sore Citie, and visit those that are fled into the country. But alas! *Decidis in Scyllam*, you are peppered if you visit them, for they are visited alreadie: the broad Arrow of Death flies there up & downe as swiftly as it doth here.' The plague was known as the *'visitation'* distinctively. See Nashe, in Mc-Kerrow's edition, ii. 166, ii. 287, etc. The year 1592-3 was one of the worst visitations: 'This yeare was no Bartholomew faire kept at London for the avoiding of concourse of people whereby the infection of the pestilence might have increased' (Stowe's *Chronicles*, Abridgment, p. 395, 1618). This plague passage is taken by Dover Wilson as evidence that the play was written in 1593. Charlton says such jesting would be impossible with the plague at its worst. He underrates the Elizabethans.

423. *tokens*] plague-spots. Cf. 'death-tokens' (*Troil.*, II. iii. 187), and 'token'd pestilence' (*Ant.*, III. x. 9). Cotgrave has '*Tac*: A kind of rot among sheep; also, a plague-spot or God's token on one that hath the Plague' (1611). In her reply the Princess takes up the implied pun on the love-tokens given by the lords, and twists 'free' (i.e. not infected) to mean fancy-free. This form of cross-talk, in which each speaker by catching up one word in his partner's sally and giving it a new turn produces as it were a surprising modulation, is characteristic of the play. The 'set of wit' between Katharine and Rosaline at ll. 20-8 above is another good example.

425. *seek not to undo us*] We are hopeless, it is useless trying to relieve us of our forfeiture.

426-7. *how can . . . sue*] The point lies in the two senses of 'sue'—to beg, and to bring a suit at law. 'You are suing', says Rosaline, 'therefore plaintiffs; how can you also be the condemned?'

434. *were you well advis'd?*] Was it a rational proceeding? Cf. *Err.*, II. ii. 215. In your sober senses.

Prin.   When you then were here,   435
       What did you whisper in your lady's ear?
King. That more than all the world I did respect her.
Prin. When she shall challenge this, you will reject her.
King. Upon mine honour, no.
Prin.   Peace! peace! forbear:
       Your oath once broke, you force not to forswear.   440
King. Despise me, when I break this oath of mine.
Prin. I will; and therefore keep it. Rosaline,
       What did the Russian whisper in your ear?
Ros. Madam, he swore that he did hold me dear
       As precious eyesight, and did value me   445
       Above this world; adding thereto, moreover,
       That he would wed me, or else die my lover.
Prin. God give thee joy of him! the noble lord
       Most honourably doth uphold his word.
King. What mean you, madam? by my life, my troth,   450
       I never swore this lady such an oath.
Ros. By heaven, you did; and to confirm it plain,
       You gave me this: but take it, sir, again.
King. My faith and this the princess I did give:
       I knew her by this jewel on her sleeve.   455
Prin. Pardon me, sir, this jewel did she wear;
       And Lord Berowne, I thank him, is my dear.
       What, will you have me, or your pearl again?
Ber. Neither of either; I remit both twain.
       I see the trick on 't: here was a consent,   460

446. thereto] *Qq,F1;* there *Ff2,3,4.*   454. the] to th' *Ff3,4.*

440. *force not*] value not. You set no value on your oath. 'I force not', 'it forceth not', 'no fors of', are common early expressions. 'No force of two straws' (*The Four Elements* [Hazlitt's *Dodsley*, i. 8], 1519); 'No force for that' (Whetstone, *Promos and Cassandra*, II. iv. and v. iv [1578]); 'If . . . blood be spilt in every place they force it not a mite' (B. Googe, *The Popish Kingdome* [repr., p. 8], 1570).

455. *jewel . . . sleeve*] See note on l. 292 above.

459. *Neither of either*] Cf. *A Yorkshire*

Tragedy, scene i (1608): 'But sirrah is neither our young master return'd, nor our fellow Sam come from London? *Ralph.* Neither of either, as the Puritan bawd says.' Tyrrell says, in a note to this passage (the play was attributed to Shakespeare): 'This quiet, good-humoured, little sarcasm is in the manner of Shakespeare.' It was more in his manner than the editor had noticed.

remit] resign, give up.

460. *a consent*] an understanding or compact, an agreement. Cf. *Tp.*, II. i. 203.

Knowing aforehand of our merriment,
To dash it like a Christmas comedy.
Some carry-tale, some please-man, some slight zany,
Some mumble-news, some trencher-knight, some Dick,
That smiles his cheek in years, and knows the trick   465
To make my lady laugh when she's disposed,

---

463. slight zany] sleight saine *Q1*.   465. smiles his] smiles, his *Q1*; smites his
Jackson conj.   years] jeers *Theobald;* fleers *Hanmer;* tears *Jackson conj.*

---

462. *dash*] frustrate, spoil. If the Muscovites (l. 121) derive from Gray's Inn, this may be a reference to the ragging of *The Comedy of Errors* there on 28 Dec. 1594. But the custom was general. See Intro., 4.33.

463. *carry-tale*] tale-bearer, spy. *N.E.D.* gives an earlier example from Holinshed's *Chronicle of Ireland* (iii. 1062), 1577. Cf. Nashe, *Pierce Penilesse* (McKerrow, i. 232), 1592: 'there are spirits called spies & tale-carriers, obedient to Ascaroth, whom the Greeks call *Daimona*, and *S. John*, the accuser of the brethren.' Shakespeare has the compound again in *Ven.*, 657; and cf. 'one Mistress Tale-porter', in *Wint.*, IV. iv. 273.

please-man] sycophant or toady.

zany] the rustic servant of the pantaloon in the Commedia dell' Arte. Florio has '*Zàne*, the name of Iohn in some parts of Lombardy, but commonly used for a silly John, a simple fellow, a servile drudge or foolish clowne in any commedy or interlude play' (*New World of Words*, 1611). And cf. Nashe, *Pierce Penilesse* (McKerrow, i. 215), 1592: 'Our Sceane is more statelye furnisht than ever it was in the time of Roscius, our representations honourable, and full of gallant resolution, not consisting, like theirs, of a Pantaloun, a Whore, and a Zanie, but of Emperours, Kings, and Princes.' See Intro., 4.32.

464. *mumble-news*] prattler. The verb was often used of repeating the paternoster. Cf. Florio: '*Novellante*, A teller of newes and tidings, a teller of tales,

fables and fond discourses. Also, a merry jester, a pleasant buffon'.

trencher-knight] Cf. *carpet-knight*. One who is a valiant man at the trencher or plate. See '*trencher-friends*' (parasites), *Tim.*, III. vi. 106; and '*trencher-man*', *Ado*, I. i. 51. Cf. Greene, *Never Too Late* (Grosart, viii. 165), 1590: 'Oh Francesco (quoth hee), how fond hast thou bene lead away with every looke, fed uppon with Trencher flies, eaten alive with flatterers.' Here the word is synonymous with the rest, a parasite, table-friend.

Dick] fellow, companion, jack. A contemptuous term, first known in the combination 'desperate *Dick*', which occurs in Wilson, *Arte of Rhetorique*, 1553; in *Triall of Treasure* (Hazlitt's *Dodsley*, iii. 280), 1567; and in Churchyard's *Queen's Reception at Bristol*, 1574, and often later. Nashe enumerates various Dicks in his attack on Richard Harvey (McKerrow, iii. 85). 'Dapper Dick' was also common, as in Greene, *Quip for an Upstart Courtier* (Grosart, xi. 239): 'I might see comming downe the hill a brave dapper Dicke, quaintly attired in velvet and Sattin.'

465. *smiles his cheek in years*] laughs his face into wrinkles. Cf. *Tw.N.*, III. ii. 79; *Mer.V.*, I. i. 80; *2H4*, v. i. 96–8; *Troil.*, I. i. 40. Farmer quotes from Webster, *Duchess of Malfi*, where a lady cannot endure to be in merry company, for she says too much 'laughing . . . fils her too full of the wrinkles'.

466. *disposed*] disposed to be merry. See above, note on II. i. 249.

Told our intents before; which once disclos'd,
The ladies did change favours, and then we,
Following the signs, woo'd but the sign of she.
Now, to our perjury to add more terror,   470
We are again forsworn, in will and error.
Much upon this 'tis:—and might not you   [*To Boyet.*
Forestall our sport, to make us thus untrue?
Do not you know my lady's foot by the square
And laugh upon the apple of her eye?   475

---

472. [*To Boyet*] Rowe.   474. square] *F4, Rowe;* squier *Qq,Ff1,2,3, Pope, Cambridge;* squire *Capell, Malone.*   475. apple] appeal *Ulrici (Furness cit.).*

---

469. *she*] mistress, woman. Cf.
AYL., III. ii. 10: 'Carve on every tree
The fair, the chaste and unexpressive
she'. And Nashe, *Have With You,* etc.
(McKerrow, iii. 110, 111), 1596: 'hee
is as infinite in commending her as
Saint Jerome in praise of Virginitie.
. . . In one place he calls her *the one shee,*
in another *the credible Gentlewoman,* in
a third *the heavenly plant,* and the
fourth *a new starre in Cassiopeia*', etc.

472. *Much upon this 'tis*] It is very
nearly this way. Cf. *Meas.,* III. ii.
242, and IV. i. 17 ('much upon this
time').

474. *know my lady's foot by the square*]
varied from the older 'have the length
of her foot'. It occurs in Lyly's *Euphues
and his England* (Arber, p. 290), 1580:
'you shall not know the length of my
foot until by your cunning you get
commendation'. And in *Pasquils Jests
and Mother Bunches Merriments* (Hazlitt
repr., p. 31): 'The counterfeiting
young mistris with kind words and
knavish wiles, finding the length of his
foote, gate many tokens of his love'.
And Dekker, *The Bachelars Banquet*
(Grosart, i. 263), 1603: 'having now
the full length of his foot, then shewes
she herselfe what she is, unmasking her
dissembling malice.' In the earlier
examples the expression has the meaning it has in the text—to know how to
win one's love; to win one's love. Later,
as in Mrs Behn's *Roundheads,* Act 1

(1682), and *The Bagford Ballads*
(Wade's *Reformation,* p. 7), etc., it had
a somewhat baser sense—to know one's
foibles, to take one's measure, for selfish
ends.

square] carpenter's rule. Halliwell
quotes from Palsgrave (*Lesclaircissement,* 1530): '*Sqyar* for a carpentar,
esquierre'; and '*Squyer* a rule, *riglet*'. See,
again, *Wint.,* IV. iv. 348, and *1H4,* II. ii.
13. The old form *squire* or *squier* is retained by most editors. By a curious
orthography the word seems to have
become 'square' in the transferred
usage earlier than this, in the expression 'wisdom's square'. Roger Ascham
has 'square, rule, and line of wisdom'
(*The Scholemaster,* 1570). Higgins's
Nomenclator has '*Norma, regula* . . . a
squire or square'. Florio and Cotgrave use both spellings indiscriminately.

475. *laugh upon the apple of her eye*]
laugh upon in an intimately affection-
ate and endearing way. Shakespeare
only once elsewhere has the expression
'apple of the eye', in *MND.,* III. ii. 104,
where it is used literally, as here, of the
pupil; not in the more familiar sense,
of the object of one's tenderest solici-
tude. It comes close to the expression
'looking babies' in one's mistress's eye.
Cf. T. Bowes's trans. of Primaudaye's
French Academy, p. 145 (1586): 'We see
our owne eies shine within the apples
of our neighbour's eies.'

And stand between her back, sir, and the fire,
Holding a trencher, jesting merrily?
You put our page out: go, you are allow'd;
Die when you will, a smock shall be your shroud.
You leer upon me, do you? there's an eye   480
Wounds like a leaden sword.

Boyet.   Full merrily
Hath this brave manage, this career, been run.

Ber. Lo! he is tilting straight. Peace! I have done.

Enter COSTARD.

Welcome, pure wit! thou part'st a fair fray.

478. allow'd] *Ff3,4;* aloude *Q1;* alow'd *F1,Q2.*   481. merrily] merely *Q1.*
482. Hath this brave manage] *Theobald;* hath this brave nuage *Q1;* hath this
brave manager *Ff,Q2.*   484. part'st] prat'st *Ff3,4.*

477. *Holding a trencher*] See above,
l. 464. The reference is not to a menial,
but to an attentive sycophant.

478. *You put our page out*] See l. 173.
you are allow'd] admitted (or per-
mitted) as a fool, you have licence. See
above, I. ii. 123. And cf. 'an allowed
fool' (*Tw.N.,* I. v. 101). See 'beg us',
below, l. 490.

479. *smock . . . shroud*] wholly effeminate. Perhaps there is a reference to an
expression occurring a couple of times
in Greene, of one sentenced by a verdict of women, 'the verdict of the
smock'; 'tried by the verdict of the
smock. Upon this they panneld a
jurie' (*The Art of Conny-catching* [Gro-
sart, x. 60]). Women will be the death
of you.

481. *leaden sword*] Swords and dag-
gers of lead or lath are commonly mentioned figuratively as mock-weapons
in Shakespeare; familiar as stage-
properties.

482. *manage*] a term from the riding-
school, an evolution to which a horse
is trained, 'specially a short gallop at
full speed' (*N.E.D.*). The term occurs
in Laneham's *Letter* (*Captain Cox,* ed.
Furnivall, Ballad Soc., 1871, p. 24),
1575: 'The Brydegroom for preemi-
nens had the fyrst coors at the Quin-

tyne, brake hiz spear *tres hardiments;*
but his mare in his manage did a littl so
titubate, that mooch a doo had hiz
manhood to sit in his sadl.'

career] a term in horsemanship, practically identical with the last in meaning. *N.E.D.* quotes from Holinshed's
Chronicle, iii. 1033/2, 1577–87: 'They
were better practised to fetch in
booties than was their manage or
careire.' Both terms belonged specially
to the tilting-yard. Gabriel Harvey
uses the term as it is here of any course
or action: 'Extra jocum, and to leave
thessame stale karreeres you knowe
full well it woulde suerly quite mare
all' (*Letters to Spenser* [Grosart, i. 133],
1573–80), and again (of the Countess
of Pembroke): 'Her hoattest fury may
fitly be resembled to the passing of a
brave career by Pegasus' (Grosart, ii.
322).

483. *Lo! he is tilting straight*] Look at
him, sparring for a wit-combat at once.
He is at it again. *Straight* is for 'straight-
way', immediately.

484. *part'st . . . fray*] occurs again in
Ado, v. i. 114. Cf. G. Whetstone,
Promos and Cassandra (pt II), III. ii
(*Shakes. Lib.,* vi. 277), 1578: 'To parte
this fraye it is hye time, I can tell, My
Promoters else of the roste wyll smell.'

Cost. O Lord, sir, they would know,   485
    Whether the three Worthies shall come in or no.
Ber. What, are there but three?
Cost.   No, sir; but it is vara fine,
    For every one pursents three.
Ber.   And three times thrice is nine.
Cost. Not so, sir; under correction, sir, I hope it is not so.
    You cannot beg us, sir, I can assure you, sir; we know
        what we know: 490
    I hope, sir, three times thrice, sir,—
Ber.   Is not nine.
Cost. Under correction, sir, we know whereuntil it doth
    amount.

491. hope, sir] hope *Ff3,4*.

See, too, Sir P. Sidney's *Masque before the Queen at Wanstead* (*The May-Lady*), 1578 (Works, ed. Feuillerat, vol. II, 330): 'Maister Rombus . . . came thither, with his authority to part their fray.'

485, 494, 497. *O Lord, sir*] See also I. ii. 6 above. The retort seems to have been seized upon by fools and fops, who found in it a means to make stylish conversation without having to commit themselves to an opinion. Jonson makes much fun of it: Asotus (*Cynthia's Revels*, I. i) uses it to fend off compliments he finds overwhelming; Orange (*Every Man out of his Humour*, III. i) to keep his end up in a learned discussion. And Orange's character is thus described: 'as dry an orange as ever grew: nothing but salutation, and "O Lord, sir!" and "It pleases you to say so, sir!" ' The phrase is ridiculed again by Shakespeare in *All's W.*, II. ii.

486. *Worthies*] See note on v. i. 109.

488. *pursents*] presents, i.e. represents. See note on ll. 499, 500.

489, 492. *under correction*] not elsewhere in Shakespeare in this form. Probably a usual rustic apology in addressing a superior. Cf. Jonson, *For the Honour of Wales* (Herford and Simpson, vii. 500): 'I am a subject by my

place, and two heads is better than one, I imagine, under correction.' See *N.E.D.* for examples, earlier, of 'I speak under correction', and 'under your correction' in serious language, as in *Meas.*, II. ii. 10, and *H5*, III. ii. 130 and v. ii. 144.

490. *You cannot beg us*] periphrastic for 'we are not fools', 'you cannot beg us for fools'. The word 'fool' is omitted here, as at l. 478. The allusion is to the begging of wardship or guardianship of idiots by favourites. See Nares (*Beg*), who refers to Blackstone (i. 8, 18) for the writ *de idiota inquirendo*. Johnson says: 'One of the legal tests of a natural is to try whether he can number.' Cf. Harington, *Metamorphosis of Ajax* (Chiswick, p. 62), 1596: '*Stultorum plena sunt omnia*: the world is full of fools, but take heed how you beg him for a fool: for I have heard of one that was begged in the Court of Wards for a fool, and when it came to trial he proved a wiser man by much than he that begged him.' And Jonson, *Every Man out of his Humour*, III. i (1599): 'He were a sweet ass: I'd beg him i' faith.' The Court of Wards was established by Henry VIII, and suppressed under Charles I.

492, 498. *whereuntil*] 'whereunto'

Ber. By Jove, I always took three threes for nine.

Cost. O Lord, sir! it were pity you should get your living
    by reckoning, sir.   495

Ber. How much is it?

Cost. O Lord, sir! the parties themselves, the actors, sir,
    will show whereuntil it doth amount: for mine own
    part, I am, as they say, but to parfect one man in
    one poor man, Pompion the Great, sir.   500

Ber. Art thou one of the Worthies?

Cost. It pleased them to think me worthy of Pompey the
    Great: for mine own part, I know not the degree of
    the Worthy, but I am to stand for him.

Ber. Go, bid them prepare.   505

Cost. We will turn it finely off, sir; we will take some care.

                                                         [*Exit.*

King. Berowne, they will shame us; let them not approach.

Ber. We are shame-proof, my lord; and 'tis some policy
    To have one show worse than the king's and his company.

King. I say they shall not come.   510

Prin. Nay, my good lord, let me o'er-rule you now.
    That sport best pleases that doth least know how.

499. they] thy *Q1*.   parfect] *Q1;* perfect *Ff,Q2;* pursent *Grant White (Walker
conj.);* present *Collier.*   in] e'en *Malone.*   502. Pompey] *Qq,Ff, Capell,
Malone;* Pompion *Rowe (ed. 2), Cambridge, etc.*   509. king's] king *Ff3,4.*
512. least] *Ff,Q2;* best *Q1.*

occurs in *Cymbeline* twice. Such compounds were often used. Greene has
'whetherto' in *Euphues his Censure*
(Grosart, vi. 228); 'whereout' occurs in Sidney's *Arcadia*, bk iii;
'whereunder' is in Petty's *Narration
of Drake's Famous Voyage* (Hakluyt),
1579; and in *Histriomastix*, Act II;
and cf. 'where against' in *Cor.*, IV.
v. 113.

495. *reckoning*] See I. ii. 39.

499. *parfect*] probably Costard
would say 'perform', or 'present'.
'Perform' for 'play' (a part) occurs
several times in Shakespeare.

500. *Pompion*] pumpkin (for Pompey). 'The earliest example of the
humour of using wrong words by
ignorant people on the stage that I

have noticed' (wrote Hart) 'is in
Promos and Cassandra, 1578.' In Sidney's
masque, *The Lady of May*, 1578
(Feuillerat, ii. 329 ff.), he attributes
this foible to Rombus, a schoolmaster;
and also 'to Lalus the old shepherd',
who says 'disnounce' for 'announce',
'bashless' for 'bashful' (like 'pursent'
for 'present'). There is no need to correct Costard any more than Dull or
Holofernes. See above I. i. 183 and IV.
ii. 90.

502. *Pompey*] Costard's indecision
about his words is rather enhanced by
the legitimate reading, which I see no
reason to alter unless we also read
'Pompion' below after he reappears
in his part. Rowe (ed. 2) made the
change.

Where zeal strives to content, and the contents
Dies in the zeal of that which it presents;
Their form confounded makes most form in mirth,   515
When great things labouring perish in their birth.
Ber. A right description of our sport, my lord.

Enter ARMADO.

Arm. Anointed, I implore so much expense of thy royal
    sweet breath as will utter a brace of words.
        [*Converses with the King, and delivers a paper to him.*
Prin. Doth this man serve God?   520
Ber. Why ask you?
Prin. A' speaks not like a man of God's making.
Arm. That is all one, my fair, sweet, honey monarch; for

513–14. contents Dies . . . presents] *Qq,Ff, Cambridge, Globe (with corrupt-passage mark)*; content Dies . . . presents *Rowe (ed. 1)*; content Dies in the zeal of that it doth present *Hanmer*; content Die in the zeal of them which it presents *Steevens*; content Lies in the zeal of those which it present *Mason conj.*; contents Die in the zeal of them which it presents *Malone, Craig.*   519. [*Converses* . . .] *Capell*; [*Talks apart with the King*] *Furness*.   522. A'] *Q1*; He *Ff,Q2*.   God's] God his *Q1*. 523. That is] *Q1*; That's *Ff,Q2*.

513–14. *contents . . . presents*] For a summary of the explanations, with or without alteration of the text, the reader may refer to Furness's Variorum edition. 'Contents' means here the subject-matter of the entertainment, which 'dies' (as we speak of a piece being 'murdered') as a result of the over-eagerness to please of those who present it. 'Dies' is a 'northern plural (see l. 309 above); and 'that' (the company of performers) is the subject, 'it' (the sport) the object, of 'presents'. The next couplet is a repetition, in another form, of the same idea—it is the collapse of an ambitious project that provides the best entertainment. It is the whole speech that Berowne finds applicable to the masque of Muscovites. Cf. *MND.*, v. i. 81–105.

519. delivers a paper] Capell inserted this in order to explain the King's speech after Armado's exit.

522. *a man of God's making*] a pro-

verbial expression. Cf. Peele, *Edward I*, II. ii (Bullen, I, p. 102), 1593: 'My masters and friends, I am a poor friar, a man of God's making, and a good fellow as you are, legs, feet, face . . . right shape and christendom.' And *The Return from Parnassus*, pt 1 (ed. W. D. Macray, p. 43), ii. 1 (1599): 'Luxurio, as they say, a man of God's makinge, as they saye, came to my house, as they saye.' Day has it in *The Ile of Guls* (1606), with variations: 'a woman of God's making and a ladie of his own, and wearing their own haire'.

523. *That is all one*] That does not matter, it is *all the same* to me. Cf. Feste's refrain at the end of *Tw.N.*: 'But that's all one, Our play is done.'

honey monarch] a common term of endearment still. Cf. *Promos and Cassandra* (pt 1), IV. vii (1578): 'Sweete honny Grimball . . . hony sweete Grimball'; and Sidney's *Arcadia* (Feuillerat, ii. 20); 'honny Dorus tell them me'. And in *Tim.* (*Shakes. Lib.*, 1875, p.

I protest, the schoolmaster is exceeding fantastical;
too, too vain; too, too vain: but we will put it, as   525
they say, to *fortuna de la guerra*. I wish you the peace
of mind, most royal couplement!   [*Exit*.

King. Here is like to be a good presence of Worthies. He
presents Hector of Troy; the swain, Pompey the
Great; the parish curate, Alexander; Armado's   530
page, Hercules; the pedant, Judas Maccabæus.
And if these four Worthies in their first show thrive,
These four will change habits, and present the other five.

Ber. There is five in the first show.

King. You are deceived, 'tis not so.   535

Ber. The pedant, the braggart, the hedge-priest, the
fool, and the boy:—

---

526. *de la guerra*] Theobald, Cambridge, New; delaguar *Qq,Ff*; della guerra Hanmer,
Hart.   527. [*Exit*] Capell.

---

443), III. v: 'Art thou well pleas'd with
this, my hony?' Shakespeare makes a
verb of it in *Ham.*, III. iv. 93: 'honeying
and making love'.

525. *too, too*] The intensive redupli-
cation occurs several times in Shakespeare, and was very common. Formerly the two words were hyphened or
written as one. See *Lucr.*, 174, *Gent.*, II.
v. 205, and *Wiv.*, II. ii. 261.

526. fortuna de la guerra] Cf. Jonson,
Case is Altered, I. i (1598): '*Juniper*.
Valentine, I prithee ruminate thyself
welcome. What, *fortuna de la guerra!*'
Juniper's business is to ridicule
'forced words'. The expression occurs
in Middleton's *More Dissemblers besides
Women*, v. i (1623); and in a letter
dated 1624 in *Court and Times of
James I*, ii. 461, but on both occasions
is given its Italian form. Sometimes it
is rendered in English: 'Once again to
prove the fortune of warre' (M. Lok,
1612 [Hakluyt (ed. 1812), v. 391]).

527. *couplement*] couple. *N.E.D.*
cites Spenser, *Faerie Queene*, VI. v. 24:
'And forth together rode, a comely
couplement'.

528. *Worthies*] See above, v. i. 109.

535. *You are deceived*] The inability to

count of the comic characters in this
play was first pointed out by the two
editors of *Cambridge*. Armado in I. ii
admits he is 'ill at reckoning', and
Costard, in ll. 489–95 above, un-
wittingly betrays the same weakness.
Here the malady seems to have spread
to the King. See Intro., 5.23.

536. *The pedant, the braggart*] These
are generic names of stock characters
in Italian comedy. They appear often
elsewhere in this play as headings to
the speeches of Holofernes and of
Armado. Both characters clearly owe
something to Italian models. See
Intro., 4.32. The heading 'Boy' is
similarly used in several places to
designate Moth, while Nathaniel and
Costard appear as 'Curate' and
'Clown'.

hedge-priest] Ascham uses this term in
The Scholemaster (Arber, p. 136): 'and
therefore did som of them at Cambridge (whom I will not name openlie)
cause hedge-priestes sette out of the
contrie, to be made fellowes in the
universitie' (1568). A contemptuous
term for those plying their business
under hedges or by the roadside. Cf.
hedge-school, *hedge-schoolmaster*. Nashe

Abate throw at novum, and the whole world again
Cannot pick out five such, take each one in his vein.
King. The ship is under sail, and here she comes amain.   540

Enter COSTARD *for Pompey.*

Cost. I Pompey am,—
Ber.   You lie, you are not he.
Cost. I Pompey am,—
Boyet.   With libbard's head on knee.

538. Abate] *Qq,F1;* A bare *Ff2,3,4;* Abate a *Malone.*   539. pick] *Q1;* prick
Ff,Q2.   in his] *Q1;* in 's *Ff,Q2.*   541. *Ber.*] *Bero. Q1; Ber. F1,Q2; Boyet
Ff2,3,4.*

has the expression 'hedge rakt up
termes' (McKerrow, iii. 27) to express
illiterateness.

538. *Abate throw at novum*] except for
the throw at 'novum'—as we might
say, 'bar a throw'.

novum] 'A game of dice properly
called *novem quinque*, from the two
principal throws being nine and five'
(Schmidt). It looks as if a throw of five
might in some circumstances stand for
nine, just as Armado's five players
were to stand for the nine Worthies—
hence Berowne's joke.

541. Ber.] The majority of editors
have unreasonably followed F2 in giving this retort to Boyet. Berowne and
Boyet here join forces in mocking the
Worthies, and it is this alliance that
reconciles them.

You lie] Staunton suggested that the
point of this must rest in a piece of
stage-business: that 'Pompey' on
entering, trips over his accoutrements
and falls prostrate. The pun is certainly
a favourite with Shakespeare; cf. *Ham.,*
v. i. 131, and *Oth.,* III. iv. 1.

542. *libbard's head*] leopard's head.
'In old French, the language alike of
heraldry and of our early statutes, the
term *leopart* means a lion passant
guardant. . . . The *leopard's head*, therefore, is properly the head of a lion
passant guardant, which in fact is a
lion's front face' (Cripps, *Old English
Plate,* p. 46 [1891]). J. Bossewell, how-

ever, *Workes of Armorie,* 1572, says a
leopard is a cross between a lion and
pard (a kind of panther). Presumably
Boyet is referring to 'arms' tradition-
ally borne by Pompey, as were the lion
and axe by Alexander (see note on
ll. 571–2). Pompey's arms are given by
S. Daniel in a preface to his translation (1585) of Paolo Giovio's *Dialogo
dell' Imprese Militari et Amorose* (B ii[v]) as
'a Lyon with a sword clasped in his
claw'; and Daniel is not alone in taking
Pompey's signet-ring, as described by
Plutarch, for an *impresa,* or badge,
'Ensifer Leo'. John Ferne, *The Blazon
of Gentrie* (1586), p. 197, describes
Pompey's 'insigne, and banner of
Armes' as 'in a field Gewles, a Lyon
erected Or, holding a swoord, point
in chefe argent, poigne de purpre'·
Though I cannot find Pompey's lion
anywhere described as 'passant guardant', I suspect that Costard bore some
such figure on his shield, and that the
text covers more stage-business (see
preceding note). As he struggles to his
feet again, Costard may hold his shield
either clutched to his knee, or out-
stretched, as if offering the Princess a
platter 'on the knee'. Theobald quoted
Cotgrave: '*Masquine.* The representation of a lion's head, &c., upon the
elbow, or knee of some old-fashioned
garments.' In Sherwood's *English-
French Dictionary* (1672) this is given
'A libbard's head (on the knees or

Ber. Well said, old mocker: I must needs be friends with
      thee.

Cost. I Pompey am, Pompey surnam'd the Big,—   545

Dum. The Great.

Cost. It is 'Great,' sir; Pompey surnam'd the Great;
      That oft in field, with targe and shield, did make my foe
        to sweat:
      And travelling along this coast, I here am come by chance
      And lay my arms before the legs of this sweet lass of
        France.   550
      If your ladyship would say, 'Thanks, Pompey,' I
      had done.

Prin. Great thanks, great Pompey.

Cost. 'Tis not so much worth; but I hope I was perfect.
      I made a little fault in 'Great.'   555

Ber. My hat to a halfpenny, Pompey proves the best
      Worthy.

Enter Sir NATHANIEL *for Alexander.*

Nath. When in the world I liv'd, I was the world's
        commander;
      By east, west, north, and south, I spread my conquering
        might:
      My scutcheon plain declares that I am Alisander,— 560

Boyet. Your nose says, no, you are not; for it stands too right.

---

elbows . . .), *Masquine.*' See note at
'vane', IV. i. 96, for an illustration of
the second suggestion.

548. *targe*] shield. Common in
earlier writers.

556. *My hat to a halfpenny*] Halliwell
quotes from Lodge, *Wits Miserie* (p.
63), 1596: 'Here is the only man living
to bring you where the best licour is,
and it is his hat to a halfe penny but hee
will be drunke for companie.' See note
at 'I'll lay my head to any good man's
hat' (I. i. 299). Berowne seems to be
fond of betting in hats. Caps were
commoner in this connection; perhaps
earlier.

561. *nose ... stands too right*] refers to a
well-known physical peculiarity of

Alexander. Cf. North's *Plutarch*, 1579:
'Lysippus ... hath perfectly drawn and
resembled Alexander's manner of
holding his neck, somewhat hanging
down towards the left side' (Temple
ed., vii. 5). And in De la Primaudaye's
French Academy, 1577 (trans. T. B.,
chap. xiii [1586]): 'Wee reade that
Alexander the Great and Alphonsus,
King of Arragon, having each of them
somewhat a wry necke, this by nature,
the other through custome, the flatterers and courtiers held their necks on
the one side, to counterfeit that imper-
fection.' This part of the *French
Academy* has been utilized by Robert
Greene, and the above passage will be
found in his *Tritameron*, pt II (1587)

Ber. Your nose smells 'no,' in this, most tender-smelling knight.
Prin. The conqueror is dismay'd. Proceed, good Alexander.
Nath. When in the world I liv'd, I was the world's
          Commander,—
Boyet. Most true; 'tis right: you were so, Alisander.   565
Ber. Pompey the Great,—
Cost. Your servant, and Costard.
Ber. Take away the conqueror, take away Alisander.
Cost. [*To Nathaniel.*] O! sir, you have overthrown Alis-
          ander the conqueror. You will be scraped out of the   570
          painted cloth for this: your lion, that holds his poll-
          axe sitting on a close-stool, will be given to Ajax: he

562. this] *Ff,Q2;* his *Q1.*

(Grosart, iii. 148). Puttenham refers to
the feature in *The Arte of English Poesie*
(Arber, p. 302), 1589: 'It was mis-
liked in the Emperor Nero, and
thought uncomely for him to counter-
fet Alexander the Great, by holding
his head a little awrie, and neerer to-
ward the one shoulder, because it was
not his owne naturall.' Steevens first
drew attention to this point.

562. *Your nose smells 'no'*] Cf. again
North's *Plutarch, ut supra*: 'I remember
I read also in the commentaries of
Aristoxenus, that his skin had a marvellous good savour, and that his
breath was very sweet, insomuch that
his body had so sweet a smell of it self,
that all the apparel he wore next unto
his body, took thereof a passing delightful savour.' Berowne suggests it
is *Boyet's* nose, and delicate sense of
smell, that detects the impostor.

571. *painted cloth*] cloth or canvas,
variously painted in oil, and used as
hangings, or for decoration, or in form-
ing partitions in interiors. This may
be taken as the exact sense here, on
account of the words 'scraped out', but
the term was also used of the arras or
tapestry (in spite of Dyce's *Glossary*)
which formed the hangings in many
cases. 'The Nine Worthies' was a
favourite subject: 'Thou woven worthy
in a piece of Arras, Fit only to enjoy a

wall' (*The Double Marriage*, IV. iii
[Waller, *Beaumont and Fletcher*, vi.
384]). Alexander was the chiefest
worthy. Cf. Whitlock, *Zootomia* (p.
171), 1654, quoted by Nares: 'That
Alexander was a souldier, painted
cloths will confesse; the painter
dareth not leave him out of the nine
worthies.'

571–2. *lion . . . close-stool*] In Gerard
Legh's *Accedens of Armourye*, 1563, the
arms of the worthies are given: 'The
fourth was Alexander, the which did
beare Geules, a lion or, seiante in a
chayer, holding a battle-ax argent.'
Legh's treatise had been republished
in 1591. See also Intro., 5.21.

572. *Ajax*] punning on a *jakes*, an old
name for a privy. The word occurs
again in *Lr.*, II. ii. 72. The quibble became very common from the title of a
work by Sir John Harington, *The Metamorphosis of Ajax*, 1596. See Nashe's
Works (McKerrow, iii. 38). 'The
pithie tractate of *Ajax*', as Henry Hutton calls it, is constantly referred to by
contemporary writers. Sir John was
forbidden the Court for it, but in 1598
his friend Robert Markham wrote to
him, saying, 'Your book is almost for-
given and I may say forgotten, but not
for its lacke of wit or satyr . . . and tho'
her Highness signified displeasure in
outward sort, yet did she like "the

will be the ninth Worthy. A conqueror, and afeard
to speak! run away for shame, Alisander. [*Nathaniel
retires.*] There, an't shall please you: a foolish mild   575
man; an honest man, look you, and soon dashed!
He is a marvellous good neighbour, faith, and a
very good bowler; but, for Alisander,—alas! you
see how 'tis,—a little o'erparted. But there are
Worthies a-coming will speak their mind in some   580
other sort.

Prin. Stand aside, good Pompey.

Enter HOLOFERNES *for Judas, and* MOTH *for Hercules.*

Hol. Great Hercules is presented by this imp,
Whose club kill'd Cerberus, that three-headed *canus*;
And, when he was a babe, a child, a shrimp,   585
Thus did he strangle serpents in his *manus*.
Quoniam he seemeth in minority,
Ergo I come with this apology.
Keep some state in thy exit, and vanish.   [*Moth retires.*
Judas I am,—   590

573. afeard] *Q1;* afraid *Ff,Q2.*   574–5. [*Nathaniel retires.*] *Capell.*   577. faith]
Q1; in sooth *Ff,Q2.*   579. 'tis] *Johnson, Cambridge;* tis *Q1,Ff;* it's *Q2;* 'tis;
Capell, Steevens.   584. *canus*] *Qq,Ff;* canis *Rowe, Cambridge.*

marrow of your book"' (*Nugæ Antiquæ,*
ii. 287) (1779). Sir John Harington
may have borrowed his quibble from
this passage, but likely enough it was
common property earlier.

576–8. *an honest man . . . and a very
good bowler*] '*An honest man and a good
bowler*' occurs in Clarke's *Paræmiologia,*
1639 (*Centurie of Prayse*). Probably in
general use before Shakespeare. 'Good
bowler' may mean no more than 'a
good sport'.

576. *dashed*] dispirited, disheartened.
See above, l. 462, for a slightly different
use. Cf. *Oth.,* iii. iii. 214.

579. *o'erparted*] given too difficult a
part. Cf. Jonson, *Bartholomew Fair,* iii.
i (1614) (Herford and Simpson, vi.
69): '*Quarlous.* How now, Numps!
almost tir'd i' your Protectorship?
overparted? overparted?' *N.E.D.*
quotes this.

583–4. *Hercules . . . club*] See note at
v. i. 109. Hercules with his club was
another favourite in the painted cloth,
or 'worm-eaten tapestry' (*Ado,* iii. iii.
145, 146).

583. *imp*] See note on i. ii. 5.

585. *shrimp*] Cf. *1H6,* ii. iii. 23:
'Alas, this is a child, a silly dwarf! It
cannot be this weak and writhled
shrimp Should strike such terror to his
enemies.' Gabriel Harvey uses it in
Pierce's Supererogation (Grosart, ii. 46),
1592: 'Agrippa was an urcheon,
Copernicus a shrimpe, Cardan a
puppy, Scaliger a baby, Paracelsus a
scab, Erastus a patch, Sigonius a toy,
Cuiacius a patch to this Termagant.'
And in *How a Man may Chuse a Good
Wife* (Hazlitt's *Dodsley,* ix. 40), 602:
'That shrimp, that spindleshank, that
wren, that sheep biter, that lean chitty-
face'.

Dum. A Judas!

Hol. Not Iscariot, sir.

 Judas I am, ycleped Maccabæus.

Dum. Judas Maccabæus clipt is plain Judas.

Ber. A kissing traitor. How, art thou prov'd Judas? 595

Hol. Judas I am,—

Dum. The more shame for you, Judas.

Hol. What mean you, sir?

Boyet. To make Judas hang himself.

Hol. Begin, sir; you are my elder. 600

Ber. Well follow'd: Judas was hang'd on an elder.

Hol. I will not be put out of countenance.

Ber. Because thou hast no face.

Hol. What is this?

Boyet. A cittern-head. 605

---

595. prov'd] *F2*; proud *Q1*; prou'd *F1,Q2*.

592. *Not Iscariot*] from John, xiv. 22, as Furnivall notes.

594. *clipt*] The two senses, to shear and to embrace, are quibbled with, as well as the word-play with 'cleped'.

595. *A kissing traitor*] A 'Judas kiss' became proverbial at an early date. Cf. *The Booke in Meeter of Robin Conscience* Hazlitt, *Early Popular Poetry*, iii. 245), *c.* 1550: 'And that you have given him many a Judas kisse Your act will declare how you have done amisse.'

How, art thou prov'd] Now then, haven't I proved you are Judas? 'Judas clipt' is kissing Judas, the traitor.

600. *you are my elder*] a proverbial bit of chaff. Cf. Lyly's *Endymion*, II. ii: 'You will be mine elder, because you stand upon a stoole.' And see *Err.*, v. i. 420. Still in use?

601. *Judas . . . elder*] an old legend. Dyce quoted *Sir John Mandevill* (E.E.T.S., p. 61), 1364: 'And faste by is zit the Tree of Eldre, that Judas henge him self upon, for despeyr that he hadde whan he solde and betrayed oure lord.' See also *The Vision of Piers the Plowman* (ed. Skeat, i. 26): 'Judas he japede with the Iewes seluer, And on an ellerne treo hongede him after.' And in Shakespeare's time in Marlowe, *Jew of Malta*, IV. vi. 68 (Case ed., p. 145): 'The hat he wears, Judas left under the elder when he hanged himself'; and Jonson, *Every Man out of his Humour*, IV. iv: 'He shall be your Judas, and you shall be his elder-tree to hang on.' Brand quotes from Gerard's *Herbal*, ed. Johnson, p. 1428: 'The *Arbor Judæ* [*Cercis siliquastrum*] is thought to be that whereon Judas hanged himself, and not upon the elder-tree, as it is vulgarly said.' It is doubtful, to say the least of it, if our elder grew within reach of Judas. It is not native in Palestine.

605–13.] This personal description of Holofernes recalls that of Gabriel Harvey by Nashe in *Have With You to Saffron Walden* (McKerrow, iii. 73, etc.). But there is much to be said against the identification. See Intro., 5.22.

605. *cittern-head*] 'The cittern had usually a head grotesquely carved at the extremity of the neck and finger-

Dum. The head of a bodkin.
Ber. A death's face in a ring.
Long. The face of an old Roman coin, scarce seen.
Boyet. The pommel of Cæsar's falchion.

609. falchion] fauchion *Q1;* faulchion *Ff,Q2.*

board' (Nares). Nares cites several parallels and compares Gargantua's lamentation for 'Badebec, who had a face like a rebec' (Motteux's *Rabelais,* ii. 24). See Marston's *Scourge of Villainy* (Bullen's *Marston,* iii. 301): 'Shall brainless citternheads, each jobbernoul, Pocket the very genius of thy soul?' And Dekker, *Match mee in London,* Act i (Pearson, iv. 137): 'Fidling at least half an hour on a citterne with a man's broken head at it, so that I think 'twas a barber surgeon'; and see Fletcher's *Love's Cure*: 'You citternhead, you ill-countenanced cur'. For a description of this musical instrument, somewhat like the guitar, see Chappell's *Popular Music* [1859], i. 101.

606. *head of a bodkin*] Bodkins, long jewelled pins for ladies' hair, appear abundantly as New Year's gifts to Queen Elizabeth from 1580 to 1590. See Nichols's *Progresses of Queen Elizabeth,* ii. 289–499. The heads or tops were various in form, often flowers in gold or small precious stones. In 1586–7 two occur: 'Item twoe bodkins of golde, th' one a flye, th' other a spider', and 'a bodkinne of silver with a little ostridge of gold'. They seem to have been very fashionable at this especial period. Cf. here Florio's *New World of Words*: '*Puntaruolo,* a bodkin, a head-needle, a goldsmith's pouncer. Also a nice, a coy, or selfe-conceited fellow, a man that stands upon nice faultes, a finde-faulte, a carper, a scrupulous, over-weening man'.

607. *death's face in a ring*] Death's head rings, with the motto *memento mori,* were in early popularity. See *1H4,* iii. iii. 34, 35; *Mer.V.,* i. ii. 55; and *2H4,* ii. iv. 255. An early example found by Hart is in Greene's *Farewell to Follie* (Grosart, ix. 239), 1591: 'The

olde Countesse spying on the finger of Seignior Cosimo a ring with a death's head ingraven, circled with this poesie, *Gressus ad vitam*'. And see Greene's *Never Too Late* (Grosart, viii. 30) for the real thing: 'I have in my cell A dead man's scull which calls this straight to mind That as this is so must my ending be.'

609. *Cæsar's falchion*] I presume this is also from a painted cloth representation of Cæsar. Cæsar's sword is, however, famous in legend. Bayle says (*Dictionary of History,* ed. 1735, ii. 419, n): 'I forgot an Act of Religion which is very curious. The Arverni boasted to have Julius Cæsar's sword, and showed it still in Plutarch's time, hung up in one of their Temples. Cæsar saw it and laughed but would not suffer his Men to take it away. He considered it a consecrated Thing' (Plutarch, in *Apoph.,* p. 720 E). It is a long jump from this to the days of Smollett. In *Peregrine Pickle,* chap. xxxiv (1750), this sword is in our own country: 'The company walked up hill to visit [Dover] castle, where they saw the sword of Julius Cæsar, and Queen Elizabeth's pocket pistol.' Cæsar was much more in evidence in Elizabethan times than now; existing popularly perhaps, only in 'as dead as Julius Cæsar'. But in those days Cæsar's wine was at Dover (H. Peacham, in *Coryat*). Cæsar's bread (gone sour) is in Beaumont and Fletcher and in Jonson. Deloney saw salt and wine in the Tower of London which had been there ever since Cæsar left it: 'the wine was grown so thick it might have been cut like a jelly.' Nashe mentions the wine also. Cæsar's salt beef is in Beaumont and Fletcher's *Love's Pilgrimage.* His money is in *The Jests of George Peele.*

Dum. The carved bone face on a flask.   610
Ber. Saint George's half-cheek in a brooch.
Dum. Ay, and in a brooch of lead.
Ber. Ay, and worn in the cap of a toothdrawer.
    And now, forward; for we have put thee in countenance.
Hol. You have put me out of countenance.   615
Ber. False: we have given thee faces.
Hol. But you have outfaced them all.
Ber. An thou wert a lion, we would do so.
Boyet. Therefore, as he is, an ass, let him go.
    And so adieu, sweet Jude! nay, why dost thou stay?   620
Dum. For the latter end of his name.
Ber. For the ass to the Jude? give it him:—Jud-as, away!
Hol. This is not generous, not gentle, not humble.

610. carved bone] carv'd-bone *Qq,Ff.*
an ass *Q2,Ff3,4.*

619. as he is, an ass] *Q1,Ff1,2;* as he is

These imaginings did not arise from any pictorial Cæsar.

610. *carved bone . . . on a flask*] See *Rom.*, III. iii. 132. Cotgrave has '*Flasque*, as *Flascon*; also, a flask, or box, for powder'. There are several prints of early flasks in Demmin's *Arms and Armour* (pp. 535, 536, Bell's ed. 1877). Some are of horn of the end of the sixteenth century, of German origin, all ornamented with carved work. One is a 'German primer' of this period inlaid with ivory, circular, with a grotesque central face.

611. *half-cheek*] profile, side-face. The same as 'half-face' in *John*, I. i. 94.

brooch] an ornament or jewel often worn in the hat; or a badge of leather or pewter to indicate the wearer's business. Cf. Dekker's *If this be not a good Play* (Pearson, iii. 289): 'The cittie water-bearers (trimly dight) With yellow oaken tankards (pind upright) Like brooches in their hats.' See next note.

612–13. *brooch of lead . . . in the cap of a toothdrawer*] Cf. Taylor, *Wit and Mirth* (Hazlitt's repr., p. 62), 1630: 'In Queen Elizabeth's dayes, there was a fellow that wore a brooch in his hat like a toothdrawer, with a Rose and Crown

and two letters: this fellow had a warrant from the Lord Chamberlaine at that time to travell with an exceeding brave ape which hee had; whereby hee gat his living from time to time at markets and fayres.' Evidently the common badge of the trade.

615. *out of countenance*] See above, l. 272.

618, 619. *lion . . . ass*] Suggested by Æsop's fable of the ass in the lion's skin. Cf. Nashe, *Foure Letters Confuted* (McKerrow, i. 290), 1593: 'steale Tully, steale Tully, away with the Asse in the Lions skinne.' And Jonson, *Case is Altered*: 'put off this lion's head, your ears have discovered you.' The application of the fable is generally as here, when the lion is found to be an ass he is told to clear out. Another quibble is suggested here by Furnivall, from Heywood's *Proverbs and Epigrams*, 1562 (Spenser Soc., p. 92): 'An ass was given to a rapacious governor named Jude', etc. A standing joke. Lyly has the same quibble on the name Mydas (iv. 1).

623. *humble*] 'courteous, benevolent, kind' (Schmidt). The context suggests this meaning, but no such sense is admitted in *N.E.D.* See l. 729 below.

Boyet. A light for Monsieur Judas! it grows dark, he may
    stumble.   [*Holofernes retires.*
Prin. Alas! poor Maccabæus, how hath he been baited. 625

Enter ARMADO *for Hector.*

Ber. Hide thy head, Achilles: here comes Hector in arms.
Dum. Though my mocks come home by me, I will now
    be merry.
King. Hector was but a Troyan in respect of this.
Boyet. But is this Hector?   630
King. I think Hector was not so clean-timbered.
Long. His leg is too big for Hector's.
Dum. More calf, certain.
Boyet. No; he is best indued in the small.
Ber. This cannot be Hector.   635
Dum. He's a god or a painter; for he makes faces.
Arm. The armipotent Mars, of lances the almighty,
    Gave Hector a gift,—

629, 667. Troyan] *Qq,Ff;* Trojan *Rowe, etc.*   632. Hector's] *Capell, Cambridge;*
Hectors *Q1;* Hector *Ff,Q2.*   634. in] with *Ff3,4.*

624. *Monsieur Judas*] The frequent
use of 'Monsieur' reminds us we are in
France.
    dark . . . stumble] perhaps refers to
John, ii. 10: 'If a man walk in the
night, he stumbleth'; and xiii. 30:
'Judas having received the sop went
immediately out, and it was night.'
    627. *come home by me*] come back on
my own head, like a boomerang.
    629. *Troyan*] merely an ordinary
kind of good fellow. See l. 667 below.
    631. *clean-timbered*] well-built. Cf.
Jonson, *Every Man out of his Humour*,
Induction: 'O, good words, good
words; a well-timbered fellow, he
would have made a good column'; and
Greene, *A Quip for an Upstart Courtier*
(Grosart, xi. 290): 'His Comrade that
bare him company was a iolly light
timber'd Iack a Napes.'
    633. *calf*] fool; as well as part of leg.
    634. *small*] the part of the leg below
the calf (Schmidt). The expression
occurs twice in Sidney's *Arcadia*, bk i

(*ante* 1586): 'in her going one might
sometimes discerne the smal of her leg,
which with the foot was dressed in a
short paire of crimson velvet buskins'
(Feuillerat, i. 75); and in bk v:
'Pyrocles came out led by Sympathus,
cloathed after the Greeke manner, in a
long coate of white velvet, reaching to
the small of his legge' (ii. 169). Craig
noted another instance in Hakluyt
(Maclehose ed., vi. 4): 'about their
armes and smalles of their legs they
have hoops of golde' (*Voyage of John
Eldred*, 1583).
    636. *He's . . . faces*] proverbial, in
Fuller's *Gnomologia*. See *Mery Tales,
Wittie Questions and Quicke Answeres,
Very Pleasant to be Readde*, 1567 (*c.*
1540), edited W. C. Hazlitt, 1864, pp.
106–7; and Taylor, *The Sculler*, 1612
(iii. 22 [1630]).
    637. *armipotent*] a title of Mars. It
occurs in Chaucer's *Knight's Tale*, ii.
24: 'Ther stood the tempul of Marz
armypotent.'

Dum. A gilt nutmeg.
Ber. A lemon.   640
Long. Stuck with cloves.
Dum. No, cloven.
Arm. Peace!
     The armipotent Mars, of lances the almighty,
     Gave Hector a gift, the heir of Ilion;   645

639. A gilt nutmeg] *Ff,Q2;* A gift nutmeg *Q1.*   643. Peace!] *not in*
Ff,Q2.

639. *gilt*] Hart wrote: 'A sense of *gild,* equivalent to the old cookery term "endore", which seems to have escaped the dictionaries and commentators. The term is used by Hugh Plat (*Delights for Ladies*), 1600; *The Art of Preserving* (ed. 1611): "a, 13. The making of sugar-plate, and casting thereof in carved moldes. . . . Set it (the paste) against the fire till it bee dry on the inside, then with a knife get it out as they used to doe a dish of butter, and drie the backside, then gilde it on the edges with the white of an egge laide round about the brim of the dish with a pensile, and presse the golde downe with some cotton, & when it is drie skew or brush off the golde with the foote of an Hare or Conie." Probably, though not so stated, saffron was used. No gold was used in this gilding. Was there ever any in the "*gilded pill*"? Yolk of egg, quicksilver and salt armoniac are the ingredients. Hence the gilded rosemary, gilt wheat, gilded bride-branches, etc., of Ben Jonson and others. And in Nichols's *Progresses,* ii. 78: "a greate pye of quynses and wardyns guilt" (1577–8).'

gilt nutmeg] Cf. Jonson, *The Gipsies Metamorphosed,* 1621: 'I have lost an inchanted nutmeg, all gilded over, was inchanted at Oxford for me, to put in my sweetheart's ale a mornings.' In an *Account of Receipts* (*Harleian Miscellany,* vii. 159) 'A dozen of gilt nutmegs' occurs in 1660. See last note. No doubt the nutmeg lasted a long time, a slight sprinkle of the strong flavour being sufficient in ale, port-wine, etc. The gilding may have been a preservative from the effects of atmosphere, from dust, and also ornamental.

640–1. *lemon. Stuck with cloves*] Oranges were more commonly used in this manner, but oranges and lemons seem to have been used indiscriminately for the same purposes. In the little volume of Hugh Plat, quoted from at l. 639, we are told what the use of the orange stuck with cloves was. It was, like the nutmeg, for the ale. See (a, 32): '*Divers excellent kindes of bottle Ale.* . . . Some commende the hanging of roasted Oranges prickt full of cloves in the vessel of ale, till you finde the taste thereof suffiicentlie graced to your owne liking.' Halliwell quotes from Bradwell, 1636, that a lemon stuck with cloves was a good thing to smell occasionally against pestilence; and Dr Rawlinson states that the executioner of Charles I found an orange full of cloves in the king's pocket. More to the purpose is Steevens's extract from Lupton's *Notable Things*: 'Wine wyll be pleasant in taste and flavour if an orenge or a lymon (stickte round about with cloaves) be hanged within the vessell that it touch not the wyne. And so the wyne wyll be preserved from foystines and evyll savor' (ii. 36 [1595]). H. B. Charlton suggested (*M.L.R.,* xii [1917]) that in offering *drinkers*' aids the jokers pun on the hint of potations in 'armi*potent*'. See *Oth.,* III. iii. 80, 'potent in potting'.

A man so breath'd that certain he would fight; yea
From morn till night, out of his pavilion.
I am that flower,—

Dum.   That mint.

Long.   That columbine.

Arm. Sweet Lord Longaville, rein thy tongue.

Long. I must rather give it the rein, for it runs against   650
Hector.

Dum. Ay, and Hector's a greyhound.

Arm. The sweet war-man is dead and rotten; sweet
chucks, beat not the bones of the buried; when he
breathed, he was a man. But I will forward with   655
my device. Sweet royalty, bestow on me the sense
of hearing.   [*Berowne steps forth.*

Prin. Speak, brave Hector; we are much delighted.

Arm. I do adore thy sweet grace's slipper.

Boyet. Loves her by the foot.   660

Dum. He may not by the yard.

---

644. fight; yea] *Qq,Ff, Steevens, Cambridge, Globe;* fight ye *Rowe (ed. 2), Dyce, etc.*
654–5. when he . . . man] *Q1, Capell et seq.; not in Ff,Q2.*   657. [*Berowne steps
forth*] *Q1;* [*Berowne steps to Costard and whispers him*] *Capell;* [*Berowne whispers
Costard*] *Steevens, Craig; om. Cambridge, Globe.*

646. *breath'd*] in such good wind and
condition that he would fight, yea from
morn to night. The alteration to 'ye'
enfeebles the sense. For 'breathed' see
Shr., Induction, ii. 50; *Ven.*, 678, etc.
Cf. the old play of *The Taming of a
Shrew*, 1594 (*Shakes. Lib.*, 1875, p. 165),
i. i: 'Make the long breathde Tygre
broken winded.'

647. *pavilion*] the ceremonial tent
from which the champion issued to the
lists. This Hector is the hero of the
medieval romances, not of the *Iliad*.

648. *columbine*] Cf. *A Twelfe Night
Merriment (Narcissus)*, 1602 (ed. M.
Lee, 1893): 'Looke, O thou flower of
favour, thou marigold of mercye and
columbine of compassion, looke, O
loke on the dolourous dewe dropps dis-
tilld from the limbeckes of loopeholes
of their eyes.' A very popular flower at
this time.

652. *Hector . . . greyhound*] This name
is given in a 'Catalogue of some general

Names of Hounds and Beagles' in *The
Gentleman's Recreation*, by Nicholas
Cox, p. 14, ed. 1721.

653. *war-man*] See *The Troublesome
Raigne of King John*, 1591 (*Shakes. Lib.*,
1875, p. 294): 'Here comes the
warmen all.' And again at pp. 306,
308.

dead and rotten] not again in Shakespeare. See Harrison's *Description of
England*, bk II, chap. iii (New Shakes.
Soc., p. 88), 1577–87: 'I tell you, sirs,
that I judge no land in England better
bestowed than that which is given to
our universities; for by their maintenance our realme shall be well
governed when we be dead and rotten.' A speech of King Henry VIII.

654. *chucks*] See v. i. 103.

657. [Berowne steps forth] See note
on l. 663.

661. *by the yard*] more 'talking
greasily'. 'Yard', like 'prick' (IV. i. 133–
9), is the organ of generation.

Arm. This Hector far surmounted Hannibal,
  The party is gone—

Cost. Fellow Hector, she is gone; she is two months on
  her way.   665

Arm. What meanest thou?

Cost. Faith, unless you play the honest Troyan, the poor
  wench is cast away: she's quick; the child brags in
  her belly already: 'tis yours.

Arm. Dost thou infamonize me among potentates? 670
  Thou shalt die.

Cost. Then shall Hector be whipped for Jaquenetta that
  is quick by him, and hanged for Pompey that is
  dead by him.

Dum. Most rare Pompey!   675

Boyet. Renowned Pompey!

Ber. Greater than great, great, great, great Pompey!
  Pompey the Huge!

---

663. *The party is gone*] Granville
Barker's explanation of this (*Prefaces to
Shakespeare*, i, p. 46) is dramatically the
most convincing. Q prints the words in
italics, and centred. They are generally
taken to be a stage-direction; but were
it not for the centring (which may be
a blunder) they would clearly be a continuation of Hector's speech (also in
italics), here interrupted by Costard. He
hears 'Hector' claim to have 'surmounted' somebody, a word that he
interprets as meaning the same as the
'mounted' of *Cym.*, II. v. 17. When
Armado proceeds to say that 'the party
is gone' in consequence, Costard cannot resist breaking in with 'Indeed she
is—two months gone.' His outburst
would then be directly prompted by
Armado's speech, and there is no need
of the elaborate preparation provided
by Capell at l. 657 except as a gloss on
the enigmatic direction in Q at that
point.

667. *Troyan*] 'Trojan' generally
stood for a 'good fellow' amongst
Shakespeare's contemporaries, and
see *1H4*, II. i. 77. This is the sense here
also, but hardly in *H5*, v. i. 20, 32,
unless Pistol means by 'base Trojan',

thou disgrace to good fellows. See l.
629, above, for another slang example.
References may be given to Jonson,
Every Man in his Humour, IV. ii; Dekker,
Gentle Craft (Pearson, p. 42); Heywood,
Woman Killed with Kindness; Marston,
Pasquil and Katherine; Kemp, *Nine Daies
Morrice*, etc. In all these the name is
friendly, or gives the idea of some
liking.

670. *infamonize*] Armado's perver-
sion of 'infamize', to defame. Nashe,
who was great at verbs in *-ize* (ee III. i.
48), seems to have coined 'infamize':
'There is no other unlascivious use or
end of poetry, but to infamize vice, and
magnifie vertue' (*Foure Letters Confuted*
[McKerrow, i. 285], 1592–3). He has
it again later in *Have With You to
Saffron Walden* (McKerrow, iii. 31),
1596: 'Baffull and infamize my name
when I am in heaven.' Gabriel Harvey, Nashe's antagonist, seized on it
in his list of expressions from Nashe
held up to ridicule in *Pierce's Supererogation* (Grosart, ii. 276), 1593: 'infam-
izers of vice'. This is a reply to Nashe's
Foure Letters Confuted.

678. *Pompey the Huge*] See above,
l. 545. Marston recalls this in *The Mal-*

Dum. Hector trembles.

Ber. Pompey is moved. More Ates, more Ates! stir them   680
  on! stir them on!

Dum. Hector will challenge him.

Ber. Ay, if 'a have no more man's blood in his belly than
  will sup a flea.

Arm. By the north pole, I do challenge thee.   685

Cost. I will not fight with a pole, like a northern man:
  I'll slash; I'll do it by the sword. I bepray you, let
  me borrow my arms again.

Dum. Room for the incensed Worthies!

Cost. I'll do it in my shirt.   690

Dum. Most resolute Pompey!

Moth. Master, let me take you a button-hole lower. Do

---

681. on! stir] *Rowe;* or stir *Qq,Ff.*   683. in his] *Q1;* in's *Ff,Q2.*   687. bepray]
Q1; pray *Ff,Q2, Cambridge.*

---

content, I. i (1604): 'And run the wild-goose-chase even with Pompey the Huge'. For a similar mock-heroic use see Jonson's *Sejanus,* v. viii. 3: 'To tender your All Hail in the wide hall Of huge Sejanus'.

680. *Ates*] the spirits of discord and strife.

684. *sup a flea*] Cf. *Tw.N.,* III. ii. 61. For 'sup' used transitively, see *Shr.,* Induction, i. 28.

686. *fight with a pole, like a northern man*] Hart's note ran: 'I am not satisfied there is any reference here to the quarter-staff, as Halliwell suggested, which was expressly a Devonshire and western game. See *N.E.D.* for quotation from *Dicke of Devonshire,* 1626, who calls it 'my own country weapon'; and see Strutt's *Sports and Pastimes* for further proof. The reference is rather to outlaws and thieves. Boorde says, speaking of 'a Scotishe man' (*Boke of Knowledge,* chap. iv [1542]): 'In these partyes be many out lawes and strong theeves, for much of their lyving standeth by stelyng and robbyng.' Add to this what Harrison says (*Description of England,* bk II, chap. xvi [1577–87]): 'I might here speake of the

excessive staves which diverse that travell by the waie doo carrie upon their shoulders, whereof some are twelve or thirteen foote long, beside the pike of twelve inches: but as they are commonlie suspected of honest men to be theeves and robbers, or at the least scarse true men which beare them; so by reason of this . . . no man travelleth by the waie without his sword, or some such weapon.' The quarterstaff was about half the length of these staves. The pole here is that of the border reavers.

692. *take you a button-hole lower*] help you off with your garment, with a reference to the proverbial phrase meaning to humiliate one. Moth means that he will expose his poverty of underwear. Cf. Nashe, *Pierce Penilesse* (McKerrow, i. 204): 'The haire shirt will chase whordome out of their boanes, and the hard lodging on the boards take their flesh downe a button hole lower.' It meant 'take one down a peg'. See Cotgrave, in v, '*Mettre de l'eau dedans le vin là.* To temper, cool, tame or take a hole lower.' Cf. also '*Serrer le bouton à*' in Cotgrave, an equestrian expression, which occurs in

you not see Pompey is uncasing for the combat?
What mean you? you will lose your reputation.

Arm. Gentlemen and soldiers, pardon me; I will not   695
combat in my shirt.

Dum. You may not deny it; Pompey hath made the
challenge.

Arm. Sweet bloods, I both may and will.

Ber. What reason have you for't?   700

Arm. The naked truth of it is, I have no shirt. I go woolward for penance.

Boyet. True, and it was enjoined him in Rome for want
of linen; since when I'll be sworn he wore none but
a dishclout of Jaquenetta's, and that a' wears next   705
his heart for a favour.

Enter Monsieur MARCADE, *a Messenger.*

Mar. God save you, madam!

Prin.   Welcome, Marcade,
But that thou interrupt'st our merriment.

Mar. I am sorry, madam; for the news I bring   710

705. a'] *Q1;* he *Ff,Q2.*   708-11.] *Prose in Qq,Ff.*

T.B.'s translation of Primaudaye's
French Academy, chap. xlix (1586). In
Chapman's *Humerous Days Mirth*
(Parrott, ii. 60), 1599, it occurs again:
'Decline me, or take me a hole lower,
as the prouerbe is.'

693. *uncasing*] undressing.

699. *bloods*] gallant fellows. Occurs
again in *Cæs.* and *John.* Greene has it in
The Carde of Fancie (Grosart, iv. 179),
1587: 'Three of the boldest blouds in
Alexandria were not able to abide the
force of Clerophontes.'

701-2. *no shirt . . . go woolward for
penance*] 'Woolwarde, without any
lynnen nexte ones body *(Sans chemyse)*'
(Palsgrave, 1530). See Skeat's edition
of *Piers the Plowman* (ii. 247) and Nares
where the word is well explained:
'Dressed in wool only, without linen,
often enjoined by way of penance'.
See a quotation from Nashe at l. 692
for the similar penance of a hair shirt.

Nashe has the phrase in the text also,
which was evidently a standard joke:
'Such as have but one shirt shall go
woolward till [while] that be a wash-
ing' (*A Wonderfull Prognostication* [Mc-
Kerrow, *Nashe,* iii. 189], 1591).
Farmer quotes from Lodge's *Wits
Miserie,* 1596: 'When his shirt is a
washing then he goes woolward.' And
Steevens, from Rowland's *Letting of
Humours Blood,* 1600: 'His shirt's a
washing: then hee must goe wooll-
ward'. Nares has it from *Witts
Recreations,* 1641.

707. *Marcade*] This gentleman may
be, as well as Navarre and his friends,
an historical person—Abel Lefranc has
found the name Mercadé or Marcadé
with that of Boyet in contemporary French records. If so, the Princess should probably give him his *e*
acute and so preserve the blank verse
line.

    Is heavy in my tongue. The king your father—
Prin. Dead, for my life!
Mar. Even so: my tale is told.
Ber. Worthies, away! The scene begins to cloud.
Arm. For mine own part, I breathe free breath. I have   715
    seen the day of wrong through the little hole of dis-
    cretion, and I will right myself like a soldier.
                             [*Exeunt Worthies.*

King. How fares your majesty?
Prin. Boyet, prepare: I will away to-night.
King. Madam, not so; I do beseech you, stay.   720
Prin. Prepare, I say. I thank you, gracious lords,
    For all your fair endeavours; and entreat,
    Out of a new-sad soul, that you vouchsafe
    In your rich wisdom to excuse or hide
    The liberal opposition of our spirits,   725
    If over-boldly we have borne ourselves
    In the converse of breath; your gentleness
    Was guilty of it. Farewell, worthy lord!

---

716. day] days *Warburton's note.*   wrong] right *Warburton.*   722. entreat,]
entreat: *Q1;* entreats: *Ff;* intreats: *Q2.*

715–17. *I have seen . . . soldier*] Hart's
note deserves reprinting if only for the
satisfaction it gave him: 'Armado's
character receives in this speech a
pathetic touch to his credit that has not
been noticed. He has been publicly insulted, and his sinfulness has found
him out; and he resolves to reform and
do justice to himself and Jaquenetta as
a soldier, a man of honour, should. See,
for the result, his next speech, as evidence of his reformation (at l. 874): 'I
am a votary: I have vowed to Jaquenetta to hold the plough for her sweet
love three years.' This is what Armado
refers to; there is no renewal here of the
preceding paltry quarrel; his thoughts
were as much deeper as they were
more creditable. "The little hole of
discretion" may be made clearer if we
give Sense 2, *N.E.D.*, "judgment of
others", to the word "discretion", a
not uncommon early use.'

716. *seen the day . . . little hole*] an 'old
saw', equivalent to 'I am no fool.'
Armado's application is, as might be
expected, somewhat stilted. Cf. Heywood's *Proverbs* (ed. Sharman, p. 45),
1546: 'I see day at this little hole. For
this blood [bud] sheweth what fruite
will follow'; and Gabriel Harvey,
Letters (Grosart, i. 138), 1573–80:
'being on that can as soone as an other
spye lighte at a little hole'; and Lyly,
Euphues and his England (Arber, p. 318),
1580: 'I can see day at a little hole,
thou must halt cunningly if thou be-
guile a Cripple'; and as late as Ravens-
croft, *Canterbury Guests,* v. 5 (1695), and
Tom Browne's *Works,* ed. 1708, iii. 27
(*Pleasant Letters,* 1700).

727. *converse of breath*] intercourse of
breath, conversation. Cf. *Oth.,* IV. ii. 5.
   your gentleness] your courtesy and
kindness encouraged us to be over-
bold.

A heavy heart bears not a humble tongue.
Excuse me so, coming too short of thanks   730
For my great suit so easily obtain'd.
King. The extreme parts of time extremely forms
All causes to the purpose of his speed,
And often, at his very loose, decides
That which long process could not arbitrate: 735
And though the mourning brow of progeny
Forbid the smiling courtesy of love
The holy suit which fain it would convince;
Yet since love's argument was first on foot,
Let not the cloud of sorrow justle it   740
From what it purpos'd; since, to wail friends lost
Is not by much so wholesome-profitable
As to rejoice at friends but newly found.
Prin. I understand you not: my griefs are double.

---

729. not] but *Collier MS.*   a humble] *Qq,F1;* an humble, *Ff2,3,4;* a nimble *Theobald, Cambridge, New.*   732. parts] past *Theobald;* haste *Singer;* dart *Staunton conj.*   735. process] process of time *Ff3,4.*   742. wholesome] holdsome *Q1.*   744. double] *Qq,Ff;* deaf *Capell;* dull *Collier MS., Dyce, Craig;* hear dully *Staunton conj.*

729. *humble*] complimentary, civil. Cf. *Lucr.*, 1093–8: 'True grief is fond and testy as a child', etc.; and see above, l. 623n. The inexcusable reading 'nimble' has nothing to recommend it except ingenuity. Furness says of the Princess: 'out of her new-sad soul she has attempted to apologize for her conduct; but she breaks off abruptly . . . saying that sorrow is not *humble*, is too self-centred for apologies, which in themselves imply humility.'

732–5. *The extreme . . . arbitrate*] the necessity of a sudden decision settles all questions and hesitations. That very instant or extremity of time's limit shapes everything to the one purpose, speedy resolve. 'Extremely' has the sense of 'to the extremity'. Cf. the King's 'latest minute of the hour', below, l. 779. 'Forms' may be a 'northern' plural, but both this and the 'his' of ll. 733, 734 are easily explained on the assumption that as the sentence proceeds the simple idea

'time' comes to stand for 'time's parts'.

734. *loose*] a technical term for the discharge of an arrow, hence 'the critical moment' (Schmidt). The term is used figuratively by Jonson in *The Alchemist*, ii. 1. See Puttenham, *Arte of English Poesie*, 1586–9 (Arber, p. 289): 'His [Cupid's] bent is sweete, his loose is somewhat soure, In joy begunne ends oft in wofull houre.' And, again, p. 185, quoted by Dyce: 'The Archers terme who is not said to finish the feate of his shot before he give the loose and deliver his arrow from his bow'. Earlier, in Lyly's *Sapho and Phao*, v. i (1581): 'this arrow . . . must Phao be stricken withal; and cry softly to thyself in the very loose, Venus!'

738. *convince*] establish, prove.

744. *double*] Can this possibly mean 'bewildering'? The sense 'deceiving' or 'ambiguous' (preserved in the modern 'duplicity') is common in Shakespeare's work. Berowne's 'honest' may pun on this meaning. If

Ber. Honest plain words best pierce the ear of grief;   745
    And by these badges understand the king.
    For your fair sakes have we neglected time,
    Play'd foul play with our oaths. Your beauty, ladies,
    Hath much deform'd us, fashioning our humours
    Even to the opposed end of our intents;   750
    And what in us hath seem'd ridiculous,—
    As love is full of unbefitting strains;
    All wanton as a child, skipping and vain;
    Form'd by the eye, and therefore, like the eye,
    Full of strange shapes, of habits, and of forms,   755
    Varying in subjects, as the eye doth roll
    To every varied object in his glance:
    Which party-coated presence of loose love
    Put on by us, if, in your heavenly eyes,
    Have misbecom'd our oaths and gravities,   760
    Those heavenly eyes, that look into these faults,
    Suggested us to make. Therefore, ladies,

745. ear] *Q1;* ears *Ff1,2,Q2;* cares *Ff3,4.*   746. badges] *Qq,Ff;* bodges *New.*
755. strange] *Capell et seq.;* straying *Qq,Ff.*   760. misbecom'd] misbecombd
Q1.   762. make] make them *Pope.*

we take 'double' literally, which is in-advisable, the Princess's second grief would be either her coming departure from the King, whose intentions she hardly understands, or a mere courtesy.

746. *badges*] emblems, symbols, the formal words by which the King (and Berowne) try to convey their real feeling. Dover Wilson's 'bodges' (i.e. patchwork, *bungled* speeches) is attractive.

752. *strains*] tendencies.

755. *strange*] Capell's emendation is generally accepted. In support of it, the Cambridge editors write: 'In the *Lover's Complaint* (ed. 1609), l. 303, "strange" is spelt "straing"; and in Lyly's *Euphues* (Arber, p. 113), 'stray-ing" is a misprint for "straunge".' More probably an old spelling than a misprint for it occurs again in Hand D's part of *Sir Thomas More* (l. 8): 'they bring in straing rootes, which is meerly to the vndoing of poor prentizes, for

what∫ a sorry psnyp to a good hart.' Cf. *Promos and Cassandra* (*Shakes. Lib.*, vi. 228), pt I, iii. 1: 'O straying effectes of blinde affected Love, From wisdomes pathes, which doth astraye our wittes', etc. Halliwell quoted the first line here, with the simple remark that 'straying' was the same misprint for 'strange'. The pun again suggests it is no mis-print but a recognized spelling. Shake-speare has expressions many times from *Promos and Cassandra*. The parallel in *MND.*, v. i. 12–17, would support either 'strange' (as the equivalent of 'things unknown') or 'straying' (as the opposite of having a 'local habitation').

756–7. *subjects . . . object*] a kind of antithesis the Euphuists delighted in. 'You shall not be as objects of warre, but as subjects to Alexander' (Lyly's *Campaspe*, I. i).

756. *eye doth roll*] Cf. *MND.*, v. i. 14.

758. *party-coated*] in motley, like a fool. See note at 'patch', IV. ii. 30.

762. *Suggested*] tempted. See *Oth.*, II.

Our love being yours, the error that love makes
Is likewise yours: we to ourselves prove false,
By being once false for ever to be true   765
To those that make us both,—fair ladies, you:
And even that falsehood, in itself a sin,
Thus purifies itself and turns to grace.
Prin. We have receiv'd your letters full of love;
Your favours, the ambassadors of love;   770
And in our maiden council, rated them
At courtship, pleasant jest, and courtesy,
As bombast and as lining to the time.
But more devout than this in our respects
Have we not been; and therefore met your loves   775
In their own fashion, like a merriment.
Dum. Our letters, madam, show'd much more than jest.
Long. So did our looks.
Ros.   We did not quote them so.
King. Now, at the latest minute of the hour,
Grant us your loves.
Prin.   A time, methinks, too short   780
To make a world-without-end bargain in.
No, no, my lord, your grace is perjur'd much,
Full of dear guiltiness; and therefore this:
If for my love, as there is no such cause,
You will do aught, this shall you do for me: 785
Your oath I will not trust; but go with speed
To some forlorn and naked hermitage,
Remote from all the pleasures of the world;
There stay, until the twelve celestial signs

770. the] *Ff; not in Q1.*   774. this in our] *Hanmer;* this our *Q1;* these are our *Ff,Q2;* these are your *Tyrwhitt conj.*   775. been] seen *Tyrwhitt conj.*   778. quote] *Hanmer, etc.;* cote, coat, coate *old editions.*

iii. 364, *R2,* iii. iv. 75, and *Gent.,* iii. i. 34; and cf. i. i. 157.

773. *bombast*] stuffing of wool for padding clothes. See *Oth.,* i. i. 13.

778. *quote*] take them as meaning so.

781. *world-without-end*] Cf. *Sonn.,* lvii. Nashe uses the expression in *Foure Letters Confuted* (McKerrow, i. 324), 1592–3: 'When I parted with thy

brother in Pierce Penilesse, I left him to be tormented world without ende of our Poets and writers about London.' Occurs in the Te Deum and in Isa., xlv. 17, where the Wyclif reading is 'everlasting'.

783. *dear*] grievous, heartfelt. But no doubt the Princess implies the sense of acceptable, forgivable.

789. *signs*] of the zodiac. This ex-

Have brought about the annual reckoning.   790
If this austere insociable life
Change not your offer made in heat of blood;
If frosts and fasts, hard lodging and thin weeds,
Nip not the gaudy blossoms of your love,
But that it bear this trial and last love;   795
Then at the expiration of the year,
Come challenge me, challenge me by these deserts,
And, by this virgin palm now kissing thine,
I will be thine; and, till that instant, shut
My woeful self up in a mourning house,   800
Raining the tears of lamentation
For the remembrance of my father's death.
If this thou do deny, let our hands part;
Neither intitled in the other's heart.
King. If this, or more than this, I would deny,   805
To flatter up these powers of mine with rest,
The sudden hand of death close up mine eye!
Hence hermit, then—my heart is in thy breast.
[*Ber.* And what to me, my love? and what to me?
Ros. You must be purged to your sins are rack'd: 810

790. the] *Q1;* their *Ff,Q2.*   799. instant] *Ff,Q2;* instance *Q1.*   804. intitled]
Ff1,2,3; intiled *Q1;* intituled *F4.*   806. flatter] fetter *Hanmer (Warburton).*
808. hermit] *New (Pollard);* herrite *Q1;* euer *Ff.*   810. purged to] purged to,
Q1; purged too, *Ff.*   rack'd] *Qq,Ff;* rank *Rowe.*

pression for the duration of a year
occurs again in *Meas.*, I. ii. 172. Cf.
Gesta Grayorum, 1594 (Malone Soc.,
ed. Greg, p. 10): 'In his Crest, his
Government for the twelve days of
Christmas was resembled to the Sun's
passing the twelve Signs.'

793. *weeds*] garments. Greene commonly applies the term to a palmer's
wear.

795. *last love*] survive as love.

804. *intitled*] having a claim (a legal
sense).

806. *flatter up . . . with rest*] indulge in
idleness and freedom from cares. If I
should refuse you anything for the sake
of my selfish comfort.

808. *Hence hermit, then*] The F reading
is clearly a feeble attempt at emendation. A. W. Pollard's suggestion

(*Library*, Oct. 1917) is close to the Q
and gives us just what the King might
be expected to say: 'You tell me to be a
hermit—very well, I will be; your
word to me is law.'

809–14. *And what . . . sick*] Rosaline's
next speech makes these lines redun-
dant. They are clearly an early draft,
somehow left uncancelled by Shakespeare although he had written new
lines for Rosaline and Berowne, and
borrowed from the old for Dumain and
Katharine. See Intro., 2.51.

810. *purged . . . rack'd*] The F punctuation demands a forced sense for
rack'd, hence Rowe's attractive emendation. *Rank* might be spelt *räcke*.
Dover Wilson suggests 'that the compositor printed "to" for "till" (a common type of error) and that the line

You are attaint with faults and perjury;
Therefore, if you my favour mean to get,
A twelvemonth shall you spend and never rest
But seek the weary beds of people sick.]
Dum. But what to me, my love? but what to me?   815
   A wife?
Kath.   A beard, fair health, and honesty;
With three-fold love I wish you all these three.
Dum. O! shall I say, I thank you, gentle wife?
Kath. Not so, my lord. A twelvemonth and a day
   I'll mark no words that smooth-faced wooers say: 820
   Come when the king doth to my lady come;
   Then, if I have much love, I'll give you some.
Dum. I'll serve thee true and faithfully till then.
Kath. Yet swear not, lest you be forsworn again.
Long. What says Maria?
Mar.   At the twelvemonth's end   825
   I'll change my black gown for a faithful friend.
Long. I'll stay with patience; but the time is long.
Mar. The liker you; few taller are so young.

816. A wife? *Kath.* A beard] *Cambridge, New; Kath.* A wife? A beard *Qq,Ff1,2,3; Kath.* A wife, a beard *F4.*

should read "You must be purged till your sins are racked." The word "attaint" in the next line seems to make the connection between "rack" and torture certain.' There is no need, however, to alter 'to', which still sometimes took the place of 'till' even at this date. *N.E.D.* quotes a deposition in a Durham ecclesiastical court, *c.* 1575: 'Umphray culd gett no reste of the said Thomas to he had cast hym doon on his bedd.' Common earlier.

816. *A wife*] The words were first given to Dumain by Clark and Aldis Wright. Their emendation is the best means of making sense of the Q punctuation; that of the fourth F suggests an Elizabethan equivalent of our 'a house, a wife, and a thousand a year', but the 'threefold' of the next line forbids this reading.

819. *A twelvemonth and a day*] 'Halli-

well gives quotations from Ducange and from Cowell's *Interpreter*, which shows that this term constituted the full legal year both on the Continent and in England. It is found in Chaucer's *Wyf of Bathes Tale* (Furness). Hence the common expression 'a year and a day'.

820. *smooth-faced*] Shakespeare has this compound twice elsewhere; of commodity (advantage), in *John*, II. i. 573; and of peace, in *R3*, v. v. 33. He may have met it in Greene's *Menaphon* (Grosart, vi. 41): 'Some sweare Love Smooth'd face Love Is sweetest sweete that men can have.' It occurs also in *The Troublesome Raigne of King John* (Hazlitt's *Shakes. Lib.*, p. 263): 'A smooth facte Nunne (for ought I know) is all the Abbott's wealth.'

826. *friend*] sweetheart. See note on l. 404 above.

Ber. Studies my lady? mistress, look on me.
    Behold the window of my heart, mine eye,   830
    What humble suit attends thy answer there;
    Impose some service on me for thy love.
Ros. Oft have I heard of you, my Lord Berowne,
    Before I saw you, and the world's large tongue
    Proclaims you for a man replete with mocks;   835
    Full of comparisons and wounding flouts,
    Which you on all estates will execute
    That lie within the mercy of your wit:
    To weed this wormwood from your fruitful brain,
    And there withal to win me, if you please,   840
    Without the which I am not to be won,
    You shall this twelve month term from day to day,
    Visit the speechless sick, and still converse
    With groaning wretches; and your task shall be
    With all the fierce endeavour of your wit   845
    To enforce the pained impotent to smile.
Ber. To move wild laughter in the throat of death?
    It cannot be; it is impossible:
    Mirth cannot move a soul in agony.
Ros. Why, that's the way to choke a gibing spirit,   850
    Whose influence is begot of that loose grace
    Which shallow laughing hearers give to fools.
    A jest's prosperity lies in the ear
    Of him that hears it, never in the tongue
    Of him that makes it: then, if sickly ears,   855
    Deaf'd with the clamours of their own dear groans,
    Will hear your idle scorns, continue then,
    And I will have you and that fault withal;

---

832. thy] *Q1;* my *Ff,Q2.*   839. fruitful] *Ff;* fructful *Q1.*   856. dear] dere
Johnson conj.; drear *Jackson conj.;* dire *Collier MS.*   857. then] them *Rann conj.,*
Dyce.

831–2. *suit . . . service*] See note at
l. 276. This recognized phrase in courtship occurs in *The Shepherdess Felismena,* in Yonge's trans. of Montmayor's
Diana (*Shakes. Lib.,* p. 289, ed. 1875),
1598: 'He should never have got any
other guerdon of his sutes and services,
but onely to see and to be seene,
and sometimes to speake to his Mistresse.' A term in Feudalism primarily.
    837. *all estates*] people of all sorts.
    845. *fierce*] ardent, eager.
    856. *dear*] heartfelt; see l. 783n.,
and cf. *Sonn.,* xxxvii. 3: 'fortune's
dearest spite'.

> But if they will not, throw away that spirit,
> And I shall find you empty of that fault,   860
> Right joyful of your reformation.

Ber. A twelvemonth! well, befall what will befall,
> I'll jest a twelvemonth in an hospital.

Prin. [*To the King.*] Ay, sweet my lord; and so I take my leave.

King. No, madam; we will bring you on your way.   865

Ber. Our wooing doth not end like an old play;
> Jack hath not Jill: these ladies' courtesy
> Might well have made our sport a comedy.

King. Come, sir, it wants a twelvemonth and a day,
> And then 'twill end.

Ber.   That's too long for a play.   870

Re-enter ARMADO.

Arm. Sweet majesty, vouchsafe me,—

Prin. Was not that Hector?

Dum. The worthy knight of Troy.

Arm. I will kiss thy royal finger, and take leave. I am
> a votary; I have vowed to Jaquenetta to hold the   875
> plough for her sweet love three year. But, most
> esteemed greatness, will you hear the dialogue that

876. year] yeare *Q1*; years *Ff,Q2*.

862. *befall . . . befall*] Cf. 'befall what
may befall' (*2H6*, III. ii. 402, and *Tit.*,
v. i. 57). Similar to 'hap what will',
'come what come may', both of which
occur in Greene's *Carde of Fancie*, 1587.

865. *bring you on your way*] conduct,
accompany you on your way. The
expression occurs again in *Wint.*, IV.
iii. 122; and in *Meas.*, I. i. 62. It is close
to the 'bring me forward' of *Everyman*,
l. 290.

867. *Jack . . . Jill*] an old saying,
occurring in Heywood's *Dialogue*, 1546
(Dyce); and see Sharman's edition of
Heywood's *Proverbs*, p. 100. And
earlier, in Skelton's *Magnyfycence*
(Dyce, i. 234), 1515: 'What avayleth
lordshyp, yourselfe for to kyll, With
care and with thought, howe Jack
shall have Gyl.' Gosson has 'Every

John and his Joan' (*Schoole of Abuse*,
1579).

874. *royal finger*] See above, v. i. 95.

875-6. *hold the plough*] See note at
ll. 715–17 above.

877. *dialogue*] This use of 'dialogue'
is not included by *N.E.D.* amongst
'dialogues set as musical compositions',
the earliest example being from J.
Playford, 1653. In *The Queen's Entertainment at the Earl of Hertford's*, 1591
(Nichols's *Progresses*, iii. 113), there is a
song of a similar structure between
'Dem'(and) and 'Resp'(onse), with
an echo to take up the closing syllables
of each quatrain. It is 'The Song presented by Nereus on the water, sung
dialogue-wise, everie fourth verse answered with two Echoes'. Shakespeare's bird-notes replace the already

the two learned men have compiled in praise of the
owl and the cuckoo? it should have followed in the
end of our show.   880
King. Call them forth quickly; we will do so.
Arm. Holla! approach.

Re-enter HOLOFERNES, NATHANIEL, MOTH, COSTARD, *and others.*

This side is *Hiems*, Winter, this *Ver*, the Spring: the
one maintained by the owl, the other by the cuckoo.
Ver, begin.   885

THE SONG.

Spring.   When daisies pied and violets blue
             And lady-smocks all silver-white
             And cuckoo-buds of yellow hue

882. S.D. *Re-enter . . .*] *Enter all Qq,Ff.*   887, 888.] *Theobald; the order is 888, 887
in Qq,Ff.*   888. cuckoo-buds] cowslip-buds *Farmer conj.;* crocus-buds *Whalley
conj.*

stale echo device. Apart from such
musical examples, the prose 'dialogue',
in which the two sides of an argument
were stated by opposing characters,
was a favourite form, particularly in
religious controversy. The fashion was
set by Erasmus and the German protestants, who were much translated
and imitated in such English examples
as the *Proper Dyalogue betweene a Gentill-
man and a Husbandman* (1530). Equivalent terms were 'debate' and 'dispute',
as in Robert Greene's *A Quip for an
Upstart Courtier, or a Quaint Dispute
between Velvet-breeches and Cloth-breeches.*
Armado's dialogue is presumably the
'antic' forecast, in case the play 'fadge'
not, in v. i. 141.

882. *Holla*] 'a shout to excite attention' (*N.E.D.*); 'a call to a person to
come near' (Schmidt). Cf. Gascoigne,
The Steel Glas (Arber, p. 72), 1577:
'But holla; here, I see a wondrous
sight, I see a swarme of Saints within
my glasse. . . . What should they be
(my lord), what should they be?'

883-4. *the one . . . the other*] the two
sides in the debate. See l. 877.

886. *When daisies pied,* etc.] Furness
writes: 'Whalley speaks of this song
"which gave so much pleasure to the
Town, and was in everybody's mouth
about seven years ago". This must
have been about 1740. Genest records
no production of *Love's Labour's Lost* at
or about this date, or in fact at any
date. But we know that this song was
introduced into *As You Like It*; which,
Genest says, was acted in Nov. 1740,
for the first time for forty years. It had
an unusual run of twenty-five nights.'

887-8. *lady-smocks . . . cuckoo-buds*]
Commentators have long argued as to
what these flowers might be. In *R.E.S.*
III (n.s.), pp. 117-29, J. W. Lever has
shown that Shakespeare took them not
from nature but from the first edition
of Gerard's *Herball* (1597). This
describes six varieties of 'water Cresses
or Cuckow flowers'. To all but one
Gerard, a native of Cheshire, also
applies the purely local name of
'Ladie smockes'. The fifth variety,
'Milke white Ladie smockes', is said to
have yellowish flowers, to grow 'in
moist medowes' and to bloom 'when

Do paint the meadows with delight.
The cuckoo then, on every tree,   890
Mocks married men; for thus sings he,
    Cuckoo;
Cuckoo, cuckoo: O word of fear,
Unpleasing to a married ear!

When shepherds pipe on oaten straws,   895
    And merry larks are ploughman's clocks,
When turtles tread, and rooks, and daws,
    And maidens bleach their summer smocks,
The cuckoo then, on every tree,
Mocks married men; for thus sings he,   900
    Cuckoo;
Cuckoo, cuckoo; O word of fear,
Unpleasing to a married ear!

Winter.   When icicles hang by the wall,
    And Dick the shepherd blows his nail,   905

---

889. with delight] much bedight *Warburton.*

the Cuckowe doth begin to sing her pleasant notes without stammering'. All this Shakespeare takes over. Gerard's 'fower leaves of a yellowish colour' (meaning the pale-green calyx?) becoming the impossible 'cuckoo-buds of yellow hue'.

890–1. *cuckoo . . . thus sings he*] The quibble on cuckold reappears in *Wiv.*, II. i. 124. This special nastiness of the cuckoo is first found in the poems of T. Howell (1568) who calls it a 'slanderous bird'; but that it brings bad luck is a superstition as old as Pliny.

895. *pipe on oaten straws*] Cf. T. Watson, *Eclogue upon Death of Walsingham* (Arber, p. 163), 1590: 'An humble style befitts a simple swain, My Muse shall pipe but on an oaten quill.' And Golding's *Ovid*, i. 842: 'Some good plaine soule that had some flocke to feede And as he went he pyped still upon an Oten Reede' (1567). Spenser speaks of the shepherd's 'oaten pipe' in *Shepheard's Calendar* for January (1579).

896. *larks . . . clocks*] 'rise with the lark' occurs in Lyly's *Euphues and his England* (Arber, p. 229), 1580; and 'up with the lark' in Greene's *Never Too Late* (Grosart, viii. 124).

905. *blows his nail*] wait patiently while one has nothing to do. Schmidt says 'to warm his hands', an accidental property of the saying, arising out of idleness in cold. The expression occurs again as descriptive of listlessness in *3H6*, II. v. 3. A few examples must be quoted: 'hee was driven to daunce attendaunce without doores and blowe his nailes' (North, *Doni's Philosophie* [edited Jacobs, p. 231], 1570); 'who sate all the while with the Porter, blowing his nailes' (*Jests of George Peele* [Hazlitt's repr., p. 276], 1607); Cotgrave explains this in v. *ceincture*: 'pull straws, pluck daisies, pick rushes, or blow their fingers; generally the phrase imports an idle and lazie fashion, or posture'. In verses by Campion from Davison's *Poetical*

And Tom bears logs into the hall,
   And milk comes frozen home in pail,
When blood is nipp'd, and ways be foul,
Then nightly sings the staring owl,
          Tu-whit;   910
Tu-who, a merry note,
While greasy Joan doth keel the pot.

When all aloud the wind doth blow,
   And coughing drowns the parson's saw,
And birds sit brooding in the snow,   915
   And Marian's nose looks red and raw,
When roasted crabs hiss in the bowl,
Then nightly sings the staring owl,
          Tu-whit;
Tu-who, a merry note,   920
While greasy Joan doth keel the pot.

---

908. foul] fall *Q1;* full *Q1 (Devon copy).*   910–11. Tu-whit; Tu-who] *Qq,Ff;*
Tu-who; Tu-whit, to-who *Capell.*

Rhapsodie, 1611 (quoted by Nichols, iii. 350), cold is specified: 'But in their brests, where Love his Court should hold, Poor Cupid sits, and blows his nailes for cold.'

910–11. *Tu-whit; Tu-who*] Holt White refers to Lyly's *Mother Bombie* (written *ante* 1590), iii. iv: 'To whit, to who, the owle does cry; Phip, phip, the sparrowes as they fly.' Nashe has it in the Song of Ver in *Summer's Last Will* (1592). Cf., again, Lyly's *Endymion,* iii. iii: 'There appeared in my sleep a goodly owle, who sitting upon my shoulder, cried twit, twit, and before mine eyes presented herselfe the expresse image of Dipsas. I marvailed what the owle said till at last, I perceived twit, twit, to it, to it.'

912. *keel the pot*] cool the pot, as a cook does by 'stirring, skimming, or pouring on something cold, in order to prevent it boiling over' (*N.E.D.*). Steevens quotes from Marston's *What You Will* (opening of the play), 1607: 'Faith, Doricus, thy brain boils; keel

it, keel it, or all the fat's in the fire.' Skeat has a note on 'keel' in his edition of *Piers the Plowman* (ii. 270). He quotes 'Kelyn, or make colde, *frigefacio*' (*Prompt. Parvulorum*).

917. *crabs*] crab-apples. See *MND.,* ii. i. 48. Nares quotes from the old song in *Gammer Gurton's Needle,* Act ii: 'I cannot eat but little meat . . . I love no roast but a nut-brown toast, Or a crab laid in the fire.' Steevens refers to Nashe's *Summer's Last Will* (McKerrow, iii. 281), 1592: 'Loves no good deeds, and hateth talke, But sitteth in a corner turning Crabbes, Or coughing o'er a warmed pot of Ale'—into which the wild apples were put when roasted. And Malone's remark that 'What is called lamb's wool is produced' is confirmed by Peele, *Old Wives Tale* (ed. Bullen, i. 306), 1595: 'Lay a crab in the fire to roast for lamb's wool' (spice and sugar being added).

917, 918. *bowl . . . owl*] For the rhyme see iv. i. 140n.

The words of Mercury are harsh after the songs of
Apollo.   [*Exeunt.*

922–3. The words . . . Apollo] *In Q1 printed in larger type, without any speech-heading;
Ff add* You that way: we this way *and heading Brag. (Armado).*

922–3. *Mercury . . . Apollo*] The larger
type of Q may reflect a different hand
in the manuscript. On this assumption
Dover Wilson suggests that the line is a
mere reader's comment on the play as
a whole. The F addition was perhaps
made by the stage-manager to ensure a
tidy *Exeunt.*